Mulatto · Outlaw · Pilgrim · Priest

The Medieval and Early Modern Iberian World

VOLUME 75

The titles published in this series are listed at *brill.com/memi*

Mulatto · Outlaw · Pilgrim · Priest

The Legal Case of José Soller, Accused of Impersonating a Pastor and Other Crimes in Seventeenth-century Spain

By

John K. Moore, Jr.

TUTA SUB AEGIDE PALLAS 1683

BRILL

LEIDEN | BOSTON

Cover illustration: Clinton Lariscy, *José Soller in the Vineyards*, 2019, watercolor on paper, 20 × 20 cm. Private collection belonging to the author. Original artwork commissioned by the author.

ACLS

NATIONAL ENDOWMENT FOR THE HUMANITIES

This research was assisted by both an ACLS Fellowship from the American Council of Learned Societies and an NEH Fellowship from the National Endowment for the Humanities.

Library of Congress Cataloging-in-Publication Data

Names: Moore, John K., Jr., 1971- author. | Soller, José, defendant. El Fiscal de su Majestad con José Soller, peregrino mulato de Santo Domingo, sobre fingirse sacerdote y otros delitos.
Title: Mulatto · outlaw · pilgrim · priest : the legal case of José Soller, accused of impersonating a pastor and other crimes in seventeenth-century Spain / John K. Moore, Jr..
Other titles: Legal case of José Soller, accused of impersonating a pastor and other crimes in seventeenth-century Spain
Description: Leiden ; Boston : Brill, 2020. | Series: The medieval and early modern Iberian world, 1569-1934 ; 75 | Includes bibliographical references and index.
Identifiers: LCCN 2020002577 (print) | LCCN 2020002578 (ebook) | ISBN 9789004417779 (hardback) | ISBN 9789004422704 (ebook)
Subjects: LCSH: Soller, José–Trials, litigation, etc. | Trials (Fraud)–Spain–Galicia (Region)–History–17th century. | False personation–Spain–History–17th century, | Blacks–Spain–Social conditions–17th century.
Classification: LCC KKT174.S (Soller) M66 2020 (print) | LCC KKT174.S (Soller) (ebook) | DDC 345.46/02633–dc23
LC record available at https://lccn.loc.gov/2020002577
LC ebook record available at https://lccn.loc.gov/2020002578

Typeface for the Latin, Greek, and Cyrillic scripts: “Brill”. See and download: brill.com/brill-typeface.

ISSN 1569-1934
ISBN 978-90-04-41777-9 (hardback)
ISBN 978-90-04-42270-4 (e-book)

This book is printed on acid-free paper and produced in a sustainable manner.

To Niki, through thick and thin, and all of my children—
Cleo, Lucas, Gabriel, Seona, and Eamon—always

It is a riddle wrapped in a mystery inside an enigma;
but perhaps there is a key.

CHURCHILL

Contents

Preface IX
Acknowledgments XII
List of Figures XVII
Chronology of José Soller XIX

PART 1
In Search of Soller

1 The Vineyards 3

2 The Legal Case against José Soller 12

3 Origins 31

4 The Nature of the Journey 64

5 Reconstructing Locales along the Way 103

6 On Trial, under Sentence, and in Absentia 163

7 Into Thin Air 203

PART 2
His Majesty's Representative versus José Soller, Mulatto Pilgrim, for Impersonating a Priest and Other Crimes: *Edition and Translation*

Note on the Translation 213

Editorial Norms 216

Edition and Translation 228

PART 3
Scholarly Supplement

Proper Names in the Dossier 313

Linguistic Variants 319

Scribal Errors 321

Case Notes 323

Bibliography 331
Index 348

Preface

This book began with a fortuitous encounter in Spain between a generous Spanish scholar named Gregorio ("Goyo") Casado González and myself. One felicitous day in June of 2012, we both happened to be conducting research in the Historical Archive of the University of Santiago de Compostela in the Spanish autonomous region (roughly equivalent to a state in the US) of Galicia. After the Archive closed for the evening, he and I stopped to talk outside. Goyo asked me what I was looking into there. I replied that I was checking the records of the Hospital of the Catholic Monarchs in Santiago de Compostela, specifically the number and nationalities of pilgrims who arrived there during the seventeenth century relative to the preceding ones. A medievalist by training, I understood that Christian pilgrimage to the shrine of Saint James the Greater, brother of John the Evangelist, was at its peak during the Middle Ages, and I wanted to investigate the extent to which a decline in the pilgrim population actually had taken place after the Protestant Reformation of the sixteenth century.

I explained that my curiosity had been piqued by a Cervantes character who dresses in the guise of a pilgrim, a Christianized Muslim (Morisco) named Ricote, an old neighbor and friend of Don Quijote's squire, Sancho Panza. In a case of fiction mirroring historical reality, Ricote and his Morisco brethren had been expelled from Spain in the early seventeenth century under the rule of the Castilian Hapsburg monarch Felipe III. The phased expulsion was complete by 1613, just two years prior to the publication of the second part of *Don Quijote* in which Ricote appears. (In history, the last remaining descendants of Iberian Muslims resided in the Ricote Valley—also called Morisco Valley on account of the ethnicity of its inhabitants—in the Spanish region of Murcia, and Cervantes seems to be echoing these tragic events in the very name of this character.) No matter how sincere or long-standing their devotion, these converts to Christianity from Islam no longer were welcome or safe in Spain, which is why Ricote only can reenter his home country in disguise. In the Cervantes novel, Ricote dresses as a pilgrim and travels with a group of pilgrims.

Two key questions stood out, I explained to Goyo. First, how significant a phenomenon was pilgrimage on the Iberian Peninsula in the seventeenth century? And second, what was the role of "ethnic" pilgrims such as Ricote? In other words, was there some larger story about pilgrims of non-European descent waiting to be told during this time and place? I thought part of the answer might be found in the archives; it lay, in fact, just outside the archive doors.

In our fateful conversation there, Goyo pressed further. He was curious as to what I had published. When Goyo ascertained that I had achieved a respectable measure of success in research and writing on Hispano-medieval pilgrimage studies, Goyo dropped the big reveal: "Do I ever have an case for you," he said in Castilian Spanish. Goyo was referring to the criminal prosecution of a "mulatto pilgrim" named José Soller in 1693, the legal case that forms the basis of the volume now in your hands.

Goyo had encountered these trial proceedings some years back while conducting archival research at the Royal Archive of Galicia in A Coruña, on the shores of northwestern Spain. He is a researcher for lawyers who represent communities that hold land in common (*montes vecinales en mano común*), whose residents communally use pasturelands and woodlands to graze cattle, gather firewood, and the like. This practice descends from Germanic law when, after the fall of Rome, the Visigoths ruled the lands that now comprise Spain. These communities sometimes engage in boundary disputes with the Church and Government, whose territory may steadily encroach upon their communal lands. In order to determine where the historical borders are supposed to lie, somebody has to be able to read a variety of ancient documents and then testify as to their contents before a judge. That someone often is Goyo, one among a handful of people in the world capable of such an undertaking. In the process of his extensive research in archives across Galicia, Goyo has encountered document after document. The Soller case stood out to him as different from any he had ever seen.

Goyo had held on to a photocopy of this legal file for years, thinking he may eventually do something with it. (God knows he could have created a marvelous edition had he the time.) But Goyo was writing a dissertation on top of working extensively for the lawyers who represent the communal landowners and realized he may never get around to addressing the Soller case. Not wanting these proceedings to be hidden from the world any longer, Goyo decided to share his knowledge of the trial with me, a gesture of magnanimity without which this book could not exist.

In July of 2014, Goyo accompanied me to A Coruña, and he aided me in accurately transcribing all of the handwriting in the court and travel documents found in the case-file bundle. He hosted me at his home in Vigo, Spain, as well as in his family's vacation residence in A Guarda, Spain, directly across the Miño River from Portugal. From there, Goyo joined me in retracing the steps of Soller's confirmed itinerary on his pilgrimage from Portugal into Spain. Together we visited churches, hospitals, archives, and other places associated with Soller's documented journey from Lisbon, Portugal to Ourense, Spain. These initial site visits with Goyo are the very foundation for the ensuing years

of research, writing, and return journeys to Portugal and Spain that would follow for me alone.

As you read Soller's story, you can follow the pilgrimage locales and the dates of Soller's visit to them in the chronology that follows here (page XIX), as well as his location during the relevant stages of the criminal trial proceedings. You likewise can follow the geographic sequence of the chronology in the map of Soller's pilgrimage itinerary (figure 1).

Acknowledgments

The present volume has its origins in the generosity of Gregorio "Goyo" Casado González, who shared with me his knowledge of the existence of the Soller case in 2012. In the preface, I tell the story of that initial encounter in Santiago de Compostela, Spain, and of our 2014 investigative adventures together in Spanish Galicia and Portugal. I owe Goyo an eternal debt of gratitude.

This book was made possible by two major external grants, an American Council of Learned Societies (ACLS) Fellowship in 2016 (for 2017) and a National Endowment for the Humanities (NEH) Fellowship in 2017 (for 2018). The purpose of both the ACLS and NEH Fellowships was to afford me the necessary time to finish researching and writing. University of Alabama at Birmingham (UAB) College of Arts and Sciences (CAS) Dean Bob Palazzo provided matching funding (in the form of a semester-long sabbatical) to enable me to receive the highest possible amount of ACLS Fellowship funding for this project. The NEH Fellowship also allowed resources for conference and additional research travel to Portugal and Spain in 2018. I thank all who wrote letters of support for my various applications: Fred de Armas, Frank Domínguez, George Greenia, Baltasar Fra Molinero, Tom Spaccarelli, and Bill Worden. Their own scholarly work and mentorship are an inspiration.

The 2012 research trip to Spain during which I learned of the Soller proceedings was funded by a UAB CAS Dean's Grant, as was my 2014 journey to Galicia and Portugal, during which I transcribed the trial documents and conducted the initial site visits and research. At present, a 2019 UAB CAS Dean's grant is funding the copyediting and indexing of this book by the unparalleled Linde Brocato. I am grateful to Dean Palazzo for his continued support of the creation of this volume. I thank Linde not only for her good humor and friendship but also for her impeccable and indefatigable efforts in helping my work shine (*lucir*, as she is fond of saying). Speaking of which, Linde's published research is a beacon of good writing in our field.

A 2015 George D. Greenia Research Fellowship from the College of William & Mary's Institute for Pilgrimage Studies awarded the funding for this book's five original maps and plans, which were created by the University of Wisconsin Cartography Lab. Tanya Buckingham, Emily Pettit, and the team of cartographers in Madison did a fantastic job. Moreover, I could not be more honored to have received a grant named for George, a dear colleague and friend. George was there in Santiago that summer of 2012 when I first learned of the Soller case, and he has been supportive to the end, providing me assistance in properly translating Soller's Latin travel documents, companionship, encouragement, and research up through the present moment.

UAB Department of Foreign Languages and Literatures Chair Julián Arribas granted funding for the creation of the five original watercolor sketches by Clinton Lariscy, one of which serves as the cover image of this book. I thank Clinton, who happens to be one of my brothers-in-law, for his fantastic artwork. Julián also has pitched in matching support for the previously described (and other) grants, awards, and fellowships, not to mention for all the books, software, and extra research travel funding that this project required. He additionally has offered outstanding feedback on my various grant applications. Julián's expertise in and advice on the scholarly editing of texts from the Spanish Renaissance has improved my edition of the Castilian Spanish case tremendously. I could not ask for a better department chair than he.

Others have contributed in important ways. Isabel Soares Alves of the Berardo Collection in Lisbon facilitated both my encounter with Renato Berardo and a high-resolution scan of *The King's Fountain* (*Chafariz d'el Rey*) painting. Renato himself opened the Berardo family home in the Bacalhoa Palace so that I might see *Chafariz d'el Rey* in person (figure 19; part 1, chapters 3 and 5), a truly irreplaceable experience. My aunt Mems and uncle Sam Bicking have been a source of abiding love and affection during some challenging moments in the course of researching and writing this volume, as have Laura Bicking and Brandon and Nancy Hartselle. Chris Brown and Kent Keyser offered logistical expertise, grant support, and recognition in their respective roles as UAB Vice President (VP) and Associate VP for Research. Delores Carlito has helped UAB's Sterne Library acquire the books, databases, and articles necessary for this project. Alison Chapman proofread my book proposal and counseled me about a pivotal decision. Jason Clements and Jill Hamilton Clements reminded me of an exquisite historical case of impersonation, that of Martin Guerre, to weave into my narrative just in the nick of time.

Maryjane Dunn and Lynn Talbot have provided insight and encouragement in response to various presentations on my research and are models in the field of the Road to Santiago and pilgrimage studies and praxis. Francisco Fariña Busto taught me about the archeology of Ourense, gave me a beautiful book that helped me trace the exact location of the Fish Market Plaza in Soller's day, and led me into the scholarly community in Ourense. Hélène de Fays and Abel Muñoz hosted me in their home for invited talks in Chapel Hill. Doña Normandina González de Casado and her daughter, María Jesús ("Chus") Casado González, also received me in their home in Vigo, Spain. Kay Jenkins and Barbette Spaeth have been supportive through their work with the Institute of Pilgrimage Studies at the College of William & Mary. Rev. Dr. Jeff Hayes has been a valued friend with whom to discuss theological concerns relevant to the Soller case and otherwise. Dr. Ed Hurley likewise has provided influential

pastoral insight. Greg Hutcheson first suggested a comparison between Soller and Eleno/Elena de Céspedes (part 1, chapter 4) and recommended Israel Burshatin's foundational essay on Céspedes in the landmark *Queer Iberia*.

Denise Joseph has facilitated my travels and grant awards by coordinating the paperwork associated with all of that; I am grateful to Joan Conway, Amy Evans, and Erin White in the same regard. Andrew Keitt and Brian Steele have been encouraging writing partners and have helped me keep my priorities in order. Jane Landers and John Lipski offered penetrating feedback on a conference paper I delivered. DeRon Lariscy, my father-in-law, has given frequent encouragement during the writing of this book, and my other brother-in-law, Scott Lariscy, has extended his kindness, as well. Eddie Luster of UAB Sterne Library's Interlibrary Loan department has steadily supplied me with many books not in our collection. John Maddox recommended several sources, many of them invaluable in aiding my understanding of Atlantic creoles in the early-modern Hispanic and Lusophone worlds, and he also taught me about the existence of Couto Mixto. Heather Martin, Duke University's Librarian for African and African American Studies, was of tremendous help over many years when she was at UAB's Sterne Library.

Francisco D'Orey Manoel, Director of the Misericórdia Archive in Lisbon, and head technician Nelson Moreira Antão greatly facilitated my research there. Dellita Martin-Ogunsola gave me deep insight into Soller's agency and how the ambiguity of his testimony can be understood as a form of resistance. Yosmar Martínez invited me to serve as a plenary speaker at an Annual Gathering of American Pilgrims on the Camino in Black Mountain, North Carolina. Teresa Raquel Azevedo Sousa Martins assisted me in the archive of Aveiro, Portugal. Ben McGowan, Esquire, explained the nature of legal cases and rulings in which a defendant is tried in absentia; moreover, Cara Gavin McGowan and he flung open their doors in an hour of need. Brad McLane gave inspiration for the book's epigraph; Amy Steiner and he have been patient and supportive through the many vicissitudes of this project. Leah Middlebrook offered words of affirmation after an MLA Convention paper I delivered on Soller in Austin, Texas.

John K. Moore, my father, offered me all the love he had right up to his passing in 2017; may he rest in peace. Mitchell Moore, my brother (and an ordained pastor himself), recommended an interesting book on Thomas L. Johnson, a formerly enslaved black-African man who became a preacher, a suggestion that guided me toward key scriptural insights pertaining to Soller's situation; Mitchell and I also accompanied our families through the National Museum of African American History and Culture in Washington, D.C., which opens with an enlarged replica of none other than the *Chafariz d'el Rey* painting and continues into the hull of a slave ship. My aunt Stokely Moore has engaged

me in many interesting and meaningful conversation on the subject of this book and related topics over the years. Antonio Monteiro of the Misericórdia of Santarém, Portugal provided guidance and a variety of helpful resources. Josita Montgomery, my mom, has been as proud of me as only a mother can be. Her husband, Felix, inspired love and motivation in unexpected ways until his departure in 2014; may he rest in peace. William Montgomery, my stepbrother, is another source of unconditional love.

Kay Morgan has been inspiring in her roles as Director of UAB's African American Studies program and as the UAB CAS Diversity Officer. María Ángeles Pacheco Fernández, Antonio Sánchez de Mora, and Manuel Ravina Martín of the Archive of the Indies (Archivo General de las Indias) in Seville, Spain provided a copy of a key ship manifest and registry on one José Soller (part 1, chapter 7). Carmen Prieto, Director of the Archive of the Kingdom of Galicia (Arquivo do Reino de Galicia) in A Coruña, Spain, where Soller's legal case is housed, helped in many ways, including facilitating the assistance of the archive's technician, Dulce M. Villares Cuba, whom I thank, as well. Manuela Redol guided me in the archive of the Misericórdia of Tomar, Portugal. Erika Hille Rinker helped me understand a text in medieval German and also the duality of meaning behind the German variant of the saying that "the clothes make the man" (*Kleider machen Leute*, a statement that can be read literally either as "clothes make people" or vice versa), which influenced the section on disguise (part 1, chapter 4), and she has been enthusiastic about this project all along. Laura Rodicio Pereira offered me assistance in the municipal archives of Ourense, Spain. Lucía Salgueiro Doce aided me in my search for Soller in the Historical Archive of the University (Arquivo Histórico Universitario) of Santiago de Compostela, Spain, and other Galician archives.

Janet Scarbrough, my mother-in-law, and Jim Hart have been wonderfully loving and supportive. Kim Schnormeier helped bring fashion to the fore of my thinking regarding Soller's sartorial transformation. David Schwebel coordinates UAB CAS Dean's Grants in his role as Associate Dean for Research in the College and has offered both congratulations and guidance. John Jeremiah Sullivan gave me critical advice at a crucial juncture and has taught me the meaning of sticking with a story over many years through his pioneering achievements in creative nonfiction. Jeff and Sarah Swann have hosted my family and me several times over the many years of this volume's creation and have offered encouragement, laughter, and loving-kindness.

Carmen Toussaint welcomed me to the Rivendell Writers' Colony in Sewanee, Tennessee, an unforgettable experience that I am grateful Adam Vines recommended I pursue. Melissa and Kevin Watt hosted me in their home in Durham, North Carolina, for talks in the Research Triangle area and have pro-

vided steady friendship. Ray Watts praised and recognized the ACLS and NEH Fellowships awarded to this project in a UAB President's Message; his supportiveness as President of UAB and that of Pam Benoit as Provost have made this project possible. Additional UAB colleagues and friends who have been supportive include: Rebecca Bach, Josh Carter, Amy Dagley, Catherine Daniélou, Colin Davis, Nevbehar Ertas, Wendy Gunther-Canada, Will Hampton, Laurel Hitchcock, Drew McKnight, Steve Miller, Pam Murray, Lourdes Sánchez López, Luciana Silva, Mary Frances Thetford, DeJohn Tellis, Tiffany Westry, Kevin Worden, and Steve Yoder. I also extend my gratitude to all of my students, several of whom have engaged me over the years in discussions on Soller's story. The many individuals at archives, national and international conferences and symposia, the UAB Department of Foreign Languages and Literatures, the Donaldson Correctional Facility, an Annual Gathering of American Pilgrims, invited guest lectures, a writing retreat, and elsewhere who offered their kindness, advice, and suggestions are too many to list in this brief note of acknowledgment, but truly receive my gratitude.

I am extremely fortunate that Brill is publishing this book in The Medieval and Early Modern Iberian World series. Isidro Rivera, who sits on the Editorial Board, helped direct my submission to Kate Hammond and Marcella Mulder, who run this outstanding series. Marcella in particular has helped shepherd my book toward publication. Working with her has been my privilege and a true pleasure. As part of the peer review process, Marcella found the best anonymous reader I could have hoped for. I am very grateful to that reviewer and to the Editorial Board for this valuable feedback, which measurably improved my final manuscript submission to Brill.

Last and certainly not least, I would like to thank my wife, Nichole Lariscy, and children—Cleo, Lucas, Gabriel, Seona, and Eamon—for their supportiveness and love, and for keeping me humble. I also am grateful to Nichole for the many sources she recommended on race theory in her capacity as my colleague, a professor of English at UAB, as well as for her intuition and vision pertaining to the autobiographies of formerly enslaved people and to narrative in general. When this project started, our children were in kindergarten, middle school, and high school. They now are in middle school, high school, college, and even graduate school! It has been my honor to watch each of them grow in such amazing ways over these past seven years and for all of us to grow closer in our love for one another in the process. This book is dedicated to you.

Figures

1 José Soller's pilgrimage itinerary, map 11
2 The legal case against José Soller, front of first folio 14
3 Sculpture of San Benito of Palermo by José Ferreiro 33
4 The Atlantic world, map 34
5 Mudéjar bell tower of San Nicolás de los Servitas in Madrid, Spain; watercolor by Clinton Lariscy 57
6 Façade, Hospital of Santiago, Zafra, Spain; watercolor by Clinton Lariscy 58
7 Statue of the Virgin of Guadalupe in Extremadura, Spain 59
8 *Adoration of the Magi* by Lourenço de Salzedo 62
9 Detail, *The Seven Acts of Mercy* by Pieter Brueghel the Younger 67
10 Illuminated charter of the Misericórdia of Lisbon, Portugal 68
11a José Soller's pilgrim's credential, front 71
11b José Soller's pilgrim's credential, back 72
12 José Soller's pilgrim's passport, or safe-conduct 74
13 José Soller's pilgrim's diploma 76
14 *The Fight between Carnival and Lent* by Pieter Brueghel the Elder 80
15 Lisbon; watercolor by Pier Maria Baldi 108
16 Lisbon, featuring All Saints Royal Hospital, the Church of the Misericórdia, and the King's Fountain in the Alfama District, map 110
17 Reconstructed portal of the old Church of the Misericórdia, Lisbon 111
18 Sculpture of a pilgrim, reconstructed portal of the Misericórdia of Lisbon 113
19 *King's Fountain*, anonymous 116
20 Interior of the Church of the Misericórdia, Santarém, Portugal 120
21 Scallop Motif, exterior, Church of the Misericórdia, Santarém 121
22 Reconstructed portal of Our Lady of the Conception, Golegã, Portugal 122
23 Reconstructed bas-relief of Our Lady of Mercy, former Misericórdia chapter house, Coimbra, Portugal 124
24 Reconstructed portal, Church of Santiago, Coimbra 125
25 Detail, scallop shell, Church of Santiago, Coimbra 126
26 Coimbra; watercolor by Pier Maria Baldi 126
27 Statue of Our Lady of Grace, or Mercy, also known as Our Lady of Prison; niche over entrance to Church of the Misericórdia, Tomar, Portugal 131
28 Main cloister, Convent of Christ, Tomar 132
29 Original patio of the Misericórdia hospital, Aveiro, Portugal 134
30 Patterned tile inside Church of the Misericórdia, Aveiro 134
31 Detail, patterned tile, Church of the Misericórdia, Aveiro 135

32 Former Hospital of the Misericórdia with fountain, Viana do Castelo, Portugal 137
33 Sculpture, the Resurrected Lord; façade niche, Old Hospital, Viana do Castelo 138
34 Bas-relief, pilgrim; entrance to Church of the Misericórdia, Caminha, Portugal 140
35 Clock tower, Caminha 141
36 Mudéjar woodwork ceiling, Church of Caminha 142
37 Tui, Spain; watercolor by Pier Maria Baldi 143
38 Santiago de Compostela, Spain; watercolor by Pier Maria Baldi 144
39 Western façade, Cathedral of Santiago de Compostela by José Vega y Verdugo 146
40 Cathedral of Santiago de Compostela, bird's-eye view of layout 150
41 Statue of Saint James, Cathedral of Santiago de Compostela 152
42 Base, original portion of Roman bridge, Ourense, Spain 154
43 Sculpture of the Holy Christ of Ourense 159
44 Ourense, map 166
45 Reconstruction of Aira Gate in Ourense; watercolor by Clinton Lariscy 167
46 Detail of gothic windows, house of the Chief Magistrate, Ourense; watercolor by Clinton Lariscy 176
47 Coat-of-Arms recovered from the house of the Chief Magistrate, Ourense 177
48 Stone Inscription recovered from the house of the Chief Magistrate, Ourense 177

Chronology of José Soller

Pilgrimage, Imprisonment, Disappearance (1693)

Date	Document	Location
February 4	Pilgrim's Passport	Lisbon, Portugal
February 11	Pilgrim's Credential	Lisbon, Portugal
February 17	Pilgrim's Credential	Santarém, Portugal
February 18	Pilgrim's Credential	Golegã, Portugal
February 22	Pilgrim's Credential	Coimbra, Portugal
February 23	Pilgrim's Credential	Tomar, Portugal
February 28	Pilgrim's Credential	Aveiro, Portugal
March 9	Pilgrim's Credential	Moreira, Portugal
March 12	Pilgrim's Credential	Viana do Castelo, Portugal
March 13	Pilgrim's Credential	Caminha, Portugal
March 14	Pilgrim's Credential	Valença do Minho, Portugal
March 25	Pilgrim's Diploma	Santiago de Compostela, Spain
April 14–September 5	Court Documents	Ourense, Spain
October 13 forward	Court Documents	Absent

PART 1

In Search of Soller

CHAPTER 1

The Vineyards

So shall the last be first, and the first last.
JESUS[1]

∴

He walks into the vineyards on April 14, 1693, this "dark-skinned man with some knapsacks and a pilgrim's staff,"[2] free, and freely wandering. The grape plantations here belong to a region supplying much of the wine the traveler had been served as an essential component, along with bread, of the Christian hospitality offered in hostels and monasteries along his journey from Portugal into Spain.[3] The same valley of vineyards provides wine to the city in whose cathedral the month prior this pilgrim, after confession and absolution, had "received the Eucharistic body of Christ,"[4] the consecrated bread offered in Holy Communion alongside wine, sanctified at the Last Supper as Jesus' blood. The swarthy sojourner traverses a landscape imbued with the sacred.

These vineyards lie in the fertile Miño River valley just south of the city of Ourense, in the northwestern Spanish region of Galicia, at that time a kingdom in Spain. All this territory is right above Portugal on the Iberian Peninsula. The following century, a prominent visitor to Ourense would observe that Ourense's fertile landscape here was a veritable garden covered in fruit trees and grapevines.[5] The vineyard the wayfarer wanders into belongs to someone named Pedro Debén and is adjacent to the Berjano family grapevines. The

1 From the Parable of the Vineyard, Matthew 20:16 (Douay-Rheims Catholic Bible).

2 1^v; "un hombre moreno con unas alforjas y un bastón de peregrino." The folio cited here comes from the facing-page edition and translation of *His Majesty's Prosecutor versus José Soller, Mulatto Pilgrim, for Impersonating a Priest and Other Crimes* (*El fiscal de Su Majestad contra José Soller, peregrino mulato, por fingirse sacerdote y otros delitos*) in part 2 of the present volume. All subsequent folio citations for which the source is not labeled are from the same case file. Unless otherwise indicated, all translations to English are my own.

3 Singul, *Vino y cultura*, 53.

4 10^r; "eucharisticum Domini corpus sumpsisse." Singul, 47.

5 Morales, *Viage*, 147. Vineyards were everywhere because wine was a principal product of the region, just as olives had been before. Barriocanal López, *O camiño real*, 298.

 | DOI:10.1163/9789004422704_002

dusky pilgrim had left the city through the Aira Gate (Porta da Aira), which had two towers, one to either side, and which above the arch bore the Spanish coat-of-arms of Castilla and León, topped by a crown and above the sheepskin symbolic of the international Order of the Golden Fleece (Orden del Toisón de Oro).[6] The Porta da Aira had been completely rebuilt roughly three-quarters of a century prior in 1616, and it served as the main southern entrance to the city for those arriving from Castile in central Spain.[7] For this traveler, the Aira Gate serves as principal exit heading toward Castile as he wends his way less than a kilometer south toward the Mariñamansa intersection—marked by a stone cross and chapel—in the direction of Seixalbo, then a town and today a suburb of Ourense. A rocky road lies ahead.[8]

He carries in a satchel several items of interest, among them the equivalent of a passport, or safe-conduct (*salvi conductus*), from the departure point of his pilgrimage in Lisbon. Also in the haversack, the pilgrim has a credential (*carta de guia*) bearing signatures from various stops along his prior Portuguese itinerary heading north into Spain, toward his primary destination, Santiago de Compostela, Galicia, whose cathedral, according to tradition, houses the remains of James the Greater, brother of John the Evangelist. The Cathedral of Santiago is the shrine of Saint James, the "Apostle of all Spain."[9] The remains of this saint lie beneath the main altar, or "high altar" of the Cathedral, which was completed twenty years prior to the pilgrim's arrival.[10] Immediately behind this altar, within the Chapel of the King of France,[11] the sojourner takes communion and then receives his sealed pilgrim's diploma (*compostela*), certifying the successful completion of his sacred journey and serving as an exhortation for the Christian faithful to offer him charity on his pilgrimage beyond the shrine.[12]

---

6 The Order of the Golden Fleece is a fifteenth-century Burgundian order, and passed into the house of Hapsburg when Maximilian I married Mary of Burgundy, Charles V's grandmother.

7 Gallego Domínguez, "Torres," 249–250, 265–267, 268n109, 278. See in particular the drawn rendering reconstructed from a contemporaneous description and figure 45 in the present volume. Gallego Domínguez, "Torres," 267; Somoza Medina, *Ourense*, 63.

8 Whether on horseback or on foot, this stretch of the Royal Road (Camino Real) was inordinately difficult to traverse in Soller's day. Among the earliest Christian sanctuaries established in Ourense, a chapel near the Mariñamansa intersection was built in honor of the early Christian martyr Saint Euphemia, whose confraternity dates to the fourteenth century. Barriocanal López, *O camiño real*, 33–38, 296.

9 10^r; "Apostoli nostri ac Hispaniarum."

10 Laffi *Journey*, 164; Laffi, *Viaggio*, 202.

11 This chapel was built in honor of the reported visit and donation of King Louis XI of France (1461–1483) to the shrine of Saint James. Laffi, *Journey*, 164; Laffi, *Viaggio*, 202.

12 García Iglesias, "Visita de Cosme III," 587, 593. Starting in 1666, the Holy Eucharist has been

The *compostela* is dated March 25, 1693, three days after Easter Sunday of that year.[13] His name on the diploma reads, *"Don Joseph Soller, Priest of the Indies."*[14]

In Santiago, José Soller (pronounced "Soh-YEHR") already bore the outline of a tonsure he had received during February in Lisbon, where he had had the crown of his head completely shaven in the manner of a clergyman.[15] Three priest-pilgrims in the chapel there, foreigners from Cataluña and possibly travel companions of Soller on his sojourn to Santiago, testified to Don Jacinto Suárez, "the diploma-granting Senior Cardinal,"[16] that their colleague indeed was a priest. By the time Soller strode into Ourense—on his way from Santiago all the way to Rome, according to his safe-conduct—in April of that year (chronology), he now had, in addition to the contour of his previously-shaven head, his newly-signed pilgrim's diploma attesting to his stature as a New-World man of the cloth.

The day prior to Soller's visit to the vineyards, on April 13, 1693, he had asked a barber in Ourense, Antonio González Siabal, to reshave his tonsure for the first time since having had it shaved in Lisbon. The barber was a short man who, like Soller, happened to be "dark-skinned in the face, and with a black and curly head of hair."[17] González Siabal could see that Soller "already bore the mark of a tonsure"[18] and did not feel compelled to inspect anything further, including Soller's documentation. For the price of just four *cuartos*,[19] the barber gave Soller a new clerical haircut.

---

administered to all pilgrims in the Chapel of the King of France who come to visit the holy sepulcher of the Apostle James the Greater, which runs on the donations these pilgrims offer for the expenses of this chapel. García Iglesias, "Visita de Cosme III," 593. Today this chapel is more frequently referred to as the Chapel of the Saviour (Salvador).

13 Easter of 1693 had fallen on the earliest possible date in the Gregorian Calendar, March 22, the first day after the vernal equinox, which had been set the century prior on March 21.

14 10^{r}; *"Don Josephum Soler, Sacerdotem Indianum."* The italics here indicate handwritten text in the mostly otherwise printed pilgrim's diploma (*compostela*). See the Editorial Norms in part 2, *His Majesty's Representative versus José Soller, Mulatto Pilgrim.*

15 By Soller's day, the Western Church had established definitively that an official tonsure permitted only a discreet, circular crown of very short hair around the lower part of the head. An orthodox tonsure did not allow any remaining curls, much less long hair, as both had been associated with paganism and heresy over the preceding centuries, in particular with the heresy of Priscillianism in Galicia during the fourth century and afterwards. Beards also were prohibited in this context. The rules governing the official tonsure applied to priests belonging to both the lower and greater orders. Conde Guerri, "La tonsura," 293–299.

16 18^{v}; "el Señor Cardenal de los pasaportes."

17 5^{r}; "moreno de rostro y el cabello rizo y negro."

18 5^{v}; "traía señal de corona en la cabeza."

19 A *cuarto* was a copper coin worth four maravedis and less than an eighth of a real.

Soller's clean-shaven and dark-complexioned head was gleaming. Although he did not yet have new pastoral attire to match his new haircut, the tonsure was at least one outward sign that Soller belonged to the priesthood. The fresh trim was all it took for a tailor in Ourense, Pedro de Castro, to determine as much later that same day. This is why Castro made Soller "a clerical collar, some sleeves or covers, and a pair of pants"[20] using the lengths of black flannel Soller had given him.[21] The next day in the vineyards, Soller carries these items of ecclesiastical finery inside his satchels.

Recognizable as a member of the clergy now by his tonsure and hopefully in the near future by his priestly regalia, Soller might have the capacity to do more than simply partake of Holy Communion, which he had received in the Cathedral of Santiago; he himself possibly could administer the Lord's Supper to others. If a major-order priest, Soller would have the power to perform the Eucharistic Celebration, raising aloft consecrated wine produced from the very vineyards where he now stands. In the Catholic Mass, this wine is symbolically transformed into the sacrificial blood of Christ given in the cup of salvation.[22] Such a pilgrim-pastor in the vineyards might be properly construed as a holy traveler set in a sacramental scene.

The various roads to Santiago complement the sacred element of this landscape inasmuch as they are reflective of the mystical way of the faithful, of their path beyond the physical realm:

> On the pilgrimage routes to Compostela, the believer, responding to the profound religious dimension of this holy space, could achieve a reconciliation with God. The physical itinerary toward the tomb of the Apostle [James] is in keeping with a spiritual journey guided by meditation, prayer, and hope in the mediating power of relics and by the monks who inhabit the angelic spaces of each shrine, considering that they live communally as the apostles did, in moderation, controlling their lust and conquering their pride.[23]

20 6^r; "un alzacuello de eclesiástico, unas mangas o fundas y un calzón."

21 Soller had three rods of this black Palencia flannel. At a cost of six-and-a-half-reals per rod (2^v), Soller had paid more than forty-one times as much for this black fabric as for his haircut.

22 This sacrament is based on Jesus' words at the Last Supper: "This is the chalice, the new testament in my blood, which shall be shed for you." Luke 22:20 (Douay-Rhiems Catholic Bible).

23 Singul, *Vino y cultura*, 18; "En las rutas de la peregrinación compostelana el fiel podía lograr una reconciliación con Dios atendiendo a la profunda dimensión religiosa de este espacio sacro. El itinerario físico hacia la tumba del apóstol se corresponde con un camino

The same might be said for Soller's journey from Santiago de Compostela to Rome, being as the latter is the burial site of Saints Peter and Paul. As Christian pilgrimage destinations, both Santiago and Rome are symbolic of the eternal resting place of the saints known as the City of God, the heavenly abode from which every Christian pilgrim is a stranger in spiritual exile while on earth.[24]

Holy places populate the way in between Christian pilgrimage destinations, including Santiago and Rome. For Soller, Ourense was one such locale, as "he came to this country journeying on pilgrimage to the Apostle Santiago and to the Holy Christ of this city."[25] The two-foot high Gothic statue called the Holy Christ (Santo Cristo) of Ourense is a devotional object located at that time and still today on an altar and underneath a canopy in its own chapel in the northern transept of the Cathedral of Ourense.[26] This and other Santo Cristo sculptures were famous among pilgrims for the excruciating realism in their depiction of the agony of the Crucified Christ, and the pathos the images evoke gave rise to legends surrounding them, including that the hair and nails grew and that they sweated and even bled.[27] This holy image was particularly popular among pilgrims from Galicia and Portugal in Soller's era, and those journeying to Santiago considered the Santo Cristo of Ourense a requisite stop along the way.[28] Many viewers understood devotional images such as the Holy Christ of Ourense to be living objects capable of revealing the transcendence of God.[29] Through the act of pilgrimage, involving as it does deprivation and hardship, Soller might well be understood to be performing an imitation of Christ (*imitatio Christi*), a ritual reenactment of the suffering of that Christ upon the cross.

---

espiritual, guiado por la meditación, la oración y la esperanza en el poder mediador de las reliquias y de los monjes que habitan los espacios angélicos de cada cenobio, pues viven en común como los apóstoles, con continencia, dominando la lujuria y venciendo a la soberbia."

24 The "great passage" affirms that the elders, "confessing that they are pilgrims and strangers on the earth," seek "a better, that is to say, a heavenly country." Hebrews 11:13, 16 (Douay-Rheims Catholic Bible). "This text in Hebrews is the basic inspiration for the countless figurations in Christian literature of Life as a Journey to a Better Country." Chew, *Pilgrimage of Life*, 175.

25 18^{r}; "vino a esta tierra peregrinando en romería al apóstol Santiago y al Santo Cristo de esta ciudad."

26 Domingo de Andrade, the architect of the canopy covering the statue of Saint James in the main chapel of the Cathedral of Santiago, designed and had completed the canopy covering the Chapel of the Santo Cristo in the Ourense Cathedral by 1679. Morales, *Viage*, 150; Yzquierdo Perrín, González García, and Hervella Vázquez, *La Catedral de Ourense*, 150.

27 Martínez Martínez, "El Santo Cristo," 212.

28 Barriocanal López, *O camiño real*, 303, 321–322.

29 Bynum, *Christian Materiality*, 35, 267.

Monastic and religious societies tended to view pilgrims in similarly favorable terms. For instance, the Benedictine Rule insists that Benedictine monks are required to take in any pilgrim, poor person, or sick individual as if he were Christ himself.[30] These and other Christian monasteries provided a significant portion of the hospitality infrastructure along the Jacobean pilgrimage routes. Religious houses of all types would have welcomed Soller on his travels between Valença do Minho, Portugal, roughly 100 kilometers downstream from Ourense on the river Miño, and Santiago, and then again between Santiago and the vineyards beyond Ourense where he is on April 14, 1693 (chronology).

The same was true for Soller's pilgrimage between Lisbon and the Portuguese border at Valença (figure 1). Issued under the authority of the then-Archbishop of Rhodes and papal delegate in Portugal, Giorgio Cornaro, the safe-conduct in Soller's knapsack, for example, insists that Soller not be allowed "to suffer harm or injury or to be harassed anywhere"[31] and that he be offered the "support of kindness, aid, and shelter"[32] on his journey from Lisbon to Santiago, and after that between Compostela and Rome. Likewise, in his pilgrim's credential issued by the Lisbon chapter of the Holy House of Mercy, or Assembly of Misericórdia, these brothers and their Director, having already provided him with assistance, insist to their fellow brethren that Soller "be provided with your charity to help him continue his journey."[33] Established in Portugal in 1498, the order of the Misericórdia patterns its generosity after the fourteen Acts of Mercy, seven spiritual and seven corporal works. Among the physical acts are "feeding the hungry," "giving drink to the thirsty," and "providing lodging to pilgrims and to the poor."[34] At the Final Judgment, these brothers and other Christians will be held accountable for their actions in this regard.[35] The message in his travel documents is clear: Soller is to be provided hospitality because he is a pilgrim.

30 Chapter 53 of the *Rule of St. Benedict* (*Regula Sancti Benedicti*), "The Reception of Guests" (*De hospitibus suscipiendis*), for example, insists that Benedictine monks welcome passing strangers as if they were Christ himself. Benedict, *Benedict in English*, 51–52; Benedict, *The Abingdon Copy*, 57–59. Such hospitality is founded on Jesus' Gospel message: "I was a stranger, and you took me in." Matthew 25:35 (Douay-Rheims Catholic Bible).

31 7^{r}; "nec patiantur damno vel injuria à quoquam vexari."

32 7^{r}; "benignitatis, auxilii, et patrocinii argumentum eidem praestare dignentur."

33 8^{r}; "favoreçaõ com suas esmolas para ajuda de passar seu caminho."

34 *Misericórdia de Lisboa*, 2^{v}, 4^{r}; "Dar de comer aos famintos"; "Dar de beber aos que ham sede"; "Dar pousada aos peregrinos e pobres." The last of these good works is based upon the biblical exhortation to welcome the "stranger" (*peregrinus*) in Job 31:16–32. See part 1, chapter 4 (The Nature of the Journey) for a lengthier discussion.

35 *Um Instrumento*, 29, 1^{r}–4^{v}; Ribeiro, *Santa Casa*, 47–49, 55.

As if to underscore the penitential component of his journey, the dates of Soller's sojourn from Lisbon to Santiago correspond to the Lenten calendar. It is part of the natural cycle to go on pilgrimage during a time of the year when the days are getting longer and when the first signs of Spring slowly begin to emerge. Beyond this seasonal rhythm and in terms of the religious calendar, Lent's emphasis on austerity and reflection parallels and provides an ideological framework for long-distance pilgrimage and its accompanying rigors as a rite of purification. In this fashion, pilgrimage transcends the physical realm as "a path of righteousness, located at the edge of the earthly world," along which hospitality, compassion, and charity are practiced and in which monasteries and abbeys become "holy spaces and antechambers of paradise. Over the course of his route, following an austere and pious lifestyle, … the pilgrim achieves his spiritual purification."[36] Having obtained his tonsure in Lisbon prior to his departure, Soller's clean-shaven crown and pilgrim's garb served as outward signs of his inner spiritual journey toward union with the divine.

Unfortunately for Soller, the Spanish in Ourense do not see him in this way. Aside from his newly-shorn tonsure, Soller lacks any other visible signs of belonging to the priesthood (insignia such as the clerical regalia he may have commissioned but has not yet donned by this point), raising doubts in the minds of the locals. Someone denounces him anonymously.

Unbeknownst to Soller there in the vineyard, Bernardo de Pando, the deputy sheriff, or bailiff of Ourense, was leading a posse in his pursuit. Hot on his trail at the Mariñamansa intersection, Pando spoke with a few boys who had heard from a woman that Soller had entered the vineyards there: "Having identified him with the assistance of Gregorio de Castro and Matías Sueyro, blacksmiths, and Miguel de Albor, barber, said pilgrim was found delousing himself half-naked, holed up in an old house in the vineyard of said Pedro Debén, with his tonsure apparently having been shaved today as if it were that of a priest."[37] Note the wording, "as if it were": the underlying assumption is that Soller's tonsure could not possibly be that of a priest. Also, the choice phrase "delousing himself half-naked" suggests an impoverished pil-

---

36 Singul, *Vino y cultura*, 18; "un camino de ascesis, situado al margen del mundo terrenal"; "espacios sagrados y antesalas del paraíso. En el transcurso de la ruta, con un modo de vida austero y piadoso, … el peregrino procura su purificación espiritual."

37 1^{v}; "Y habiendo pasado a su reconocimiento asistido de Gregorio de Castro, Matías Sueyro, herradores, Miguel de Albor, barbero, se halló a dicho peregrino recogido, espulgándose medio desnudo en una casa vieja de la viña de dicho Pedro Debén, con su corona abierta al parecer de hoy día como si fuera la de un sacerdote."

grim performing a ritual purification[38] in advance of putting on the recently-acquired clerical garb that was right there in his knapsack. But time has run out.

The Chief Magistrate in Ourense, Lord Don Juan Antonio Covillas, Esquire, believes that Soller's wanton display constitutes a crime committed "in offense of the holy priesthood"[39] and desires that the alleged impersonator be punished accordingly.

Note that Soller is accused of looking like a priest rather than acting like or saying he is one. The importance of dress and appearance in this culture is paramount in this context. Early-modern Spain was a deeply visual society with a stringent dress code providing complex layers of validation of social identity, and used to maintain the established social order.

To Covillas, Soller is not a priest at all but rather "a mulatto pilgrim who seems to be a slave."[40] No evidence or indication of Soller's purported enslavement is provided—none, that is, except the word "mulatto." The fact that the pilgrim is partially of black-African ancestry means that at least in Covillas's mind, Soller is more likely to be a fugitive than a priest.

The bailiff apprehends Soller and questions him right there in the vineyard: "He responded that *he was not a priest*, that he had shaved *the tonsure* to apply *on it a poultice for the maladies from which he suffered*, and that his profession was that of a barber."[41] Soller may mean to imply that he intends to apply ointment to his bare head in an attempt to cure headaches and the like,[42] but he is not under oath at this point. The bailiff seizes Soller's belongings (the aforementioned knapsacks and their contents) and brings the pilgrim to the royal jail, located in a tower attached to the residence of Ourense's Chief Magistrate, who would be deciding Soller's case.

So begins the criminal trial against Soller.

---

38 George Greenia counts medieval pilgrims' removal of lice (and fleas, presumably) from their bodies as a key ritual ablution prior to entering a shrine of the saints. "The Bartered Body," 38, 38n2. In a seventeenth-century example of the poverty of everyday Spaniards, Esteban Murillo's painting *The Young Beggar* (*El joven mendigo*) depicts a young street urchin nit-picking his body.

39 1^{r}; "en vituperio del santo sacerdocio."

40 1^{r}; "un peregrino mulato que parece ser esclavo."

41 1^{v}; "Respondió *no era sacerdote, que la corona* la había abierto para poner *en ella un emplasto por achaques que padecía* y que su oficio era de barbero."

42 Soller could assume that his means of applying a remedy would have been a credible alibi inasmuch as "[t]he normal mode of using supposedly therapeutic substances was to ingest them or apply them to the skin in the form of ointments, poultices, and so on" during this period. Siraisi, *Renaissance Medicine*, 149.

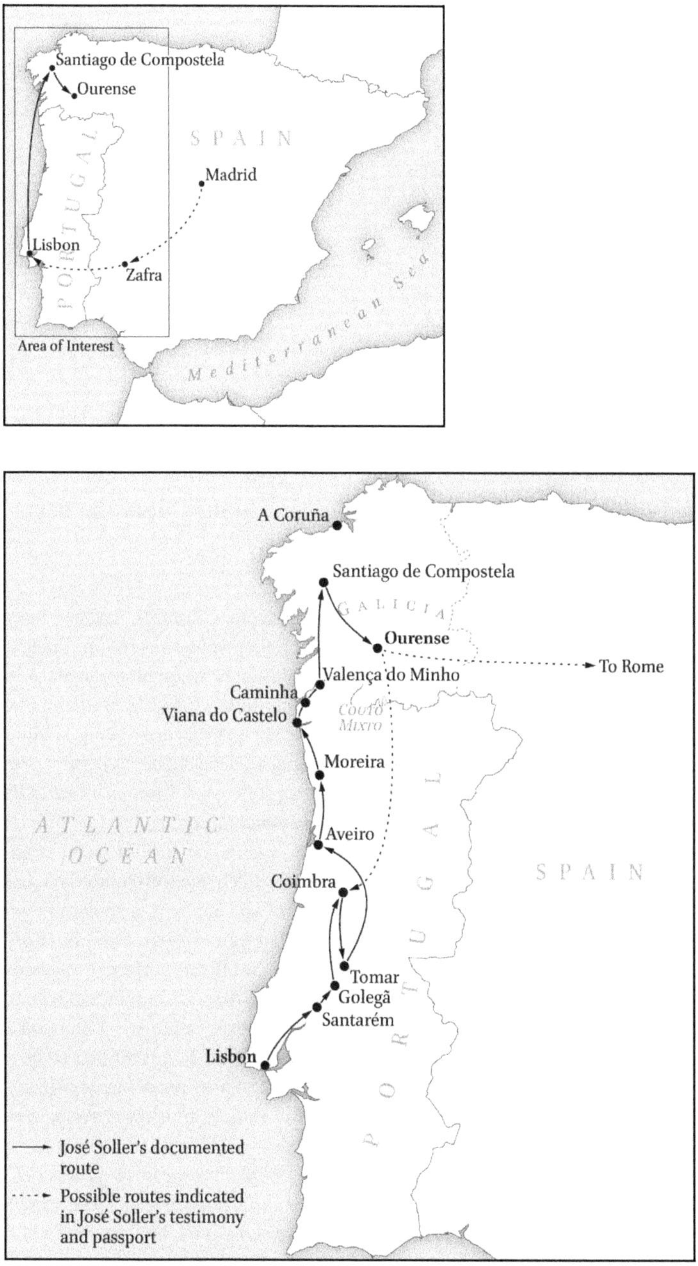

FIGURE 1 Map of José Soller's 1693 pilgrimage itinerary on the Portuguese Way from Lisbon, Portugal, to Santiago de Compostela, Spain, and on the Silver Way from Compostela to Ourense, Spain
MAP BY THE UNIVERSITY OF WISCONSIN–MADISON CARTOGRAPHY LAB

CHAPTER 2

The Legal Case against José Soller

Negro, an inspection.
Bogotá policeman[1]

∴

The main title of the trial proceedings against this protean man of color is revealing: *His Majesty's Representative versus José Soller, Mulatto Pilgrim, for Impersonating a Priest and Other Crimes.*[2] Soller is identified from the begin-

---

1 In September of 2015, Carlos Angulo, a black carpenter in Bogotá, Colombia, was hurriedly walking, rushing to get to work on time, when he heard a police officer say to him, "negro, an inspection" (*negro, una requisa*). Although such inspections are a frequent occurrence in Angulo's experience, this day he felt compelled to speak out against what he viewed as racial profiling: "My hurriedness is suspicious, while yours is not because you all are citizens ... More than two-hundred people come passing by every five minutes, and you choose to inspect precisely the two black people who are approaching." (*Mi prisa sí es sospechosa, mientras la de ustedes no lo es porque ustedes son ciudadanos ... Vienen pasando cada cinco minutos más de doscientas personas y escoges exactamente a los dos negros que vienen pasando para requisarles.*) These remarks happened to be captured on cell-phone video and subsequently "went viral" on the social media site Facebook. In the aftermath of the incident, a spokesperson for the Bogotá Police Department declared to BBC *Mundo* that there was no discriminatory intent in detaining Angulo and inspecting his belongings, that the officers perform thousands of inspections daily regardless of race or ethnicity. Nonetheless, Angulo's comments equate citizenship with the authorities and seemingly with whiteness itself, or at least with people who are not black. Angulo's usage of the term "citizen" (*ciudadano*) is very similar to how the authorities use the word "resident" (*vecino*) in the Soller case. These residents, or citizens, have rights, while Soller—a vagabond, outsider, and mulatto—would appear to have next to no rights.

2 *El fiscal de Su Majestad contra José Soller, peregrino mulato, por fingirse sacerdote y otros delitos.* Other titles listed for the case include: *The Justice Office and His Majesty's Representative in This Kingdom with Joseph Soller Chivo, Mulatto Pilgrim, Concerning His Impersonation of a Priest and Other Matters* (*El Oficio de la Justicia y el fiscal de Su Majestad en este reino con Josef Soller Chivo, peregrino mulato, sobre fingirse sacerdote y otras cosas*); *The Justice Office and His Majesty's Representative in This Kingdom with Joseph Soller Chivo, Mulatto Pilgrim, Concerning His Impersonation of a Priest and Other Matters* (cover 1; *El Oficio de la Justicia y el fiscal de Su Majestad en este reino con Josef Soller Chivo, peregrino mulato, sobre fingirse sacerdote y otras cosas*); as well as *Judgment and Proceedings against Joseph Soller, Mulatto Pilgrim, and*

 | DOI:10.1163/9789004422704_003

ning as both a mulatto and a pilgrim, two types of people often perceived to have fluid identities, to be outsiders. Mulattos and pilgrims usually did not stay in their place, so to speak, or stay in one place for long. For Soller to be labeled both at once makes him a double threat. Especially through its use of the descriptor "mulatto," the case title hints at the story of a man marked by the law, by systematic racial profiling, who would need to use his cunning voice and other "tricks of the weak"[3] to survive and possibly to be free.

The court documents of Soller's trial constitute a previously unedited and unpublished legal case that dates from 1693 and 1694, during the waning days of the Hapsburg Spanish empire. The case is housed in the Archive of the Kingdom of Galicia[4] in A Coruña, Spain, and is catalogued in the document series of the King's Representative[5] to the Royal Appellate Court of Galicia[6] under file bundle[7] 26.339/13. This legal case illuminates the discrimination people of black-African descent could face—that Soller did face—while attempting to cross the rigid lines of estate and caste.

The main text consists of thirty-seven two-sided folios written in a late-seventeenth-century form of Spanish italics (*bastardilla española*) derived from the Italian humanistic (*humanística italiana*) script (figure 2). The writing belongs to a variety of hands, mostly of the different actors involved at different points in Soller's trial and appeal: judicial secretaries, lawyers, and justices. The signature and/or rubric following each section usually indicates in whose hand the text is written.

Consorts, concerning His Impersonation of a Priest and Other Matters (cover 2; *Auto y procedimiento de oficio contra Josef Soller, peregrino mulato, y consortes sobre fingirse sacerdote y otras cosas*).

3 I borrow the term "tricks of the weak" from Ludmer, "Las tretas del débil."

4 Arquivo do Reino de Galicia.

5 "Letra fiscal." This series of documents contains 680 cases contained in 29 file bundles from the years 1580–1861 organized alphabetically by plaintiff. The cases therein deal with many different types of matters including criminal proceedings such as the Soller case. Since the time of King Felipe II (1556–1598), in each tribunal there were two representatives of the interests of the King, one for civil cases and another for criminal trials. The King's Representative was responsible for compiling each set of proceedings in which he was involved into a book. López Gómez, *Real Audiencia*, 2:1135–1136.

6 Real Audiencia de Galicia.

7 "legajo." There are different types of court documents. Simple records (*documentos simples*) form a single unity of action, time, and place. Dossiers (*expedientes*) consist of multiple records with multiple actions organized chronologically in sequence. Such file bundles gather different types of documents connected administratively. In a criminal trial, these documents constitute a lawsuit (*causa*). López Gómez, *Real Audiencia*, 2:745–746, 1317, 1320.

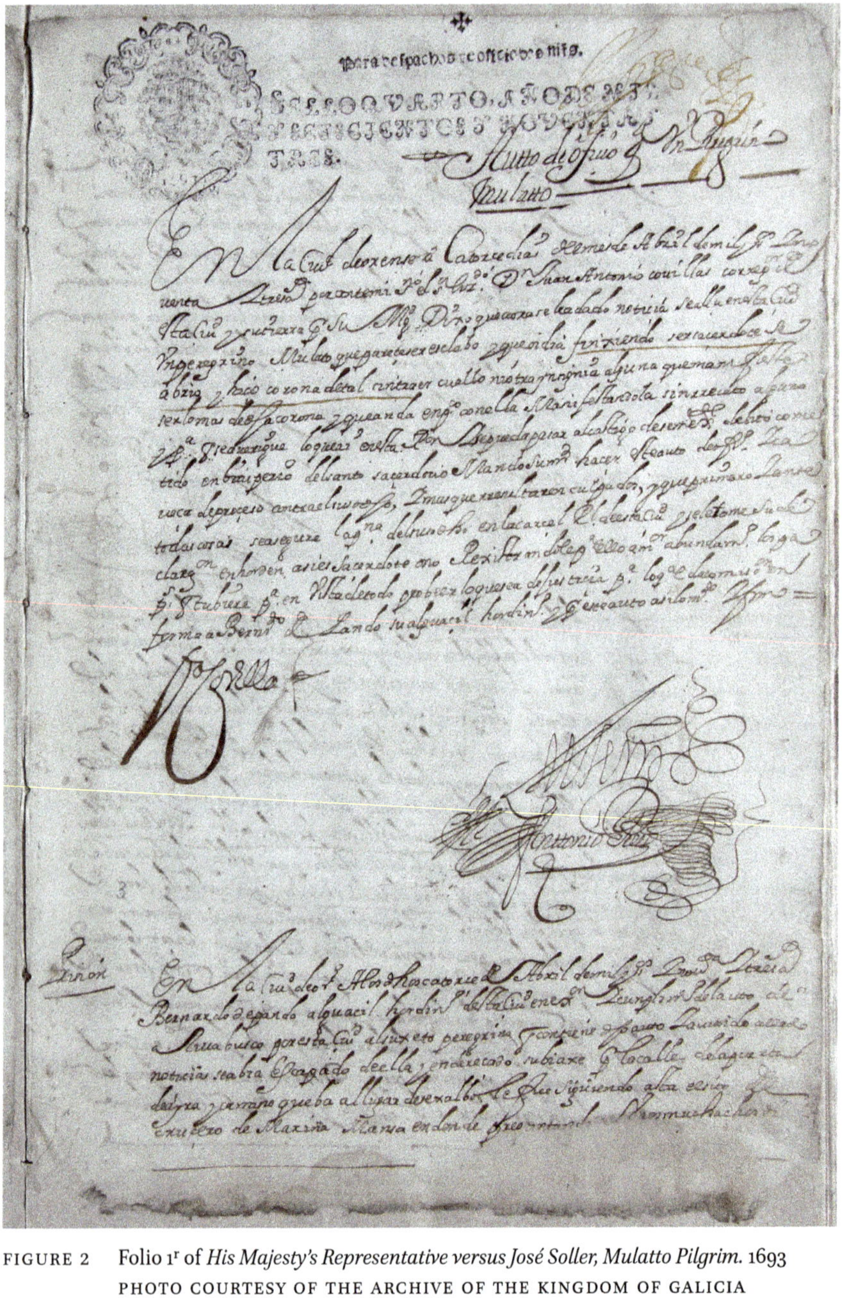

FIGURE 2 Folio 1^{r} of *His Majesty's Representative versus José Soller, Mulatto Pilgrim*. 1693
PHOTO COURTESY OF THE ARCHIVE OF THE KINGDOM OF GALICIA

Since the restoration of the binding of this dossier in the Archive of the Kingdom of Galicia, all of the folios have been trimmed to the same dimensions, 220 mm by 335 mm.[8] Most folios are stamped with the "fourth seal" (*sello cuarto*) and the year, 1693 (subsequently 1694, beginning at folio 36ʳ), all of this to the right of the ten-maravedi seal of the Kingdom of Galicia.[9] The *sello cuarto* is for the most basic type of official document, including "for legal offices" (*para despachos de oficio*).[10] The case file additionally contains previously-discussed documents (not transcriptions of them) relevant to the proceedings: Soller's safe-conduct (*salvi conductus*), which bears a melted-wax seal on the front; his pilgrim's credential (*carta de guia*); and the pilgrim's diploma (*compostela*) he obtained in Santiago de Compostela, Spain, which also has a melted-wax seal on front of it.

Mulatto · Outlaw · Pilgrim · Priest comprises a study, critical edition, and scholarly translation of the legal case of José Soller. To my knowledge, the only academic citation of the criminal proceedings dates to 1996 in Pedro López Gómez's two-volume book on the Royal Appellate Court of Galicia and the Archive of the Kingdom of Galicia. López Gómez includes a sometimes-erroneous transcription of brief extracts from some of the legal documents found in Soller's trial, presenting these select passages as an example of four of the stages of conduct in a criminal proceeding. There is no analysis of Soller's case in the five pages that López Gómez writes about the matter.[11] That said, López Gómez's book is indispensable as an overview of the Royal Appellate

---

8 These dimensions are 10 mm wider and 38 mm longer than the international standard paper size A4 used in offices in Spain and Europe today.

9 Different categories of seal had been required on all official documents since earlier in the seventeenth century under the rule of Spanish Hapsburg King Felipe IV, father of reigning monarch Carlos II, the "His Majesty" alluded to in the case title, the final Hapsburg ruler in Spain.

10 Felipe IV's Royal Charter of December 15, 1636, expressly states its intent to combat "forgeries" (*los instrumentos y escrituras falsos*) and that its effective date of enforcement is January 1, 1637. Through this charter and also via subsequent royal charters from February 4 and May 16, 1637, as well as from May 18, 1640, Felipe IV establishes four different classes of seal, in descending order: first, or greater (*mayor*); second; third; and fourth. To prevent fraud, the seal is labelled with the year it is stamped and is valid only for that year. In fact, a royal charter of April 7, 1637, stipulates that no court document is allowed to be written on anything other than sealed paper. The Crown levied a tax in the amount of two maravedis to scribes, notaries, and others obliged to use this specific kind of paper, which was forbidden for any other purpose. Felipe IV, "Título XXIV," 5:149, 5:151, 5:161. The maravedi of course is the main economic unit of Castile in the sixteenth and seventeenth centuries.

11 López Gómez, *Real Audiencia* 1:248–252.

Court of Galicia, the legal entity whose justices heard Soller's appeal of the Chief Magistrate's original ruling in Ourense.

The initial value of documents such as those in this dossier lay in serving the interests of the entity that produced and/or preserved them, the Royal Appellate Court. Today, however, the case files' historical worth far eclipses the documents' original importance. This is because these document troves disclose much about the world beyond their pages. Of particular interest is what these proceedings reveal about what life was like for a variety of social classes, especially the common people. Such proceedings even may uncover "the hidden world of peasant sentiment and aspiration" that Natalie Zemon Davis studies via the famous sixteenth-century French legal case of Martin Guerre in her classic book *The Return of Martin Guerre* or possibly even the "ways of thinking[,] … not merely what people thought but how they thought," that Robert Darnton examines by means of police inspection reports, folklore, and other morsels from the culture of everyday people of eighteenth-century France in his exemplary *The Great Cat Massacre and Other Episodes in French Cultural History*. Considering how many records and file bundles have been lost over the years due to the poor conditions of their preservation, investigators and readers are fortunate to have this case at all.[12] The Soller trial is all the more valuable for revealing at least in part the *de facto* and *de jure* treatment of mulattos in early modern Spain and the broader Atlantic World.

This bilingual edition and study is the first book to address the case in full and to assess its scope and import. To make the dossier's contents accessible, the present volume includes the requisite critical apparatus: a thorough introductory study, the main focus of which is to present an extended investigative analysis and a richly textured contextualization of Soller's narrative (here in part 1, In Search of Soller); images of the manuscript and of the pilgrim's passport and other documents found in the case file (figures 2, 11a, 11b, 12, and 13); a Note on the Translation, Editorial Norms, and a facing-page edition and translation of the trial proceedings (part 2, *His Majesty's Representative versus José Soller, Mulatto Pilgrim*); and end matter including Proper Names in the Dossier, Linguistic Variants, Scribal Errors, and Case Notes (part 3, The Scholarly Supplement). This material will benefit scholars in all disciplines who want to focus on the text itself with the support that the critical apparatus provides.

Mulatto · Outlaw · Pilgrim · Priest adds to the growing but still small body of narratives on people of color in early modern Europe and the Atlantic

12 Darnton, *Great Cat Massacre*, 3; Davis, *Martin Guerre*, 4; López Gómez, *Real Audiencia*, 2:1385–1387, 2:1438.

World, heeding Kate Lowe's call for "an intensification of historical investigation centring on those records which, for all their drawbacks, both allowed some notional black African voices to be heard, and permitted some recreation of the biographical details of black Africans in Europe (for example, some trial documentation (civil, criminal, and Inquisitorial) …)."[13] For obvious reasons, Soller did not initiate, much less author this case (nor could he have, given his apparent illiteracy, "the ignorance he confesses to have of reading and writing"[14]). The document's chief limitation is that the viewpoint of the authorities continually mediates the speech of the accused; yet while Soller's voice is not the dominant one, with a careful assessment of the file's contents in their historical context, something of his genuine perspective can be discerned, as William D. Phillips indicates is the case with notarial documents pertaining to slavery during this same time and place.[15] Detecting these voices is all the more critical considering that not only in all of Cuba and Latin America but also in the entire Hispanic world, there is but one autobiographical narrative written in Spanish by an enslaved person, that of Juan Francisco Manzano, a mulatto enslaved in mid-nineteenth-century Cuba who later obtained his freedom.[16]

One might make the same points about the criminal case against Soller and the voice—his?—that emerges from it. Moreover, there are clear glimpses of Soller's direct experience in his pilgrimage passport, credential, and diploma, all of which accompany his legal file. However limited in scope the view of the

13 Lowe, "Black Africans," 14.

14 20r; "la ignorancia que confiesa tener en leer y escribir."

15 Phillips, *Slavery*, 8, 79.

16 Such a paucity of slave autobiographies in Spanish stands in contrast to the various slave narratives written in English and is due to a variety of factors including the virtually complete lack of literacy among these enslaved people, and the prevailing bigotry against them and the stories of their enslavement. Manzano, *Autobiography*, 6–7, 21; DeCosta-Willis, "Afro-Cuban Slave Narrative," 6–7. And yet other key narratives by and about people of black-African descent in the seventeenth- and eighteenth-century Hispanic World have begun to emerge. For example, the diary of Afro-descended Peruvian nun Úrsula de Jesús is reproduced in Nancy van Deusen's bilingual edition and translation, *The Souls of Purgatory*. Meanwhile, Joan Cameron Bristol's *Christians, Blasphemers, and Witches* lays out Afro-Mexican ritual practice in New Spain during the seventeenth century. In a third example, Sue Houchins and Baltasar Fra Molinero present the hagiography (*Vida*) of an eighteenth-century black-African nun living in Spain named Teresa de Santo Domingo, who was given the name Chicaba at birth, in their groundbreaking edition, translation, and study, *Black Bride of Christ*. Also important are the black-African voices that Nicholas R. Jones recovers from the early-modern Spanish stage in his important new book, *Staging* Habla de Negros.

entirety of Soller's life that these documents provide, an analysis and presentation of the criminal case against him are important as an example of the lived experience of those of black African descent in the early modern Ibero-Atlantic world.

The first and only instance of Soller's "voice," that is, in the first person (even if mediated by his attorney, a public defender named Baltasar de Lisasueta), appears on May 2, 1693, a little over half-a-month past April 14, 1693, the day Soller lands in jail:

> I, José Soller, native of the island of Santo Domingo, kingdom of Perú, imprisoned in the royal jail at the order of Your Grace for impersonating a priest without being one, declare that Your Grace must grant the favor of releasing me freely on account of what results from the proceedings and my confession, which I uphold, which is the naked truth and without pretense, without there being in me any malice: yes, it does contrive for me to pass freely on pilgrimage amid the dangers of such a long journey. In awareness of which, I beseech Your Grace to deem just to proclaim as I have requested, taking pity on my uncommon simplicity, poverty, long pilgrimage, and prison. I ask for justice and for merciful pardon, et cetera.[17]

There is a lot to unpack here, and unpack it we shall in due course. But for now, suffice it to say that Soller quite literally is begging pardon, petitioning for the mercy of the Chief Magistrate, and with good reason. It was, after all, at the discretion of this municipal justice whether or not to grant clemency to a defendant. And beyond the authority of this magistrate, the royal pardon was still in active use at this time. Hapsburg kings knew all too well the Machiavellian coupling of the two most potent weapons in their arsenal: justice and grace.[18]

Clemency was really important to defendants because trials at this time in Spain did not connote any sort of presumption of innocence. Not concerned with protecting a possibly innocent defendant or with limiting the bias toward

17 21^r; "Josef Soller, natural de la isla de Santo Domingo, reino del Perú, preso en la cárcel real con orden de Vuestra Merced por decir me finjo sacerdote sin serlo, digo que Vuestra Merced se ha de servir darme soltura libremente por lo que resulta de los autos y de mi confisión, en que me afirmo que es la verdad desnuda y sin fingimiento, sin que en mí hubiese malicia: sí, traza para pasar libre mi romería por los peligros de tan larga viaje. En cuya atención suplico a Vuestra Merced se sirva declarar como tengo pedido, usando de piedad por mi sencillez única, pobreza, y larga perigrinación y prisión. Pido justicia y piadosa merced, etcétera."

18 Heras Santos, *La justicia penal*, 34, 52–53.

presumed guiltiness as much as with the search for the truth via the inquisitorial method, "judges, prosecutors, and the injured party herself or himself would come together in the trial and combine efforts to achieve the conviction of the accused" in Hapsburg-era Castile.[19] This is the primary difference between an adversarial trial, in which all parties, accusers and accused, face one another and proceed to openly argue before a judge (and sometimes jury) for their positions in a contest thought to reveal the truth, and an inquisitorial procedure, in which testimony is presented confidentially to the judge, and without accusers and the accused facing one another openly in court to present their arguments and evidence.

In this case, the complaint made against Soller was anonymous. The impersonal phrasing that the Chief Magistrate "has been notified" (*se le ha dado noticia*)[20] about Soller's dress-code violation means that no one wanted to be cited as the person who gave the information. This is why charges are brought by the authorities (*de oficio*) rather than on behalf of an individual (*de parte*).

In Old Regime Spain, the idea eventually took hold that public misconduct harmed not only the individuals involved but also the Sovereign, as well as society as a whole. The King demanded justice for particular victims and additionally sought to set an example for society, that is, to satisfy the "public vengeance" (*vindicta pública*) cited twice in the accusation of Soller made by the Deputy Prosecutor, a secondary official usually appointed by a municipal-court magistrate.[21] When an offended party chose to denounce someone anonymously, she or he simply made the municipal justice aware of some facts without having to become involved in the case as a plaintiff. The informer did not have to prove anything and could not ask for any specific penalty as a result. The Crown promoted the mutual repression of its subjects through the protection of such informants.[22] This disciplinary model provides the nascent "rituals of exclusion" (*rituels d'exclusion*) Michel Foucault describes through which Old-Regime societies systematically began to shun outcasts including lepers, delinquents, and last but not least, vagabonds.[23]

Inasmuch as the King sought to protect society from harmful conduct and bad example, an inquisitorial criminal trial could begin just like this: with

19 Heras Santos, *La justicia penal*, 174; López Gómez, *Real Audiencia*, 1:246; "jueces, fiscales, y la propia parte ofendida concurrían en el proceso y aunaban esfuerzos para conseguir la condena del reo."

20 1^{r}.

21 20^{r}, 27^{r}; Heras Santos, *La justicia penal*, 167, 174.

22 Heras Santos, *La justicia penal*, 164, 175.

23 Foucault, *Discipline and Punish*, 198; Foucault, *Surveiller et punir*, 200.

no more than an accusation and a judge's decision to intervene. A complex regular proceeding (*procedimiento ordinario complejo*) such as this one was comprised of three basic parts: the indictment, the full trial, and the sentence. In the initial indictment, the judge launched an investigation, deposing the witnesses and the like, and the accused was interrogated in accordance with the inquisitorial proceeding, which dominated all kinds of trials at this time (part 1, chapter 6). The magistrate required that the accused give one statement immediately upon his capture and another formal one under oath.

The inquisitorial process is a procedure that was adopted by civil courts across Europe after the 1215 decision of the Fourth Lateran Council to ban ordeals, although there is some evidence that an early version of it was already used by ecclesiastical courts before that date. Michel Foucault traces this "investigation procedure" (*procédure d'enquête*) to a later moment, the birth of the national monarchies.[24] Regardless of its date of origin, Foucault asserts that the process of private interrogation is "an authoritarian search for a truth observed or attested"[25] and that the method represents "the sovereign power arrogating to itself the right to establish the truth."[26] For Enrique Villalba Pérez, this "inquisitorial" (*inquisitivo*) process (separate from that of the Inquisition but adopting the same method, as the Monarchy learned much from ecclesiastical and Inquisitorial bureaucracy) was "promoted by the Crown as an instrument of its repressive politics subject only to itself."[27] Despite its bad reputation, the inquisitorial process was meant to systematize the collection and evaluation of evidence. It includes rules regarding how to analyze proofs and logically add them together to create a full proof that would justify conviction. The Spanish Inquisition also used it, but so did all courts everywhere, independently of the question whether they dealt with criminal or civil procedures. Though mixed in with the accusatory principle that governs civil

---

24 In keeping with Foucault's suggested timeline, Isabel brought the Inquisition to Castilla in 1478, the year before Fernando's father died to make Fernando King of Aragón as Fernando II. Since Isabel and Fernando had wed previously in 1469, Aragón and Castilla effectively combined to form "Spain" in 1479. Foucault's chronology is about right as far as the Inquisition is concerned, but it is late inasmuch as the inquisitorial method had begun to be developed centuries earlier in continental Europe.

25 Foucault, *Discipline and Punish*, 225; Foucault, *Surveiller et punir*, 226; "recherche autoritaire d'une vérité constatée ou attestée."

26 Foucault, *Discipline and Punish*, 225; Foucault, *Surveiller et punir*, 227; "le pouvoir souverain s'arrogeant le droit d'établir le vrai."

27 Villalba Pérez, *La administración de justicia*, 84; "promovido por la Corona como instrumento de su política represiva sólo sujeto a ella."

trials, the inquisitorial method is the dominant process employed in criminal proceedings such as Soller's.[28]

In the full trial phase, the alleged criminal was identified and denounced. In theory, the purpose of the formal accusation was to elaborate upon the alleged crime; in practice, it allowed the judges, prosecutors, and accusers to build their case against the defendant. This phase involved witness testimony, which in many instances was false, followed by the oral hearing, in which the parties and their lawyers made their allegations and defended their rights.[29]

The conclusion of a criminal trial was the sentencing phase. Sentences were established by a judge's decision after examining the facts of the case, and they almost never were in favor of the defendant. In their sentences, judges may have been informed by but never cited established law—the synthesis of Roman (civil) and canon law known as *ius commune* that formed the backbone of continental European jurisprudence from the twelfth through the seventeenth centuries[30]—which gave these magistrates maximum flexibility. Such indeterminacy meant that the sentences "lacked an explanation, a justification, and objective validity."[31] These sentences were as terse as could be,[32] leaving plenty to the imagination as a result. Such is the sentence in this case. We can observe all of the phases of complex regular proceedings in Soller's criminal trial.

Soller was up against a legal structure that was discriminatory to the core. Under the Spanish Hapsburg dynasty, the cases of the Spanish courts were organized according to a system of privileges that differentiated individuals by status, lineage, birthplace, place of residence, school, type of employment, and so on. In other words, there were not any universally applied criteria but rather different rules for different classes of people. The social body did not consist of individuals as much as it did of confraternities, guilds, schools, town halls, et cetera. The privilege of an individual emanated from the group to which he or she belonged and its concomitant prerogatives, monopolies, and freedoms. The

---

28 López Gómez, *Real Audiencia*, 1:223.

29 Heras Santos, *La justicia penal*, 176; López Gómez, *Real Audiencia*, 1:247–249, 1:251; Villalba Pérez, *La administración de justicia*, 85–87.

30 Jusdado Ruiz-Capillas, "Ius Commune y Common Law," 333, 335–336; Tomás y Valiente, "El 'Ius Commune Europaeum'," 13. Whereas English Common Law is based on precedent (*stare decisis*, still used in the United States of America), *ius commune* is the steadily accumulated gloss, commentary, and interpretation of Justinian jurisprudence (*Corpus Iuris Civilis*) on the civil side, and of canon law (*Corpus Iuris Canonici*) in the Christian component of this hybrid Common Law of continental Europe during the Old Regime.

31 López Gómez, *Real Audiencia*, 1:252; "Carecían de explicación, de justificación, y de valor científico."

32 Villalba Pérez, *La administración de justicia*, 90.

system largely rewarded the members of the upper classes, who received preferential treatment.[33] Such blatant favoritism of the elite was consistent with broader Spanish society, the rules of which at this time were rigged against poor people such as Soller.

Take, for example, the social pyramid and financial structure of those involved at all stages of the trial. At the appellate level, the King's Representative (*fiscal*) sits at the apex. He is a member of the eternal elite who, along with his officers, pays no taxes whatsoever. It is perhaps no coincidence that the *fiscal* serves as the King's permanent representative to the higher courts principally in fiscal cases concerning the Royal Treasury.[34] At the level of the municipal court, neither the Chief Magistrate deciding the original case nor his functionaries has to render economic tribute to the King. Among those appearing in Soller's original trial, these individuals would include the Deputy Prosecutor, as well as the court reporters, judicial secretaries, and bailiff—literally everyone who works in the legal system. In other words, the entire court bureaucracy at the municipal and appellate levels and above is comprised of a tax-exempt class of people.[35] This financial disparity is emblematic of the unequal class and economic structure not only of Spain as a whole[36] but also of Ourense, Galicia, the city in this northwestern kingdom of Spain where the initial trial takes place.

At this time, Ourense had devolved into a source of profit for those at the top of the social pyramid—the nobility, bureaucracy, and high clergy—none of whom paid any taxes. Meanwhile, members of the ordinary population—including small merchants, farmers, and artisans—saw themselves subjected to increasingly onerous tribute payments, which stifled their ability to improve their lot financially. At the bottom of the pyramid were the dirt poor, beggars, and those who depended upon the charity of others for their survival.[37]

---

33 López Gómez, *Real Audiencia*, 2:1105.

34 Heras Santos, *La justicia penal*, 167.

35 Gallego Domínguez, *A cidade de Ourense*, 18; Somoza Medina, *Ourense*, 59–60; Somoza Medina, *Historia de Ourense*, 56–57.

36 As early as the mid-sixteenth century, Spain's first political economist, Luis de Ortiz, pointed out to King Felipe II how financially detrimental it was for the kingdom to have so many members of the upper echelons of society be exempt from taxes. Cruz, *Discourses of Poverty*, 42. "Because so much tax revenue was mortgaged, the government found it impossible to rely on ordinary sources of money. Soaring inflation, a decreased population, the relentless rise in war costs, all forced statesmen to realise that an expensive foreign policy was no longer possible and that the Castilian taxpayer was contributing more than his fair share." Kamen, *Spain in the Later Seventeenth Century*, 359–360.

37 Somoza Medina, *As Lagoas*, 38; Somoza Medina, *Ourense*, 55–58, 62–63, 65–66; Somoza Medina, *Historia de Ourense*, 42, 57.

The only taxpayers out of everyone in the criminal trial would have been Antonio González Siabal, the barber, and Pedro de Castro, the tailor, both of whom are indicted for aiding and abetting Soller's perceived deception. These two are the ones who provide the tonsure and tailored fabric meant to enable Soller to feign membership in the clerical class. The crushing economic burden of a colossal empire fell on the shoulders of people in this class of small merchants and tradesmen.

Although the barber and tailor are indicted along with Soller for their complicity, both are released from jail on bail and eventually are exonerated after testifying against Soller. They have to pay court costs in order to make bail, and the barber has to post bond for the tailor who cannot afford to do even that. Meanwhile, the magistrate, judicial secretary, and bailiff—who pay no taxes at all—each get paid: fifteen, twenty-seven, and six reals respectively.[38] The fact that González Siabal and Castro are able to post bail in part explains why these two are bonded and released by April 17, 1693, only two days after having entered jail on April 15, 1693.[39] Meanwhile, Soller rots in his cell for at least four-and-a-half months, from April 14, 1693, the day he is apprehended in the vineyard, until September 5, 1693, his sentencing date.

Soller is at the bottom of the social hierarchy. As a pilgrim reliant upon the charity of others and who is not a member of any local polity, he also pays no taxes at all (except for the customs, tolls, and fees on services that *everyone* pays at this time). Neither is he charged any court costs since he is unable to pay. Were Soller to have exercised his stated profession of "herbalist barber" in Ourense, he surely would have had to contribute to the King's coffers. But Soller is lumped in with the beggars and other indigents at the foot of the social and economic hierarchy by virtue of his status as a pilgrim. By impersonating a priest, Soller nearly leapfrogged many of those above him and joined the ranks of another class of people exempt from making tribute payments, the clergy. He even may have succeeded in doing so for a time.

As someone who is black(ish), Soller is presumed to be a runaway slave. As a pilgrim, he is viewed as an outsider and vagabond in a society that has lost the capacity to distinguish between the legitimately poor and mere delinquents (much like our own society today). A "plague" of vagrants has torn the social

38 In the Middle Ages, when power over a town was granted as a royal favor (*merced*) to a noble, there was negotiation about what income streams (*rentas*) were part of that *merced*. Usually, the Crown reserved the income from the court and the administration of justice. But the legal system provided, in fact, an income stream from the fines and fees paid by those who became entangled in it.

39 15^{r}–17^{v}.

fabric of Spain to such an extent that the perceptions of the country's citizenry regarding the itinerant poor are altered irrevocably, and not for the better.[40] The odds never did look good for this priest impersonator.

Meanwhile, the kingdom is hemorrhaging money from an unsustainable degree of foreign wars and internal rebellions. The King requires free labor for his many galleons. His chief representative in Ourense is the one designated to decide the case in a system that frequently issues utilitarian sentences geared toward service to the Crown.[41] From this standpoint there is a judgment so easy, a sentence so commonly issued, it almost seems preordained: send Soller to row in the King's galleys, unpaid, for an unbroken period of two years, "on penalty of death by hanging."[42]

The deck was stacked from the beginning. And yet Soller is an Afro-Caribbean man of the spoken word, a creole storyteller with agency and adaptability, who maybe, as his final act, employs his wiles to slip free of his jail cell in the tower attached to the Chief Magistrate's house, the Royal Residence, as it was known. Prisoners here and all over Galicia broke free and escaped to the Portuguese border with such frequency in the seventeenth century that the Royal Appellate Court was forced to take measures in the following century to attempt to counteract this persistent problem.[43] Jails were porous throughout Spain during the Hapsburg regime, apparently: between the years 1531–1700, as many as 72% of inmates escaped after conviction.[44]

And maybe, just maybe, Soller made it to the extremely nearby territory of Couto Mixto (figure 1 and part 1, chapter 7), which we might refer to as an "In-between Land"[45] (literally "mixed domain" or "combined fief"), an aspirational (or ambiguous) Andorra situated between Spain and Portugal geographically, between the laws of these two empires legally. Rather than a full-blown principality, Couto Mixto operated at times as a nearly independent micro-state where both Spaniards and Portuguese lived and enjoyed privileges in both kingdoms as if they were natives.[46] In other words, locals could assume Galician/Spanish or Portuguese identity as it suited their interests and needs

40 Cruz, *Discourses of Poverty*, 5.

41 López Gómez, *Real Audiencia*, 1:252; Heras Santos, "Los galeotes," 289.

42 32^{r}; "pena de muerte de horca."

43 López Gómez, *Real Audiencia*, 1:255–256; Ortego Gil, "La pena de muerte," 154, 167.

44 Heras Santos, *La justicia penal*, 39.

45 To describe Couto Mixto as an "in-between" space is suggestive of its unique status as "a distinct and autonomous world" (*un mundo distinto y autónomo*), that is, as a type of "third space" (*tercer espacio*). Paül and Trillo Santamaría, "La construcción literaria," 311.

46 García Álvarez and Puente Lozano, "Las Comisiones Mixtas," 78n24; García Álvarez and Puente Lozano, "La frontera hispano-portuguesa," 763.

at the time.[47] This blended or hybridized jurisdiction explains the meaning behind Couto Mixto's name, "mixed place." Because these residents did not fully belong to either kingdom, "their territory was a refuge for criminals and smugglers, even rebels."[48] Many sought asylum and immunity from further prosecution here, as, according to at least one testimony, neither Spanish nor Portuguese sentries were allowed entrance to apprehend outlaws residing in Couto Mixto.[49] Perhaps this In-between Land is one of the only places in Europe an in-between man such as Soller—between worlds, between ethnicities, between social statuses—could live free.

The Spanish empire was in a state of utter decadence by the time of Soller's entrance: a sizeable population of men depleted by war; gold leaving faster than it ever arrived; inflation and disease rampant; and as we have seen, an unequal tax burden. Just a century before, Spain's possessions had constituted the empire where the sun never set, from the Philippines to Italy and in between, but the brightest star dropped quickly on Spain's global dominion in the century that followed. Now, the brokenness of the Hapsburg political and economic system was on full display throughout Spain and the Americas. On the Iberian mainland, there was abject poverty, a decreasing population, and the outright abandonment of agriculture, industry, and business. Across the Atlantic, Spain was unable to protect her overseas holdings from other nationalities eager to fill the void.[50] The absolute crisis at this time led to "the country's anxieties towards the economy's decline internationally … [and] continued to implicate the views on poverty that circulated at the national level."[51] It is therefore no coincidence that "the process of incriminating the poor was completed in the seventeenth century."[52] The indigent were made scapegoats for the broader problems of society. During the final Hapsburg century, writers and thinkers commented on a general feeling of disenchantment with the fall of Spanish hegemony, which seemed to vanish as swiftly as it had appeared, as if everything had been some sort of cruel dream.

At the head of it all stood Carlos II, last of the Hapsburg line in Spain. He was inbred, rickety, and incapable of producing an heir. This Spanish monarch

---

47 Herzog, *Frontiers of Possession*, 228.

48 Herzog, *Frontiers of Possession*, 229.

49 Paül and Trillo Santamaría, "La construcción literaria," 300.

50 Costa Buján, "Santiago de Compostela," 58; Landers, *Black Society*, 20. For a nuanced portrayal of "The Years of Crisis" under Carlos II, see especially Kamen, *Spain in the Later Seventeenth Century*, 357–375.

51 Cruz, *Discourses of Poverty*, 76.

52 Heras Santos, *La justicia penal*, 148; "en el siglo XVII se completó el proceso de acriminación de los pobres."

additionally continued his father and grandfather's ill-advised practice of outsourcing his authority to the King's favorite. Known by his enemies as "the Bewitched one," he was widely assumed to be cursed on account of his impotence. This is the King in question here, the one whose representative in Galicia pursues the most severe verdict possible in the Soller appeal: the death penalty. And yet by this point, much of the King's power had devolved to municipal authorities such as the Chief Magistrate who decided Soller's original case: "it is clear that 'decline' tells only half the story of Castilian justice in the seventeenth century; 'devolution' would be much more exact."[53]

Early-modern Spanish society was obsessed with rules. That regulations repeat themselves time and again is a testament to their inefficacy. Consider, for example, the numerous sixteenth-century Poor Laws that failed to stem the tide of peripatetic poor wandering across Spain, whose cities and towns continued to host more vagabonds than any other kingdom in Europe.[54] Or take, for instance, Carlos II's multiple seventeenth-century orders attempting to recruit galley oarsmen (1670, 1675, 1687, 1692, 1693, and 1699), including the year of Soller's sentence, 1693, when only thirteen defendants are recorded as having been sentenced to the galleys in Castile. These royal decrees were a direct response to the fact that convicted defendants tended not to serve their sentences and benefited from negligence and even corruption at the highest levels of society.[55] Authorities in an empire experiencing the throes of its own demise desperately wanted to make an example of Soller. They seem to have failed.

1 To Be a Mulatto Priest

Soller is a precursor, one of the mulattos who attempted to become priests in the early modern Spanish empire and were foiled. Ann Twinam reads through the historical record to chart members of lower social castes, especially people of black-African descent, who sought to scale the social ladder: "Although these attempts to attend university, to hold public office, to practice occupations such as public notary, or to enter the priesthood proved mostly unsuccessful, they

53 Kagan, *Lawsuits and Litigants*, 211.

54 Cruz, *Discourses of Poverty*, 40. For more on the relentless twin problems of vagrancy and pauperism in Spain at this time, see the first part of Henry Kamen's chapter on "The Underprivileged" in *Spain in the Later Seventeenth Century*, 276–280.

55 Sánchez Gómez, *Delincuencia y seguridad*, 177–178, 180.

preshadowed eventual successes."[56] Twinam is referring to the eighteenth century, and Soller's case dates from the late seventeenth century. In this sense, Soller can be seen as among the earliest mulatto pioneers who sought to move up the social ladder. Though his efforts failed, such failures are the building blocks of the ultimate achievement of upward mobility among people of color.

There were no explicit prohibitions on people of black-African descent entering the priesthood until authorities thought there needed to be barriers erected once people from all backgrounds began to demonstrate a certain degree of social maneuverability. The birth of a class of free mulattos in Hispano-America created a cascade of restrictions on this population including one prohibition from 1636 barring those of black-African descent, of blended ethnic ancestry, and/or born out of wedlock from joining the clergy. This ban was in place throughout all of the Spanish viceroyalties in the Americas.[57] It was not until after Soller's day that the ministry became a path to whiteness for mulattos:

> Among their highest aspirations was entrance to the priesthood. Anyone associated with the sacred chrism essentially became white, for his status meant that elites had to treat him with respect. As a local cleric, he would participate in public ceremonies and receive a coveted place. Evidence suggests that at the beginning of the eighteenth century a few mulattos were beginning to bypass such prohibitions.[58]

This is a compelling explanation for why Soller or any other person of color would have wanted to impersonate a priest. Ordainment would have been a way for Soller to join the holy, or greater orders (*órdenes mayores*), and thus to whiten himself; or at least entering the priesthood held that promise. Moreover, there were several types of priesthood within the lesser orders (*órdenes menores*) that did not even require literacy, much less ordination. Soller would have seemed much more plausible to the broader populace as one of these lower-order priests.

It would take until the first Spanish legislature, called the Cortes of Cádiz, and the Spanish Constitution of 1812 for the authorities to grant blacks and mulattos an avenue for becoming citizens and priests.[59] There emerged "a

56 Twinam, *Purchasing Whiteness*, 118.
57 Fra Molinero, "Ser mulato," 127n7.
58 Twinam, *Purchasing Whiteness*, 119.
59 Twinam, *Purchasing Whiteness*, 413, 420.

consensus that the state had an obligation to diminish barriers and provide opportunities for mobility, including access to higher education and the priesthood."[60] Absent such an opportunity granted by his society, Soller seizes it anyway.

Soller himself articulates his motive for attempting to pass as a priest in the inverse of these terms. In the first-person passage cited earlier, what he says via his public defender, Lisasueta, is that dressing as a priest "does contrive for me to pass freely on pilgrimage amid the dangers of such a long journey."[61] The meaning of Soller's statement to the Chief Magistrate is made clear if we hone in on the word "freely." Elsewhere in his defense, Soller says that he pretends to be a priest because he is exhausted from repeatedly being arrested while he travels, as he perpetually is assumed to be a runaway slave for his skin color; he seeks "with this clerical habit to manage to move freely so that they should not apprehend him as a slave according to the physiognomy of his dark-skinned face and curly hair, as they had done on other occasions."[62] As much as pursuing whiteness, Soller is fleeing blackness and the concomitant struggles being black presents him with in his everyday social reality.

Unfortunately, there is reason to believe Soller in this regard. In Renaissance Europe, "manumission could not free black Africans from slavery because society at large equated black skin colour (of whatever hue) with slavery, and many freed ex-slaves were apprehended as fugitives and were forced to negotiate their freedom all over again through the courts."[63] Despite the fairly significant numbers of freed persons (*libertos*), "Europeans persisted in imagining all black Africans in Europe as slaves. So the first, most fundamental and most deep-seated stereotype (one that was patently incorrect) was that all black Africans in Renaissance Europe were (and by extension were only fit to be) slaves."[64] In keeping with this unjust reality, we see this assumption borne out in the Soller case.

The authorities do not hesitate to categorize Soller as a fugitive solely on the basis of his ethnic features. This may be because "In sixteenth-century Spanish the word *negro* denoted both a person of black appearance and a black person who was a slave, without distinction."[65] In Spain, Portugal, and their

60 Twinam, *Purchasing Whiteness*, 416.

61 21^{r}; "traza para pasar libre mi romería por los peligros de tan larga viaje."

62 3^{v}; "con este hábito pasar libre y que no le prendiesen por esclavo según la fisonomía de su rostro moreno y *cabelo* rizo como lo habían hecho en otras ocasiones."

63 Lowe, "Stereotyping," 20; see also Phillips, *Slavery*, 144–145.

64 Lowe, "Stereotyping," 21.

65 Fra Molinero, "Juan Latino," 328.

colonies during this period, "almost until very recently, the person of black-African descent persisted in people's mental conception as synonymous with or the archetype of a slave."[66] It did not matter to the ruling powers that a significant portion of the population in southern cities on the Iberian peninsula (i.e., Seville) consisted of black Africans, some whom were enslaved but many of whom were free.[67] This reality clashed with their official narrative of blacks as slaves.

In the Soller case, there is a vast disconnect between this racist theory and the practice of everyday people's lives. For example, the attitudes of the barber and tailor toward ethnicity seem much more relaxed than those of the authorities. Each of the former changes his story. The tailor, Pedro de Castro, initially says that Soller already was wearing a priest's habit upon arrival to his tailor shop.[68] Later under oath, however, Castro mentions only the outline of Soller's tonsure.[69] At first the barber, Antonio Gonzales Siabal, likewise claims Soller to have worn the priestly habit,[70] but the authorities pressure the barber to say that Soller wore no such clerical garb. González Siabal then claims not to have paid attention to that detail. The presumption of the questioners is that Soller could not have been a priest and must have been a slave due to his black-African features.

In taking the confession of Antonio González Siabal, the judicial secretary Antonio Pérez asserts that this barber should have known better than to shave Soller's beard and tonsure: "by his physiognomy, dark-skinned face, and curly head of hair, he [González Siabal] could have determined he [Soller] was a slave and not a priest."[71] The barber responds that he did notice that Soller "was dark-skinned in the face and curly in the hair,"[72] but this may not have mattered to González Siabal because this barber himself is described earlier in virtually identical terms: "dark-skinned in the face, and with a black and curly head of hair,"[73] to quote again. Also, fellow resident of Ourense Juan Bautista had told the barber that Soller was a priest. Moreover, Soller already had "the outline of

66 Franco Silva, "La mujer esclava," 290; "casi hasta nuestros días, el negro ha quedado en la mentalidad de la gente como sinónimo o prototipo de esclavo."
67 Landers, *Black Society*, 8.
68 11^r.
69 11^v.
70 12^r.
71 13^r; "por su fisonomía, rostro moreno y cabello rizo, pudo hacer juicio era esclavo y no sacerdote."
72 13^r; "era moreno de cara y rizo de pelo."
73 5^r; "moreno de rostro y el cabello rizo y negro."

a priest's tonsure" that he said he had not shaved since his departure from Lisbon.[74] This ordinary sort of person, a barber, does not seem bothered by Soller's ethnic features.

The very different perspective of the judicial secretary, however, is by extension the viewpoint of the Crown: he acts on behalf of the court presided over by the Chief Magistrate, who is the principal royal representative in Ourense. In effect, "certain external biological traits (skin, hair, nose, mouth) eventually became a sign or *signifier* of the social condition of slavery."[75] Moreover, these signs were overlaid by the moral stigma of "natural inferiority. In this fashion, black skin color acquired a new meaning: black people were not completely human."[76] To these judicial authorities, it is intolerable for Soller to have impersonated a priest as a person of color. The Deputy Prosecutor makes it clear in his accusation that Soller's unpardonable act was "offending the priestly caste, being mulatto."[77]

To reiterate, for Soller to appear dressed as a priest matters far more than do his deeds or words because of how deeply visual this culture was and because of how stringent its dress code was. The Royal Appellate Court of Galicia did not seek to protect the weak but rather to maintain the established hierarchy and to safeguard the system of privileges belonging to the powerful in Hapsburg Spain.[78] The same is true of the municipal court authorities in Soller's original trial. Among these seventeenth-century Spanish authorities, the designated keepers of the social order, Soller's desire to be upwardly mobile is a form of self-fashioning that flies in the face of their prevailing stereotypes regarding the "proper" societal role for those of black-African descent.

74 12^{v}; "el cerco de corona de sacerdote."

75 Fra Molinero, *Imagen del negro*, 2; "ciertas características biológicas externas (piel, pelo, nariz, boca) pasaron a convertirse en marca o *significante* de la condición social de esclavitud."

76 Fra Molinero, *Imagen del negro*, 2; "inferioridad natural. De esa forma el color negro de la piel adquirió un nuevo sentido: los negros no eran humanos completamente."

77 20^{r}; "menospreciando el estado sacodertal, siendo mulato."

78 López Gómez, *Real Audiencia*, 2:1391.

CHAPTER 3

Origins

> I noticed that none of the black people in the marketplace had been marked with the brand. In Seville, the color of their skin—the color of my skin—was a sign in itself.
>
> ESTEBANILLO[1]

Even after studying the case, there is plenty one does not know about this man: exactly how old he is (forty-two, forty-four, or forty-six years), precisely where he's from (Italy or the Americas), specifically where he visited prior to his confirmed journey (Madrid and Zafra, Spain, and/or France), where he was headed (back to Coimbra, Portugal, as Soller says he intends, or on to Rome, as his pilgrim's diploma states), what his actual profession is (an herbalist barber or a priest), or in which circumstances he truly wound up after the case ends (at the oars of the galleys, dead, or free). The documents Soller carries with him add to the stories that he himself tells the authorities, widening the glimpse into his reality. As in Natalie Zemon Davis's multifaceted presentation of the com-

1 Lalami, *The Moor's Account*, 110. Laila Lalami's book is a work of historical fiction, and in this case the fictional part is the first-person narrative she places in the mouth of Estebanillo. And yet this person of color from Africa named Estebanillo did exist. In history as in Lalami's novel, Estebanillo became a slave to the Spaniard Andrés Dorantes, and wound up being forcibly enrolled in the ill-fated Spanish Expedition of 1528 led by the first governor of Spanish Florida, Pánfilo de Narváez, and chronicled by Álvar Núñez Cabeza de Vaca. The Spaniards came to rely on Estebanillo as a cultural liaison between themselves and the native tribes on the way from Florida into Texas.

Estebanillo was far from an anomaly and can be considered an "Atlantic creole" in the parlance of Ira Berlin. In fact, "Men of color drawn from creole communities of Europe accompanied Columbus to the Americas and marched with Balboa, Cortés, De Soto, and Pizarro … Other Atlantic creoles traveled on their own, as sailors and interpreters in both the transatlantic and African trades … Wherever they went, Atlantic creoles extended the use of the distinctive language of the Atlantic, planted the special institutions of the creole community, and propagated their unique outlook." Berlin, *Many Thousands Gone*, 25–26; Berlin, "Creole to African," 275. In other words, free blacks and African slaves lived and worked alongside one another within the same society across the centuries in both Spain and Spanish America.

 DOI:10.1163/9789004422704_004

peting narratives of Martin Guerre and the doppelgänger who impersonated him in sixteenth-century France, so in the Soller case must one develop the capacity to absorb multiple possible and plausible storylines. Some are more confirmable and more probable than others. All of them tell about a black life that may not have mattered to many people then, but which matters to us today.

1 The Island of Santo Domingo in Peru of the Indies

The question of Soller's place of origin is muddled from the beginning of the document. He swears in his initial affidavit "that he is from the Island of Santo Domingo, *although previously he had said he was from Italy or Naples*,"[2] a statement that perhaps sows doubts about his reliability as an informant (despite the information not having been recorded in his direct speech). Soller's mention of Italy is nonetheless an intriguing prospective place of origin for him given the devotion among those of black-African descent in Europe to San Benito de Palermo (1526–1589), a black Franciscan monk born to enslaved black-African parents in sixteenth-century Palermo, Italy. This Franciscan brother died at the end of the sixteenth century, and by the seventeenth century, a hundred years prior to his eventual beatification in 1743, he was the object of fervent devotion above all other black saints, particularly in Spain and the Iberian peninsula, and especially among the numerous free blacks and slaves here: "The immense majority of slaves and free persons lived in cities, and their concentration facilitated the diffusion of the image of one whose exemplary life comprised a model to follow."[3] The Franciscan brotherhood has fostered devotion to this saint up to the present day in Galicia,[4] and there is an eighteenth-century statue of San Benito by José Ferreiro in the Church of San Francisco in Santiago de Compostela (figure 3). That said, Soller presumably was not under oath when he previously had claimed to be from Italy (not to mention that there is instability around anything not transcribed as someone's direct words). If Soller's confirmed response, the Island of Santo Domingo, is taken at face value, it is easy enough to understand: this island is Hispaniola (Española), which today is comprised of the Dominican Republic and Haiti (figure 4).

2 1^{v}; "que es de la isla de Santo Domingo, *aunque antes había dicho era de Italia o Nápoles*" (emphasis that of the judicial secretary).

3 Vincent, "San Benito de Palermo," 25; "La inmensa mayoría de los esclavos y libertos vivía en ciudades y su concentración facilitaba la difusión de la imagen de un ser cuya vida ejemplar constituía un modelo a seguir."

4 Vincent, "San Benito de Palermo."

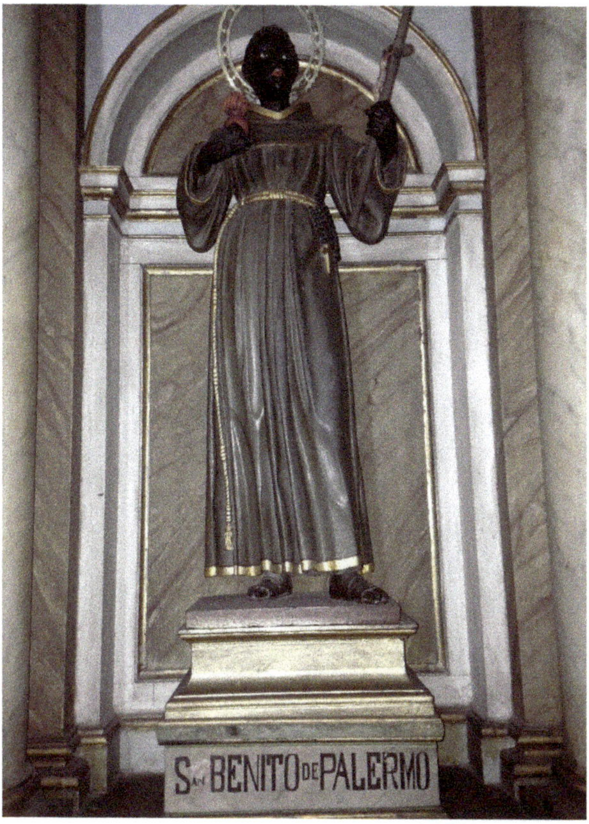

FIGURE 3 Sculpture of San Benito of Palermo by José Ferreiro. Church of San Francisco, Santiago de Compostela, Spain. Eighteenth century
PHOTO BY THE AUTHOR

The issue becomes further complicated just two folios later in the document when we find Soller saying in his subsequent affidavit that he is a "native of the island of Santo Domingo in Perú of the Indies."[5] A variation of this assertion is repeated three more times: once in his confession, "the island of Santo Domingo in Perú";[6] again in his only first-person testimony of the entire case, rendered as "the island of Santo Domingo, kingdom of Perú";[7] and a third time in Soller's appeal of the original ruling: "the island of Santo Domingo, kingdom

5 3^{v}; "natural de la isla de Santo Domingo en el Perú de Indias."
6 18^{r}; "la isla de Santo Domingo en el Perú."
7 21^{r}; "la isla de Santo Domingo, reino del Perú."

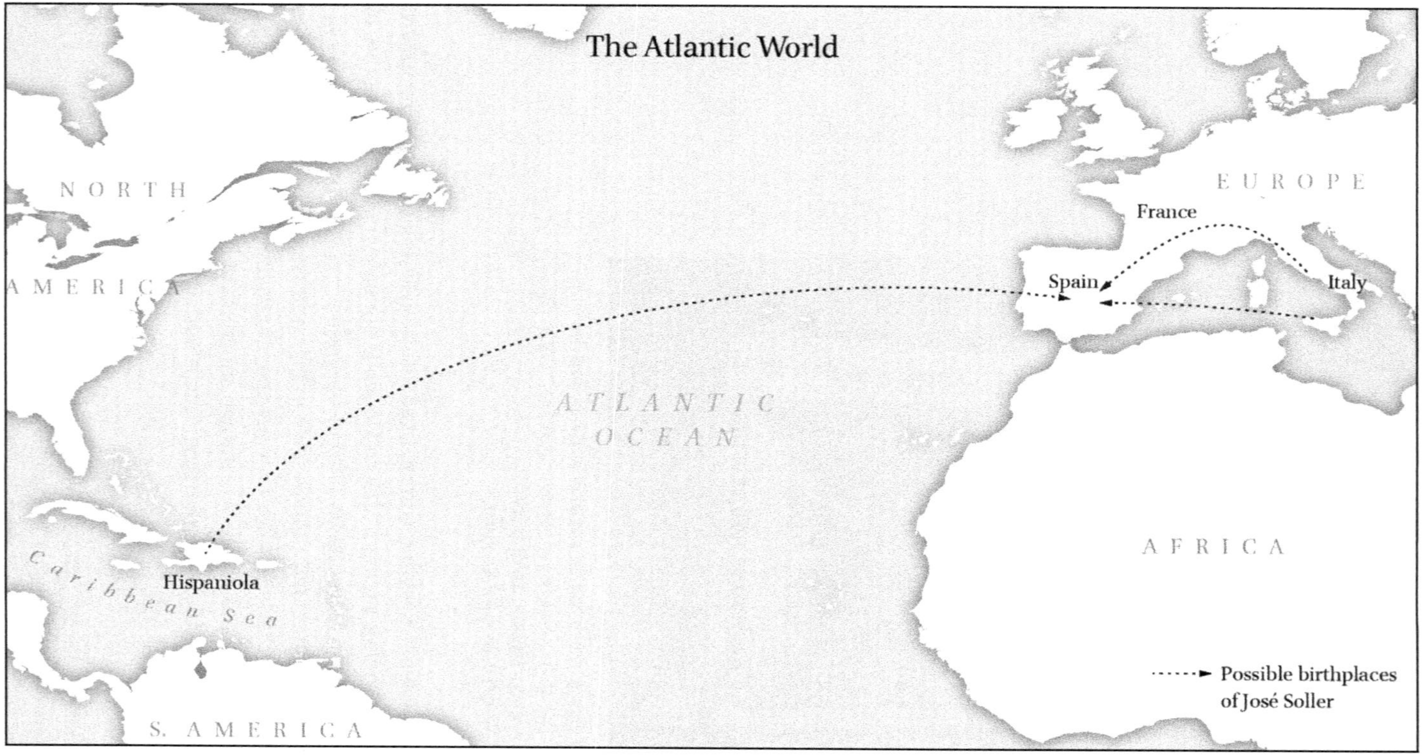

FIGURE 4 Map of the Atlantic world illustrating Soller's claimed origins prior to his arrival in Spain
MAP BY THE UNIVERSITY OF WISCONSIN–MADISON CARTOGRAPHY LAB

of Perú."[8] The confusion lies in the fact that Santo Domingo did not belong to the Viceroyalty of Peru but rather to that of New Spain,[9] the latter of which comprised the land masses in this portion of the Caribbean basin then under Hapsburg rule.[10] It also arises out of Soller's inconsistent testimony. It would seem that if Soller had come from Española he would have known it was part of Nueva España and not Peru. This coupled with other inconsistencies—as to whether or not he actually was pretending to be a priest, for example—may give the initial impression that Soller is lying or at least confused.

One noticeable item upon rereading is the apparent interchangeability of "Perú/Pirú" and the "Indies" (Indias) in the legal case. Peru appears again on Soller's passport, or safe-conduct, in which he is described as a "*Spanish subject of the Indies from the kingdom of Perú*."[11] This safe-conduct is an ecclesiastical printed document that has handwritten text inserted in blanks left for that purpose. The Indies appear in Soller's pilgrim's diploma, where he is described as a "*Priest of the Indies*."[12] From one of his confessions: "finding himself in the city of Santiago, he asked two or three foreign priests to testify before the diploma-granting Senior Cardinal that the confessant also was a priest so that it would be so written on the diploma that was given to him. It was executed in this fashion."[13] Throughout the case, the notaries public repeat attributions for "Priest of the Indies" (*Sacerdotem Indianum, sacerdote indiano*). With one lapse (before he was under oath), Soller has maintained from February (in Lisbon) through March (in Santiago) and now in April of 1693 (in Ourense) that he is from some variation of or locale within "Perú," which is to say, the West Indies.

---

8 33^r; "la isla de Santo Domingo, reino del Pirú."

9 Hispaniola was not so much a colony of Spain as part of one of its co-equal realms, New Spain (Nueva España), as was the case between Castile and its other ultramarine territories: "Such peninsular-overseas relationships evolved from seventeenth-century Hapsburg constructions that viewed the American kingdoms as equal." Twinam, *Purchasing Whiteness*, 66.

10 In Felipe II's landmark inventory of territorial holdings, the *Relaciones topográficas*, there is a town in the kingdom of Toledo that alternately goes by the names Santo Domingo, Santo Domingo del Valle, or Val de Santo Domingo. Campos y Fernández de Sevilla, "*Relaciones topográficas*," 493, 493n211, 512, 516, 533. This monarch's ultramarine holdings, however, are not included here.

11 7^r; "*indianus del cividade del Perú*." The Old Portuguese word *cividade* ("*Ciuidade*" in the original handwritten text in this document) can have multiple meanings, and this one corresponds to what is rendered elsewhere as "kingdom" (*reino*) in the Castilian Spanish vernacular portions of the legal case.

12 10^r; "*Sacerdotem Indianum*."

13 18^v; "hallándose en la ciudad de Santiago, pidió a dos o tres sacerdotes estranjeros declarasen ante el Señor Cardenal de los pasaportes que también lo era el confesante para que se le escribiese así en el despacho que se le diese. Y así se ejecutó."

One source that seems to indicate a similar usage of Peru is the seventeenth-century English poet Andrew Marvell's "The Mower":

> The tulip, white, did for complexion seek,
> And learn'd to interline its cheek;
> Its onion root they then so high did hold,
> That one was for a meadow sold.
> Another world was search'd, through oceans new,
> To find the Marvel of Peru.

Marvell's usage of the botanical term "marvel of Peru," the flower, "Mirabilia Peruviana, or Admirabilis planta,"[14] is presented as a metaphor for the conquest of the Americas. What is of interest regarding these lines of the poem is not the narrator's criticism of hybrid flowers and cultivated gardens per se, but rather the poet's use of Peru as a synecdoche for the entire New World. One parallel would be the use of the term "Guinea" as a stand-in for all of black Africa. During the early modern period, for example, Guinea is described as "The land of black people, or Ethiopians, in Africa."[15] In the Marvell poem, Peru likewise would seem to stand for all of the Americas.

As it turns out, at least three seventeenth-century authors writing in Spanish—Buenaventura de Salinas, Juan Meléndez, and Francisco de Montalvo—employ the term Peru as a synonym both of the "New World" and of the "Indies."[16] Additional corroboration is found in definition number 3 of the term *perulero* in the *Dictionary of Latin American Racial and Ethnic Terminology*: "person from SA [Spanish America]."[17] Sebastián de Covarrubias, in his landmark seventeenth-century encyclopedic etymological dictionary, the *Treasury of the Spanish Language* (*Tesoro de la lengua castellana o española*), defines the word *perulero* as "he who has become wealthy from the Indies of Perú."[18] Note that the phrase "Indies of Perú" refers to all of the Indies, that is, the Americas.

---

14 Marvell, "The Mower," n1. Note that this is the common garden plant "Four O'Clock."

15 Covarrubias 1016; "La tierra de los negros o etiopes, en África." See Fogelman and Goldberg, particularly with regard to Congo's interchangeability with Guinea. "'El rey de los *congos*,'" 155 and *passim*. Also, Schwartz cites a late sixteenth-century judge in Ecuador who equates Guinea with Africa as a land of savagery. *All Can Be Saved*, 161. Finally, the royal account of Gomes Eanes de Zurara (ca. 1453–1454) on the Portuguese conquest of Africa is entitled *The Chronicle of the Discovery and Conquest of Guinea*.

16 Mazzotti, "El Dorado," 404.

17 Stephens, *Ethnic Terminology*, 431.

18 1359; "el que ha venido rico de las Indias del Perú."

This region of course eventually came to be associated with the legend of El Dorado. The myth began with Diego de Ordás, who, based on his expedition to the Orinoco River in 1529, "was the first to make references ... to a rich, New World kingdom lying beyond the jungle and the mountains of the coast."[19] Covarrubias associates Peru with material wealth from the first sentence of his entry on this region: "Extremely famous region in the West Indies, conquered and ruled by the Catholic Monarchs of Spain, from where so many millions have been brought in gold and silver."[20] This association between Peru and the legend of El Dorado shows why It would have been used to stand for all of the Americas; this is an aspirational rhetorical gesture, as if to say, all of the Americas should be so fortunate as to have the wealth of Peru.

2 The Agency of a Creole Man-of-Words

Much of the uncertainty in Soller's story seems by design, in large part by his own design. As the linguist John Lipski remarked after attending a presentation I once gave on Soller, "this guy has changed his position so many times, it sounds like he could have run for office."[21] Why would Soller have done this? Well, for starters, disguise has its advantages. The pilgrim's outfit he wore could have been one form of concealment, while the priest's habit may have been another. Beyond appearances, though, oral discourse certainly falls within the repertoire of this great cultivator of ambiguity.

Suffice it to say that it may not have been in Soller's best interest to be straightforward and transparent with the authorities in a society that has it in for him before he even opens his mouth. In other words, Soller may have been trying to throw off the authorities intentionally through changing the details of his story. This is a form of signifying, as Henry Louis Gates, Jr. elucidates in his landmark *The Signifying Monkey*. It is also the case in folktales descended from African oral tradition, tales such as that of Brer Rabbit, who asks not to be thrown in the briar patch when the briar patch is *exactly* where Brother Rabbit is most at home and where he can escape. Rhetorical ruses count among the tricks of the weak.

19 Mazzotti, "El Dorado," 379.

20 1358–1359; "Provincia famosísima en la India Occidental, conquistada y señoreada de los Católicos Reyes de España, de donde se han traído tantos millones de oro y plata."

21 Conversation at the Colloquium on Black Resistance and Negotiation in Latin America: Runaway Slave Communities, University of Alabama at Birmingham, October 8, 2016.

The fact that questions remain concerning Soller's origin, profession, and the like shows what a capable performer he is and was, in keeping with the art of the Creole storytellers of the region from which Soller purportedly hails, the West Indies. The ethnographer Roger D. Abrahams uses the moniker "man-of-words" to convey the performative nature of the speech act in Afro-descended communities in the Caribbean. He describes the "good arguer" as a type of "man-of-words who is capable of turning any conversation into a show,"[22] someone who would seem to have much in common with Soller. In Afro-descended communities, Abrahams observes that words matter greatly and that each group takes very seriously their economy of speech.[23] Abrahams argues black-African speech communities are systematic in their verbal expression and that these Afro-descended cultural groups consistently retain these communication patterns over time throughout the Atlantic world.[24] He goes on to note that:

> The importance of effective speaking in Afro-American communities has been testified to repeatedly by multiple outside observers ... Men-of-words are given respect and approval for quickness of wit and for eloquence ... What I have called, for convenience's sake, "broad talkers" are the ones who rely primarily on wit and other economical verbal devices, and who commonly use creole as their medium.[25]

Soller would appear to be a man-of-words steeped in this same tradition.

A parallel exists between the elusive nature of Soller's narrative and the slippery mode of the Creole storyteller, and the reason lies in their shared background of hardship. In his introduction to *Creole Folktales*, Patrick Chamoiseau explains that these stories originated during the colonial period and that their deeper significance only is revealed against the historical backdrop of slavery in the Caribbean. The Creole person-of-words is the voice of the enslaved, of the oppressed, of those struggling to survive the brutality of the slaving society, which is why in these folktales:

> through cunning, patience, nerve, and resourcefulness (which is never a sin), the weak may vanquish the strong or seize power by the scruff of the neck. The Creole tale splatters the dominant system of values with all the immoral—or rather, amoral—guile of the poor and downtrodden.

---

22 Abrahams, *Man-of-Words*, xvi.
23 Abrahams, *Man-of-Words*, xix.
24 Abrahams, *Man-of-Words*, xxi.
25 Abrahams, *Man-of-Words*, 21.

> Yet these stories contain no "revolutionary" message, and their remedies for misfortune are not collective ones. The hero is alone, and selfishly preoccupied with saving his own skin.[26]

Soller's approach can be understood as part of this structure of opposing purposes, a system that simultaneously recognizes the futility of its goal of total freedom and yet refuses to abandon its pursuit of liberty despite all odds. Akin to Soller's testimony, which the authorities scrutinize in the utmost detail, the Creole person-of-words must dissimulate in his or her speech, using veiled, deceptive phrasing that intends to camouflage even as it discloses the underlying message. Similar to the manner in which the Creole storyteller is swift to laugh at him or herself, emphasizing the speaker's lowly status,[27] Soller is self-deprecating in the extreme once his testimony is concluded. Understanding the mode of storytelling helps us better comprehend the meaning of the story.

Soller's presentation of himself in a variety of different lights betrays his sense of awareness regarding how others perceive him as a man of color, what W.E.B. Du Bois describes as "double-consciousness, this sense of always looking at one's self through the eyes of others ... One ever feels his two-ness, ... two souls, two thoughts, two unreconciled strivings; two warring ideals in one dark body, whose dogged strength alone keeps it from being torn asunder."[28] The cosmology of a modern American black intellectual seems crucially relevant to Soller's multiple narratives and to his struggle in early-modern Spain.

The ambiguity Soller cultivates is itself a mode of resistance. In other words, Soller appears to have been intentionally trying to throw off the authorities through changing the details of his story, similar to the dance of a crab seeking to evade capture. Hence the Puerto Rican art of approaching issues indirectly, called "the crab dance" (*jaibería*), can be yet another lens through which to more clearly view Soller's inconsistent testimony: "A subtle intransigence, it undercuts control by acceding to one position and then to another. Refusing to stay in a fixed place can be confusing to interlocutors, who then become

---

26 Chamoiseau, *Creole Folktales*, xii–xiii. Chamoiseau, *Au temps de l'antan*, 10; "à force de ruse, de détours, de patience, de débrouillardise qui n'est jamais péché, peut vaincre le fort ou saisir la puissance au collet; le conte créole éclabousse le système de valeurs dominant, de toutes les sapes de l'immoralité, que dis-je: de l'a-moralité du plus faible; Il n'a pourtant pas de message 'révolutionnaire', ses solutions à la déveine ne sont pas collectives, le héros est seul, égoïste, préoccupé de sa seule échappée."

27 Chamoiseau, *Creole Folktales*, xiii–xiv. Chamoiseau, *Au temps de l'antan*, 11.

28 Du Bois, *Souls of Black Folk*, 3.

anxious and more controlling. But the gain is some space and some time to maneuver."[29] Soller's slipperiness is his means of self-protection.

These explanations additionally connect with Zora Neal Hurston's arguments in *Mules and Men*, which are cited in Doris Sommer's book *Proceed with Caution* as an admonition to those who aspire to gather African-American folk tales.[30] Hurston observes that "the Negro … is particularly evasive … The Indian resists curiosity by a stony silence. The Negro offers a feather-bed resistance. That is, we let the probe enter, but it never comes out. It gets smothered under a lot of laughter and pleasantries."[31] In response, Sommer asks us to "notice the double move to engage and deflect outsiders. And if reliable knowledge cannot be gotten, control is impossible."[32] It is in exactly this sense that the double discourse of Soller can be understood as a means of eluding the authorities' grasp.

3 Blackness and Slavery

One can sympathize, especially considering that Soller seems to have been racially profiled inasmuch as it is his skin color and Africanized features that attract the attention of the authorities and cause them to assume he is a slave. Once Soller arouses the attention of the authorities for being a "dark-skinned man" (*hombre moreno*) with the freshly shaven tonsure of a priest, the following is his initial response: "Having apprehended and secured him, he was asked whether or not he was a priest and what motive he had for having shaved said tonsure. He responded that *he was not a priest*, that he had shaved *the tonsure* to apply *on it a poultice for the maladies from which he suffered*, and that his profession was that of a barber."[33] Upon being brought in for questioning, Soller adds a new twist to this storyline in his first affidavit, saying "that he only was a poor barber who had shaved the tonsure for ailments from which he suffered and for being the fashion of his country."[34] The next day, however, Soller's story

29 Sommer, *Proceed with Caution*, 20.
30 Sommer, *Proceed with Caution*, 16.
31 Hurston, *Mules and Men*, 18.
32 Sommer, *Proceed with Caution*, 17.
33 1^v; "Y habiéndole aprehendido y asegurado se le preguntó si era sacerdote o no y que motivo tenía para haber abierto dicha corona. Respondió *no era sacerdote, que la corona* la había abierto para poner *en ella un emplasto por achaques que padecía* y que su oficio era de barbero."
34 1^v; "que sólo era un pobre barbero; que la corona la había abierto por achaques que padecía y ser estilo de su tierra."

changes dramatically: "he shaved the priest's tonsure and commissioned that a clerical neckband be cut for two priest's collars that he had, with this clerical habit to manage to move freely so that they should not apprehend him as a slave according to the physiognomy of his dark-skinned face and curly hair, as they had done on other occasions"[35] on his prior travels through France and elsewhere. This final rationale is the one Soller sticks with in subsequent confessions and statements.

Although it is difficult to divine a "true" response here, there is some historical reason to believe Soller's final explanation. It would not have been a complete surprise for him to have been presumed a slave in Spain or Portugal, as "during the sixteenth and seventeenth centuries, the bulk of Europe's population of African descent resided on the Iberian peninsula, and the vast majority of them there lived the demeaning life of slaves."[36] This surely has something to do with why many formerly enslaved persons were caught and arrested for being runaways simply by virtue of the melanin content of their skin.[37] And yet in Spain there were enslaved people of other ethnic backgrounds besides African. Some black Africans arrived here of their own recognizance on business or for diplomacy; numerous others who came in shackles via the slave trade later obtained their freedom.[38]

Without papers documenting free status, however, a black person easily could be "returned" to slavery, as dark-skinned freed persons regularly were confronted with the calamity of being confused with still-enslaved people.[39] William Phillips cites an example from 1693, the same year as Soller's travels, in Jaén, Spain:

> María de la Concepción had to go before a town clerk to have a legal document drawn up. She described herself as a free widow of African origin with two adult sons of mixed race. She stated that "my sons and I go about in different places working and seeking a living, and many people doubt that we are free, and many problems arise from that, and they arrest us,

35 3^v; "abrió la corona de sacerdote y mandó hacer un alzacuello de tal para dos cuellos que tenía y lograr con este hábito pasar libre y que no le prendiesen por esclavo según la fisonomía de su rostro moreno y *cabelo* rizo como lo habían hecho en otras ocasiones."

36 Berlin, *Many Thousands Gone*, 25.

37 This same legacy certainly holds true in the United States, where slavery gets racialized so profoundly. The remaining cognitive pollution is the assumption that any person of color is either low-level hired help or "dangerous."

38 Landers, *Black Society*, 8.

39 Phillips, *Slavery*, 144.

saying we are slaves. And to avoid such inconvenience and so that we are held to be free people and not slaves," she had the document prepared.[40]

And consider an unpublished list of cases having to do with black and enslaved people in the Archive of the Kingdom of Galicia, where the Soller dossier is preserved. These case titles virtually conflate "black people" (*negros*) and "enslaved persons" (*esclavos*), a confusion that reflects the association between blackness and slavery in the worldview of the authorities. For example, a case from 1696 deals with "Juan Antonio Somoza, a dark-skinned man, with Jerónima Monsuriu, widow of Antonio Somoza. She wants to oblige the former [Somoza] to serve as a slave."[41] Here *moreno* is the word used to denote Sr. Somoza's blackness, and Sra. Monsuriu most certainly thinks of him as a slave.

Dark skin came to be associated with slavery as early as the fifteenth-century in continental Europe. The original linkage stems from the royal account of Gomes Eanes de Zurara (ca. 1453–1454) in which he describes the arrival of the first large group of black African people (some 250 of them) on August 8, 1444, at Lagos, in the Algarve region of southern Portugal. These captured and enslaved human beings were bound in shackles and almost entirely naked: "The message could not have been clearer: it was not only permissible but right for Europeans to capture and enslave black Africans, and to treat them in an inhuman way; it was also financially rewarding and led directly to royal favours."[42] Zurara's text linked together notions of Africa, darkly pigmented skin, and human bondage in a chain of misery that would take centuries to decouple.[43] His insistence on the marked difference of the captives due their dark skin color, however, is belied by the lighter tones of mulattos and indigenous people: "Zurara's description of the skin color of the captives admits this connection at the same time that it attempts to isolate brownness as a separate or discrete pigmentational category. Brownness in this taxonomic perspective functions as a buffer zone between black and white and allows a racial hierarchy to remain in place, however temporarily."[44]

But skin-tone is not the only factor in play here. Europeans considered wearing clothes to be the only civilized thing to do. European sumptuary laws of the times clearly linked clothing to social status, and Europeans viewed Africans

40 Phillips, *Slavery*, 145.

41 "Juan Antonio Somoza, moreno, con Jerónima Monsuriu, viuda de Antonio Somoza. Querer obligar a servir a aquél como esclavo."

42 Lowe, "Introduction," 10–11.

43 Lowe, "Introduction," 11.

44 Blackmore, *Moorings*, 29.

without clothing through this cultural lens of human worth based on attire.[45] Hence the potency of Zurara's account of the first large group of black slaves arriving on the mainland: because they were scantily clad, they were seen as primitives fit for slavery.

Zurara's book, *The Chronicle of the Discovery and Conquest of Guinea*, i.e., of Africa, is the first official chronicle to espouse blatantly racist ideas against black people. This text circulated widely throughout Europe, and as a result, so did his attempt to ennoble the Portuguese enslavement of black Africans as part of an evangelistic mission. Zurara's portrayal cast these enslaved persons as lowly savages in need not only of religious salvation but also of redemption by civilization. Unfortunately, Zurara's concept of slavery persisted alongside the expansion of the slave trade itself.[46] After Bartolomé de las Casas, the great "liberator of indigenous people" (*libertador de los indios*), read Zurara's account, he came to repent for his previous advocacy of the enslavement of Africans in lieu of Native Americans: "Las Casas tried to close the door on African slavery, after opening it for so many Spanish slaveholders. He failed."[47]

Zurara was the principal Portuguese proponent of the idea that black Africans were justifiably enslaved due to their inherent sinfulness, which Zurara believed to have been caused by their descent from the lineage of Noah's son Ham. In Genesis, Ham laughs at his drunken father, Noah, who is passed out naked. As a result, Noah curses not only Ham but also Ham's son Canaan and all their subsequent generations, condemning the lot to slavery in perpetuity.[48] And yet while the story of Noah and his sons, especially the "sons of Ham" trope, is a biblical antecedent to the racialized categorization of the social hierarchy,[49] the idea that black Africans descended from Canaan is not canonical, that is to say, scriptural. Rather, this interpretation of the curse theory evolved over subsequent centuries and into the next millennium.

Ibram Kendi traces the theory regarding the "curse of Ham" from Hebrew and Islamic sources through the renowned Persian scholar Tabari (838–923): "God had permanently cursed ugly Blackness and slavery in to the very nature of African people, curse theorists maintained ... The shift to solely enslaving Black people, and justifying it using the curse of Ham, was in the offing."[50] Lynn Ramey tracks the cultural process of Ham's blackening and of his association

45 Lowe, "Stereotyping," 21.
46 Kendi, *Stamped from the Beginning*, 23–25.
47 Kendi, *Stamped from the Beginning*, 27.
48 Saunders, *Black Slaves*, 38.
49 Genesis 9:18–29; Genesis 10. See Harney, *Race, Caste, and Indigeneity*, 42–45.
50 Kendi, *Stamped from the Beginning*, 21.

with Africa to the fifteenth century. Crucially, she notes that the story containing Ham's curse in Genesis never mentions race at all. The color black, however, did have negative connotations in medieval Hebrew and Christian writings, and it was only a matter of time before Ham was painted as a black African in the fifteenth-century Arragel Bible, as well as in medieval maps designating the African continent, also referred to as Ethiopia, as the locus of Ham and his descendants. Devils and evil spirits were painted black and/or referred to as Ethiopians in illuminated manuscripts and medieval letters.[51] In European literature, I would trace the depiction of blackness as evil to a few centuries earlier in the epic poem of the *Song of Roland* (*Chanson de Roland*), the foundational work of France's national literature.

By the fifteenth century, "A movement had begun to point a moralizing finger at black Africans as a group."[52] Their observable differences in phenotype, language, and customs were mistaken for paganism, primitiveness, and underdevelopment, all of which were understood to require remedy in the form of colonization, evangelization, and enslavement. In other words, the social hierarchy supported the unequal proposition that white people were superior to people of color.[53] All in all, "Slavery converts black people into a unified Other, eliminating national differences, emphasizing *color*, and deemphasizing language, culture, national origin or whatever other individualizing circumstance."[54] Although pigmentation is an amorphous concept, any coherence it may have in historical documents primarily is a function of discriminatory intent,[55] as well as an aesthetics, in which what is unmarked—whiteness—is held as superior.

This type of racialization is a variant of the pogroms against the Jews in Valencia in 1391—building up to their eventual expulsion in 1492 under Fernando and Isabel—and against the New Christians (*conversos*) in Toledo in 1449. These massacres and the Edict of the Expulsion are the product of an "ethnic cleansing" complicated by various factors: economic (Jews collected taxes from the Christian laborers), geographic (there was a rural/urban divide, and Jews tended to live in cities), and religious (zealots such as Vicente Ferrer preached against the Jews for supposedly having murdered Christ, which

51 Ramey, *Black Legacies*, 42–45.

52 Ramey, *Black Legacies*, 45.

53 Fra Molinero, *Imagen de los negros*, 9.

54 Fra Molinero, *Imagen de los negros*, 17; "Los negros son convertidos por la esclavitud y para la esclavitud en un Otro unificado, eliminando las diferencias nacionales, enfatizando el *color* y desenfatizando lengua, cultura, origen nacional o cualquier otra circunstancia individualizadora."

55 Martín Casares, "Repensar," 21.

fomented violence and riots against them). With the *conversos* the situation was different because the Old Christians (*cristianos viejos*) resented the New Christians for suddenly being able to ascend the ranks of the nobility on account of their conversion to Christianity from Judaism. This is why Isabel brought the Inquisition from Italy in 1478, to ascertain whose conversion was sincere and whose was made out of self-interest.

Classifying people by skin color, on the other hand, attempts to make social inequalities seem "natural," that is, biologically or scientifically determined, since such racial categories are strategically necessary for the ruling powers in slaving societies.[56] That is to say, it is the social context of slavery that creates the perceived need for racial categories, not vice versa. Such racial constructs are an ideal tool for domination and subjugation.[57]

4 Analogues and Exceptions

This rude reality accounts for how the black protagonist presents himself in *The Gallant Negro of Flanders* (*El valiente negro de Flandes*), a seventeenth-century play by the minor Spanish playwright Andrés de Claramonte. This hero, named Juan de Mérida, feels compelled to state in contrast to societal expectations, "though black, I am not a slave." To prove the fact of his liberty despite the "disgrace of his color," Mérida displays his free papers, "this letter … of my liberty."[58] This passage is designed to reinforce the official viewpoint of Spanish Imperial authorities, of whose outlook the Spanish Golden Age theater is a chief proponent.[59] To be certain, the expectation Mérida expresses, that a black person normally is (or ought to be) an enslaved person, aligns with the views of the Deputy Prosecutor and the Representative of the King of Spain in the Soller case and appeal.

Society's conflation of blackness with slavery impacts even the greatest exceptions to the rule in early modern Spain and Portugal, Juan Latino being the most obvious example. In the sixteenth century, Latino is a truly extraordinary personality in Renaissance Spain. He came to Europe an enslaved black African, worked hard to get a classical education (studying alongside his then-master), and subsequently earned his freedom. Latino's acquired surname

56 Martín Casares, "Repensar," 22.

57 Martín Casares, "Repensar," 22.

58 Claramonte y Corroy, *Valiente negro*, 85, 87; "pues aunque negro soy, no soy esclavo"; "la infamia del color"; "esta carta … de mi libertad."

59 Fra Molinero, *La imagen de los negros*, 16.

comes from what he eventually became, a Latin teacher in southern Spanish city of Granada; his poetry also is in Latin. In fact, Juan Latino is the first black African from south of the Sahara to publish a book-length volume of poetry in a European language.[60] Moreover, Latino is the earliest intellectual of black-African ancestry in Europe to generate a rhetoric of black dignity.[61] This black pride is manifest in Latino's continual reframing of metaphors with the color black in his poetry: an Ethiopian converts to Christianity; a raven sings a song hailing auspicious events; the black Latino himself is a bard. In Latino's verse, "Blackness here has shed its baggage as a marker of slave status or disdain."[62]

This poet's masterpiece is the *Austrias carmen*, a song of triumphalist glory basking in the victory of the Spanish Armada over the Ottoman Turks in the Mediterranean battle of Lepanto. While it may seem plausible to see such an epic poem as a puff piece praising the Spanish "empire where the sun never set" under Felipe II, Chantell Smith explains Latino's deeper goal of supporting those on society's fringes vis-à-vis the back-story of Juan de Austria, whose leadership in this battle is the topic of this epic. Juan de Austria and King Felipe II are half-brothers, both the sons of Charles V, but the former was born out of wedlock and as such must prove himself all the more in battle. Being a black African in Renaissance Europe, Juan Latino identifies with Juan de Austria as an illegitimate son: both types of people live at the margins of society. Smith proposes that this is why Latino chooses Austria as the hero of the epic poem.[63] Latino was respected and well-known among some of the greatest writers of his day for his educational attainment and for his mastery in composing poetry in Latin. Regardless of these formidable achievements, however, Juan Latino's influence perpetually would be diminished by virtue of his dark phenotype.[64] Latino would attempt to discredit any perception of his debased and subjugated status through his achievements in the world of letters, most notably by praising of a member of the house of Austria in Latin verse.[65] "Being a bard worthy to write the *Austrias carmen*, Latino established himself as an authoritative, exceptional figure in a society where *black* was akin to *slave*."[66]

Even Latino's remarkable achievements as a person and a poet are not enough to combat the tide of racial prejudice based on skin color that would

60 Latino, *Carmen Austria*, 428.
61 Phillips, *Slavery*, 144.
62 Wright, *Epic of Juan Latino*, 112.
63 Smith, "Juan to Juan," 232.
64 Smith, "Juan to Juan," 236.
65 Fra Molinero, "Juan Latino," 336.
66 Smith, "Juan to Juan," 243.

come to prevail in seventeenth-century Spain. This current of racial discrimination was so strong that norms barring admission of black people and mulattos to professions in the Church and Palace were practically unnecessary prior to the mid-seventeenth century. For example, Afro-descended painter Juan de Pareja, disciple of the seventeenth-century Spanish master Diego de Velázquez, would need to enlist the help of powerful allies, namely Velázquez and his protectors (who were part of the nobility), in order to succeed as a member of his profession.[67]

Extreme forms of such racism persisted well beyond this time and beyond Iberian shores, for instance in the nineteenth-century United States story of Solomon Northup, whose autobiography is popularized in the Academy-Award winning film of the same title, *Twelve Years a Slave*. You may recall that Northup lives in the free state of New York and obtains papers confirming his status as a free man for a trip to Washington, DC. These free papers constitute the only evidence Northup has of his free status until he is drugged and kidnapped.[68]

> My impression is there were then three persons with me, but it is altogether indefinite and vague, and like the memory of a painful dream. Going towards the light, which I imagined proceeded from a physician's office, and which seemed to recede as I advanced, is the last glimmering recollection I can now recall. From that moment I was insensible. How long I remained in that condition—whether only that night, or many days and nights—I do not know; but when consciousness returned, I found myself alone, in utter darkness, and in chains.[69]

Moreover, these crucial documents, the only proof of his free status, have been stolen: "What had I done to deserve imprisonment in such a dungeon? … I felt of my pockets, so far as the fetters would allow—far enough, indeed, to ascertain that I had not only been robbed of liberty, but that my money and free papers were also gone!"[70] The year is 1841.

Northup subsequently is sold into slavery and shipped off to Louisiana in this inhumane capacity for twelve years. During the period of his enslavement

---

67 Fra Molinero, "Ser mulato," 127n7. Exceptional figures of black-African descent in early modern Portugal include the black surgeon Mestre António and the mulatto playwright and grammar teacher Alfonso Álvares. Saunders, *Black Slaves*, 146.

68 Northup, *Twelve Years*, 33.

69 Northup, *Twelve Years*, 37–38.

70 Northup, *Twelve Years*, 38.

in Louisiana, it is the stolen free papers that Northup seeks in order to obtain once again documentary proof of his status as a free person, and on his behalf "master Bass" secretly sent a letter, which Northup saw after the fact:

> "Having been born free, just across the river from you, I am certain you must know me, and I am here now a slave. I wish you to obtain free papers for me, and forward them to me at Marksville, Louisiana, Parish of Avoyelles, and oblige
>
> "Yours, SOLOMON NORTHUP.
>
> "The way I came to be a slave, I was taken sick in Washington City, and was insensible for some time. When I recovered my reason, I was robbed of my free-papers, and in irons on my way to this State, and have never been able to get any one to write for me until now; and he that is writing for me runs the risk of his life if detected."[71]

After twelve brutal years, it is the eventual delivery of these free papers that allows Northup to return to his family a free man. Despite its later date and location at a remove from that of Soller, Northup's situation is parallel to that of Soller at least in one regard: "liberty is going to be a very slippery condition for all people of African descent during the Colonial era because having black blood in one's veins means it is possible to return to slavery one day."[72] For the same reasons, neither can Soller afford to take his freedom for granted.

5 Free Papers

Soller's removal from the vineyards of Ourense and his subsequent imprisonment may bear a direct relationship to his ethnicity. In other words, what makes him look like an "outsider" (*forastero*) is his being "mixed-raced" (*mestizo*) and mulatto. The Deputy Prosecutor in the criminal proceedings, Joan del Rodicio, eventually states as much in one of his later formulations: "José Soller's personal appearance and figure are that of a mulatto, from which he is inferred to be a fugitive slave, unless he should prove the contrary with documents, and

71 Northup, *Twelve Years*, 264, 275.

72 Fra Molinero, "Ser mulato," 146–147; "la libertad va a ser una condición muy resbaladiza para todas las personas de ascendencia africana durante la época colonial; porque tener sangre negra en las venas equivale poder volver a la esclavitud en algún momento."

more so when he is from a foreign kingdom."[73] The "documents" of this passage probably are a reference to free papers; in their absence, Soller is presumed to be a runaway slave based solely on his blackness and foreignness.

The problem is, Soller *already has* the documents he thinks will provide him liberty. Soller says he seeks to have his pilgrim's diploma (*compostela*) indicate he is a priest in order to act as a sort of equivalent to free papers protecting him from imprisonment.[74] But the Deputy Prosecutor dismisses this possibility outright. Despite the fairly significant numbers of *libertos*, many white Europeans stubbornly continued to take for granted that all people of black-African ancestry were slaves. This deeply ingrained yet provably false stereotype was coupled with the abhorrent notion that black Africans not only were slaves but also were *meant to be* enslaved.[75] One sees this assumption borne out in the Soller case. For the Spanish authorities, Soller's apparent ethnicity trumps all the other factors, including the documents he actually has in his possession. The Deputy Prosecutor, for example, presumes all of Soller's papers to be forgeries[76] despite the "lawful motive" (*justis de causis*) cited in his passport.[77]

What Soller does not have, though, are free papers, or "a freedman's letter of manumission":[78] "Manumission in Portugal, as in other societies, was a popular and secure method of attaining freedom, and by the sixteenth century the population of freed slaves amounted to some 10 percent of the slave population. The manumission document was called the *carta de alforria*, usually given only by the master himself, either in his lifetime or by will."[79] As a result of the lack of notarial documents from the early modern period, very few of these free papers exist today; many unregistered *cartas de alforria* may have existed and simply not survived.[80]

Over the course of Soller's trial proceedings and appeal, he is twice labeled a "fugitive slave."[81] Including these instances, there are ten mentions total

---

73 24^{r}; "su aspecto personal y forma es de mulato, de que se infiere ser esclavo fugitivo, menos que no acredite lo contrario con papeles, y más cuando es de reino estraño."

74 3^{v}.

75 Lowe, "Stereotyping," 21.

76 20^{r}.

77 7^{r}.

78 These free papers are known as an *ahorría* or as a *carta de alforria*. Lawrance, "Black Africans," 73; Phillips, *Slavery*, 132.

79 Phillips, *Slavery*, 132. Others list the freed population of Portugal at this time as closer to seven percent. Berlin, "Creole to African," 276n58.

80 Saunders, *Black Slaves*, 141.

81 24^{r}, 33^{r}.

describing him as a "slave,"[82] most of these by the Deputy Prosecutor and the King's Representative. Not once, however, is Soller described as bearing the brand of a slave or of a fugitive slave outlaw on his cheeks:

> Slave owners and public officials certainly branded some slaves, but it appears that it was usually unsuccessful fugitives who suffered the branding. Such marks obviously would diminish the value of the slave, and masters would have kept that in mind. A common marking for fugitives was a mark of an "s" on one cheek and an "i" on the other, signifying the Latin slogan *sine iure*, or outside the law. Often the marks were popularly interpreted to mean "s" and a straight-line symbol of a nail (*clavo* in Spanish), so that when combined they read as *esclavo*, Spanish for slave. Many modern scholars have followed the popular interpretation. Other brand marks included whole words indicating ownership.[83]

In the absence of such markings, there is no hard evidence to show that Soller has ever been a slave. Soller effectively is branded an outlaw by the color of his skin—Juan de Mérida's "disgrace of his color" in Claramonte's play.

Scarcely is Soller referred to in the case without the descriptors *mulato* or *mestizo*, the latter of which means "mixed-race" in the Soller case. Moreover, the Deputy Prosecutor's language here—José Soller is "a mulatto, from which he is inferred to be a fugitive slave"—represents a departure from standard descriptive usage during the period. "In the Portuguese and Spanish colonies there rapidly developed a social hierarchy structured according to degrees of intermixture of Negro and European blood, replete with a complicated battery of terminology to facilitate definition."[84] These categories followed a basic pecking order: those of European descent born in Spain and Portugal on the Iberian Peninsula (*peninsulares*); those of European heritage born in the New World (*criollos*); those of blended indigenous and European ancestry (*mestizos*); natives (*indios*); those of mixed black-African and European backround (*mulatos*); black people (*negros*); and those of mixed black and indigenous ancestry (*zambos*). The continued blending of these ethnicities, however, created myriad racial varieties, which led to a colonial caste system that attempted to categorize and hierarchize these various mixtures of European, indigenous, and African ancestry. Mulattos and mestizos were but two of a whole host of

---

82 1^r, 3^v (twice), 5^v, 13^r, 18^v, 20^r, 24^r, 30^r, 33^r.

83 Phillips, *Slavery*, 76; see also Claramonte y Corroy, *Valiente negro*, 85n39.

84 Jordan, Winthrop, *White over Black*, 167.

ethnicities coexisting with those of a European background,[85] so much so that *mestizo* could refer to any blend, including black and white.

The early-modern caste system in Europe and the Americas is an extension of the medieval estates model: those who toil (*laboratores*); those who pray (*oratores*); and those who fight (*bellatores*). The model itself has much in common with the caste order in India: "Like its subcontinental counterpart, the medieval European system articulated hierarchical categories and postulated a system-wide participation of all members of society …; any notion of changing one's position was seen as inherently subversive."[86] Hence the disruptiveness of Soller's disguise. What Soller ultimately resists is the scaffolding of this caste system superimposed onto the deep structure of the three estates.

This terminology was not at all precise: "when one talked about the population of mixed descent the most common practice was to resort to all-encompassing expressions such as '*mestizos*, *mulatos*, and other castes,' which without a doubt corresponds much better to the general image deduced from letters, reports, rosters, documents, … that is, the prevailing official discourse."[87] In keeping with this reality, the Soller case indiscriminately refers to him as either a *mestizo*[88] or, more commonly, as a *mulato*[89] person. But Rodicio's use of *mulato* is pejorative vis-à-vis its association with slavery. While Soller is viewed as threatening by virtue of being a pilgrim-outsider, it is not at all clear that he actually is a runaway slave. Soller simply may have sought out the disguises that pilgrimage and the priesthood afforded him in order to move about—in order to live—freely.

6 Mulatto

Mulatto. The word itself derives from "mule," the animal a blend of two species, horse and donkey, the mulatto an admixture of people who are white and black.[90] The association between *mulato* and *mulo* was common in the early

85 Harney, *Race, Caste, and Indigeneity*, 10, 190–191.

86 Harney, *Race, Caste, and Indigeneity*, 13.

87 Ares Queija, "Mestizos, mulatos y zambiagos," 84; "a la hora de hablar de la población de origen mixto lo más común era recurrir a expresiones englobantes del tipo 'mestizos, mulatos y demás castas', que sin duda corresponden mucho mejor con la imagen generalizadora que se desprende de cartas, informes, relaciones, cédulas …, esto es, del discurso oficial predominante."

88 Four times: 1^{v} (twice), 5^{v}, 6^{r}.

89 Nineteen times from beginning to end in the dossier.

90 Covarrubias, *Tesoro*, 1302.

modern period.[91] Yet the comparison is to an animal, which means the word in its origin arguably is racist in its animalization, in its dehumanization of the person. By the same token, Javier Irigoyen-García, in *The Spanish Arcadia*, shows how sheepherding contributes to Old Christian identity and therefore its others through the language of sheep breeding focused on whiteness of wool, in which terms like *raza* and *ralea* first refer to the unwanted presence of dark wool and come to be synonyms for the innate taint of impure (non-white) race. He is talking about Muslims and Moriscos, but the animal terminology clearly applies here, as well.[92] The etymology accounts for the mental leap (for some, such as Deputy Prosecutor Rodicio in Soller's trial) from mulatto to slave: subhuman and therefore manacled, worked, controlled.

Early modern Spanish authorities perceived mulattos as a threat. Their very presence in society points to the existence of miscegenation, as the mothers of mulattos usually were black slave concubines, the fathers typically the Christian white masters: "Historians have amply documented how slave-owners took the bodies of their female slaves for sexual pleasure as well as the profits assured in slave offspring."[93] The characterization of mulattos as "bastards" largely was a result of their fathers (and in turn, the rest of society) not acknowledging their progeny as legitimate offspring and also because they usually were the product of a sexual union outside of wedlock. In baroque Spain, the very existence of mulattos generates discomfort: they are visible, living proof not only of fornication but also of miscegenation.[94] Phenotype signals the "illegitimacy" of mulattos, whose presence therefore compromises the obsessive claims to blood purity (*limpieza de sangre*) of the Old-Christian elite. In this sense, Soller's very existence as a mixed-race individual jeopardizes the foundation of the power structure.

In an extension of the *limpieza de sangre* strictures, blackness of any shade was sneered at and stereotyped as the embodiment of shamefulness, immorality, and lawlessness in early modern Spain and Portugal. Dark skin was viewed as "impure," and simply having it was sufficient to preclude one's ability to rise in the ranks of society.[95] As the population of mulattos, dark-skinned people (*pardos*), and blacks grew, the Spanish monarchy issued a number of royal mandates to keep them in their sunken place: "Blacks, pardos, and mulattos

---

91 Earle and Lowe, *Black Africans*, xv.

92 See especially Irigoyen-García's analysis of "Sheep Herding and Racial Terminology" in *Spanish Arcadia*, 38–43.

93 Burshatin, "Written on the Body," 422; see also Franco Silva, "La mujer esclava," 293, 298.

94 Fra Molinero "Ser mulato," 124.

95 Sweet, *Domingos Álvares*, 192.

could not hold any public or royal offices (1549, 1584); practice most professions … (1535); or become notaries (1621). They could not attend the university."[96] The legal code was designed to ostracize and prosecute people of black-African ancestry, including mulattos. Moreover, the law was engineered for people of color effectively to be defenseless.[97]

These laws for blacks and mulattos included restrictions on the type of clothing they could wear. Ethnic minorities were not allowed to dress as Spaniards in the Americas, prohibiting people of color from donning the clothes of elite whites: "Even though sumptuary laws might sometimes be breached, they nonetheless set normative visual markers attempting to sustain hierarchy."[98] This is exactly the social barrier Soller runs up against when putting on the priestly habit.

Soller's impersonation of a priest as a mulatto meant that he was dressing beyond his station:

> Westerners felt that slaves' [*sic*] appropriated European formal wear in order to partake in vainglorious displays that did not conform to bond people's debased status. When field slaves wore dress clothing, they failed to comply with white perceptions of how they should look. Slavery was a labor institution, and whites felt bond people should wear clothing that indexed their debased status. Coarse clothing, like blackness, symbolized savagery and oppression, punctuating white perceptions of Africans. When slaves wore dress clothing, many whites concluded that they challenged their debased status and assumed privileges whites reserved for themselves.[99]

And yet all was not doom and gloom for people of black-African descent as they forged new identities.

As Jane Landers has documented meticulously, free people of black African descent occupied a variety of roles in Hispano-America: adventurers such as Juan Garrido, who fought alongside Hernán Cortés in the conquest of Mexico, and Juan González (Ponce) de León, who helped conquer natives in revolt; Francisco Mejías, a mulatto who was an overseer for the Spanish in Puerto Rico; Francisco Galindo and Juan de la Cruz, two additional mulatto overseers; Captain Diego Martín (also known as Diego el Mulato), who served in a military

96 Twinam, *Purchasing Whiteness*, 102; see 105, as well.
97 Fra Molinero, "Ser mulato," 137.
98 Twinam, *Purchasing Whiteness*, 102.
99 Dawson, "Enslaved Ship Pilots," 174.

capacity equivalent to the rank of admiral in the Spanish fleet; and a host of Spanish militia soldiers, rebels against the Crown, and maroons (*cimarrones*), who formed entire communities of runaway slaves.[100] Revolt and runaways are a common thread throughout the slave-holding societies in Atlantic basin.

In what today is Colombia, for example, these communities of *cimarrones* freed other slaves, traded with the enemies of the Spanish such as pirates, and

> also challenged Spanish notions of civilized living, and the desired racial and social order. When their *palenques* (palisaded camps) became large, fortified, and somewhat permanent, Spaniards tried to eradicate them in major military campaigns that adopted the language and character of Christian crusades. In these expeditions, St. James, the patron saint of the Spanish Reconquest, once known as Santiago Matamoros [the Moor-slayer], or Mataindios [the Indian-slayer], took on a new aspect as Matanegros (the Negroslayer).[101]

Of course it was the shrine of this same St. James to which Soller was traveling on pilgrimage. The irony of Soller making a journey to the shrine of the slayer of his own kind deepens the cruelty in this case study.

There seems to have been greater leeway for the upward mobility of those of blended African ancestry in Portugal. For example, "Mulattoes who were not only Christians but also resembled Europeans in their features—and who often had the advantage of prolonged acquaintance with Portuguese culture—were esteemed."[102] A key sixteenth-century example is the "half-caste" known as Brás de Albuquerque, born out of wedlock to a white Portuguese nobleman and his African mistress. King Manuel I later dubbed Brás de Albuquerque "Afonso" after Albuquerque's deceased father, himself descended from Portuguese royalty. It did not hurt Afonso (Brás) de Albuquerque's standing that his family tree on his father's side additionally intersects with that of the fourteenth-century Queen of Castile Catherine of Lancaster, she who was tutored by Geoffrey Chaucer (a dear friend of her father, John of Gaunt, Duke of Lancaster). This aristocratic lineage seems to have enabled Brás de Albuquerque's upward mobility, acting as a counterweight to the blackness in his background. Like so many mulattos, Brás de Albuquerque technically was an illegitimate child, a bastard. And yet "there are systems within systems," to quote Renato Berardo, the man who now administers his family estate at the Bacalhoa Palace (Palácio

100 Landers, *Black Society*, 10–22.

101 Landers, "Cartagena," 152.

102 Saunders, *Black Slaves*, 175.

da Bacalhôa) in Azeitão, Portugal, just south of Lisbon, the selfsame palace that Afonso (Brás) de Albuquerque acquired and embellished during his lifetime. This Albuquerque also constructed the intriguing four-story House of Spikes (Casa dos Bicos) in the Alfama District of Lisbon.[103] These premier properties complement Albuquerque's leadership roles as a writer, as Minister of Finance (Vedor da Fazenda), as President of the Lisbon Senate, and as a member of the board of directors of none other than the Misericórdia brotherhood,[104] the institution that provided the hospitality infrastructure that directly benefited José Soller on his journey north from Lisbon. Afonso (Brás) de Albuquerque's sixteenth-century story illustrates as well as anyone's the impressive degree of upward mobility people with African ancestry could achieve within the ranks of Portuguese society.

7 Atlantic Creole

As a *mulato* in Portugal and Spain who possibly hails from the Caribbean or Italy, Soller's identity can be understood as *creole*, a word borrowed from the Portuguese *crioulo*, used to indicate someone of black-African ethnicity native to the Americas. The term also has been used to mean someone of blended European ancestry, that is, mixed with another type of ethnic background, as well as to refer to black Africans living in Europe.[105] More broadly, Soller can be understood as what Ira Berlin has termed an "Atlantic creole" for his apparently extensive contact with trans-Atlantic societies.[106] "Although the countenances of these new people of the Atlantic—Atlantic creoles—might bear features of Africa, Europe, or the Americas in whole or in part, their beginnings, strictly speaking, were in none of these places. Instead, by their experiences and sometimes by their persons, they had become part of the three worlds that came together along the Atlantic littoral."[107] These Atlantic creoles often "played fast and loose with their diverse heritage, employing whichever identity paid best."[108] One sees this strategy in Soller's adoption of the priest's tonsure and fabric, and also in his responses and statements over the course of the criminal proceedings against him.

103 Conversation with Renato Berardo in the Bacalhoa Palace, Azeitão, Portugal, June 22, 2018.
104 Historical markers in the museum inside the Bacalhoa Palace.
105 Berlin, "Creole to African," 253n5.
106 Berlin, "Creole to African," 254.
107 Berlin, "Creole to African," 254.
108 Berlin, "Creole to African," 255.

Aurelia Martín Casares charts the ethnic and geographic origin of enslaved peoples on the Iberian peninsula, among whom are included for the sixteenth and seventeenth centuries Hindus, Filipinos, Native Americans, as well as Afro-descended peoples of myriad backgrounds: sub-Saharan, Afro-Portuguese, Afro-Spanish, Afro-Brazilian, Afro-Caribbean, and Afro-Latin American.[109] Soller claims to be Afro-Caribbean and may be Afro-Portuguese or Afro Spanish. He definitely is on the more assimilated end of the spectrum.

In his second affidavit, Soller says that he left Santo Domingo roughly sixteen years prior in the company of one Count of Alayos and "that for a long time he was present in Madrid and other parts" (figure 5). Soller must have had flawless Spanish. Otherwise, a text such as this would have indicated he was someone who was not fluent (*bozal*). In fact, "in Spanish society, there were not mulattos who were not fluent because the vast majority were Spanish or Portuguese, that is to say, culturally integrated."[110] It is logical that Soller not only would have had a good familiarity with Spanish culture but also that he would have been fully acculturated. The repeated references to Soller as a native of the New World (*indiano*) supports the notion of his acculturation.

Soller says "that he came to this country from the villa of Zafra on pilgrimage to the Apostle Santiago, as will be manifest in his documents."[111] These papers, however, only document his route north from Lisbon to Santiago. Zafra is very close to the Portuguese border, and Soller's confirmed itinerary begins in Lisbon (figure 1). Once called "little Seville" for its wealth, Zafra is situated along the north-south axis of the pilgrimage route to Santiago de Compostela known as the Silver Way (Vía de la Plata),[112] which begins to the south in Seville and heads north from Zafra (via Mérida, Cáceres, Plascencia, Salamanca, and Zamora, Spain). Zafra's whitewashed walls and Islamic-influenced (Mudéjar) architecture remain in the medieval heart of the city to this day, and the façade of the former Hospital of Santiago, one of two hospices serving pilgrims during Soller's time, is still standing (figure 6). This route could be what Soller meant to indicate. Given the pilgrim's documented itinerary, however, it seems much more likely that Soller would have come to Lisbon first on a westerly path

---

109 Martín Casares, "Repensar," 19.

110 Fra Molinero, "Ser mulato," 126; "no había mulatos bozales en la sociedad española, porque la inmensa mayoría eran españoles o portugueses, es decir, seres culturalmente integrados."

111 3ᵛ; "que a esta tierra vino desde la Villa de Zafra en romería al apostol Santiago, como constará de sus papeles."

112 Estrada, *Población general de España*, 328.

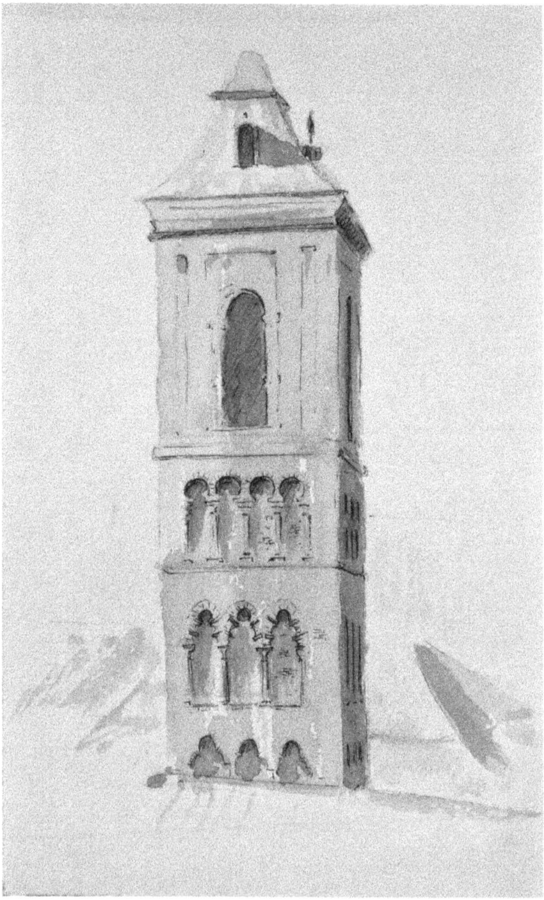

FIGURE 5 Mudéjar bell tower of the Church of San Nicolás de los Servitas, Madrid, Spain. Twelfth century
WATERCOLOR SKETCH BY CLINTON LARISCY

(via Badajoz, Spain at the Spanish-Portuguese border, and subsequently Elvas, Évora, Setúbal, and Azeitão, Portugal), as shown in the map of figure 1.

Soller presumably arrived in Zafra from Madrid. The pilgrimage destination of Guadalupe lies in between these two places geographically in the heights of the Guadalupe mountain range in the Spanish region of Extremadura. There is a mythical black Madonna and Child here, the original Virgin of Guadalupe—whose holy image represents "freedom for captives, a file for their chains, and relief from their suffering"[113]—she who gave rise to the eponymous patron

113 Cervantes, *Trials of Persiles*, 220; "libertad de los cautivos, lima de sus hierros y alivio de sus pasiones." Cervantes, *Persiles*, 294.

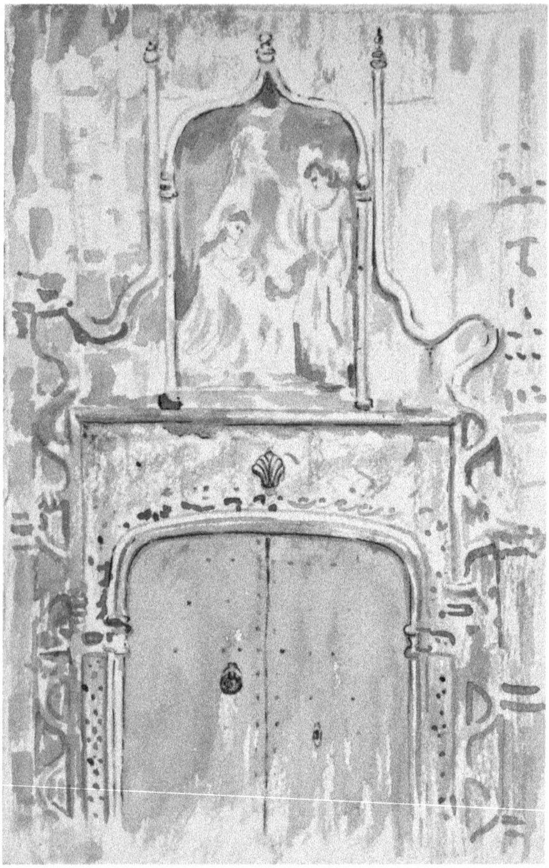

FIGURE 6 Façade of the former Hospital of Santiago, Zafra, Spain. Fifteenth century
WATERCOLOR SKETCH BY CLINTON LARISCY

saint of the Americas, among her myriad other New-World manifestations.[114] Though this Virgin's features are not Africanized per se (in the way of curly hair or a broad nose, for example), an audience of some African descent may have identified and may identify still with the statue nonetheless, if only for the dark pigmentation of Mary and Jesus (figure 7). The Virgin of Guadalupe in Mexico, of whom an eighteenth-century painting adorns the shrine to Our Lady of Guadalupe in Extremadura, likewise is famous (apart from her miracles) for her dusky complexion, a source of particular pride among the majority population of mestizos (mixed indigenous and European in this case).

114 García, *Guadalupe de Extremadura*.

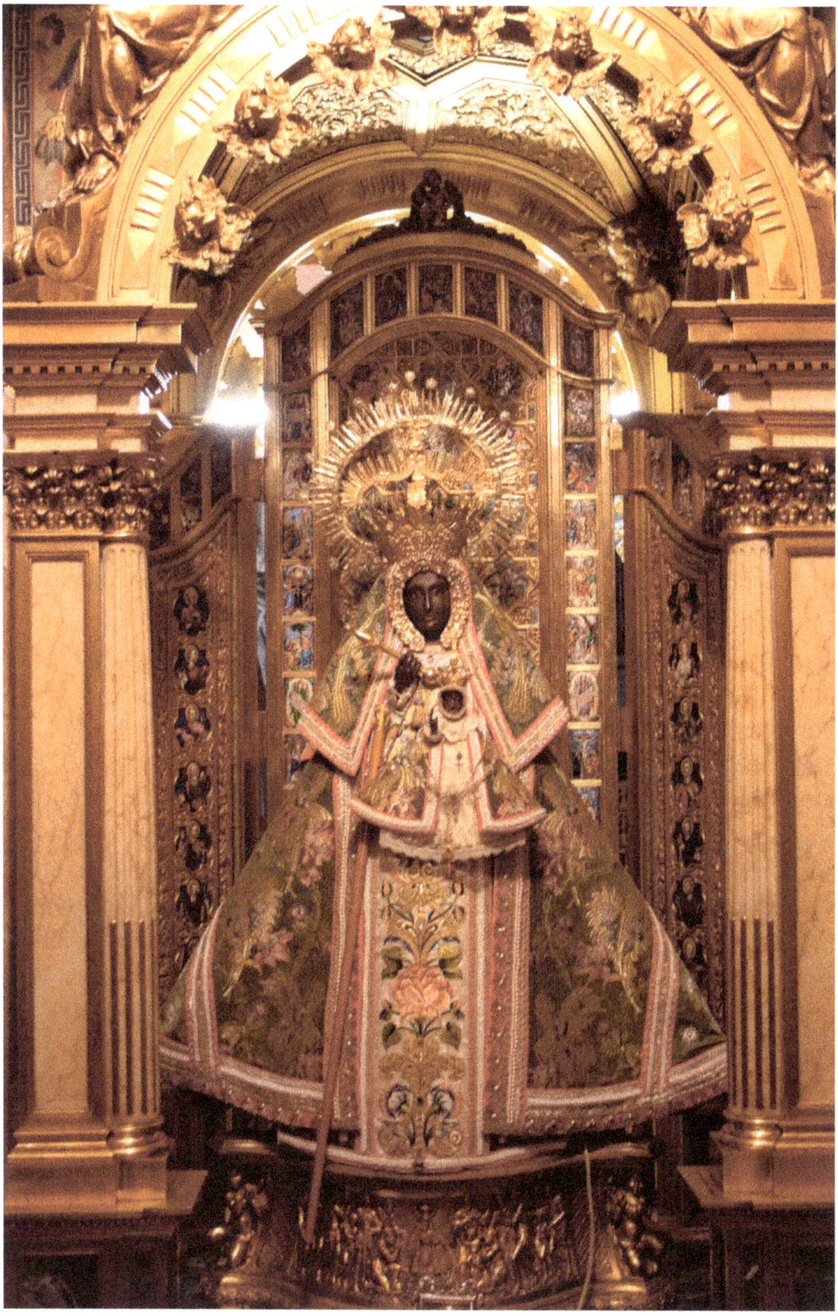

FIGURE 7 Statue of the Virgin of Guadalupe, Guadalupe, Spain. Circa twelfth century
PHOTO BY THE AUTHOR

There is no documentary evidence to support Soller's claims regarding Madrid or Zafra, but he possibly would not have stood out in either location. There was a high number of people of black-African descent enslaved in Zafra,[115] and Madrid had a broad variety of slave owners and types of slaves during this period.[116] Soller could have completed the better part of a circular route from Madrid southwest to Zafra, west to Lisbon, north to Santiago de Compostela, southeast to Ourense, then through the Aira Gate heading back toward Castile and Madrid.

The fluidity of Soller's identity is in keeping with that of the "Atlantic creoles," especially with regard to the point that the Atlantic Creoles' "liminality, particularly their lack of identity within any one group, posed numerous dangers" for this population, including their possible enslavement. Authorities tended to view the potential for subversion posed in the indeterminacy of the Atlantic creoles' principal traits, namely "their linguistic dexterity, cultural plasticity, and social agility."[117] The criminal prosecution against José Soller reveals how this figure's hybrid identity as a mulatto and pilgrim—two types of liminal figures in and of themselves—made him a double threat in the eyes of officials in baroque Spain. Soller is met with the probes of the authorities, but his liminality and agency enable him to offer a resistance of his own in return.

Given the inconsistency of the testimony—direct and indirect, sworn and not—in these criminal proceedings, one cannot be sure of Soller's place of origin, whether it be Italy, Hispaniola, or somewhere else. Such uncertainty might exist even if we had a bonafide autobiographical account from Soller, as authors so often cast themselves in the most favorable light possible. With regard to Olaudah Equiano's foundational slave narrative of his own life, for example, Vincent Carretta has shown that research does not bear out the most fundamentally accepted and frequently cited portions of Equiano's autobiography: that he was born in Africa; that he crossed the Middle Passage in a harrowing manner; even whether he spent the majority of his adult years in America, England, or on the ocean. Carretta describes Equiano as an "Atlantic creole" (à la Ira Berlin) for the reason that he bears within himself the essence of Africa, Europe, and the Americas, which explains his self-described status as a cosmopolitan man.[118] Soller likewise can be understood as one of the "Atlantic creoles" in geographic terms: "by their experience and sometimes by their person, they had become part of the three worlds that came together in the Atlantic lit-

115 Phillips, *Slavery*, 69.
116 Phillips, *Slavery*, 119.
117 Berlin, *Many Thousands Gone*, 24; "Creole to African," 263.
118 Carretta, *Equiano the African*, xii–xv.

toral. Familiar with the commerce of the Atlantic, fluent in its new languages, and intimate with its trade and cultures, they were cosmopolitan in the fullest sense."[119] Part of the significance of this story involving "the island of Santo Domingo in Perú of the Indies" is that it places a figure of black-African descent along a triangular geographical vector from, at some point in his lineage, Africa to the New World, and then in the place of origin he claims under oath, from the Caribbean to Europe. Soller is a citizen of the black urban Atlantic, a creole in the Atlantic world.

Soller's acculturation in this community can be seen in his reference to his initial Atlantic crossing from the island of Santo Domingo with the otherwise unidentifiable Count of Alayos, and after his sentencing, in Soller's mention of the Admiral of Castile, the chief maritime authority in Spain (part 1, chapter 7). Soller was one of a host of people of African origin in the Atlantic world who became more or less culturally adapted: "These processes of Africanization and creolization did not exclude—and may even have encouraged—the circulation of individuals across ethnic and racial lines in ways that further hybridized these urban communities. Slaves of crown officials crossed and recrossed the Atlantic, connecting black communities in various Atlantic ports."[120] This reality was certainly the case in Lisbon, from where Soller begins his pilgrimage.

In terms of their assimilation, some Spaniards considered creoles born in the Americas to be "domesticated" due to their adoption of Christianity.[121] Another type of Atlantic creole, the "acculturated, Spanish-speaking Catholics,"[122] goes by the name *ladino*: "Blacks, pardos, and mulattos gradually began to belong to the larger Catholic 'us.'"[123] Soller himself purports to be devoutly Catholic, a "*mixed-race-Catholic-Christian who believes firmly in the law* of God,"[124] and as such, one who is "very fearful of God."[125]

In Portugal, most slaves of black African descent, unlike the Moorish ones, converted to Christianity.[126] The large numbers among the black population of those who adopted Christianity are reflected from the first part of the sixteenth century forward in paintings of the Epiphany scene, in which the Christ child is revealed to the traveling wise men, among whom Balthasar typically

---

119 Berlin, *Many Thousands Gone*, 17.
120 Cañizares-Esguerra, "Demons, Stars," 14–15.
121 Landers, "African Landscape," 155.
122 Landers, "African Landscape," 156.
123 Twinam, *Purchasing Whiteness*, 106.
124 1^v; "*mestizo cristiano católico que cree firmemente en la ley* de Dios."
125 18^v; "muy temeroso de Dios."
126 Saunders, *Black Slaves*, 59.

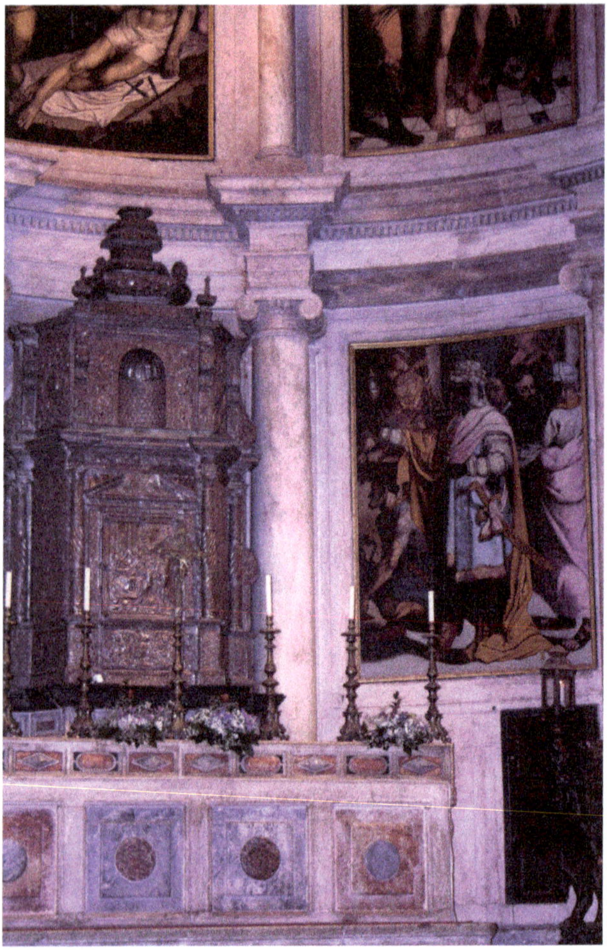

FIGURE 8 *Epiphany* (*Adoration of the Magi*) by Lourenço de Salzedo. Church of the Hieronymite Monastery of Bethlehem (Belém) in Lisbon, Portugal. 1572–1574
PHOTO BY THE AUTHOR

is depicted as a black man.[127] One such painting is the *Adoration of the Magi* by Lourenço de Salzedo found in the Church of the Hieronymite Monastery of Bethlehem (Belém), present in Lisbon during Soller's day (figure 8). Participation among the "Atlantic creoles" in the life of the Catholic Church was a key part of the process of their acculturation in European society. This population became somewhat integrated through church attendance, marriage in the

127 Saunders, *Black Slaves*, 168. See also Vincent, "San Benito de Palermo," 27.

Church, and raising their children in contact with these religious and societal norms.[128] Religious assimilation or "creolization" of this sort might best be considered a form of cultural adaptation.[129] Soller's pilgrimage and his dressing as a priest take such a strategy for survival to new heights.

128 Berlin, "Creole to African," 259.

129 Cañizares-Esguerra, Childs, and Sidbury, *Black Urban Atlantic*, 15.

CHAPTER 4

The Nature of the Journey

> And now I recognize and know by experience what they say—that "the love for the fatherland is sweet."
>
> RICOTE[1]

∵

Pilgrimage in the Middle Ages produced large waves of travelers to and from the various shrines of the saints. By the early modern period, "pilgrimages continued to serve as a pretext for people, whether individually or in groups, to leave their homes in order to go encounter the sanctuary of their devotion."[2] The three most important pilgrimage destinations in Christendom were Jerusalem, Rome, and Santiago de Compostela; of these, Compostela probably was the most popular. And in Europe during Soller's day, Santiago was without a doubt the second most-important pilgrimage destination in Europe after Rome.[3]

Santiago de Compostela had been attracting pilgrims internationally since the twelfth century and had existed as a devotional site from centuries before. Around the year 830 after Christ, a tomb was discovered on a local hillside that was claimed to be—on what today are regarded as shaky grounds—that of Saint James, brother of John the Evangelist. The significance of this discovery

1 Cervantes, *Don Quixote*, 750; Cervantes, *Don Quijote*, 2:435; "y agora conozco y experimento lo que suele decirse: que es dulce el amor de la patria." These are the words of the Christianized Moor (Morisco) Ricote in the second part of *Don Quijote* to his friend and former neighbor Sancho Panza. Speaking on behalf of his Morisco brethren who have been expelled from Spain, Ricote expresses his extreme love of country. His use of the term "fatherland" (*patria*) emphasizes the connection to spiritual pilgrimage: this *patria* symbolizes Heaven, from which every Christian pilgrim is in spiritual exile while on earth. The cruel irony here is that despite Ricote's essential Spanish-ness, he remains alienated from his homeland even while talking with an old friend inside Spanish borders.

2 Lobo de Araujo and Esteves, "Pasaportes de caridad," 211; "las peregrinaciones continuaban sirviendo de pretexto para que, de manera individual o en grupo, los hombres abandonasen sus casas para ir al encuentro del santuario de su devoción."

3 Taín Guzmán, *La ciudad de Santiago*, 11.

 | DOI:10.1163/9789004422704_005

radiated outward and devotion to the apostle increased to the extent that at its zenith during the twelfth century, Compostela attracted multitudes of international pilgrims.[4]

The cult of Saint James and pilgrimage to Compostela were more deeply rooted and popular in Portugal than in any other European country from the ninth century on, and there was an elaborate hospitality network to care for pilgrims throughout this kingdom.[5] In addition, a portion of society became aware of the need to take care of its destitute population in light of the Gospel mandate to do so,[6] even if by the sixteenth century, "the poor were becoming not solely a moral and religious concern, but were increasingly looked on as a social disease."[7] Partially to abate the spread of this societal contagion, hostels and hospitals took in not only the indigent but also all types of travelers, pilgrims and merchants alike, and offered anonymous charity. It was an important service given the difficulty of finding a suitable place to shelter when traveling.[8]

In some parts of Europe, particularly the Protestant north, long-distance travel to pilgrimage shrines had abated severely after the Reformation. The mid-sixteenth-century Council of Trent encouraged pilgrims to visit local shrines over making long-distance pilgrimages. And in the seventeenth century, the Thirty Years' War impacted religious travel until 1659 in France and Spain.[9] This decline in long-distance Christian pilgrimage, however, seems *not* to have impacted travelers from southern Europe, including Italy, in the late seventeenth century.[10] The pace of arrival of pilgrims to Santiago from Portugal also was particularly brisk in Soller's day.[11]

Taken together, the documents in the case file reveal that Soller traveled as a pilgrim, at least part of the way "on horseback" (*com cavalgadura*),[12] from Lisbon, Portugal, to Santiago de Compostela and beyond to Ourense, Spain, just beyond which he was apprehended for impersonating a priest. Soller's

---

4 Laffi, *Journey*, 11–12.

5 Cunha, "A devoçaõ," 85.

6 2 Corinthians 8:9; Matthew 8:20; John 13:15 and 13:35; see Cunha, "A devoçaõ," 94.

7 Cruz, *Discourses of Poverty*, 47.

8 Cunha, "A devoçaõ," 97–98.

9 Laffi, *Journey*, 12.

10 Laffi, *Journey*, 12. Pilgrimage from parts of Italy to Compostela persisted into the following centuries, as well. The travel diary of the eighteenth-century Italian pilgrim Giacomo Antonio Naia is a key example. Read his take on *Journey to the West* in *Viaje a Santiago de Compostela*.

11 Cunha, "A devoçaõ," 107.

12 8^r; literally, "on a saddle animal"; alternatively, "on a mount."

confirmed itinerary for the year 1693, with the document that provides this information, is found in the chronology and is illustrated in the map of figure 1. In 1694, Soller remains absent during what remains of his appeal of the original ruling.

1 The Holy House of Mercy

Throughout that portion of his journey as a pilgrim in Portugal, Soller relied on the hospitality and charity of the Holy House of Mercy (Santa Casa de Misericórdia), a religious brotherhood committed to carrying out the Corporal Works of Mercy (alongside the spiritual ones) traditional to Catholicism. As depicted in the painting *The Seven Acts of Mercy* by Pieter Brueghel the Younger (figure 9), these observable, physical actions are performed in body and include: feeding the hungry, giving drink to the thirsty, providing lodging and help to pilgrims on the road, clothing the naked, visiting the sick, feeding the imprisoned, and burying the dead.

The particular Santa Casa in Lisbon—the first—was instituted in 1498 by Queen Leonor.[13] The brotherhood and various chapters of this confraternity provided an essential social safety net for the poor, especially beggars, orphans, and the sick who came to pervade the streets in urban areas throughout Portugal. Local communities would take matters of controlling poverty into their own hands by founding their own chapter without having to depend on whatever government policies happened to be in effect at the moment.[14] There eventually would be so many mendicants that they would form three confraternities of their own in Lisbon, one of which gathered in the Church of the Misericórdia. The existence of these confraternities points to just how protected the beggars were, who were estimated to number around a thousand in early sixteenth-century in Lisbon.[15] The Misericórdia hospitals in Lisbon and Portugal served as a model for what sixteenth-century Castilian reformers wished to implement in cities across Spain in their attempt to remedy the social ill of pauperism.[16] The increasing association between poverty and delinquency helps explain why, in the words of Foucault, "Religious groups and charity organizations had long played this role of 'disciplining' the population."[17]

13 2^{v}; *Compromisso*.

14 Lobo de Araujo and Esteves, "Pasaportes de caridad," 211–212; Ribeiro, *A Santa Casa*, 46; Maciel, "Misericórdia de Viana," 25.

15 Ribeiro, *A Santa Casa*, 59–60.

16 Cruz, *Discourses of Poverty*, 55, 63, 77.

17 Foucault, *Discipline and Punish*, 212; Foucault, *Surveiller et punir*, 213–214; "Des groupes

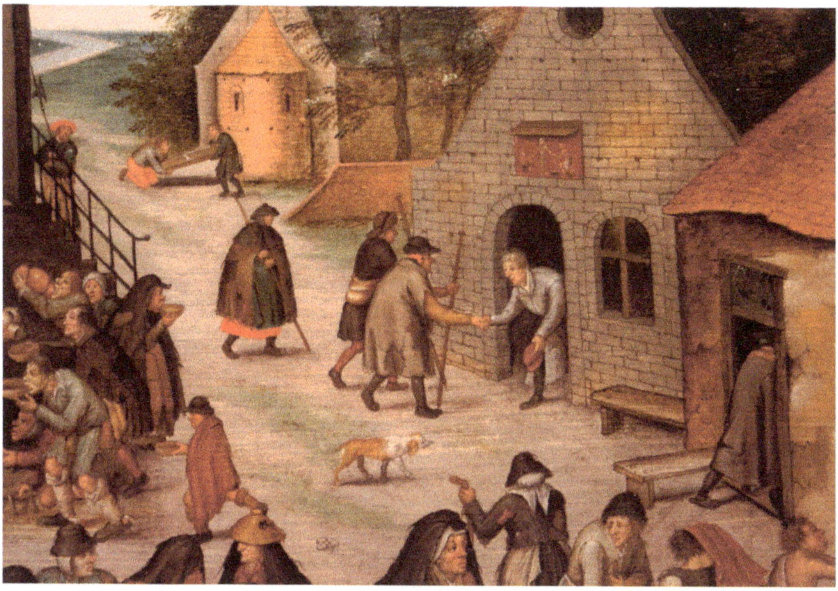

FIGURE 9 Detail of the *The Seven Acts of Mercy* by Pieter Brueghel the Younger, 1564, Brussels–1637/8, Antwerp. Late sixteenth–early seventeenth century
PHOTO BY THE AUTHOR

The Lisbon *Charter*, or *Compromisso da Confraria da Misericórdia*, founding the brotherhood declares that the institution must: care for prisoners; bury the unclaimed dead; and help the needy, providing shelter, clothing, food, and medicine, as well as offering important religious involvement in the way of prayers, masses, and processions.[18] This charter additionally establishes that there are to be thirteen men who govern this institution: one Director, nine councilmen, one scribe, and two stewards or majordomos. The chapter also provides wine and the host to priests for the purpose of saying Mass.[19]

The Corporal Works of Mercy are laid out in this, the founding document of the Order itself.[20] The earliest extant copies of the *Compromisso* include an incunabulum from 1516 still held by the Misericórdia of Lisbon and an illuminated manuscript commissioned by King Dom Manuel I in 1520, also held by the Lisbon chapter. Although the text of the *Compromisso* had been for-

religieux, des associations de bienfaisance ont longtemps joué ce rôle de 'mise en discipline' de la population."

18 *Compromisso*, 4^{r}; Ribeiro, *A Santa Casa*, 46; The original document, or *Compromisso*, founding the Lisbon chapter, approved by King Manuel and Pope Alexander VI, was lost in the in the earthquake-tsunami-fire that consumed Lisbon in 1755.

19 *Compromisso*, 8^{r}, 15^{v}.

20 *Compromisso*, 3^{v}–4^{r}.

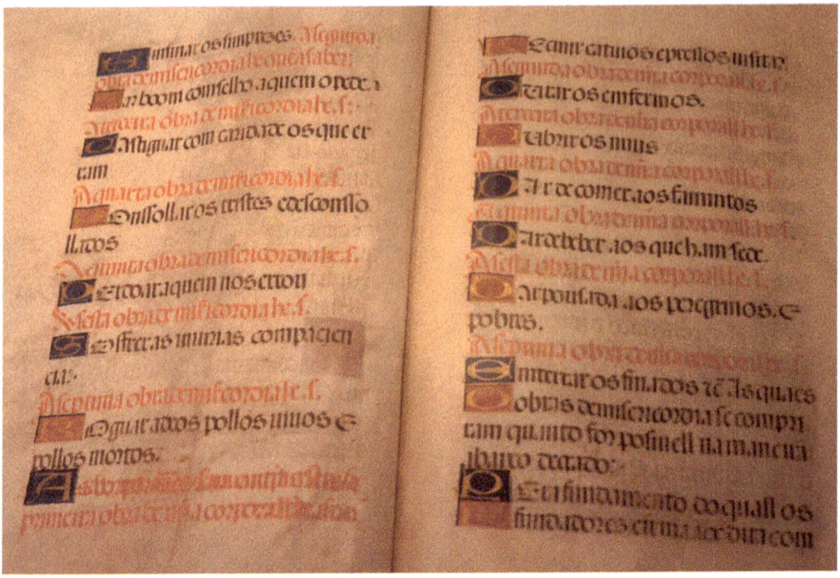

FIGURE 10 Illuminated manuscript of the *Charter* (*Compromisso*) of the Lisbon chapter of the Misericórdia assembly. 1520
PHOTO BY THE AUTHOR. COURTESY OF THE MISERICÓRDIA OF LISBON

mally approved since the inception of the Misericórdia in Lisbon in 1498, the 1516 version is the first known printed book belonging to the Lisbon chapter of the confraternity. King Manuel I directed that the 1520 manuscript of the *Compromisso* be written and illuminated, and then bound in crimson velvet (figure 10).[21]

The manuscript version sent by this king of Portugal and of the Algarve specifies the fourteen Works of Mercy, seven spiritual ones and seven corporal acts. Among the seven corporal works are feeding the hungry (*Dar de comer aos famintos*), giving drink to the thirsty (*Dar de beber aos que ham sede*), and providing lodging to pilgrims and to the poor (*Dar pousada aos peregrinos e pobres*). The last of these good works is based upon the admonition to welcome the stranger in the book of Job:[22] "The stranger did not stay without, my door was open to the traveler."[23] All of these actions are presented as what the brothers and other Christians will be held accountable for at the Final Judgment.[24]

21 For a codicological description of the manuscript version, see Ribeiro, *A Santa Casa*, 50.

22 Job 31:16–32. Monteiro, "Obras de Misericórdia," 10.

23 Job 31:32 (Douay-Rheims Catholic Bible); "Foris non mansit peregrinus: ostium meum viatori patuit" (Latin Vulgate). Note the equivalency between "pilgrim" (*peregrinus*) in the Latin and "stranger" in the English translation.

24 *Um Instrumento*, 29, 1^r–4^v; Ribeiro, *A Santa Casa*, 47–49, 55.

This sphere of action expanded in tandem with the institution, especially after the reform of 1582, which added such good works as rescuing orphans, providing dowries to spinsters, and the ransom and transport of captives. This reform was approved by king Felipe II of Spain (Filipe I of Portugal) once Portugal had become a kingdom within his domain and once he had offered his full protection of the Misericórdia. This monarch's son and successor, King Felipe III of Spain (Filipe II of Portugal), offered the same level of support as his father had before him. Unfortunately, the expansion of the institution's responsibilities seems to have generated financial hardship. The Misericórdia was not solvent for virtually the entirety of the rule of Felipe II despite his protection and despite the support of the municipality of Lisbon, which came to the chapter's financial rescue on numerous occasions during this period.[25]

Among those to be sheltered are pilgrims, poor tradesmen and travelers, those searching for a lord or other accommodation, and convalescents.[26] Wherever the chapter house, the structures of the Misericórdia would have to accommodate: a hospital to care for pilgrims and the sick; a church in which to hold daily liturgical ceremonies and the requisite masses; and an administrative office for those who governed the confraternity to meet.[27] On the whole in Soller's day, travelers with credentials received better treatment than those without.[28] Soller's travel documents give him access to the hospitality network offered by the Misericórdia and other charity-granting institutions. Moreover, his pilgrim's diploma proclaims him to be a priest from the New World.

2 Pilgrim's Credential

Soller's itinerary from February 11 through March 14 of 1693, can be gleaned from his pilgrim's credential (*carta de guia*) in the list of signatures of the Director or another brother in the assembly of the indicated location where Soller would furnish this document (figures 11a, 11b). Such pilgrims' credentials from this time are extremely rare to find today since these documents typically remained in the hands of individuals and were not handed over to archives. For example, one of only four other pilgrim's credentials I found is listed in the catalogue of the archive of the Misericórdia in Viana de Castelo, Portugal. The credential attests to the journey from Cascaes, Portugal (a charming coastal

25 Pinho, "As Casas da Misericórdia," 1:111n297; Ribeiro, *A Santa Casa*, 83–85, 115.
26 Pinho, "As Casas da Misericórdia," 1:101.
27 Pinho, "As Casas da Misericórdia," 1:187.
28 Arribas Briones, *Pícaros y picaresca*, 255.

town to the west of Lisbon on the Atlantic Ocean) to Viana in the century after Soller's.[29] If it were not for the legal case of Soller, this and his other travel documents may not have been preserved in the Archive of the Kingdom of Galicia's Prosecutor's Documents series or for that matter, preserved at all.

Every chapter of the Santa Casa de Misericórdia distributed these *cartas de guia* to the needy who had to move or who chose to travel, and their documents allowed these poor travelers to receive hospitality and charity at any member organization in route to their destination: "Fundamental tools for pilgrims and travelers, the pilgrim credentials acquired the status of an act of mercy and became a highly sought-after instrument throughout the Modern Age."[30] These instruments had to be solicited in writing, and since the poor frequently were illiterate, others wrote petitions on their behalf to the confraternity. For the wealthy, offering charity of this sort to the needy was a way to approximate oneself to Christ and help ensure one's salvation. In addition to the spiritual benefits, helping the poor additionally served as a way of controlling the poor.[31]

Soller's pilgrim's credential is furnished to him by the Assembly of Misericórdias, which includes all the Portuguese chapters of this brotherhood. Handwritten text filling in the blanks in the printed document lists his destination as Valença do Minho, located on the Miño River, which at that point forms the northern Portuguese border with Spain. It is a given that Soller's starting point was Lisbon. First of all, his safe-conduct is issued in this city. Secondly, in 1690, the Assembly of the Misericórdia in Lisbon was given sole authority to print and issue credentials as the mother house (*casa mãe*) of all the other chapters in Portugal. The Lisbon chapterhouse served as the model even for the overseas branches of the Misericórdia:[32] "No fewer than sixty-one branches had adopted the Lisbon rule (*compromisso*) by the time of D. Leonor's death in 1524" both within Portugal and abroad.[33] The statutes of all the other chapters of the Misericórdia were modeled on those of the Lisbon charter, and these statutes themselves constituted the legal foundation on which all their actions were based.[34]

---

29 I viewed the remaining three credentials in an exhibit at the Lisbon chapter of the Misericórdia in July of 2014, all three of which date to after the earthquake/tsunami/fire that hollowed out the city in 1755. Extremely ephemeral, these *cartas de guia* are exceedingly scarce documents.

30 Lobo de Araujo and Esteves, "Pasaportes de caridad," 225; "Instrumentos fundamentales para los peregrinos y viajeros, las cartas de guía adquirían status de obra de misericordia y se convirtieron en un instrumento muy solicitado a lo largo de la Edad Moderna."

31 Lobo de Araujo and Esteves, "Pasaportes de caridad," 208–209.

32 Lobo de Araujo and Esteves, "Pasaportes de caridad," 213–214; Ribeiro, *A Santa Casa*, 40.

33 Saunders, *Black Slaves*, 151.

34 Maciel, "Misericórdia de Viana," 33.

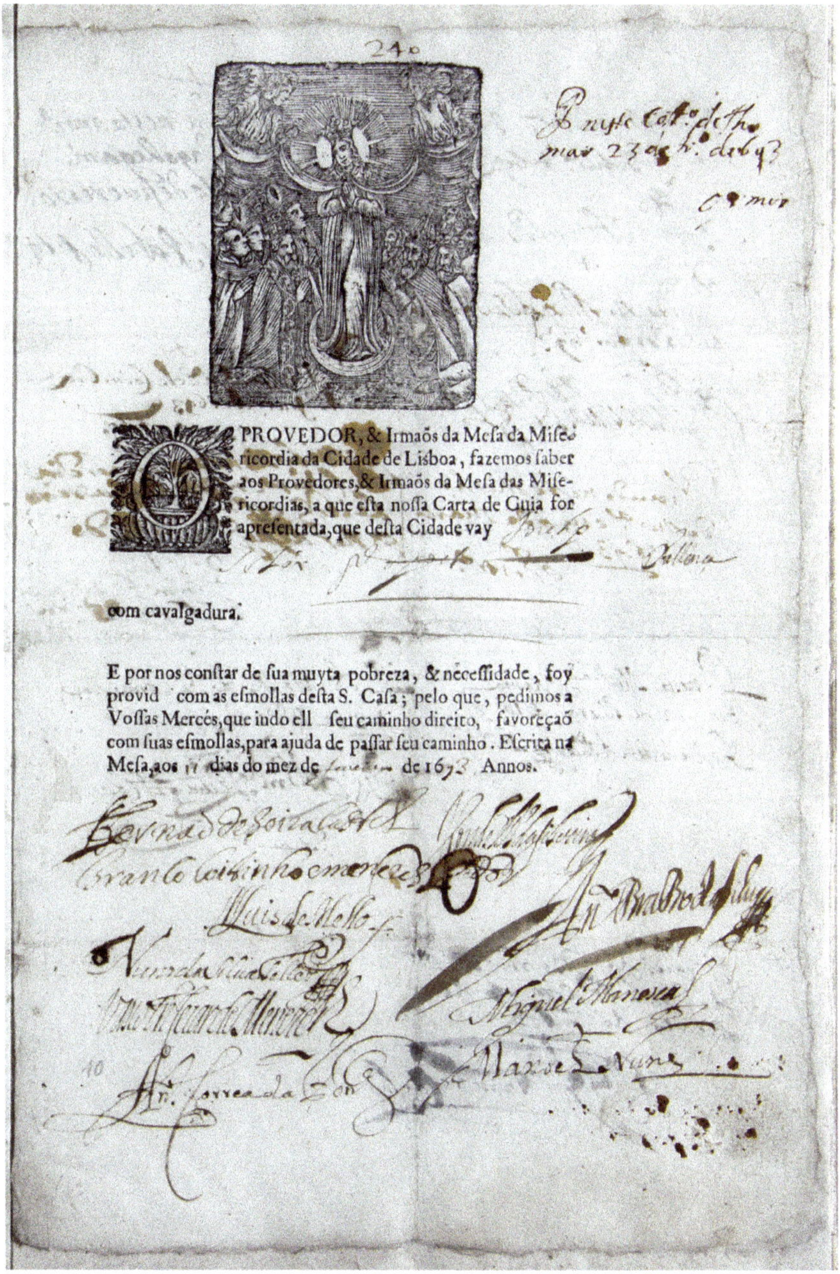
O PROVEDOR, & Irmaõs da Mesa da Misericordia da Cidade de Lisboa, fazemos saber aos Provedores, & Irmaõs da Mesa das Misericordias, a que esta nossa Carta de Guia for apresentada, que desta Cidade vay

com cavalgadura.

E por nos constar de sua muyta pobreza, & necessidade, foy provid com as esmollas desta S. Casa; pelo que, pedimos a Vossas Mercés, que indo ell seu caminho direito, favoreçaõ com suas esmollas, para ajuda de passar seu caminho. Escrita na Mesa, aos 17 dias do mez de [illegible] de 1693 Annos.

FIGURE 11A Soller's pilgrim's credential (*carta de guia*), front. Folio 8r of *His Majesty's Representative versus José Soller, Mulatto Pilgrim.* 1693
PHOTO COURTESY OF THE ARCHIVE OF THE KINGDOM OF GALICIA

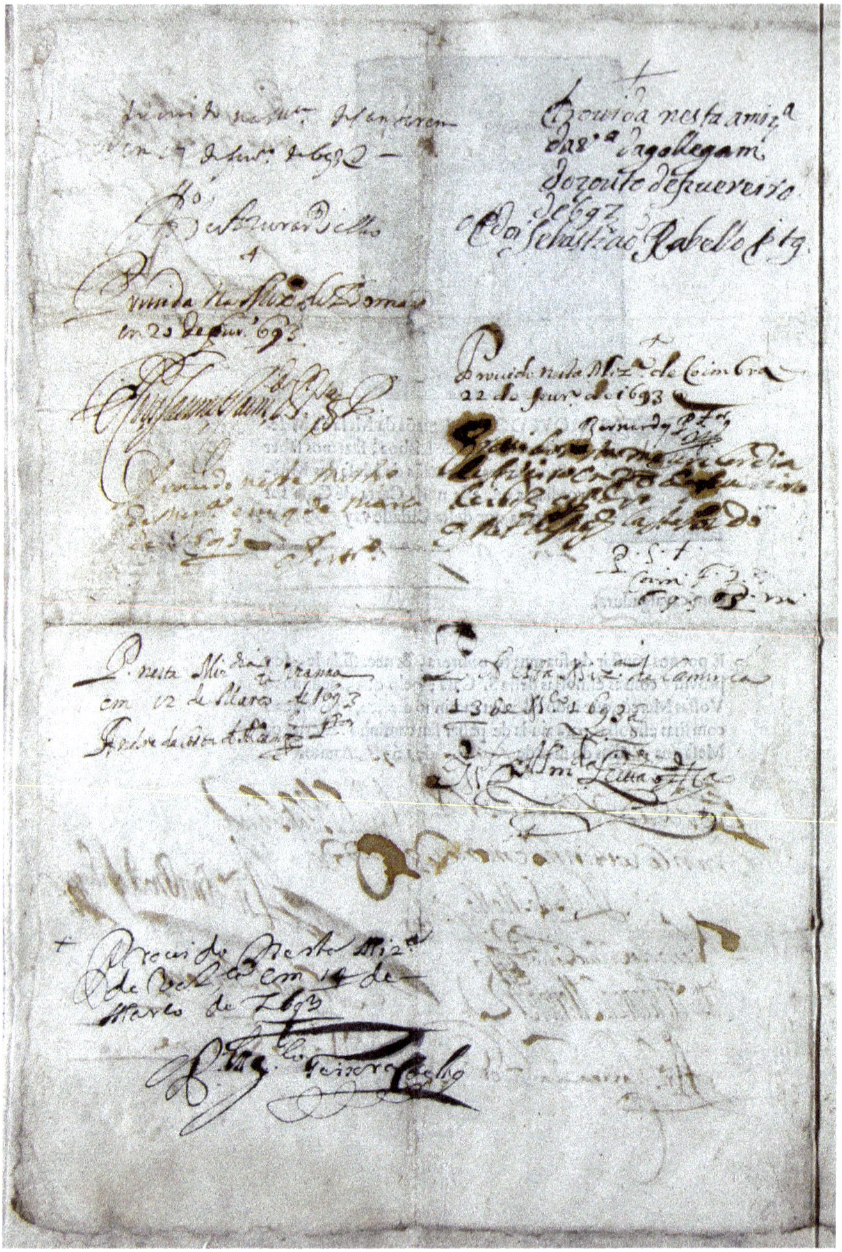

FIGURE 11B Soller's pilgrim's credential (*carta de guia*), back. Folio 8[v] of *His Majesty's Prosecutor versus José Soller, Mulatto Pilgrim*. 1693
PHOTO COURTESY OF THE ARCHIVE OF THE KINGDOM OF GALICIA

An abbot of Fleury considered the first chapter of the Misericórdia in Europe to be in fifteenth-century Rome. Its purpose was to accompany those condemned to death and to bury them. Pope Innocent VIII granted this institution many privileges and indulgences. Others give primacy to the Misericórdia of Florence, which they claim to have been founded in 1350. Regardless, the first Misericórdia chapter originated in Italy. Despite having their Italian roots, the Misericórdia of Lisbon and the others in the kingdom that would follow suit bore the stamp of Portugal's unique and independent character. The brotherhood's Italian origin is confirmed in the last will and testament of João II of Portugal, husband to Leonor, as the document recommends that the Hospital of Lisbon model itself after that of Florence. Though under different norms than the Italian institution, as expressed in the *Compromisso*, the King's wife carried out the same ideals of Christian charity in her founding of the Misericórdia in Portugal.[35]

Soller's credential functioned in tandem with his safe-conduct to allow him access to the charity services at each stop: "Those who carried pilgrim's credentials were sure to receive assistance … The beneficiaries of this help would travel from Misericórdia to Misericórdia, renewing these 'passports' of charity."[36] Even though travelers could be sent off by coach or even by boat, pilgrims often were issued a mount along with their *cartas de guia*.[37] This is why the expression "on horseback" (*com cavalgadura*) was printed in the text, not a handwritten part of Soller's safe-conduct; pilgrims regularly received a saddle animal for their travels at this time.[38]

3 Safe-Conduct

Soller obtained his pilgrim's passport, or safe-conduct (*salvi conductus*), on Ash Wednesday, which in the year 1693 took place on February 4 (figure 12).[39] The

35 Ribeiro, *A Santa Casa*, 40–42. Italian chapters of the Misericórdia persist and are widely admired to this day. Ribeiro, *A Santa Casa*, 42.

36 Lobo de Araujo and Esteves, "Pasaportes de caridad," 212–213; "Los portadores de las cartas guías estaban seguros de que recibirían auxilio … Los beneficiarios de esta ayuda se desplazaban de Misericordia a Misericordia, renovando estos 'pasaportes' de caridad."

37 Lobo de Araujo and Esteves, "Pasaportes de caridad," 215.

38 As noted previously, I viewed three post-1755 credentials in an exhibit at the Lisbon chapter of the Misericórdia. Two of these likewise include the expression "com cavalgadura," but the text is handwritten.

39 Gregorian calendar tables show Easter Sunday occurred on March 22 in 1693. Every year Ash Wednesday takes place forty-six days prior to Easter to allow forty days of abstinence

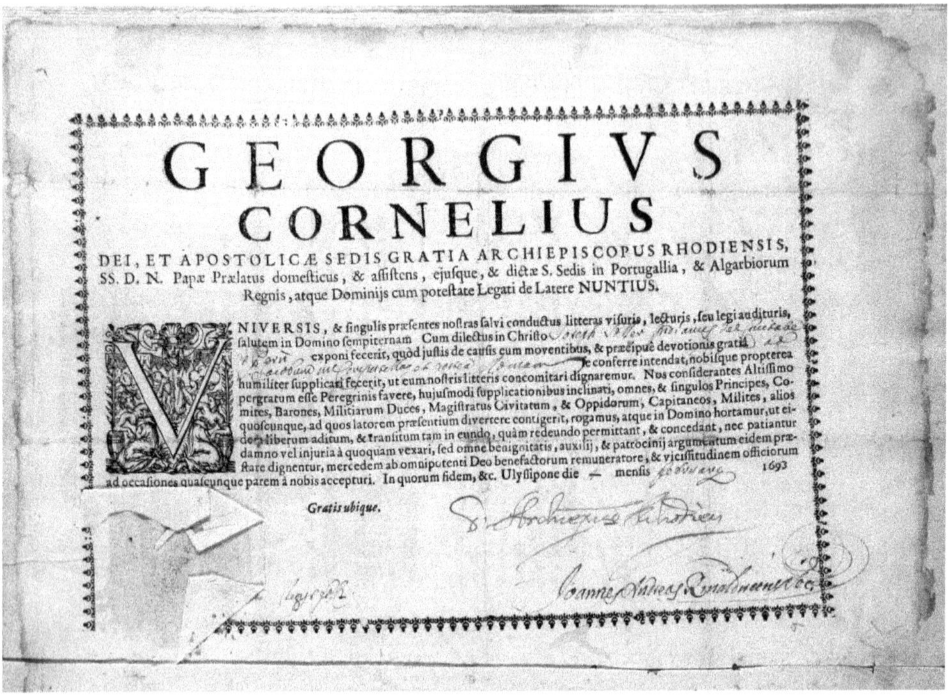

GEORGIVS
CORNELIUS
DEI, ET APOSTOLICÆ SEDIS GRATIA ARCHIEPISCOPUS RHODIENSIS,
SS. D. N. Papæ Prælatus domesticus, & assistens, ejusque, & dictæ S. Sedis in Portugallia, & Algarbiorum
Regnis, atque Dominijs cum potestate Legati de Latere NUNTIUS.

VNIVERSIS, & singulis præsentes nostras salvi conductus litteras visuris, lecturis, seu legi audituris, salutem in Domino sempiternam. Cum dilectus in Christo exponi fecerit, quòd justis de causis eum moventibus, & præcipuè devotionis gratiâ se conferre intendat, nobisque propterea humiliter supplicari fecerit, ut eum nostris litteris concomitari dignaremur. Nos considerantes Altissimo pergratum esse Peregrinis favere, hujusmodi supplicationibus inclinati, omnes, & singulos Principes, Comites, Barones, Militiarum Duces, Magistratus Civitatum, & Oppidorum, Capitaneos, Milites, alios quoscunque, ad quos latorem præsentium divertere contigerit, rogamus, atque in Domino hortamur, ut eidem liberum aditum, & transitum tam in eundo, quàm redeundo permittant, & concedant, nec patiantur eum damno vel injuria à quoquam vexari, sed omne benignitatis, auxilij, & patrocinij argumentum eidem præstare dignentur, mercedem ab omnipotenti Deo benefactorum remuneratore, & vicissitudinem officiorum ad occasiones quascunque parem à nobis accepturi. In quorum fidem, &c. Ulyssipone die — mensis 1693

Gratis ubique.

FIGURE 12 Soller's passport, or safe-conduct (*salvi conductus*). Folio 7^r of *His Majesty's Representative versus José Soller, Mulatto Pilgrim.* 1693
PHOTO COURTESY OF THE ARCHIVE OF THE KINGDOM OF GALICIA

following Wednesday, on February 11, 1693, the brothers of Mercy in Lisbon issued the pilgrim's credential (*carta de guia*) contained in Soller's file. This document, which bears a wax seal on its front, together with his safe-conduct granted Soller unencumbered passage throughout Portugal and in territories beyond, helping him arrive in Santiago de Compostela in the neighboring kingdom of Galicia. According to the barber's testimony elsewhere in the court documents, Soller already "bore the outline of a tonsure on his head" and said "he said he had not shaved it since Lisbon,"[40] meaning Soller most likely obtained a tonsure at some point prior to his departure from Lisbon. The safe-conduct indicates that from Compostela, this "*Spanish subject of the Indies from the kingdom of Perú*" had intended to follow his pilgrimage "*to Santiago de Compostela,*

plus six feast days on Sundays, when fasting is forbidden. Since the year 1693 was not a leap year (yes, leap years did exist then), Ash Wednesday had to have taken place on February 4 of that year.

40 5^v–6^r; "traía señal de corona en la cabeza"; "dijo no la había limpiado desde Lisboa." See also 12^v–13^r.

and afterwards to Rome,"[41] a projected itinerary that suggests he intended to stay on the pilgrimage road for an extended period, perhaps in a manner similar to those who effectively made a career of being pilgrims.

4 Pilgrim's Diploma

Soller acquired his pilgrim's diploma (*compostela*) in the Cathedral of Santiago three days after Easter Sunday, on Wednesday, March 25, 1693 (figure 13). This document, which also bears a wax seal on its face, describes Soller as a "Priest from the Indies,"[42] a geographical detail in keeping with Soller's claims elsewhere to be originally from the island of Santo Domingo, or Hispaniola.[43] As for the indication on the diploma that he is a cleric, Soller testifies that "at his request, some Catalan pilgrim-priests claimed that he who is testifying also was a priest, and considering all of that, they wrote it for him in this fashion on the diploma."[44] It is unlikely Soller actually was a greater-order pastor given all the canon law that governs apostolic succession to ordain a bishop and the authority of the local ordinary (the bishop) to ordain and grant faculties to confect the sacraments within his jurisdiction. (This technical vocabulary is still in use today.) Once again, Soller would have been more credible as a member of the minor-order clergy, who could not administer Holy Communion. Anywhere Soller would have visited as a "priest," he would have had to check in with the local chancery to get faculties before saying Mass or hearing confessions.

5 Ethnicity and the Priesthood

Compound this difficulty with the fact of his blended African ancestry and his inability to read, and the prospect of Soller having become a priest of the greater orders seems all the more unlikely—unlikely, but not impossible. In early modern Portugal, for example,

41 7^r; "*indianus del cividade de Perú*"; "*ad Jacobum in Compostella, et postea Romam.*"

42 10^r; "Sacerdotem Indianum."

43 1^v, 3^v, 18^r, 21^r, and 33^r; Soller's possible geographic origins are discussed at length in the previous chapter (Origins).

44 3^v; "a pedimento suyo unos sacerdotes peregrinos catalanes aseguraron en la ciudad de Santiago que el que declara era también sacerdote. Y en vista de ello, se lo escribieron así en el despacho." See also 18^v.

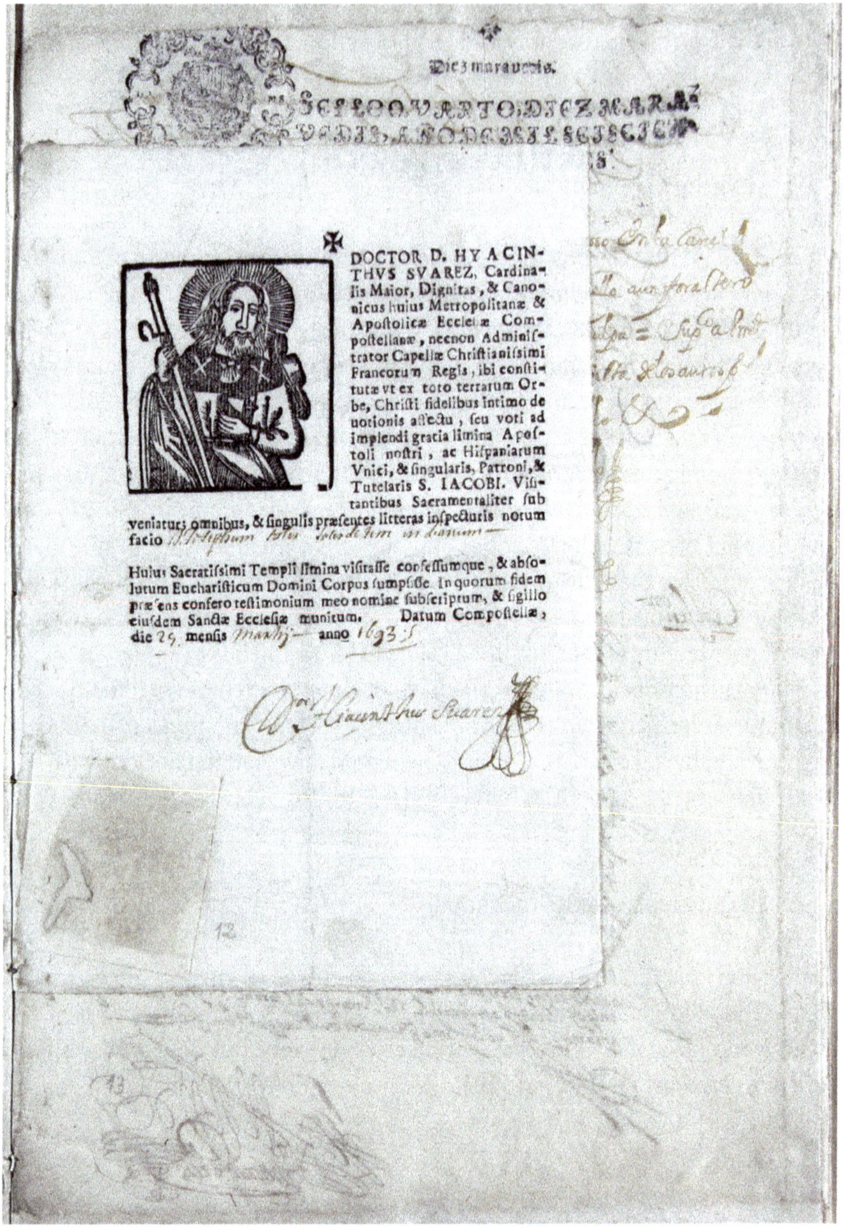
DOCTOR D. HYACINTHVS SVAREZ, Cardinalis Maior, Dignitas, & Canonicus huius Metropolitanæ & Apostolicæ Ecclesiæ Compostellanæ, necnon Administrator Capellæ Christianissimi Francorum Regis, ibi constitutæ vt ex toto terrarum Orbe, Christi fidelibus intimo deuotionis affectu, seu voti adimplendi gratia limina Apostoli nostri, ac Hispaniarum Vnici, & singularis, Patroni, & Tutelaris S. IACOBI. Visitantibus Sacramentaliter subveniatur; omnibus, & singulis præsentes litteras inspecturis notum facio

Huius Sacratissimi Templi limina visitasse confessumque, & absolutum Eucharisticum Domini Corpus sumpsisse. In quorum fidem præsens confero testimonium meo nomine subscriptum, & sigillo eiusdem Sanctæ Ecclesiæ munitum. Datum Compostellæ, die 29 mensis Martij anno 1693

FIGURE 13 Soller's pilgrim's diploma, or *compostela*. Folio 10ʳ of *His Majesty's Representative versus José Soller, Mulatto Pilgrim*. 1693

PHOTO COURTESY OF THE ARCHIVE OF THE KINGDOM OF GALICIA

> Very few blacks and other former slaves were admitted to the holy orders and they did not advance rapidly within the secular Church … In Portugal itself the only way an ordained black could legally follow his vocation was as a member of a monastic order, where there were no benefices or cures of souls … Mulattoes seemed to have fared better both as regular and secular churchmen and could even secure the administration of church property.[45]

A.C. de C.M. Saunders provides examples of a mid-sixteenth-century mulatto priest and of a mulatto prior in Portugal.[46] In the Americas, however, whites predicted that their own kind would abandon the priesthood, universities, and other professions if the Council of the Indies allowed dark-skinned people (*pardos*) and mulattos to join their ranks: "They would not want to debase their own social status by mingling familiarly with inferiors."[47]

Despite this resistance to mulatto clergymen, there are later historical examples from the Spanish Americas. For example, on Hispaniola in the early eighteenth century, the state allowed the church to ordain people of black-African ancestry due to a shortage of priests on this island. The elevated number of mulatto clergymen produced great anxiety among the authorities, who considered the numerous mulatto priests to be unqualified and unlettered. The monarchy revoked these privileges for mulattos by the end of the eighteenth century and commanded archbishops not to ordain anyone with dark pigmentation thereafter.[48] In another instance, Diego Mexias Bejarano, a member of the *pardo* upper echelon, petitioned Rome in 1793 for a dispensation allowing his son Diego Lorenzo to enter the priesthood. Having acquired documents attesting to the virtual elimination of African ancestry in his lineage through intermarriage, the family "would face a firestorm of protest at their attempts to whiten and have a son enter the priesthood."[49] In a third example, an educated pardo named Pedro Crisólogo was able to become a priest in Panama during this period. Once again, his success is at least partially attributable to a paucity of priests in his locale. This shortage may also have helped him obtain the position of vicar in his hometown by 1809 instead of having to serve in a

45 Saunders, *Black Slaves*, 158.

46 Saunders, *Black Slaves*, 158.

47 Twinam, *Purchasing Whiteness*, 64. Mestizos additionally tended to be excluded from among the ranks of priests despite Felipe II's formal approval of a measure allowing qualified mestizos to become ordained. Konetzke, "Mestizaje en América," 62.

48 Twinam, *Purchasing Whiteness*, 120.

49 Twinam, *Purchasing Whiteness*, 146.

remote backwater.[50] A final example of an Afro-descended figure who wanted to become a priest is found in José Manuel Valdés, a highly esteemed surgeon in early nineteenth-century Lima who happened to have both black-African and indigenous ancestry (*zambo*) and to be the product of an out-of-wedlock, or "illegitimate" birth. While Valdés was able to obtain a "whitening decree" (*gracias al sacar*), enabling him to purchase whiteness, his illegitimacy remained a problem. A papal dispensation solved this issue, but the archbishop of Lima warned him of a mutiny among the church canons who would not want to associate themselves with a dark-skinned person. Rather than face such outright hostility to his ordainment, Valdés abandoned his effort to become a priest.[51] These accounts illustrate how difficult it still could be for a person of color to become a priest in the late eighteenth-, early nineteenth-century Hispanic world.

Rising to the ecclesiastical ranks was hard enough for people of color with all the qualifications; it would have been that much more difficult for Soller: "mulatto mobilities figured in 1620s, 1700s, 1760s, and 1790s benchmarks as they, respectively, received respect for their defense of the empire, aspired to perquisites such as priesthood and the university, sought occupational exemptions to practice white professions, and first applied for the whitening gracias al sacar."[52] Soller was not alone in recognizing the advantage of being or seeming to be a priest, but a key difference is that it was via unofficial channels that he sought the advantage, likely solely on the basis of his clerical haircut and attire. Also, "The whitening gracias al sacar could only have existed because it rested on the real mobilities of unknown thousands of slaves, free blacks, castas, pardo, and mulatto vassals and soon-to-be citizens who leveraged those potentials inherent in their worlds to seek better lives for themselves and their children."[53] Soller is one of these who sought mobility and a better life even if not through anything as official as the late eighteenth-century's whitening decree.

Soller declares in his affidavit "that he did not have the status and rank of priest, neither major nor minor orders (neither did he know Latin)."[54] There were several types of priesthoods within the greater orders (*órdenes mayores*) and lesser orders (*órdenes menores*), and some of these did not require ordina-

50 Twinam, *Purchasing Whiteness*, 400.
51 Twinam, *Purchasing Whiteness*, 407.
52 Twinam, *Purchasing Whiteness*, 417.
53 Twinam, *Purchasing Whiteness*, 421.
54 1^{v}; "no tenía el estado y dignidad de sacerdote ni órdenes mayores ni menores, ni tampoco sabía latín."

tion. Soller additionally claims an inability to read,[55] which might seem on its face to be an immediate disqualification for any member of the clergy. In early modern Europe, however, "many of the nobles and the clergy could not read or write, or could do so only with difficulty, just like the peasants."[56] Moreover, "The style of life of some rural nobles and parish priests was not so different from that of the peasants around them. They were also more or less cut off from the great tradition,"[57] meaning excluded from formal training or university training. Lesser orders tended be conferred upon individuals of humbler origins and preparation, many of whom were illiterate, and so the likelihood of people believing that Soller had *órdenes menores* was greater than if we imagine a priest only as a "real priest," that is to say, ordained. Even if Soller was not already a member of the cloth, which he may not have been, his will to become a priest-*cum*-pilgrim at least entails a convenient synchronization with the Western Christian calendar.

6 Lent

Soller's pilgrimage to Santiago de Compostela is a decidedly Lenten affair. His travel documents date from Ash Wednesday to just past Easter Sunday. In Portugal, Soller's confirmed itinerary begins in Lisbon one week after Ash Wednesday, February 11, and proceeds to Santarém on February 17 all the way to Valença on the Portuguese–Spanish border by March 14. From there, Soller went across the Miño River on to Santiago de Compostela, where he arrived by no later than March 25, three days after Easter Sunday. Soller spent Holy Week in Spain and probably most of that in Santiago since Easter Sunday fell on March 22 and because the journey from Tuy, Spain, just across the river from Valença, Portugal, is only a few days' walk to Santiago, and fewer if riding. Soller easily could have arrived to Compostela by March 17 or 18, 1693, during the middle of Holy Week.[58]

In addition to coinciding with Lent, the months of Soller's travels occur during that season of the year when people usually would go on pilgrimage—additionally providing the cover of crowds on the road. The timing is predictable inasmuch as popular festivals in medieval and early-modern soci-

55 1^v.

56 Burke, *Popular Culture*, 27.

57 Burke, *Popular Culture*, 28.

58 A roughly contemporary pilgrim of Soller's who also crossed the Miño at Tuy to head to Santiago is Cosimo III de' Medici. Taín Guzmán, *La ciudad de Santiago*, 15.

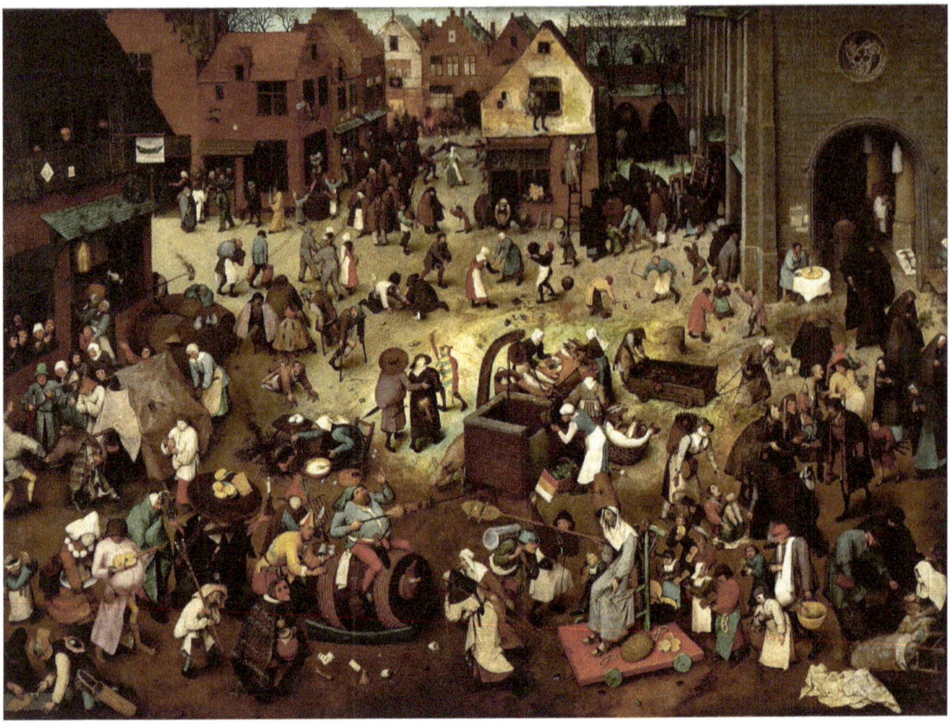

FIGURE 14 *The Fight between Carnival and Lent* by Pieter Brueghel the Elder. 1559

eties tend to follow the seasons of the year: Carnaval (called Entrudo in Portugal) at Winter's end, pilgrimages at the start of Spring from February to May, and with the arrival of summer the feasts of Saints John the Baptist and Paul.[59] Literary and artistic works of the period reflect how deeply imbued this pattern was in the life cycle, rhythms, and mentality of the people of the period and their social reality. Juan Ruiz provides a famous medieval example in the episode of the battle between Lady Lent (Doña Cuaresma) and Sir Carnality (Don Carnal) from *The Book of Good Love* (*Libro de buen amor*). Centuries later in 1559, Pieter Brueghel the Elder paints this allegorical conflict in *The Fight between Carnival and Lent* (figure 14). The Carnival–Lent cycle determines the structure of whole chapters in Francisco de Quevedo's *The Grifter* (*El buscón*) just as this calendrical rhythm is determinative for major episodes in Pedro Calderón de la Barca's *Life is a Dream* (*La vida es sueño*).[60]

59 Vélez-Sainz, "Alternancias de carnaval," 50; Río Barredo, "Burlas y violencia," 112.
60 Vélez-Sainz, "Alternancias de carnaval"; Blue, "Carnival and Lenten Alternations."

In the calendar cycle Lent also marks the start of springtime and is associated with the rebirth its culmination represents symbolically in the Resurrection. In any event, Soller's travels follow this pattern. The cycle could explain why and how Soller does what he does during the time of year he does it. It also could provide a set of circumstances of which he took advantage as camouflage. If Soller is a mock-priest, what better cover could he have than to undertake a penitential pilgrimage during the Lenten season?

At least as long as Lent lasted, the nature of the season likewise makes it understandable how this tonsured mulatto pilgrim was able to fit into his surroundings on the way from Lisbon to Santiago. This is because social hierarchy is eliminated or reduced during Lent, but for opposite reasons than those of Carnival. Whereas the latter involves heterogeneous spontaneous expression that manifests itself in a variety of idiosyncratic ways across a multitude of individuals, the former effects a homogeneous flattening of social roles in harmonious fraternity. Consider, for example, the multiplicity of carnival masks juxtaposed against the absolute uniformity of the pointed hoods in the penitential processions during Holy Week, the culmination of the Lenten cycle. Lent insists on "the radical equality among all men"[61] and nullifies "the value of differences in beauty or social rank."[62] In the Soller case, such an egalitarian Lenten spirit perhaps is made manifest in the declaration of the Catalan pilgrim-priests to the cardinal in charge of the pilgrim passports in Santiago de Compostela that their mulatto friend, possibly their traveling partner along the way, is a priest just as they are.

During Lent, all are made equal in their abstinence, and the pilgrimage of Soller is in harmony with the symbolism of the season. Pilgrimage involves hardship and deprivation, trials and challenges, and is a time for repentance and penitence. Pilgrimage was (and still is) *literally* a "penitential" practice, that is, used in the reformation of criminals: "arising as a counterthrust to the corruption of ordinary life in manor and village and town, pilgrimage became built into the structure of Christian culture as a 'penitential system,' as a rite of passage for readmitting criminous and reprobate individuals to the *Unam Ecclesiam* and, indeed, into civil society."[63] Pilgrimage as a penitential activity is highly appropriate for the Lenten season with its emphasis on fasting, abstinence, and sacrifice to remind believers of the ultimate sacrifice. The question

61 Gutiérrez Estévez, "Una visión antropológica," 55; "la igualdad radical de todos los hombres."

62 Gutiérrez Estévez, "Una visión antropológica," 55; "el valor de las diferencias de belleza o posición social."

63 Turner, "Variations on a Theme," 46.

remains as to whether or not Soller was an authentically penitential pilgrim—but in this respect he was no different than many other pilgrims.

These facets of pilgrimage help explain why taking in pilgrims is one of the Corporal Works of Mercy traditional to Catholicism and why the Misericórdia brotherhood considers it imperative to help pilgrims. This confraternity's spirituality is intimately linked to Lent and to Christ's Passion, and Lenten processions figure prominently in the Santa Casa's celebrations from Ash Wednesday through Good Friday.[64] These processions were essential not only as devotional practices but also as a public testimony of the fraternal and spiritual life of the various Misericórdia chapters. This is why such religious celebrations were anticipated, defined, and structured in the *Compromisso*.[65] Both pilgrimage and Lent clear the way for the new beginning that the Easter Resurrection represents. Be he devout or not, Soller's penitential journey to Santiago de Compostela encapsulates the fresh start he seems to have sought on his journey.

Although Soller was in Lisbon on Ash Wednesday (February 4, 1693) and already in Spain by Holy Thursday (March 19, 1693), Lenten rituals of other chapter houses are suggestive of what Soller may have experienced in Lisbon and beyond. For instance, the *Procession of the Holy Steps* [*of Christ*] (*Procissão dos Santos Passos*) in the Archive of the Misericórdia in Tomar lays out the sequence and nature of this march during the Lent season of 1697. The description indicates: the brother who is to lead the doleful march with his trumpet; the brother set to guide the thirteen angels (*anjos*) carrying articles and instruments associated with the Crucifixion (a hammer and nails; a ladder and lance; rods and whips; a sponge and the cloth with Christ's visage, or Veil of Veronica; and a rooster, among other items); the brothers in charge of the angels; and the brothers who are to carry the Holy Christ images and sculpture of the crucified Christ, called a Calvary (Calvário).[66] The procession evokes and reenacts the Passion of Christ.

In another example, the Misericórdia of Viana, Portugal, provides a privileged space for this brotherhood's penitential processions on Ash Wednesday and Holy Thursday during which penitents flagellated themselves,[67] and the Holy Thursday penitential march constituted a primary obligation in all the

64 Pinho, "As Casas da Misericórdia," 1:113–114.

65 Pinho, "As Casas da Misericórdia," 1:113–114. Magalotti describes a procession in Lisbon Cosimo III attended in which a fragment of wood from the Holy Cross was displayed under a canopy on February 23, 1669 (267). This would have been in the early days leading up to Ash Wednesday of that year, which would have been on March 6, 1669.

66 Misercórdia de Tomar, *Procissão dos Santos Passos*, 167–168^{v}.

67 Maciel, "Misericórdia de Viana," 27.

chapter houses.[68] In this procession, as many as a thousand men and women dressed in black and marched bearing candles and participating in the rite of the mortification of the flesh—to the point of copious bloodshed. This lugubrious procession was divided into three or four stations with an altar featuring the crucified Christ at each one. Many men bore iron rods, wooden crosses, and large stones on their backs. By the time the penitents returned to the chapter house, they were covered in blood. Others carrying water would wash and clean the wounds of the marchers.[69] All were made equal in their suffering in imitation of the Passion of Christ.

Later observers have noted the persistence of the Lentenesque attire of the brothers of the Misericórdia. The merchant Ch.V. de Hautefort noted in 1814 that these men wrapped themselves in black cloth with hoods of the same fabric as that used in funerary processions.[70] In 1866, Eugenio Müntz notes more Lentenesque attire in Pisa, describing the brother he saw as a type of ghost, covered top to bottom in a blue tunic and wearing a blue mask with two holes for eyes. Müntz observes that the brothers of the Misericórdia in the Algarve region (in southern Portugal) wear similar outfits during their Holy Thursday procession from church to church and in numerous other penitential marches throughout the Lent season. These hooded figures often undertake nocturnal processions by candlelight in solemn fashion at the slow pace of a funeral dirge and in sad contemplation of the Passion of the Christ. For Müntz, this funerary march conveyed a profound sense of melancholy and sorrowful contrition.[71] Note that this type of costume for Lenten processions—virtually identical to the outfit of the *penitentes* of Seville during the Holy Week processions—subsumes the identity of the individual and levels the hierarchy among the participating brothers.

The most crucial and representative period of Lent is Holy Week and its processions displaying the Passion of Christ.[72] One of the principal social phenomena of this time is "the indiscriminate fraternity of Lenten spirituality."[73] This wholesale camaraderie is manifest in the hood (*capirote*) of the penitents (*penitentes*), the very emblem of homogeneity, as opposed to the heterogeneity of the Carnival mask:[74] "During Lent, preaching on the situations at the end

68 Ribeiro, *A Santa Casa*, 55.
69 Ribeiro, *A Santa Casa*, 57–58.
70 Ribeiro, *A Santa Casa*, 42.
71 Ribeiro, *A Santa Casa*, 42, 44–45.
72 Gutiérrez Estévez, "Una visión antropológica," 51.
73 Gutiérrez Estévez, "Una visión antropológica," 53; "la fraternidad indiscriminada de la espiritualidad cuaresmal."
74 Gutiérrez Estévez, "Una visión antropológica," 54.

of one's life, '*novísimos*,' especially the reminder of death, fulfills an analogous function to that of the *capirote* upon accentuating the perception of radical equality between all mankind and annulling the value of differences in beauty or social position."[75] Perhaps this is, as noted, the dynamic found immediately following the Lenten period in the Catalan priests attesting to the Senior Cardinal of the Passports that Soller also is a priest. But well after Lent, the return to ordinary time, what with its rules and differentiation, would not allow Soller to sustain the ruse: weeks after Easter in Ourense, he no longer was shielded by the egalitarian homogeneity of the Lenten season.

7 Pilgrimage-as-Disguise

To a limited extent, pilgrimage itself is a liminal and an egalitarian phenomenon, as well, meaning that pilgrims are thrown out of their everyday circumstances and the regular order of their lives, that they are thrust into new situations in which different relationships and identities can emerge. This is not to say that all hierarchy is eliminated but rather that the possibility of new structures and modes of interaction comes into play. It is the fluidity of Soller's identity as a pilgrim that poses a threat to the ruling class. Foucault articulates the reason why this would be so: "discipline fixes; it arrests or regulates movements; it clears up confusion; it dissipates compact groupings of individuals wandering about the country in unpredictable ways …; it must neutralize … horizontal conjunctions."[76]

Accordingly, Soller is viewed with suspicion for not having an occupation, a nationality, or even an ethnicity that are recognized as legitimate in the eyes of the Spanish authorities. Regarding his occupation, Soller describes himself as an "herbalist barber" (*barbero arbolario*) yet is seen as a mixed-race slave and vagabond (and as the latter, a probable delinquent). As for his nationality, Soller is repeatedly dubbed an "outsider" (*forastero*). And with regard to ethnicity, we have seen in the previous chapter (Origins) that "mulatto" is synonymous

75 Gutiérrez Estévez, "Una visión antropológica," 55; "Durante la Cuaresma, la predicación sobre los 'novísimos', y en especial el recuerdo de la muerte, cumple una función análoga a la del capirote, al acentuar la percepción de la igualdad radical de todos los hombres, y anular el valor de las diferencias de belleza o posición social."

76 Foucault, *Discipline and Punish*, 219; Foucault, *Surveiller et punir*, 221; "la discipline fixe; elle immobilise ou règle les mouvements; elle résout les confusions, les agglomérations compactes sur les circulations incertaines …; elle doit neutraliser … des conjonctions horizontales."

with illegitimacy. As is the case with mulattos, pilgrims often are viewed as dangerous for existing in a realm somewhat beyond the strictures of the legal code.

The various hospitals, hostels, and monasteries in Portugal that played such an indispensable role in aiding pilgrims housed not only these religious travelers but also ruffians, robbers, false penitents, women of all types, businessmen, noblemen, people without scruples, in short, everyone.[77] As Jan Van Herwaarden notes, "As long ago as St Jerome, the danger of falling into bad company had formed an important part of the criticism of pilgrimages."[78] The twelfth-century *Book of Saint James* admonishes that "All iniquity and fraud abounds on the routes of the saints,"[79] in part for the picaresque nature of many of the travelers.

Despite outward appearances, not all pilgrims are penitential or devout. Both the authentically poor and fraudulent vagabonds find a way to make a living along this route, and pilgrim's attire became a way of masking one's intentions. Mixed in with pious travelers were a number of picaresque wayfarers such as merchant-pilgrims, false penitents, and sellers of bulls and relics.[80] In the words of Pablo Arribas Briones, "mendacity, idleness, and roguishness gradually take over this formerly sacred route."[81] In broader society, confusion reigned as to who actually was poor and who pretended to be; as a result, all marginalized populations generally came to be shunned. Despite numerous efforts to restrict the flow of vagabonds, Anne Cruz observes that these idle wanderers "continue to circulate freely as unbounded signs of social unrest throughout the vast expanse of the Habsburg Empire" during the sixteenth and seventeenth centuries.[82] Not even the imperious-sounding "constable of vagabonds" (*alguacil de vagabundos*) appointed by magistrates in cities across Spain helped stem the tsunami of vagrants.[83] In short, more than just a few pilgrims live by the "law of deceit"[84] renounced by the tailor and the barber in the Soller case.

---

77 Cunha, "A devoçaõ," 97–98, 101.

78 Herwaarden, *Saint James and Erasmus*, 252.

79 *Liber Sancti Jacobi*, 98, fol. 87^{v}; "Omnis iniquitas et omnis fraus habundat in sanctorum itineribus."

80 Arribas Briones, *Pícaros y picaresca*, 25. Pedro Talonario refers to these false pilgrims as lawless vagabonds. López Santaolalla, "Picaresca y peregrinaje."

81 Arribas Briones, *Pícaros y picaresca*, 29; "La mendacidad, la vagancia, la picaresca en suma, se van adueñando poco a poco del otrora camino sacro."

82 Cruz, *Discourses of Poverty*, 45.

83 Heras Santos, *La justicia penal*, 163.

84 15^{r}, 17^{r}; "ley del engaño."

According to a proclamation issued by the Hapsburg monarch Felipe II, it was illegal by the end of the sixteenth century for Spaniards to wear the pilgrim's habit due to its abuse by a significant contingent of grifters among the Spanish populace. Under Law VI of this legal compilation, pilgrims and foreigners traveling directly to and from the Cathedral of Santiago may beg alms freely along the pilgrimage road, but they are not allowed stray to places off the route and solicit charity in the manner of vagabonds, as this is not allowed to citizens of the realm.[85] Such laws reflect the historical reality that not all pilgrimage activities are purely penitential; some journeys constitute picaresque wanderings.

A good example from Soller's century would be three pilgrim-thieves who pilfered coins from the offering box of the Royal Hospital (Hospital Real) of Santiago; two travelers were from France, Pierre Esculi (1611) and Pablo Baron (1613), and one was from Navarra, Juan de Casanueba (1617). The two Frenchman stole from an alms receptacle in the main chapel, while the Navarrese man looted from a donation container in the hall chapel. We know about all three pilgrim-delinquents because they were caught, jailed, and tried. The judicial proceedings clarify that the thieves attached the sticky sap of mistletoe to the end of a wooden rod, which they put inside the opening of the offering box to harvest the coins from inside.[86] Bearing in mind that these rods may have been their own pilgrim staffs, it could be that the very attire of these pilgrims was used as an instrument of criminality.

Consider, as well, the unholy travels of the exile Diego de Torres Villaroel on his pilgrimage to Santiago in the mid-eighteenth century:

> I began to satisfy various vows I had made for my liberty and my life in my time of enslavement and pain. The most painful vow I undertook was traveling on foot to visit the sanctuary of the Apostle Santiago, and it was without a doubt the most unworthily fulfilled one because the undevout, vain, and ridiculous circumstances of my pilgrimage spoiled part of the merit and value of my promise. I left Salamanca brimming in pilgrim attire, with a staff, a cloak, and a fairly expensive outfit … After the weariness of our journey [each day], we would have tremendous fun in the houses of the nobility, in convents, and elsewhere, where the only task was to listen to music, arrange dances, and prepare all kinds of games, diversions, and amusements.[87]

---

85 Felipe II, "Romeros y peregrinos," 198.

86 Santos Fernández, "Tres peregrinos," 33, 35, 37.

87 Torres Villaroel, *Vida*, 166–167; "empecé a satisfacer varios votos que había hecho por mi

The pious pilgrim's habit of Torres Villaroel masks to the outside world his jocular lack of devotion.

The false pilgrims Auristela and Periandro in the Cervantes novel *The Trials of Persiles and Sigismunda: A Northern Story* (*Los trabajos de Persiles y Segismunda*) constitute another example of pilgrimage as disguise. Periandro expresses the desire for them to don the pilgrim's habit instead of barbarian attire for their trip from Lisbon to Rome: "So, they made just that change and in two days' time looked like perfect pilgrims."[88] This is the "pilgrimage as a pragmatic disguise" to which Barbara Fuchs alludes in her commentary on the episode.[89] Fuchs goes on to note with regard to their pilgrim's garb that "their disguise rids them of the marks of otherness and affords them a relative anonymity."[90] In light of narratives such as these, Miguel Ángel López Santaolalla describes the traveler's dress as the "perfect tool and disguise of the pilgrim."[91]

The ease with which the pilgrim's cloak could be used to conceal one's true identity—as a vagabond, for example—resulted in the Crown's keen interest in discerning authentic pilgrims from false ones.[92] Law VII in Felipe II's proclamation addresses the prohibition against citizens of the Spanish realm wandering in the habit of pilgrims even if undertaking an authentic Christian pilgrimage within or beyond Spanish borders. This law stipulates that Spanish residents should wear their normal outfit and carry official documentation from their local judge. They are not allowed to depart more than four leagues from the pilgrimage route begging alms. These Spanish pilgrims must carry licenses signed by their local bishop, called a dimissory letter.[93] (Church dignitaries also grant dimissory letters to their clergymen so they can be ordained

---

libertad y mi vida en el tiempo de mi esclavitud y mis dolencias. Fue el más penoso el que hice de ir a pie a visitar el templo del apóstol Santiago, y fue sin duda el más indignamente cumplido, porque las indevotas, vanas y ridículas circunstancias de mi peregrinación echaron a rodar parte del mérito y valor de la promesa. Salí de Salamanca reventando de peregrino, con el bordón, la esclavina y un vestido más que medianamente costoso ... Divertíamos poderosamente las fatigas del viaje en las casas de los fidalgos, en los conventos de monjas y en otros lugares, donde sólo se trataba de oír músicas, disponer danzas y amontonar toda casta de juegos, diversiones y alegrías."

88 Cervantes, *Trials of Persiles*, 200; Cervantes, *Persiles y Segismunda*, 269; "Hízose así, y de allí a dos días se vieron peregrinamente peregrinos."

89 Fuchs, *Passing for Spain*, 102.

90 Fuchs, *Passing for Spain*, 103.

91 López Santaolalla, "Picaresca y peregrinaje"; "instrumento y disfraz perfecto para el peregrino." See also Arribas Briones, *Pícaros y picaresca*, 47.

92 Heras Santos, *La justicia penal*, 156.

93 Felipe II, "Romeros y peregrinos," 198–199.

by a foreign bishop.) Foreigners were allowed to wear the pilgrim's habit when entering Spain; they, too, were required to carry dimissory letters from their local bishop. Foreign pilgrims were then supposed to present this paperwork to a judge within four leagues of the border through which they entered Spain and to declare their intention to undertake a pilgrimage before a notary.[94] A traveling clergyman also is required to carry a dimissory letter commending the upstanding character of the itinerant priest to his ecclesiastical superiors.

Soller's case file is missing these documents. Soller has the safe-conduct and credential, but he lacks a license from his local justice and does not appear to have presented any such document before the authorities within four leagues of the Spanish frontier. Neither does he have any sort of dimissory letter supporting his outward appearance as a priest what with his clerical tonsure and priestly regalia. Soller is able to obtain his *compostela* without this paperwork, and moreover, this pilgrim's diploma describes him as a priest.

In Ourense, Soller is recognized as a pilgrim from his attire, especially his satchels and pilgrim's staff.[95] But contrary to the saying in English that "the clothes make the man," the meaning in Spanish more commonly is inverted: "the habit does not a monk make" (*el hábito no hace al monje*). In other words, the clothes most certainly do not make the man, and appearances often disguise an underlying reality. The latter saying is more in line with what mediates the viewpoint of the Spanish authorities in the Soller case, as they do not trust in the slightest that the fabric for the priest's habit and tonsure Soller has acquired for himself mean that Soller is in reality a priest, in part because of the incongruence with his skin.

The value of clothing in seventeenth-century society was real and pervasive in the Latin world, long before the age of mass production. One's attire was correlated with that person's degree of affluence and prominence in society, regulated by law to equate with identity (and to limit conspicuous consumption). Apparel also had the ability to confer the appearance of rank and position.[96] Clothing, alongside eating, was the most significant indicator of social status during the early modern period. Men's fashion became increasingly extravagant from the sixteenth to the seventeenth centuries, and so obtaining the proper type of clothes was an important challenge if one wished to look the part of the nobility or clergy.[97] In the end, sartorial regulations governing consumption in the way of attire and other expenditures could not deter the unbri-

94 Felipe II, "Romeros y peregrinos," 199.
95 1^v.
96 Erauso, *Lieutenant Nun*, ix.
97 Quevedo, *The Grifter*, xxviii–xxix.

dled upward maneuverability that clothing allowed.[98] The intentional act of impersonation, sometimes referred to as "passing," is a way for Soller to resist these sumptuary laws and to navigate upward within the caste system.

Clothing is a motif throughout the criminal proceedings. When the bailiff first apprehends Soller, this pilgrim is "half-naked,"[99] probably about to change into the priestly clothing in his possession. This clerical garb in itself is a topic referenced repeatedly by a variety of parties throughout the case.[100] While in prison, Soller expresses his previous desire to obtain clothing as a reward from the merchant in Coimbra whose cashbook is in his possession.[101] The last time Soller appears in the case as a prisoner, he is "naked" in both a literal and metaphorical sense.[102] His nakedness evokes "the body of the guilty man set up against the body of the King" that Foucault describes as so typical of Old-Regime justice;[103] Soller's shackled nudity is suggestive of "the strongest power over the body of the greatest criminal, whose total destruction made the crime explode into its truth."[104] In the attempt of the Corregidor—a municipal royal delegate—to reveal the underlying reality, Soller's body quite literally is laid bare in the process.

Prior to his criminal trial, passing as a priest gives Soller the opportunity to "dress across" the boundaries of his identity.[105] Soller's act of wearing the tonsure and, if we believe the initial statements of the barber and tailor in his trial (part 1, chapter 3),[106] the clerical garb itself does not cross gender lines in the manner of the Lieutenant Nun Catalina de Erauso or the transgender and transsexual surgeon-soldier Eleno/Elena de Céspedes, but Soller's actions most assuredly traverse the bounds of identity. Erauso's disguise is no passing fad but rather an issue of vital importance. Her uniqueness resides in her attempt to create her own identity through the crossing of gender boundaries

98 Fuchs, *Passing for Spain*, 5.

99 1^{v}; "medio desnudo."

100 *ropa*: 3^{r}, 4^{v}, 5^{r}, 6^{r}, 11^{v} (twice); *traje*: 11^{r}, 12^{r}, 14^{r}, 16^{r}, 24^{r}; *se vestían*: 2^{v} (margin); *vestirse*: 18^{v}; *vestiduras*: 20^{r}.

101 18^{v}.

102 30^{r}.

103 Foucault, *Discipline and Punish*, 227; Foucault, *Surveiller et punir*, 228; "le corps du coupable dressé contre le corps du roi."

104 Foucault, *Discipline and Punish*, 227; Foucault, *Surveiller et punir*, 228; "pouvoir le plus fort sur le corps du plus grand criminel dont la destruction totale fait éclater le crime dans sa vérité."

105 This is the etymological root of *transvestism*. The prefix *trans* means "across," as in "trans-oceanic," while the morpheme *vest* (from *vestism*) is related to clothing, as in "vestments."

106 11^{r}, 12^{r}.

at a time when any type of border crossing was dangerous.[107] The same is true of Céspedes, who conducted a major identity transformation—from female to male; from a dark-skinned, branded house slave to a soldier in Hapsburg King Felipe II's army, not to mention to becoming the first licensed female surgeon in Spain and probably in all of Europe. Elena/Eleno de Céspedes not only dressed and acted as a male would have, she actually modified her own sex in the first gender reassignment surgery in history. The intervention was successful enough to convince the King's personal physician, Dr. Francisco Díaz, who wrote the first medical treatise on urology, that she was a male after a direct examination of Eleno's private parts. Until undergoing trial by the Spanish Inquisition, Eleno successfully leapt beyond the frontiers that kept marginalized groups (underground Jews, ostensibly converted Muslims, women, enslaved people, et cetera) on the fringes of society.[108] The question for Soller likewise would seem to be an existential one, a matter of survival. He enacts his own change of fashion in order to overcome similar societal barriers to those Erauso and Céspedes faced. Whereas Erauso and Céspedes received formal royal authorization for their change of habit and gender roles, in contrast Soller received no sort of monarchical permission to dress as a priest.

The crime the Spanish Inquisition in Toledo found Céspedes guilty of was not transgenderism, transsexuality, or even sodomy, but rather bigamy, a conviction based on the technicality that he (Eleno) was really a she (Elena), and that *she* had gotten remarried without the proper paperwork certifying *his* widowed status (that of Eleno).[109] The trial documents use the expression "to adopt the habit of" (*tomar hábito de*)—a stricter legal term that conveys the direct relationship between one's attire and social position in institutions ranging from convents and monasteries to military orders—to refer to Céspedes's disguise.[110] In Soller's case, the *hábito* repeatedly cited throughout is that of a priest.

Soller's trial proceedings show that impersonation was simultaneously a powerful and a potentially perilous approach to upwardly transcending society's hierarchical borders. As with Céspedes, Soller's disguise is a challenge to the exclusionary racism of the prevailing dogma in the Spanish empire, his retailored identity unbound to the dominant culture's master narrative

107 Erauso, *La historia*, 61.

108 On Elena/Eleno de Céspedes, see Burshatin, "Written on the Body," as well as Hernández Delgado and Ruiz Rodríguez, *Elena o Eleno*.

109 Burshatin, "Written on the Body," 424.

110 Burshatin, "Written on the Body," 437.

regarding ethnicity and caste.[111] Soller's cross-dressing act complicates where he belongs Spanish society and unsettles the hierarchical categories that otherwise might have been used to more readily classify and exclude him.[112] Soller has an uncertain status that is difficult or impossible to resolve in early modern Spain.

In the second part of *Don Quijote*, such is the case with Sancho's friend and former neighbor Ricote, a Morisco, one of the Christianized Moors in history forced into exile from Spain in the early seventeenth century under Felipe III by his royal edict of expulsion. The Christian elite, which considered itself "pure" (i.e., free of Jewish and Muslim lineage) and who had retaken the Iberian peninsula from the Muslims over the previous centuries, could not tolerate the presence of the Moriscos, who were essentially ethnically cleansed from seventeenth century Spain.[113] Though his pilgrim attire is standard—a staff for support and protection from wolves; a cape for protection from the cold; and haversacks for the transportation of victuals—Ricote is so well disguised that even Sancho does not recognize him at first.[114] For Ricote, his pilgrim's outfit is merely to prevent being recognized when entering territory forbidden to "the unfortunates of my race,"[115] as he puts it. For his German travel companions, however, their pilgrim dress serves to dissimulate their true purpose, which is to accumulate enough charity to return home with a profit. In fact, when the Germans stop Sancho upon their initial encounter, they seek to elicit his generosity by singing and begging for alms. Sancho shares all that he has to offer, which is his bread and cheese, but these pilgrims want money: "*¡Geld, Geld!*" is their cry. They consider Spain to be their Indies, a reference to the conquest of the Americas, a place viewed by many a colonial Spaniard as ripe for plunder. The Germans' outfits cannot hide that they are more rogue than pilgrim, and Ricote's travel companions are just a few in a long line of con artists (*pícaros*) who populated the Spanish pilgrimage routes since at least as early as medieval times. Ricote, on the other hand, is an exile, a pilgrim in the truest sense of the word. Just as pilgrims are symbolic exiles in the same sense that Christians, while on earth, perceive themselves to be in exile from their true homeland, Heaven, so does Ricote's pilgrim dress reinforce his status as a stranger in his own land.

While pilgrims are by definition foreigners, Ricote's manners and speech are revealed to be authentically Spanish next to those of his German travel

---

111 Burshatin, "Written on the Body," 440.

112 Fuchs, *Passing for Spain*, 7.

113 Burshatin, "Written on the Body," 439.

114 Cervantes, *Don Quijote*, 2:432; *Don Quixote*, 747.

115 Cervantes, *Don Quixote*, 748; Cervantes, *Don Quijote*, 2:433; "los desdichados de mi nación."

companions. Ricote was so disguised that he is described as having acquired a new identity, specifically that he "had been transformed from a Moor to a German, or a *tudesco*."[116] And yet he remains a Spaniard to the core: while the Germans get drunk, Sancho and Ricote stay awake to talk because they have drunk wine in moderation. Ricote's character is not fully revealed except in the context of hospitality. In this setting, Ricote speaks native Spanish, eats pork, and is revealed to be a sincere convert to Christianity. All of these traits defy the very basis the ruling fundamentalist Christian ideologues used to justify Ricote's expulsion along with his ethnic group.[117] Despite Sancho's initial perception of Ricote's appearance as that of a foreigner (*franchote*), their picnic/communion scene shows that Ricote is Spanish through and through. In Ricote, Cervantes presents us with an exceedingly sympathetic figure caught in an impossible bind inside Spanish borders.[118] Hospitality has transformed Ricote from a stranger into a friend, one with whom the audience in Spain's imperial age could both identify and empathize.

Categories such as *mestizo* and *mulato*, which the caste system seeks to fix into a rigid hierarchy, are unstable when confronted with people such as Soller who take their identities into their own hands despite the limited roles society allows them to perform. In the words of Barbara Fuchs, "The passing subjects actively intervene in the creation of their own identities, even if their agency is limited by the roles and categories that the culture makes available to them … Even as it emphasizes how identity is socially constructed, passing serves to recognize the role of individual agency in that construction."[119] In other words, this individual's appropriation of a new identity is an active response to societal stereotyping that seeks to conflate mulatto with slave.

Such passing and the use of disguises additionally are a reaction to the exclusionary racism that seeks to bar mulattos and other marginalized groups from elite professions such as the priesthood. One might camouflage his or her status for a variety of motives, but most of the time the aim is to play a role that otherwise would be forbidden. The drive to transgress society's prohibitions is the underlying force behind ruses that mask profession, status, literacy,[120] and in the case of Soller, ethnicity and race, a daring gesture given his patent phenotype. Put another way, Soller's primary motivation may be to improve his status

116 Cervantes, *Don Quixote*, 748; Cervantes, *Don Quijote*, 2:433; "se había transformado de morisco en alemán o tudesco."

117 Marchante-Aragón, "The King," 116.

118 Fuchs, *Passing for Spain*, 11.

119 Fuchs, *Passing for Spain*, 112.

120 Hotchkiss, *Clothes Make the Man*, 10.

in society as he seeks not to hide but rather to transcend the limitation that his ethnicity imposes on his movement, power, and life.

8 Exploiting Hospitality

On no other pilgrimage route in Christendom was there a greater amount of charity than on the Camino de Santiago. This social safety net was essential to the massive number of people who were hungry, especially in the sixteenth and seventeenth centuries. The charity network was irresistible to the numerous rogues who took advantage of the pilgrim's habit as a way to get fed for free: "This pilgrim attire … often is the trickster's accomplice, providing him protection, safe passage, and frequently—without any other documentation—access to the organized charity of hostels and monasteries, just as with private charity from pious persons."[121] In other words, the pilgrim's habit-as-disguise enables hospitality.

In fiction, Cervantes' novel *The Trials of Persiles and Sigismunda* illustrates this historical reality. Auristela's devotion is such that she vows to go from Lisbon to Rome on foot, begging door to door if necessary. This is how she and her entourage ultimately proceed, enabled by a beast of burden. They additionally procure pilgrim staffs that double as defense weapons, that is, as sheaths for hidden rapiers.[122] Periandro identifies the group as foreign pilgrims from far away who are going first to Our Lady of Guadalupe in Spain (figure 7), whose miracles wind up making a dramatic impression on the awestruck travelers, then on to Rome.[123] Remember that Guadalupe lies along Soller's possible route from Madrid to Zafra (part 1, chapter 3) and that his safe-conduct states his intention to proceed to Rome from Santiago.

The narrator describes these characters as "our pilgrims" (*nuestros peregrinos*).[124] Antonio, unrecognized by his father, asks if any lodging for the weary travelers can be found somewhere in town. His father replies: "'The people who live here are good Christians, … so all the houses are pilgrims' hostels, but if there weren't any other, mine, which is spacious, could take the place of all of

121 López Santaolalla, "Picaresca y peregrinaje"; "Este atuendo peregrino … es muchas veces cómplice del pícaro facilitándole protección, salvoconducto y muchas veces—sin otra documentación—acceso a la caridad organizada de hospitales y conventos, así como la caridad privada de gentes piadosas." See also Arribas Briones, *Pícaros y picaresca*, 47.

122 Cervantes, *Persiles y Segismunda*, 272.

123 Cervantes, *Persiles y Segismunda*, 276. See Book 3, Chapter 5 of the *Persiles* for a description of the tremendous impact Guadalupe has on the pilgrims.

124 Cervantes, *Trials of Persiles*, 242; Cervantes, *Persiles y Segismunda*, 277.

them. I have some precious treasures out there in the wide world, and I don't know but that right now they might be looking for someone to take them in.' "[125] The irony of course is that one of the "precious treasures" about whom Antonio's father speaks is hidden in plain sight under the cloak of a pilgrim.

The concept of a hospital in the sixteenth and seventeenth century essentially maintained its multi-purpose medieval identity as a center for treatment of the sick, a hostel for pilgrims, and an inn for travelers. Not all hospitals were only centers for the ill, as many were destined to furnish lodging in hostels for weary sojourners and in hospitals for the sick, and sometimes both in the same building. Due to their function and to advances in medical practices, most hospitals belonging to the Misericórdia were completely remodeled or rebuilt from the eighteenth through the twentieth century, and almost no vestiges remain of the original structures.[126] These hospitals were created by princes and monarchs to provide charity. Further, monastic houses nearly always had an annex used as a hospital or pilgrims' hostel. Similar institutions followed suit in hosting pilgrims and the poor in structures annexed to a church or to the Bishop's residence.[127] Hospitality-granting institutions were ubiquitous along the various routes of Saint James throughout Spain and Portugal.

In the seventeenth century, Italian pilgrim-priest Domenico Laffi notes the extreme charity offered to as many as 2,000 people at a time in the King's Hospital (Hospital del Rey) in Burgos. Two centuries beforehand, Hermann Künig von Vack likewise notes the generosity of the thirty-two hospitals then in existence, the Hospital del Rey above all the rest. The various pilgrim menus tended to offer some variety of bread, meat, wine, and stew.[128]

Künig von Vach discusses where to find wine, bread, and lodging at every turn:

> In Burgos there are thirty-two hospitals. The King's Hospital is the best of them all; they give you plenty to eat and drink. Do not overlook the Hospital or the Little Hen; they have good beds and give food and drink. You can also go to the Knights' Hospital. The city has many beautiful large buildings. Many pilgrims will want to see the pillar at which the hospital master

---

125 Cervantes, *Trials of Persiles*, 243; Cervantes, *Persiles y Segismunda*, 323; " 'Según es cristiana la gente que le habita, … todas las casas dél son hospital de peregrinos, y, cuando otra no hubiera, esta mía, según su capacidad, sirviera por todas: prendas tengo yo por esos mundos adelante, que no sé si andarán agora buscando quien las acoja.' "

126 Pinho, "As Casas da Misericórdia," 1:481, 483.

127 Ribeiro, *A Santa Casa*, 21.

128 López Santaolalla, "Picaresca y peregrinaje." Laffi's figure of 2,000 is an exaggeration simply meant to indicate the hospital's large size. Laffi, *Journey*, 142.

> who poisoned [350] pilgrims was put to death. If you cross the bridge on the right it is near the King's Hospital.[129]

In reference to the King's Hospital from Künig von Vach's account, Laffi describes a "hospice" in Burgos that offers "much charity to pilgrims."[130]

With regard to hospitality toward pilgrims throughout Spain in the seventeenth century, Laffi notes:

> I should like also to explain to needy pilgrims something very useful to them, which demonstrates the great charity that they extend in Spanish cities and other places in the kingdom. When a pilgrim arrives at a place where there is no hospice he may go to the local constable, whom they call the alguazil, in other words the justice, to appeal to him. The constable will then call one of his men who will lead the pilgrim to an inn that has a good bed. Also, if he needs bread or wine they will give it to him without hesitation. Whatever the pilgrim needs, if he asks the constable, that they will provide without any question. If he falls ill he may ask those who have horses to give him bread and wine, and then take him on horseback to the nearest village, or carry on to another if need be, until they come to one that has a good hospital where the sick man may be taken care of.[131]

129 Künig von Vach, *Pilgrimage and the Path*, 12; Künig von Vach, *Die Straß*, 83; "In der Stadt gibt es 32 Spitäler. Das königliche Spital übertrifft alle anderen, darin bekommt man satt zu trinken und zu essen. Hennikynß Spital sollst du auch nicht übersehen, darin findest du gute Betten und Almosen. Du kannst aber auch das Spital der Ritter aufsuchen. Die Stadt hat viele schöne Türme. Der Bruder, der die Saule sëhen will, an der man den Spitalmeister erschossen hat, der 350 Brüder vergiftet hatte, halte sich, wenn er über die Brücke geht, rechts, nahe bei des Königs Spital steht sie dann gleich."

The translation erroneously numbers the pilgrims at 450.

130 Laffi, *Journey*, 141.

131 Laffi, *Journey* 142–143; Laffi, *Viaggio*, 184; "Voglio ancora avvertire li poveri pellegrini d'una cosa molto utile per loro e ancora per mostrare le gran carità che si fanno in Spagna e per tutti i luoghi e città di detto regno: arrivando alcun pellegrino in qualche loco dove non sia l'ospitale, vadi dal barigello di quel loco che lora chiamano l'alguazil, overo la giustitia, raccomandatosi a lui, questo chiama uno delli suoi huomini e gli dice che conduchi quel pellegrino alla tale hosteria e che gli diano un buon letto e ancoa, se ne ha bisogno, pane e vino e che gli diano quello che comanda e che ha di bisogno questo poveretto, comandando cosi il barigello, quali lo fanno senza replica alcuna e, se fosse amalato, comanda a quelli che hanno cavalcature, che gli diano pane e vino e poi lo conduchino a cavallo fino ad un altro luogo, il più vicino che sia, e così fanno tutti gli altri successivamente fin che questo venghi condotto in un buon ospitale per essere curato."

Additional accommodations included providing resident linguists "so that confessions could be heard in several tongues" for the international group of pilgrims staying here.[132]

Hospitals took measures to avoid pilgrims doubling their ration, or having seconds, ordinances that may have worked in small towns but which were largely ineffective in the big cities that were the main targets of rogues and vagabonds. In the sixteenth century, several brotherhoods in Astorga convened to discuss how to prevent being taken advantage of by false pilgrims. Pablo Arribas Briones describes the art of deception these professional beggar-pilgrims have mastered, including such practices as falsifying credentials and pilgrim's diplomas.[133] This type of fraud is the very "law of deceit" (*ley del engaño*) in the Soller case that the barber and tailor formally renounce before being released from jail.[134] The Deputy Prosecutor believes that Soller lives by such a nefarious code.

These facts of existence also are reflected in the fiction of the day. Take the seventeenth-century picaresque novel *Estebanillo González*, in which the pilgrim's habit is a ready disguise for this eponymous rogue, as well. Estebanillo's attire for his pilgrimage to Santiago de Compostela made him unrecognizable. His chief ambition as a pilgrim is far from holy, as it served mainly as an opportunity for him "to eat at all hours and not to fast at all times."[135] His pilgrim's dress and cloak are long, his pilgrim's staff reinforced, and his drinking gourd of a substantial size.[136] And this disguise succeeds in getting him stew and wine as alms for pilgrims passing through the Escorial monastery north of Madrid.[137] With the advantage this disguise afforded them, Estebanillo and his fellow group of trickster travelers took what they wanted in the way of wine, stray chickens, and money on their very short daily journeys. As for the bread they obtained, they would eat it, feed it to the chickens, or even sell the poor-quality loaves.[138] Such practices may help explain how Soller would have been able to afford the fabric for the priest's habit and the tonsure.

After passing through Galicia and arriving to Valença, Portugal, Estebanillo obtains a credential (*carta de misericordia*) of the sort given to all poor travelers.[139] This pilgrim's credential (*carta de guia*) from the Santa Casa de

132 Laffi, *Journey*, 142.
133 López Santaolalla, "Picaresca y peregrinaje"; Arribas Briones, *Pícaros y picaresca*, 254.
134 15^r, 17^r.
135 *Estebanillo González*, 170; "por comer a todas horas y por no ayunar a todos tiempos."
136 *Estebanillo González*, 170.
137 *Estebanillo González*, 171.
138 *Estebanillo González*, 174.
139 *Estebanillo González*, 177.

Misericórdia would be identical to the one given to Soller in Lisbon. Estebanillo says that with this credential "one can navigate very well throughout that entire kingdom, as in whichever city or village one shows it, any honorable man is provided with whatever he wants to eat."[140] Once in Oporto, Portugal, Estebanillo trades in his pilgrim's habit for the guise of a peddler. He has enough money left over from his pilgrimage that he can buy all the component parts of his petty merchant's disguise, though not enough to keep the constable of vagabonds from asking Estebanillo how he could get by as a merchant with so little merchandise.[141] *Estebanillo González* and other seventeenth-century picaresque novels, such as Mateo Alemán's *Guzmán de Alfarache*, Quevedo's *Buscón*, and Francisco López de Úbeda's *The Female Rogue Justina* (*La pícara Justina*) reflect the mistrust broader Spanish society felt toward the growing population of vagabonds, who increasingly came to be regarded as social outcasts.[142] Estebanillo, this picaresque pilgrim from fiction, lives by the same "law of deceit" followed by so many false pilgrims in history.

In *La pícara Justina*, Justina associates pilgrimage with freedom. The allegorical poem that opens the first chapter of the second part reads, "May Liberty overtake Justina by her being a pilgrim."[143] Justina says her feeling is that the best pilgrimage is the one that is from the furthest away, and she quotes the witticism "The Saint I most frequently visit is Saint Far-away" (*El Sancto que yo más visito es San Alejos*).[144] (Note the wordplay between the name Alejo and *a lejos*, meaning "far away.") One trait of picaresque antiheroes is their mobility. They prize their freedom above all, and the Road to Santiago provided this to a great degree.[145] Justina becomes a pilgrim to gain not only freedom but also mobility and agency.

Justina becomes a semi-permanent pilgrim, as she herself says: "I found occasion to wander from pilgrimage to pilgrimage."[146] Moreover, it did not take much of anything for Justina to go on so many pilgrimages: "for me to go each week on seven pilgrimages of nine leagues apiece, no more reason was needed than for the southwest wind to blow the weathervane."[147] This type of perpetual

---

140 *Estebanillo González*, 178; "se puede marear muy bien por todo aquel reino, pues en cualquier ciudad o villa que la muestran, juntan y dan con que puede comer cualquier hombre honrado."

141 *Estebanillo González*, 178–179.

142 Cruz, *Discourses of Poverty*, 44–45.

143 López de Úbeda, *La pícara Justina*, 114; "Libertad saque a Justina por romera."

144 López de Úbeda, *La pícara Justina*, 115.

145 Arribas Briones, *Pícaros y picaresca*, 26.

146 López de Úbeda, *La pícara Justina*, 118; "tomé ocasión de andarme de romería en romería."

147 López de Úbeda, *La pícara Justina*, 119; "para hacer yo cada semana siete romerías de a nueve leguas cada una, no había menester más razón que ver andar la veleta de ábrego."

wandering is exactly what was feared by the authorities: hence the numerous Spanish laws against vagabondage.

On the surface, this picaresque novel criticizes the type of pilgrim motivated by idle curiosity: "Many of those in our time who go on pilgrimages, which the female pilgrims undertake solely out of curiosity and leisure, are justly reprehensible and compared to those Israelite pilgrims who, walking through the desert to which God was leading them, became idolaters."[148] The narrator warns time and again of the perils of pleasure-seeking pilgrimage.[149] Such a moral of Justina's story would have made the picaresque elements of the tale more palatable to authorities such as the Inquisition. For our purposes, the key point is the underlying historical reality of perpetually wandering pilgrims on which admonishments such as this are based. These deceptions were and are employed as strategies for survival or simply to improve one's lot in life along the way.

9 Priest Impersonators

The population of artful dodgers was far from limited by nationality. An eighteenth-century Italian pilgrim to Santiago de Compostela named Nicola Albani impersonated a priest in Pontevedra, Spain. On his first pilgrimage in 1743, Albani was able to live very well—being provided with food and drink, accommodations, and noble treatment—all the while satisfying his travel lust. His cynicism was such that he returned two years later, this time with the false credentials of a priest to receive even better treatment.[150] Per Albani's autobiographical travel diary: "I was admitted to the priests' quarters, with a good bed and dinner, as is provided in that guesthouse. It was certainly a clever act on my part to pass myself off as a priest, since I was not one, with the only goal of receiving better treatment, which another traveler taught me, because the other time I passed through here, I had to sleep on a wooden floor without as much as a candle."[151] Albani's devotion coexists with his proclivity for the

148 López de Úbeda, *La pícara Justina*, 121; "*Muchos y muchas de las que en nuestros tiempos van a romerías, que van ellas con sólo espíritu de curiosidad y ociosidad, son justamente reprensibles y comparados a aquellos peregrinos israelitas que, caminando por el desierto a donde Dios les guiaba, dieron en ser idólatras.*"

149 López de Úbeda, *La pícara Justina*, 165.

150 López Santaolalla, "Picaresca y peregrinaje"; Arribas Briones, *Pícaros y picaresca*, 53–54.

151 Albani, *Viaje de Nápoles*, 126; "fui ammesso nella Stanza de Sacerdoti con buen Letto, e Cena, secondo passa detto Ospedale, benchè fù mia politica passar per Ecclesiastico qual'Io non ero tale, à sol fine d'esser più ben trattato, qual cosa mi fù insegnata da un'altro

picaresque. Soller likewise would have been able to obtain improved lodging in the Santa Casa with his tonsure and any other elements of the priest's habit he may have had with him.

Any lentenesque deprivation of pilgrimage would have been lessened for men of the cloth. This is because the benefits of the priesthood, feigned or not, could be financial, as well. For example, the ordained pilgrim-cleric Domenico Laffi "is happy to accept alms after officiating as a priest" and "welcomes the thought of a free meal."[152] Such is the case as well for Martín Garatuza (Martín de Villavicencio y Salazar), a con-man and priest-impersonator active in seventeenth-century New Spain, or Mexico, who received payments for giving false Mass. Ever since his exploits, Garatuza has become the "archetype of the picaresque creole."[153] This is so much the case that in Mexican popular culture, "Garatuza" is synonymous with "swindler."

Garatuza's priest impersonation was successful over a period of years. Toward the end of 1642, at forty-one years of age, he stole the certificates of ordination belonging to a priest he knew in Mexico City. Though not quite as dramatic as Arnaud du Tilh's incredible impersonation of Martin Guerre—even with the latter's family and wife!—in sixteenth-century France,[154] these clerical papers nonetheless allowed Garatuza to impersonate this particular priest in the weeks that followed in the various towns he passed through on his way to Oaxaca. (By contrast, Soller is not impersonating any specific priest.) Garatuza was captured along the way a short time later in January of 1643. After a period of being detained by the Inquisition and transferred to Mexico City, he obtained permission to visit some relatives in Puebla in 1645. But instead of returning to Mexico City, Garatuza continued his wanderings on to Michoacán and Nueva Galicia, once again pretending to be a priest for the next two years. Garatuza was apprehended in Cuernavaca in September of 1647, taken back to the capital, and sentenced by the Mexican Inquisition to 200 lashes of the whip, which he received at an auto-da-fé in 1648. The Inquisition also condemned him to five years in the galleys in the Philippines. Impersonating a priest was a punishable offense under the Inquisition in Mexico, but it remained a strategy that picaresque figures in addition to Garatuza would resort to throughout the seventeenth century.[155]

Viandante, che già nell'altra volta, che da quì passai, mi toccò dormire sopra d'un Tavolato, senza ne pur Candela."

152 Laffi, *Journey*, 11.

153 Moro, "Las transformaciones," 211; "prototipo del pícaro criollo."

154 Davis, *Martin Guerre*.

155 Cordero y Torres, "Martín Garatuza," 271.

In Vicente Riva Palacio's fictionalized version of Garatuza, the chapter in which Garatuza disguises himself as a priest is entitled "In which Garatuza Proves that the Clothes Make the Man."[156] This variant inverts the popular Spanish version of the saying, "The clothes do not make the man," or literally, "The habit does not a monk make." (*El hábito no hace al monje.*) The saying can go either way, depending on what happens. The habit may make the monk, but only to a point. The clothes may make the man, until they do so no longer.

In Riva Palacio's novelization, Garatuza fills the void left by the absence of the priest and vicars in Acapulco: "The Spaniards residing in Acapulco wanted a religious service to offer thanks [to God], and Martín appeared to them as if heaven-sent and a godsend."[157] His success is unmitigated: "Once Martín decided to play the role of a clergyman, he lacked neither the knowledge nor the audacity to be successful in his effort … [:] in a single day, he became the favorite priest in the whole town."[158] The priest impersonator successfully remembers key Latin phrases he had known. He knew the rhetoric well from having lived among church people for a long time: "Martín, with all the devotion of a saint, imitated the rites of the mass; … as a preacher, Garatuza had achieved great success, and the most flattering offers came one after the other."[159]

Garatuza's employment of pseudo-Latin is reminiscent of that of the infamous pardoner (*buldero*) from the Fifth Treatise in *Lazarillo de Tormes*. The most shameless of all of Lázaro's corrupt masters, this church official orchestrates a singularly deceitful strategy based on his license to sell indulgences. Like Garatuza, the pardoner pretends to know Latin and tag-teams with the constable (*alguacil*) to swindle the people out of bundles of money in exchange for his fake indulgences. Their ruse succeeds in converting a skeptical public into a credulous and malleable group. Wherever the pardoner goes, the parishioners buy up all his indulgences without him having to preach so much as a single sermon. This literary story reflects a historical reality, for the advent of

156 Riva Palacio, *Martín Garatuza*, 267; "En el que Garatuza prueba que el hábito hace al monje."

157 Riva Palacio, *Martín Garatuza*, 268; "Los españoles avecindados en Acapulco querían función religiosa en acción de gracias, y Martín les venía como llovido del cielo y como enviado por Dios."

158 Riva Palacio, *Martín Garatuza*, 268; "Una vez decidido Martín a representar el papel de clérigo, no le faltaban ni conocimientos ni audacia para salir airoso del empeño … [:] en un día se hizo el sacerdote favorito de toda la población."

159 Riva Palacio, *Martín Garatuza*, 269; "Martín, con toda la devoción de un santo, imitaba las ceremonias de la misa …; como predicador había Garatuza adquirido un gran triunfo, y las más lisonjeras ofertas se sucedían."

print technology made the production and dissemination of bulls and credentials much easier, and the sale of these documents became a lucrative business for forgers. The result: "'How many stunts like this must pranksters play among the innocent people!'"[160] This fictionalized account is meant to criticize the hypocrisy of actual priests in sixteenth-century Spain.

In this historical fiction, Garatuza is able to enrich himself through the abundance of donations provided to him for offering communion and preaching: "Mass, the sermon, the offerings of escudos that were given in such abundance in those days, had considerably increased Martín's fortune."[161] In his role as a priest, he is welcome wherever he goes: "he found doors open to him everywhere."[162] A clear incentive for anybody wanting to appear as a priest would have been money, as Riva Palacio's novelized version of Garatuza's story illustrates: "Prosperity rained down; there hardly was a day in which he would not celebrate a mass, which if it should be an extraordinary [form of the Roman Rite], would pay better."[163] And important to vagabonds and rogues of all stripes, Garatuza never stays in any one place long enough to arouse actionable suspicions for his priest impersonation: "But since he would barely stay even a few hours in the towns after mass, it resulted from this situation that although the people there may have felt some disquiet, their comments and suspicions would arise after he already was on his way. And very few thought to pursue him, and nobody did."[164] Garatuza's financial motivation is highly relevant to the accusation of the Deputy Prosecutor in the Soller trial, Juan de Rodicio.

In the legal case of José Soller, Deputy Prosecutor Rodicio accuses the defendant of wanting to use his priestly habit and tonsure to seek financial contributions for his services:

> Making a true statement on the matter, I say that the abovementioned, offending the priestly caste, being a mulatto, which is known from his

---

160 *Lazarillo de Tormes* in Quevedo, *The Grifter*, 47; *Lazarillo*, 125; "'¡Cuántas déstas deben hacer estos burladores entre la inocente gente!'"

161 Riva Palacio, *Martín Garatuza*, 270; "La misa, el sermón, las galas de escudos que con tal abundancia se daban en aquellos tiempos, habían aumentado considerablemente el caudal de Martín."

162 Riva Palacio, *Martín Garatuza*, 270; "por todas partes encontraba las puertas abiertas."

163 Riva Palacio, *Martín Garatuza*, 271; "La bonanza seguía deshecha; casi no se pasaba un día en que no celebrara una misa, que, por lo mismo que era extraordinaria, se pagaba mejor."

164 Riva Palacio, *Martín Garatuza*, 271; "Pero como apenas permanecía unas cuantas horas en los pueblos después de la misa, de aquí resultó que aunque no quedaran allí muy tranquilos, los comentarios y las sospechas se formaban cuando él iba ya en marcha, y a muy pocos les ocurrió, y nadie lo puso en práctica, emprender su persecución."

> appearance, impersonated a priest, enabling this wickedness with the vestments and regalia of the clergy, obliging that he be given a tonsure in order to deceive those with whom he should communicate, and to burden his conscience by this means, soliciting donations for mass.[165]

Soller's lack of knowledge of Latin certainly is relevant,[166] as well, but what most bothers the Deputy Prosecutor is Soller's professed illiteracy in relation to the priesthood: "It even can be inferred from this act that such a depraved man would try to preach in some town despite the ignorance he confesses to have of reading and writing, which further aggravates the crime and the deceit and cunning, because he persuaded Doctor Don Jacinto Suárez, cardinal in the Holy Church of Santiago, from whom he brings certification of having fulfilled his pilgrimage."[167] Deputy Prosecutor Rodicio wants to punish Soller more harshly for pretending to be a pastor while not knowing how to read or write.[168]

Once beyond Santiago in Ourense, Soller's tonsure gives him away as a priest (or priest impersonator). Meanwhile, he is recognized as a pilgrim from his attire, especially his satchels and pilgrim's staff.[169] His journey has been a long one, full of sights, adventures, and misadventures in his various stops along the Portuguese Way to Santiago de Compostela beginning in Lisbon.

---

165 20^{r}; "Y haciendo del caso verdadera relación, digo que el sobredicho, menospreciando el estado sacerdotal, siendo mulato, que se conoce de su aspecto, se fingió sacerdote, acreditando esta maldad con las vestiduras e insignias de tal, obligando que se le abriese corona para engañar a las personas con quien comunicase, y por este medio cargar su conciencia pidiendo limosna para misas."

166 1^{v}.

167 20^{r}; "Y aún se puede inferir de este hecho que hombre tan depravado intentara en alguna aldea hacer sacrificio no obstante de la ignorancia que confiesa tener en leer y escribir, lo cual le agrava más el delito y el engaño y cautela porque persuadió al Doctor don Jacinto Suárez, cardenal en la Santa Iglesia de Santiago, de quien trae certificación de haber cumplido con su romería."

168 29^{r}.

169 1^{v}.

CHAPTER 5

Reconstructing Locales along the Way

> Give me my scallop shell of quiet,
> My staff of faith to walk upon,
> My scrip of joy, immortal diet,
> My bottle of salvation,
> My gown of glory, hope's true gage,
> And thus I'll take my pilgrimage.
>
> SIR WALTER RALEIGH

There were myriad routes to Compostela from Lisbon.[1] Soller's journey north is fairly typical except for the abrupt switch southward from Coimbra on February 22, 1693, to Tomar on February 23, 1693 (figure 1; chronology). When traveling north toward Santiago, one perforce arrives at Tomar prior to Coimbra by virtue of its closer proximity to Lisbon, unless, that is, one is going out of one's way to reverse course. Regardless of direction, however, the journey in between—a mountainous 50 or so miles (some 80 kilometers)—should take at least two days on foot or on horseback. Soller traverses that same distance over that same rugged country in a single day. I offer an explanation to this effect under the heading on the town of Tomar in the following reconstruction of locales along the Portuguese Way of Saint James, as well as beyond, from Santiago to Ourense on the Silver Way (Vía de la Plata).

The reconstruction of this and other settings contains images and a discussion of places associated with pilgrimage that Soller is likely to have seen, including hospitals and churches belonging to the Misericórdia. These are structures, works of art, and sights existing in Soller's day. This reconstruction additionally avails itself of contemporaneous accounts and paintings that inform what Soller himself may have experienced.

It nonetheless can be difficult to state with certainty in what capacity Soller would have engaged these places and the people therein. The various itin-

1 Cunha, "A devoçaõ," 113.

DOI:10.1163/9789004422704_006

eraries of the pilgrims who visit the Misericórdias and shrines are accounted for on the pilgrims' credentials, safe-conducts, and diplomas themselves, usually not in the archives of the various Misericórdias or hospitals. For example, I have been able to find the only *List of Travelers and Accompanying Expenses* (*Lista dos passageiros de despesa com os mesmos*) in the Archive of the Misericórdia of Tomar that exists there, but the dates are from 1808–1817, not 1693.[2] Of the records remaining at the Santa Casa in Aveiro for the year 1693, none contains information concerning where passing pilgrims may have stayed or on which date.[3]

Books such as those containing revenue and expenses (*receita e despesa*) of the confraternity's chapters are valuable for illustrating a full range of activities of the Misericórdia: alms for the poor; celebrations of the Holy Mass; the conferral of pilgrim credentials (*cartas de guia*) such as the one in Soller's possession; and expenses such as the Holy Thursday procession, among others.[4] None of these sources, however, records the comings and goings of the various pilgrims and their names. Teresa Raquel Azevedo Sousa Martins, archivist of the Casa de Misericordia in Aveiro, informs me that there never was a registry of pilgrims or a book of *acordos* here that would have recorded the passage of pilgrims. There are, however, books of minutes (*actas*) that record the decisions of the brothers regarding their charitable activities. This usually is the case for other monasteries, as well.[5]

So it is with the chapter-house in Viana do Castelo, Portugal (often referred to simply as Viana). The catalogue of the District Archive here (Arquivo Distrital de Viana) houses the historical documents belonging to the Misericórdia of Viana, including holdings from the sixteenth through the twentieth centuries

2 Manuela Redol, archivist of the Misericórdia of Tomar, was kind enough to share the contents of this volume with me during my return visit on June 28, 2018. This book contains valuable information regarding passing pilgrims, including birthplace and nationality, travel destination, arrival date, and the type and amount of alms provided to the individuals and/or their mounts. Misericórdia de Tomar, *Lista dos passageiros*, 27, 88–89v. It is not relevant, however, to Soller's journey since the dates are from the first quarter of the nineteenth century.

3 Sousa et al., "Misericórdia de Aveiro," 9, 14, 20. The remaining records for dates comprising 1693 include: the chapter's record-keeping book (*Livro dos assentos*) by its members and the Director (Provedor), from 1688–1703; the inventory of the chapter's assets (*Livro dos bens*), especially in terms of bread and funds, from 1654(?)–1694(?); the book of revenue and expenses (*Livro do rendimento e despesa*) from 1693–1694; a book of offerings made to St. Caetano of the Church of the Misericórdia 1689–1724; a file containing notebooks of deadlines, rulings, and translations of written documents from 1690–1699; and a register of conditions, clauses, charters, and licenses of this chapter of the Misericórdia from 1615–1825.

4 Pinho, "As Casas da Misericórdia," 1:114–115.

5 I consulted the online proceedings (*actas*) of the Aveiro brotherhood for 1693.

pertaining to the old hospital. Those containing books of revenue and expenses (*libros de receita e despesa*) are what remain from the Viana chapter of the Santa Casa de Misericórdia. The volume from 1693 contains the accounting of income and expenditures both large and small for that year: i.e., what the brothers paid the organist that year, inventories, the decisions of the brothers, and so on. But as with nearly every bit of archival material throughout Soller's known itinerary in Portugal and Spain, the comings and goings of the pilgrims are not tracked; this book is, after all, a budget document.

In Santiago de Compostela, one can determine that José Soller did not receive a direct charitable payout from the canons of the Cathedral. One may consult the chapter proceedings (*actas capitulares*) for the town council (*cabildo*) of Santiago, the body which commissions its religious administrator (*mayordomo*), a priest or layman who acts as their accountant—and strictly distinct from the churchwarden (*fabriquero*) in charge of corporate bookkeeping for the maintenance of the building and its routine operations, including liturgies, and, uniquely for Santiago, the funding of the substantial body of musicians and vocalists who had their own separate allowances handled by a music income manager (*administrador del depósito de música*). Antonio López Ferreiro transcribed the authorized donations made by the assembly of the town council (*mesa del cabildo*) to needy visitors, and for all of 1693, this is the record: "1693. February 7—Twelve reals to Father Brother Antonio Falco, Italian priest. June 19—A gold doubloon worth two escudos, or in their place four pesos at fifteen reals apiece, to the Illustrious Sir Don Thomas Gregorio Badapur, Archbishop of the Holy Cross, in Greater Armenia, robbed of his church by infidels and who is soliciting donations for its rescue."[6]

Soller also does not appear to have been admitted to the Royal Hospital of the Catholic Monarchs (Hospital Real de los Reyes Católicos). In case Soller had arrived visibly ill to Santiago de Compostela, I also thought some record might exist in the Historical Archive of the University (Archivo Histórico Universitario), which holds the records of the Hospital Real de los Reyes Católicos.[7] That archive is near the Chapel of the Souls (Capilla de Ánimas) near Plaza Cervantes. Lucía Salgueiro Doce, director of the archive, searched without success for a mention of Soller throughout the entire holdings—including the notary's

6 López Ferreiro, *Iglesia de Santiago*, 9:appendix 33:165; "1693. Febrero 7.—Doce reales al P. Fr. Antonio Falco, religioso italiano. Junio 19.—Un doblón de oro de á dos escudos ó en su lugar cuatro pesos de á 15 reales cada uno, al Illo. Sr. D. Thomas Gregorio Badapur, Arzobispo de Santa Cruz, en la Armenia mayor, despojado de su Iglesia por los Infieles y que anda pidiendo para su rescate." George Greenia, e-mail correspondence, June 21, 2017.

7 Fernández Catón, *Archivo del Hospital*, 276.

registry and its few documents on the sale of enslaved persons, which would not apply to a free man in any event.[8] I consulted the manuscript registry entitled *The Sick of the Royal Hospital* (*Hospital Real Enfermos*) for the dates of Soller's stay in Santiago. Having already consulted this volume in person in 2012, I searched the relevant folios again in 2017 and corroborated the archivist's findings. As far as I can discern, there is no mention of any José Soller.

There additionally are records from the Hospital de San Roque, which is now the rehabbed home of the High Council of Scientific Research (Consejo Superior de Investigaciones Científicas, or CSIC) "Father Sarmiento" Institute for Galician Studies (Instituto de Estudios Gallegos "Padre Sarmiento"). It is unlikely that Soller was housed there unless he arrived with a venereal disease! Those records are kept in the Archive of the Cathedral (Archivo de la Catedral), but inconveniently there are no records for the years around 1693.[9]

Soller's travel dates and locales throughout Portugal and Spain are known exclusively from the documents detailed in the previous chapter (The Nature of the Journey). This reconstruction of the locales he visited is therefore tentative and often relies on an examination of extant material contemporaneous with Soller's pilgrimage.

1 Lisbon

Much of the Lisbon Soller would have known no longer exists due to the worst natural disaster in the history of all of Europe, which took place over six decades after Soller's time in Lisbon. A significant portion of the old city is gone. Lisbon was the center of an empire described by Antonio in the Cervantes novel the *Trials of Persiles and Sigismunda* as "'Europe's leading and busiest trading city; here the riches of the Orient are unloaded, from here they're distributed throughout the whole world.'"[10] Beginning All Saints' Day, or November 1, 1755, most of the buildings of the Misericórdia together with its records there were destroyed, along with the rest of littoral Lisbon, in a cataclysmic earthquake-tsunami-fire.

8 Lucía Salgueiro Doce, email correspondence, June 26, 2017.

9 See *Hospitales de San Roque*, 559. Entries 2380 and 2381 show a gap between the years 1645 and 1720. There is no published catalog but there is a complete inventory prepared by Arturo Iglesias Ortega in March of 2011. George Greenia, e-mail correspondence, June 21, 2017.

10 Cervantes, *Trials of Persiles*, 198; Cervantes, *Persiles*, 267; "'la mayor de Europa y la de mayores tratos; en ella se descargan las riquezas del Oriente, y desde ella se reparten por el universo.'"

The Misericórdia of Lisbon celebrates one of its two main feast days on All Saints' Day, the very day of the earthquake (the other is on Holy Thursday, the procession of the penitents, as in the marchers in the pointed hoods that are famous for their Holy Week processions in Seville today).[11] Tapers were lit for mass to illuminate all the churches across the city. Once knocked over in the earthquake, many of the candles were in close proximity to curtains and other flammable material. The result was a veritable firestorm throughout the lowland basin of Lisbon on the shores of the Tagus River once the waters of the tsunami receded.

The earthquake itself, originating just a few hundred kilometers to the southwest of the city under the Atlantic in tectonic plates that clashed together with a force "the equivalent of 475 megatons of TNT or 32,000 Hiroshima bombs. It was at least three times more powerful than the volcanic eruption of Krakatoa and a thousand times more potent than the devastating Haitian earthquake of 2010."[12] As noted, the earthquake not only collapsed entire buildings but also triggered both an enormous tsunami that flooded the entirety of the lower part of the city on the banks of the Tagus river and a catastrophic fire that engulfed the entire city, leaving most of it a pile of charred rubble: "One of the most destructive conflagrations of European history, it gutted the principal institutions of Lisbon's political, religious, and economic life."[13] The fire spread in earnest the next day, All Souls Day, November 2. Whole buildings were reduced to ash, as were libraries, valuables, and so much of Lisbon's artistic and archeological heritage.

While the fire was especially destructive, all three elements of this natural disaster made a tremendous impact: "Various testimonies exist that prove that the building of the Misericórdia was among the most damaged on the day of the great earthquake that destroyed the coastal part of Lisbon."[14] In less than an hour, the tsunami hit, reaching approximately nine feet high in the Church of the Misericórdia, the base of which itself stood at 33 feet above sea level.[15] Even worse, the fire that began the morning of November 2 set off a conflagration throughout the stricken area, including the Church of the Misericórdia brotherhood, burning the church from the inside, effectively hollowing it out and

---

11 Ribeiro, *A Santa Casa*, 94–96.

12 Molesky, *"This Gulf of Fire"*, 6. See also Ribeiro, *A Santa Casa*, 63.

13 Molesky, *"This Gulf of Fire"*, 7.

14 Serrão, Joaquim Veríssimo, *Misericórdia de Lisboa* 205; "Existem vários testemunhos a comprovar que o edifício da Misericórdia foi dos mais atingidos no dia do grande terramoto que destruíu a parte ribeirinha de Lisboa."

15 Molesky, *"This Gulf of Fire"*, 133–134.

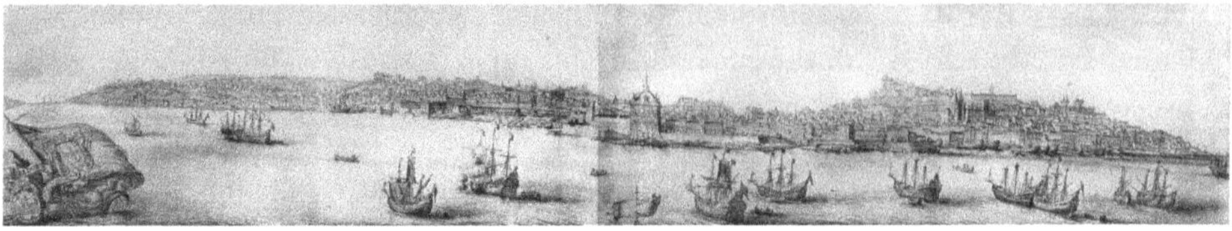

FIGURE 15 Lisbon. 1669
PANORAMIC WATERCOLOR BY PIER MARIA BALDI

destroying its notary office and records.[16] This same fire, more than the earthquake or the tsunami, destroyed many churches and institutions.[17] Yet even though the Misericórdia was lost in this apocalyptic catastrophe, what remains of the historical record, particularly traveler's accounts, enables a reconstruction of some of what was there in Soller's time in Lisbon and the Misericórdia chapter complex there.

In 1669, the architect-painter Pier Maria Baldi, part of the entourage of Cosimo III de' Medici, painted a panoramic watercolor of Lisbon from the perspective of the Tagus river. The Archduke and Prince of Tuscany visited here as part of his European tour, which included visits to Portugal, Spain, Ireland, England, Holland, and France. As befit the prince and heir to the Tuscan throne, his retinue was a sort of itinerant court comprised of an exaggerated number of noblemen and women, intellectuals, and servants. Among the members of this entourage was Cosimo III's chronicler, Lorenzo Magalotti. Another was Baldi, whose mission it was to illustrate cities and towns along the way, and whose work has served as an outstanding visual representation of seventeenth-century Europe—especially of Spain and Portugal, of which Baldi made 120 drawings distributed across seventy-one sheets. Baldi painted all of these vistas in black and/or sepia tones on paper.[18] From Baldi's representation of Lisbon (figure 15), one clearly sees the magnificence of this city very near the time Soller was there.

Cosimo III was impressed by the city of Lisbon and its structures, and remarked on the exquisite Manueline Hieronymites (Jerónimos) Monastery of

---

16 Serrão, Joaquim Veríssimo, *Misericórdia de Lisboa*, 206.

17 Molesky, *"This Gulf of Fire"*, 270; Serrão, Joaquim Veríssimo, *Misericórdia de Lisboa*, 208. Saunders mistakenly believes all of this institution's records in Lisbon perished as a result. Saunders, *Black Slaves*, 55. This was nearly but not entirely the case: the Director of the Misericórdia of Lisbon from 1751–1752, Don Lourenço Filipe de Mendonça e Moura, had kept some of the notarial records of the Misericórdia in his home. Serrão, Joaquim Veríssimo, *Misericórdia de Lisboa*, 208.

18 The one of Compostela is an ink drawing. Baldi appears to have painted all of these landscapes and cityscapes after the fact in his studio in Florence based on the multitude of sketches he made *in situ*. Taín Guzmán, *La ciudad de Santiago*, 14–15, 43–44.

Santa Maria de Belém along the Tagus. But he did not care for the Cathedral, which he criticized for being Gothic and dark. The Archduke of Tuscany particularly preferred the Italianate design of the modern architecture of the period over the city's medieval structures.[19] From Lisbon, the Archduke of Tuscany would go north to Coimbra, Porto, and Viana, crossing into Galicia at Tui, and overnighting at Pontevedra on his way to Santiago de Compostela.[20] Soller also crossed the Minho River into Spain from Valença, Portugal, opposite Tui.

As for the Misericórdia, King Manuel I had recognized the value of caring for the poor and wanted to endow the mother house in Lisbon with a building befitting its status and the importance of its works. The chosen location was between the Episcopal See and the Tagus river at a site called the Ribeira, meaning shoreline, located to the southeast of Lisbon's old Jewish quarters (Judiaria Velha), known at that time as the Vila Nova de Gibraltar. King Manuel I did this in part to help satisfy this brotherhood's expansionist aims. The headquarters were built on lands reclaimed from a landfill, as were those of the public square (*terreiro*) on the south-facing bank of the Tagus River. The small Misericórdia hospital was relocated to the enormous All Saints Royal Hospital (Hospital Real de Todos os Santos). The whole Misericordia complex, including its church and hospital, took roughly twenty years to complete. The new structure was completed in 1534 under the reign of King João III, who attended the solemn procession marking the grand opening. These festivities constituted what perhaps were the most magnificent ones that João III ever witnessed.[21] One can appreciate the location, scope, and grandeur of the Misericórdia compound, especially the hospital, in the following map of Lisbon (figure 16).

The Church of the Misericórdia, oriented West to East as so many churches are (to symbolize the Resurrection and to anticipate the Second Coming of Christ), was among the most sumptuous churches of all Lisbon, after only that of Santa Maria de Belem. Contemporaneous travelers from the world over remarked on the splendor of the quarry-rock church and on the magnificence of the polished-stone hospital, shining examples each of Manueline, or Portuguese late-Gothic architecture. One of these, father Manuel Bernardes, considered the buildings of the Misericórdia to be greater than some of the Seven Wonders of the World, including the Colossus of Rhodes and the Pyramid of Giza.

So much grandeur was reduced to mere rubble in 1755. Only the main entrance, the southern door, of the church survived the damage. This portal

19 Serrão, Vitor, "Portugal," 548.
20 Taín Guzmán, *La ciudad de Santiago*, 15.
21 Ribeiro, *A Santa Casa*, 60–61; Serrão, Joaquim Veríssimo, *Misericórdia de Lisboa*, 56–57.

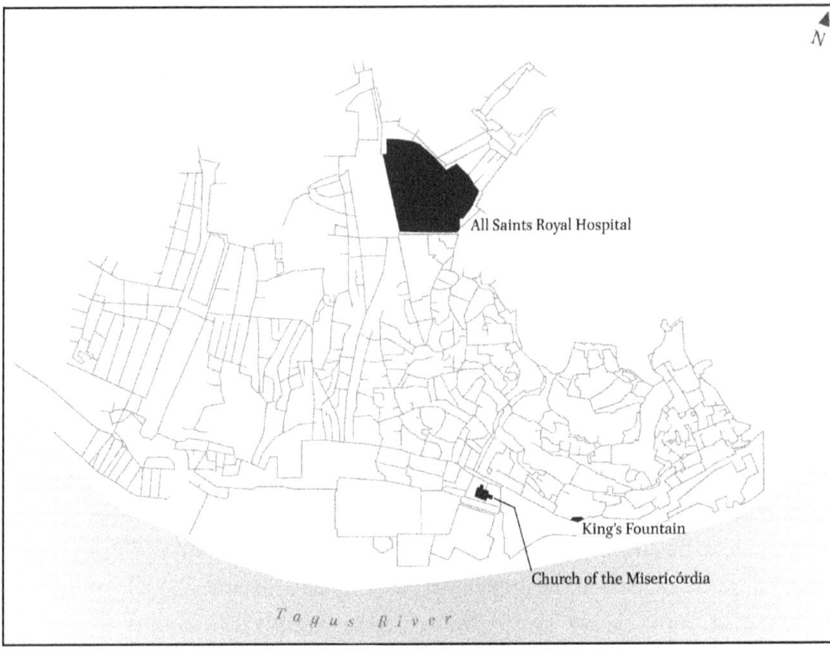

FIGURE 16 Map of Lisbon circa 1693 based on contemporaneous maps and drawings from the period. Detail of All Saints Royal Hospital, the Church of the Misericórdia, and the King's Fountain in the Alfama District
MAP BY THE UNIVERSITY OF WISCONSIN–MADISON CARTOGRAPHY LAB

and its marvelous tympanum featuring the Virgin and her protective mantle were reconstructed and placed as the façade of the main entrance of the old Church of Our Lady of the Conception (Nossa Senhora de Conceição Velha), built on top of the former site of the Misericórdia. This rebuilt portal is located today on Customs House Street (Rua Alfândega) on the block between it and the Street of the Codfishermen (Rua dos Bacalhoeiros).[22] This portal, which once opened into the chapel of the Church of the Misericórdia, now opens into the chancel of Nossa Senhora de Conceição Velha (figure 17).[23]

The Misericórdia's chapel referred to here is the Chapel of the Holy Spirit (Capella do Espírito Santo), a confluence of ethnicity, class, and caste in Lisbon and the African colonies, founded by the donation of Dona Simôa Godinho, a black, African woman from São Tomé, and her husband, a Portuguese noble-

22 Ribeiro, *A Santa Casa*, 62–64, 69, 78; Serrão, Joaquim Veríssimo, *Misericórdia de Lisboa*, 57. After the natural disaster occurred, the Misericórdia was relocated to its current location atop the heights of Saint Roque.

23 Serrão, Joaquim Veríssimo, *Misericórdia de Lisboa*, 206.

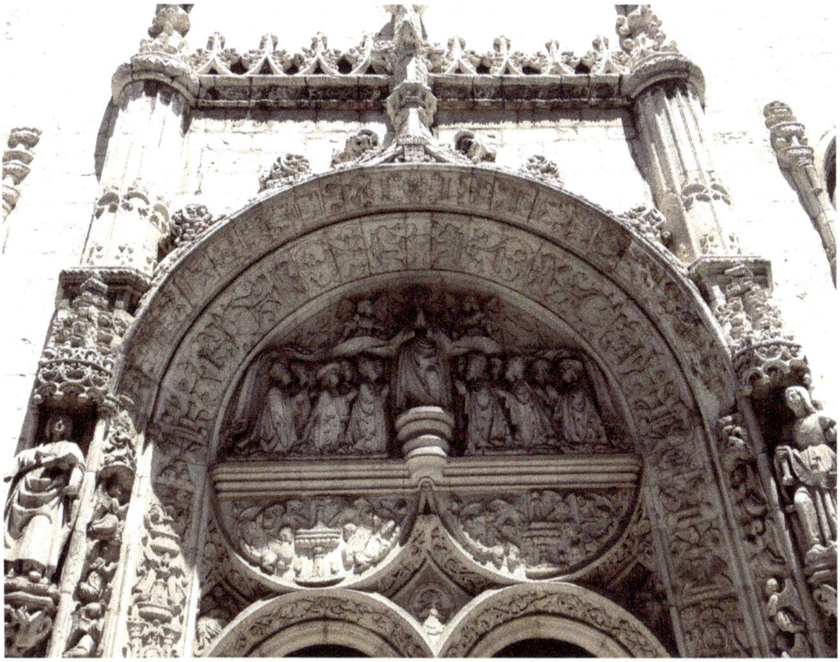

FIGURE 17 Reconstructed portal of the former Church of the Misericórdia, now belonging to the old Church of Nossa Senhora da Conceição. Lisbon, Portugal. Sixteenth century
PHOTO BY THE AUTHOR

man. After he died at the end of the sixteenth century, Dona Simôa asked to be buried with him. This dark-skinned woman (*preta*) with her husband still had their tombs in this chapel at the time the 1755 fire burned it to the ground. As we have seen, the former chapel of the Church of the Misericórdia was reconstituted as the chancel of Conceição Velho after the natural disaster.[24]

One notes in the tympanum of this portal what came to be the most prominent symbol of the Misericórdia, that is, the Virgin sustained by two angels and with her cloak open, shielding on the one hand earthly powers including kings, queens, and princes—among these King Manuel and Queen Maria, all of them on their knees—and on the other hand spiritual authorities such as Popes, bishops, cardinals, and clergymen—brother Miguel Contreiras and various prelates among these figures.[25] This bas-relief statue of the Virgin measures

24 Serrão, Joaquim Veríssimo, *Misericórdia de Lisboa*, 208; Ribeiro, *A Santa Casa*, 117.
25 Ribeiro, *A Santa Casa*, 79.

three feet tall. The entire group measures 20 palms in length (some 14 feet) and consists of seven stones. The name of the architect of this Portuguese national treasure is unknown.[26]

The Virgin Mary is an appropriate patroness of the Misericórdia brotherhood considering that in her capacity as merciful mediator between her Son and humanity, she is the very personification of the charity the brothers had a mandate to provide.[27] It is in this spirit that the cloak of Mary's protection expands beyond the privileged to include the needy, children, the indigent, the sick, prisoners, and others, including pilgrims. In a lateral column to the right of this portal, one sees the figure of a pilgrim with his staff and scallop shell, a clear allusion to the pilgrimage road to Santiago as well as to the mandate to shelter pilgrims along their journey (figure 18).

The brotherhood made a huge impact on Lisbon's population. For example, Magalotti writes in 1669 that the Misericórdia of Lisbon consists of 600 brothers, 300 laymen and 300 noblemen; offers as many 300 masses daily for the deceased; and takes care of 600 sick people in its hospital there.[28] He also describes the process of distributing alms to the many priests required for this endeavor in the sacristy of the church.[29] To this day, it is customary for the bereaved to provide a stipend to pastors for their services in helping them bury their dead. As a priest or mock-priest, Soller additionally would have had the potential to receive similar perquisites.

The Santa Casa de Misericórdia additionally would care for the imprisoned slaves of those masters who refused to feed and clothe them. But not everything about the Misericórdia was geared toward charity: if the slave was acquitted and the master refused to pay the cost in arrears, then the Misericórdia would sell the slave to cover the amount.[30] Sometimes "black slaves" would become part of the family, as it were, of a particular master, and "Free blacks, both men and women, and their families were allowed to join by themselves."[31] In theory, however, no black people, including mulattos, were allowed leadership roles in this or in many other brotherhoods. In a "society which classified its slave and freed population by colour,"[32] this ritual of exclusion was attributable solely to

26 Ribeiro, *A Santa Casa*, 80, 82.

27 Cruz, *Discourses of Poverty*, 52.

28 Magalotti, *Viaje de Cosme*, 1:289–290.

29 Magalotti, *Viaje de Cosme*, 1:290.

30 Saunders, *Black Slaves*, 129.

31 Saunders, *Black Slaves*, 151.

32 Saunders, *Black Slaves*, 153. As if to drive home the point regarding the exclusion of blacks from leadership roles, the brothers of the Misericórdia voted with a system of white beans and black beans, and any candidate for Director or brother with a majority of white beans

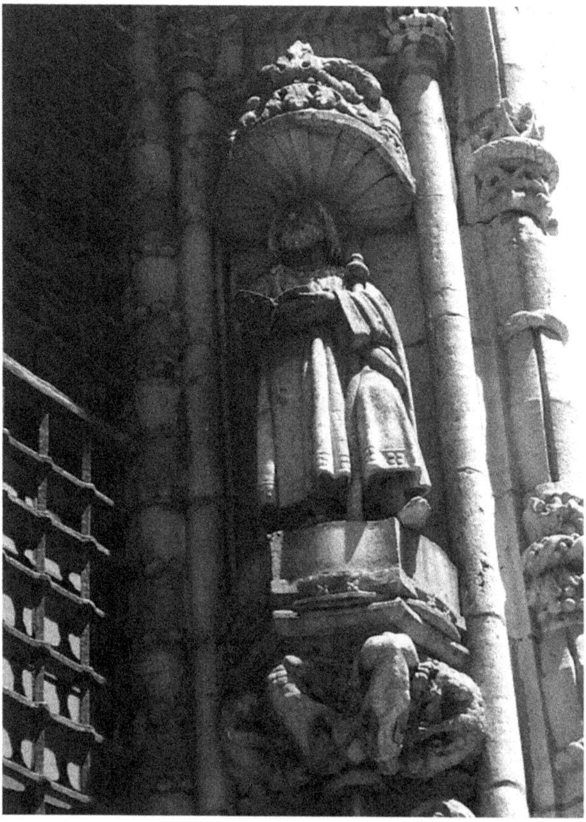

FIGURE 18 Sculpture of a pilgrim to Santiago. Detail from the reconstructed portal of Conceição Velha, formerly the southern entrance to the Church of the Misericórdia. Lisbon, Portugal. Circa 1534
PHOTO BY THE AUTHOR

the pigmentation of their skin, to their phenotype. And yet the story of Brás de Albuquerque, an Afro-Portuguese man who joined this group's Board of Directors in the sixteenth century (part 1, chapter 3), reminds us that the reality is far more complicated, particularly for those of privileged lineages yet of mixed African descent.

---

could be admitted to the Order. A black bean constituted a negative vote, as has long been traditional for the color. Misericórdia of Coimbra, *Compromisso*, 4.

2 The King's Fountain Plaza in Lisbon

The location of the Church of the Misericórdia of Lisbon during Soller's stay there was only a short distance downriver from the plaza of the King's Fountain (Chafariz d'el Rey) in the Alfama District (figure 16). As a principal source of potable water for the city, residents of all ethnic backgrounds gathered here. This population included a sizeable percentage of people of black-African descent.

Lisbon, Seville, and Valencia were the largest slave ports in the Iberian Peninsula throughout the sixteenth century and beyond.[33] In Seville by 1565, there were more than five thousand Africans, most enslaved persons. Meanwhile in Lisbon at the tail end of the sixteenth century, Africans and their children were present throughout most parts of the city. A few decades later, by 1630, there were around fifteen thousand enslaved people and two thousand freed people of black-African descent in Lisbon.[34] The black population was intermingled across the non-ghettoized neighborhoods of the city, and black and white Lisboners and their families became friends and even stood as godparents to one another's children.[35] Despite the paucity of historiography on "black Lisbon" during the seventeenth and eighteenth centuries, James Sweet estimates that by the 1700s, the population of people with some degree of black African ancestry was close to 20 percent, that is, as high as a fifth of Lisbon's total population.[36] "Whatever the exact numbers, outsiders perceived that the black genetic contribution was changing Lisbon irrevocably."[37]

The Afro-descended population accounts for such a high percentage of the total in large measure due to the fact that Lisbon is a port city, and black people were hired or forced to be workers in such a setting, in particular during the moment in history Soller was there.[38] James Sweet expounds on the ethnic background of trans-Atlantic port workers at this time:

> Especially after the middle of the seventeenth century people of African birth or descent became increasingly numerous residents of British, Dutch, French, Spanish, and Portuguese port cities and of American ports, even those that served non-plantation hinterlands … [F]ree and enslaved

33 Franco Silva, "La mujer esclava," 291.

34 Schwartz, *All Can Be Saved*, 160.

35 Saunders, *Black Slaves*, 146.

36 Sweet, *Domingos Álvares*, 159; Sweet, "African Lisbon," 236–237.

37 Sweet, "African Lisbon," 237.

38 Cañizares-Esguerra, Childs, and Sidbury, *Black Urban Atlantic*, 3–4.

> blacks became increasingly important maritime workers … In addition, blacks worked in domestic service, in the many crafts necessary to serve transoceanic commerce …, and in the nonartisanal work that took place around the docks … But the vast majority of Africans living in European or American ports had been involuntarily drawn into those urban centers either directly or indirectly by the transatlantic slave trade.[39]

Unsurprisingly, the people of African descent did not receive equal treatment in Lisbon.

The Chafariz d'el Rey Plaza on the Naus Shoreline (Ribera da Naus), for instance, was rebuilt in 1517 with different water outlets for separate use by the white and black populations.[40] Certain water fountains were set aside specifically for black people irrespective of their free or enslaved status and regardless of their sex. White women also had their own fountain, "so as to avoid disorder."[41] While Lisbon had over four hundred years on the Jim Crow American South in the racial segregation of its water fountains, early-modern Portuguese society nonetheless allowed for a far greater degree of upward mobility among people of color.

An anonymous late-sixteenth-century Flemish painting of this place depicts a number of blacks, mostly slaves, serving in different social stations, including a black-African knight of Santiago on horseback (figure 19). White slaves are present, as well. In this scene at the King's Fountain, there are water-bearers (*aguadeiros*) working, that is, uniformed servants or house slaves fetching water, and many different classes of over 200 people, both free and enslaved, more than half of these persons of color. The free black knight wearing a cape emblazoned with the blood-red cross of the Order of Santiago illustrates that being an Afro-descended person was not a wholesale blockade from being able to rise in the social ranks of the cosmopolitan scene in sixteenth-century Lisbon, even in what was among the most prestigious military orders.[42]

Indeed, João de Sá Panasco, a sixteenth-century man of black African descent, was himself appointed to the Order of Santiago for his military service in the Maghreb on behalf of the Crown.[43] The mounted black knight of this painting, resplendent in sword and cape, could be this same man. Panasco's days in

39 Sweet, "African Lisbon," 237.
40 Massing, *"Age of Discovery"*, 231.
41 Lawrance, "Black Africans," 117.
42 Jordan, Annemarie, "Images of Empire," 159–160; Lahon, "Black African Slaves," 276–277; Massing, *"Age of Discovery"*, 232.
43 Jordan, Annemarie, "Images of Empire," 160–161.

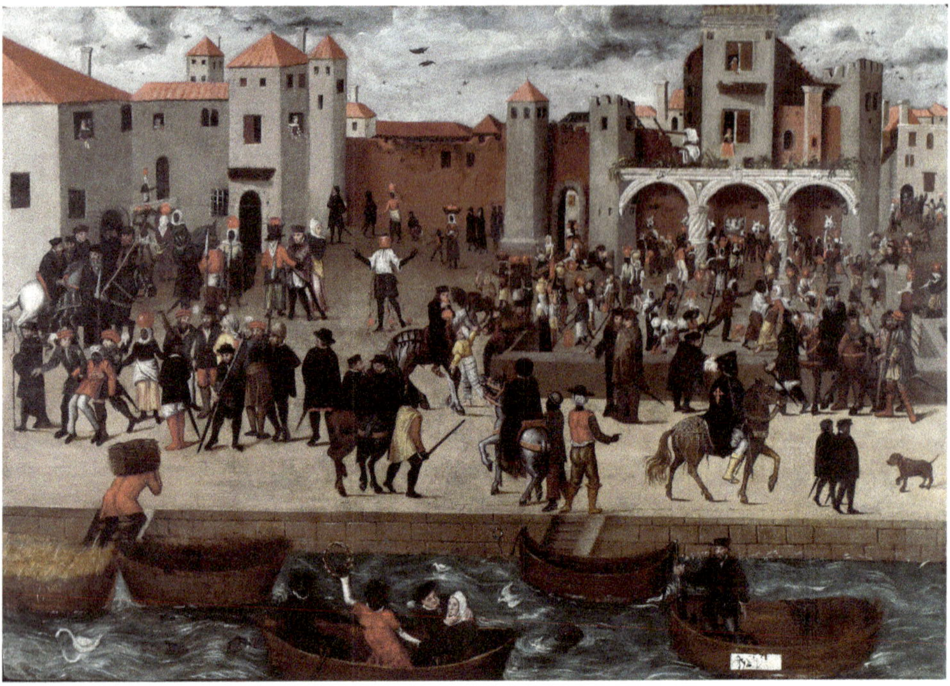

FIGURE 19 *Chafariz d'el Rey*. Anonymous Flemish Painting. Lisbon, Portugal. Circa 1570–1580. Oil on wood, 93×163 cm
COURTESY OF THE BERARDO COLLECTION, LISBON, PORTUGAL

Portugal began with him as an enslaved jester in the Portuguese royal court. He got promoted to courtier and the King's personal valet by 1547, and Panasco joined the nobility around mid-century.[44] (In Spain, by contrast, restrictions limiting access to this military order had tightened completely by the seventeenth century.[45]) In the painting, his sword represents his power, his cape his status, his horse his wealth. To the right of this knight, two elegantly dressed noblemen of black-African descent also carry swords as symbols of their stature. The black knight is not exceptional for being a powerful man of color in this society.

What is more, the private residence in which this painting is displayed, the Bacalhoa Palace (Palácio da Bacalhôa in Azeitão, located on a wine estate just south of Lisbon), epitomizes this story of upward mobility among people of African descent in early-modern Portuguese society. The *Chafariz d'el*

44 Garber, "Africans in Renaissance Europe."
45 Lahon, "Black African Slaves," 277n52.

Rey is part of the vast Berardo Collection, which is larger than that of the Guggenheims and is the second largest private collection in all of Europe. Portuguese businessman and collector José ("Joe") Manuel Rodrigues Berardo owns both the painting and the palace. His son, Renato, kindly welcomed me to the Berardo family home to view the painting. As scion of the estate, the younger Berardo emphasized that their residence once belonged to the Albuquerque family, in particular to Afonso (Brás) de Albuquerque, the Afro-Portuguese son of conqueror and second viceroy to India Afonso de Albuquerque (part 1, chapter 3). In the niche above the lintel over the main doorway to the home, a terra cotta bust of the younger Albuquerque oversees all who enter and exit the premises. Renato Berardo was careful to point out Afonso (Brás) de Albuquerque's tight curls, which would have come from Albuquerque's African mother. By virtue of his father's stature and with the blessing of King Manuel I, this part-African, part-European man not only assimilated but moreover ascended to the very heights of sixteenth-century Portuguese society with all the accompanying rights, privileges, and honors.[46] Afonso (Brás) de Albuquerque's effective whitening and resulting rise in rank and authority in Portugal is not at all unlike the hard-earned privileged position enjoyed by João de Sá Panasco, the probable Afro-Portuguese knight of Santiago in the *Chafariz d'el Rey* painting housed here.

The further north Soller went in Portugal, the whiter the population would have become. This is because there were fewer blacks in northern Portugal as compared to Lisbon:[47] "The geographic distribution of slaves in Portugal resembled that elsewhere in southern Europe: large concentrations in the cities and ports, few slaves in the mountains and poorer regions."[48] Along Soller's itinerary, there were slaves in the coastal city of Aveiro by the mid-fifteenth century and further south in the interior in Coimbra by the first third of the sixteenth century:[49] "within a few decades after the first blacks were brought to Portugal, they also could be found well inland in rural districts" such as Santarém, just upriver from Lisbon.[50] Enslaved people also worked the vineyards of Coimbra. By the mid-sixteenth century, roughly ten percent of Lisbon's population consisted of slaves (about 10,000) compared to roughly five percent of the total population of Aveiro and Tomar.[51] In gen-

46 Conversation with Renato Berardo in the Bacalhoa Palace, Azeitão, Portugal, June 22, 2018.
47 Lawrance, "Black Africans," 116; Saunders, *Black Slaves*, 53.
48 Saunders, *Black Slaves*, 177.
49 Saunders, *Black Slaves*, 53.
50 Saunders, *Black Slaves*, 54.
51 Saunders, *Black Slaves*, 59–60, 69.

eral terms, "Slaves were much less common north of the valley of the Tagus. Some worked on farms in the coastal belt as far north as Coimbra, probably because the work was unattractive to freemen who could easily go to Lisbon."[52] In places where Soller traveled in Portugal such as Santarém, religious institutions held slaves,[53] not that all of these subjugated individuals would have been descended from sub-Saharan Africans. Indeed, it is crucial not to conflate an enslaved person with a person of black-African descent, even if these individuals of color formed a majority among the slave population. As far north as Galicia, there were enslaved individuals of black-African ancestry, as well as of Turkish, Morisco, and Berber backgrounds. There even is documentation of slaves of Asian descent in seventeenth-century Vigo, Galicia, just north of Portugal in Spain.[54] Regardless of the demographic distribution, residents of Lisbon and of Portugal in general "were more used to contact with Africans than were Northern Europeans."[55]

Lisbon, like any big city, would have afforded Soller a certain degree of anonymity, as opposed to a smaller town or city neighborhood where most people would have known one another. Soller might have played the slippage between identities and locations, being one place where he could be assumed to be someone's servant and being somewhere else where perhaps he could be something greater. Despite the relative freedom of movement dark-skinned people had in Spanish and especially in Portuguese society during this time, a dark-skinned person donning the attire of the more privileged classes would have been subjected to closer scrutiny than otherwise might have been the case. Even today, the whitening of the population is readily noticeable the more one moves toward the interior and the north in Portugal and Spain. Put another way, the further north and inland Soller traveled, the more he would have stood out as person of color and the more he would have had to employ the "tricks of the weak."

3 Santarém

Santarém is not so far north for Soller to have stood out. In sixteenth-century Portugal, enslaved people of black-African descent here regularly received permission to invite other black people to celebrate religious feasts and Sundays

---

52 Saunders, *Black Slaves*, 87.
53 Saunders, *Black Slaves*, 67.
54 Ménard, "'Un esclavo.'"
55 Fonseca, "Black Africans," 121.

together. However, once it was discovered that these reunions enabled these slaves to plot their escape, such gatherings became outlawed (see below, part 1, chapter 6).[56]

Magalotti describes Santarém as famous in Portugal for being an important center of miracles and as a town set atop a smooth hillock skirting the banks of the Tagus River.[57] In one of Baldi's watercolors,[58] one can observe the wall of the city surrounding the town. Historic Santarém was decorated in Soller's day with beautiful polychromatic tiles.[59] The historical marker outside the sixteenth-century Church of the Misericordia here describes it as "One of the most beautiful examples of Renaissance architecture in the city, Mercy Church constitutes a perfect example of the 'large-hall churches.' The interior is richly ornamented with grotesques on the columns and on the ribbings of the vaulted ceiling." The church and its architectural elements from this time period are extremely well preserved (figures 20 and 21).

By the mid-seventeenth century, Santarém came to have around fifty assistance centers, including hospitals, hostels, leper-hospitals, confraternities, and inns. The last of these were able to offer longer stays for the ill or wounded. Most of these institutions were located on the heights of Santarém above the shoreline of the Tagus. Santarém differed from other places in that the hospitality infrastructure was located in the city center, not so much along the periphery of the city, which is where military and religious orders typically would build their hospitals to receive pilgrims and the poor.[60] Indeed, a reconstructed map of a central city block in Santarém during the medieval or early modern period shows a pilgrims' hospital, the Original Poor Pilgrims Hospital (Primitivo Hospital dos Pobres Caminhantes), located at the corner of what today are the streets (*ruas*) João Alfonso (previously Arco de Manços) and Miguel Bombarda (previously Santo Estevão). This hospital was comprised of a variety of infirmaries belonging to religious orders and third parties, its previously existing structure but half a block from the Church of the Misericórdia.[61]

A reconstructed medieval map of Santarém during from the thirteenth through the fifteenth centuries shows two entrances to the south from Lisbon

---

56 Saunders, *Black Slaves*, 106.

57 Magalotti, *Viaje de Cosme*, 1:309–310.

58 Magalotti, *Viaje de Cosme*, 2:LVIII.

59 Serrão, Vitor, "Portugal," 549.

60 Quintino, "Santarém Medieval."

61 The section of street where this church is located since has been renamed the First of December Street (Rua Primeiro de Dezembro), which becomes that of João Alfonso, along which the former hospital was located. Both refer to the same street despite their different names.

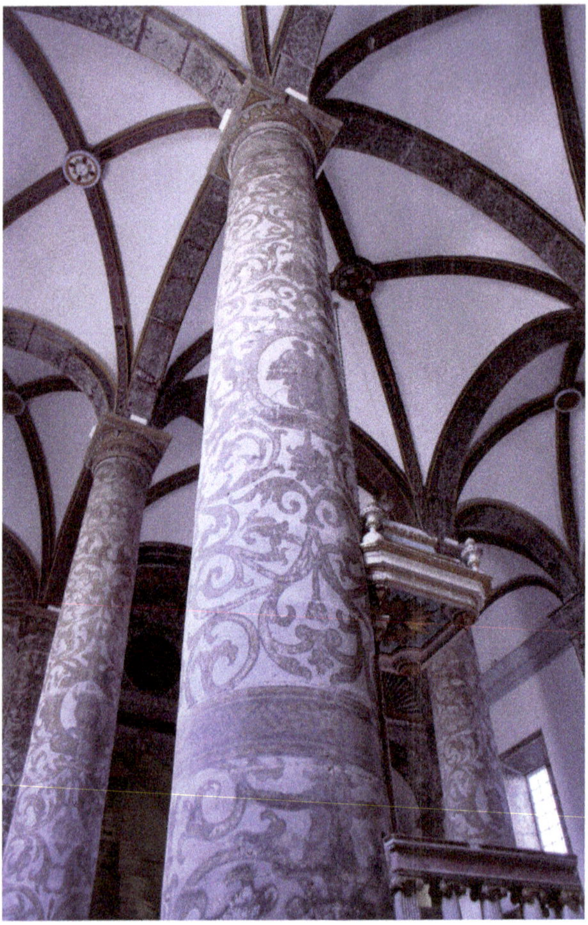

FIGURE 20 Ribbed vault and columns with frescoes. Interior, Church of the Misericórdia, Santarém, Portugal. Sixteenth century
PHOTO BY THE AUTHOR

and one to the north toward Tomar and Coimbra. All are fairly close to or just beside the Tagus river. These riparian routes are what Soller would have taken.

4 Golegã

Magalotti is especially impressed by the beauty of the landscape between Golegã and Tomar, whose features he describes in superlative terms: olive groves, wheat fields, forests, pasture lands, and livestock interspersed among

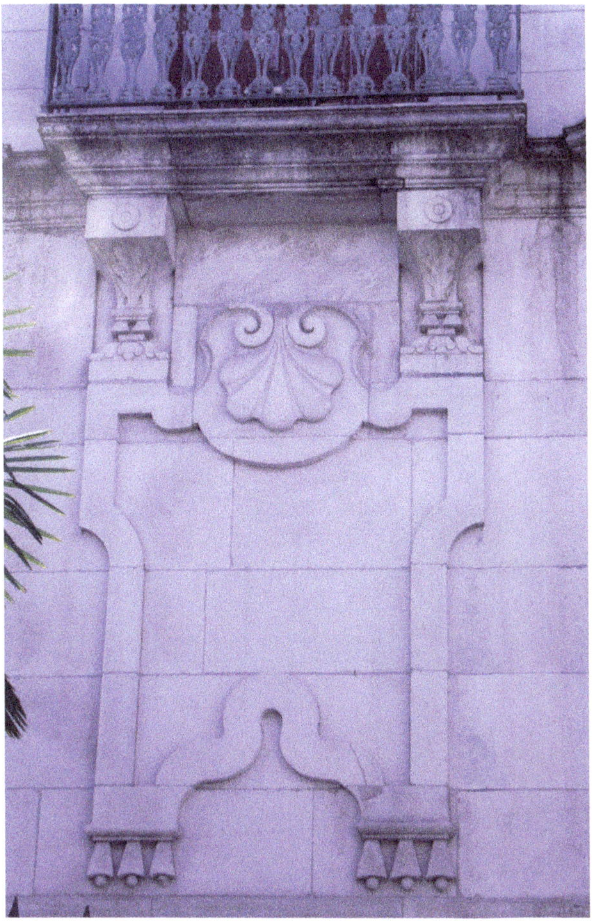

FIGURE 21 Close-up of scallop motif. Exterior, Church of the Misericórdia, Santarém, Portugal. Sixteenth century
PHOTO BY THE AUTHOR

small towns, rolling hills, open plains, abundant creeks, and fresh air.[62] I can attest that the journey today is lovely in similar ways. Cosimo III admired an unfinished yet opulent palace in this town.[63] What remains today is the fifteenth-century Manueline Church of Our Lady of the Conception (Nossa Senhora da Conceição). Although the interior of the church underwent extensive remodeling in the seventeenth and eighteenth centuries, its main portal

62 Magalotti, *Viaje de Cosme*, 1:311.
63 Serrão, Vitor, "Portugal," 549.

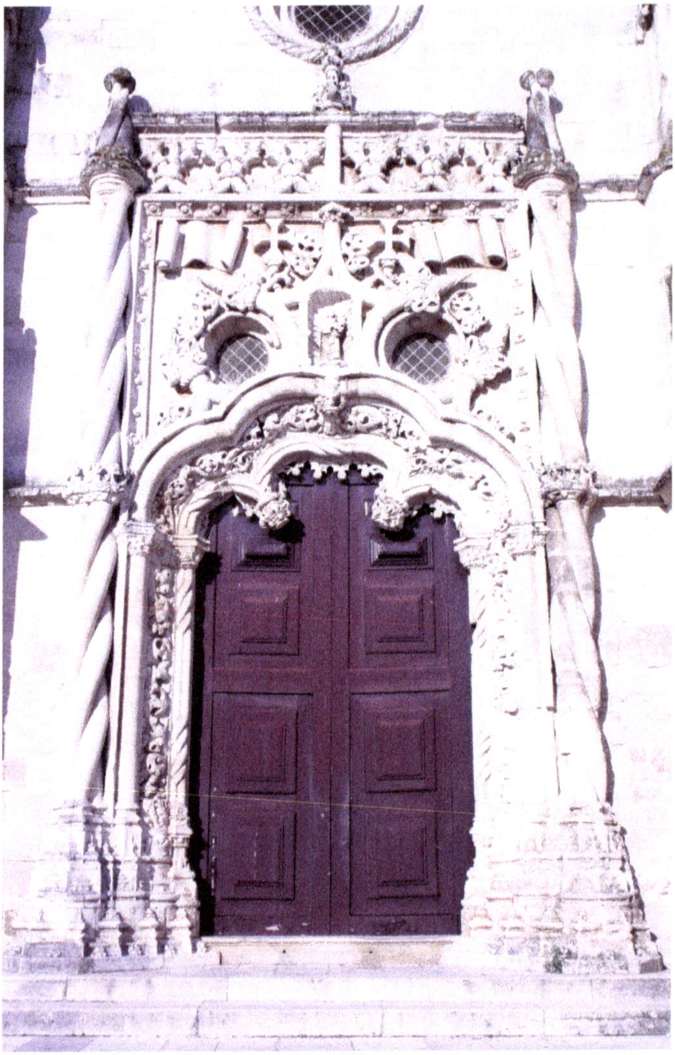

FIGURE 22 Manueline portal of Our Lady of the Conception (Nossa Senhora da Conceição). Golegã, Portugal. Fifteenth century
PHOTO BY THE AUTHOR

has been restored to its original form and is as it would have been seen in Soller's travels through Golegã (figure 22).[64]

64 Historical marker outside the Church of Our Lady of the Conception in Golegã.

5 Coimbra

The Coimbra chapter of the Portuguese Confraternity of the Misericórdia was approved by King Manuel in September of 1500, two years after the establishment of the Lisbon chapter in August of 1498. The primary mover and shaker of establishing the Misericórdia brotherhood in Lisbon was Manuel's sister Leonor, widow of King João II, who was governing as Queen in her brother Manuel's name in 1498.[65] This is only the second Portuguese chapter of the brotherhood. The epigraph to the Coimbra chapter's *Charter* (*Compromisso*) comes from the apostle Paul's letter to the Corinthians: "And now there remain faith, hope, and charity, these three: but the greatest of these is charity."[66] It is charity—often translated as love—that dominates the seven acts of Mercy performed by the brothers of the Misericórdia, at least as far as fellow Christians are concerned. In not so charitable a spirit, however, the Coimbra chapter additionally had a blood purity policy explicitly excluding those tainted with Moorish or Jewish blood.[67]

The chapter initially was headquartered in the then-Cathedral of Coimbra and later was relocated to this city's Church of Sant-Iago by 1526 (figures 23, 24, and 25). It was arranged for the structures of the Misericordia to be built atop the roof of this church in 1546 so as not to interrupt religious services in the Old Cathedral (Sé-Velha) after initially having been installed there in 1526.[68] This chapter's Misoricórdia was in this location during Soller's visit to the city at the end of the seventeenth century, and remained there until halfway through the nineteenth century.[69]

One of the University's buildings was adjacent to the new location of the Misericórdia and the Church of Santiago.[70] In the first half of the twentieth century, every post-medieval architectural element was demolished, including the installations of the Misericórdia headquarters here in the sixteenth and seventeenth centuries. Only the reconstructed medieval church remains.[71]

Formerly in Lisbon, the University relocated to Coimbra, where it became the only medical university that granted diplomas to physicians in the Por-

---

65 Misericórdia of Coimbra, *Compromisso*, 81.

66 1 Corinthians 13:13 (Douay-Rheims Catholic Bible). Misericórdia of Coimbra, *Compromisso*, IV; "a Fé, a Esperança, a Caridade: estas tres virtudes, porém a maior dellas é a Caridade."

67 Misericórdia of Coimbra, *Compromisso*, 2.

68 Misericórdia de Coimbra, *Compromisso*, 81–82.

69 Loureiro, *Toponímia de Coimbra*, 1:238.

70 Loureiro, *Toponímia de Coimbra*, 2:319.

71 Historical plaques in the Museum of the Misericórdia in Coimbra.

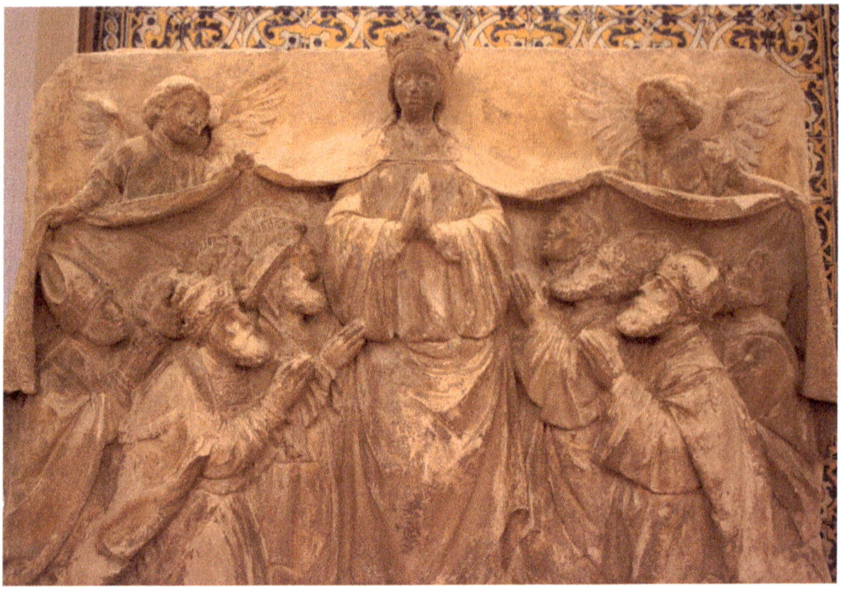

FIGURE 23 Reconstructed bas-relief of Our Lady of Mercy from the then-chapter house prior to its dismantlement from the Church of Santiago. João de Ruão. Coimbra, Portugal. Circa 1550
PHOTO BY THE AUTHOR

tuguese Empire.[72] In Coimbra, the Archduke of Tuscany visited the University, the convents of Santa Clara and Santa Cruz, the old cathedral, and the College of the Jesuits, the last of which awed the Prince with its façade. The new sacristy and chapel of Saint Teotónio in the monastery of Santa Cruz of Coimbra impressed him quite a bit, and the University was of particular interest.[73] Magalotti describes the University of Coimbra as the most illustrious in Portugal.[74]

In other words, Coimbra was a university town, which meant there would have been plenty of students partying (and plenty of servants, as well), creating enough hubbub for Soller to remain hidden, in addition to being big enough to allow him to be anonymous. The anonymity to be found in the city is a sought-after commodity among the shamefaced nobility (*nobles vergonzosos*)

---

72 Soares 209, 216; Serrão, Joaquim Veríssimo, *Misericórdia de Lisboa*, 59.

73 Serrão, Vitor, "Portugal," 549.

74 Magalotti, *Viaje de Cosme*, 1:318–319. In 1732, Diego de Torres Villaroel was exiled by the Spanish crown to Portugal where he first lived in Coimbra, which he, too, describes as extremely beautiful and possessing a great and glorious university. He lived for a few years there, and made that vow to undertake a pilgrimage to Santiago de Compostela, fulfilled in 1737. Torres Villaroel, *Vida*, 16, 159–161.

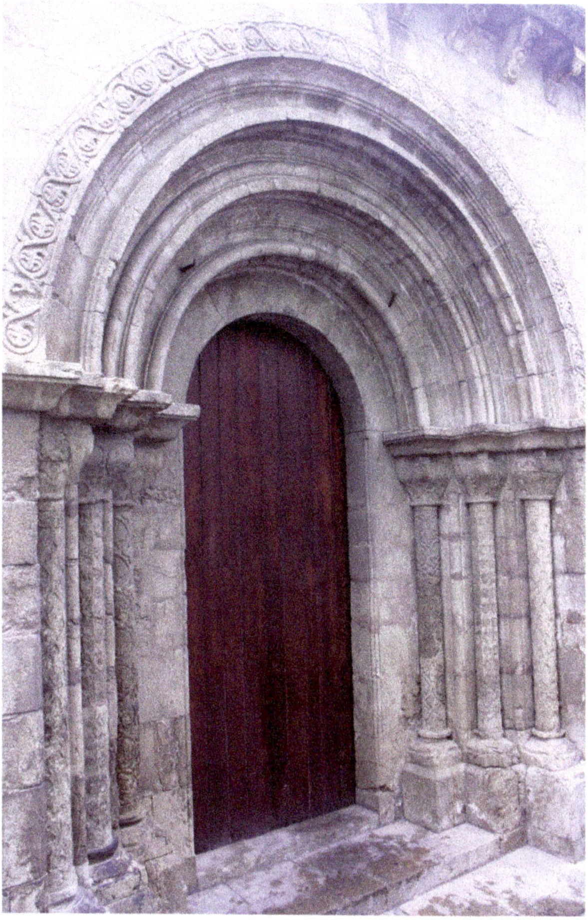

FIGURE 24 Reconstructed portal of the Church of Santiago, over which the Misericórdia chapter house was located in Soller's day. Coimbra, Portugal. Nineteenth century rebuilt to its original medieval form
PHOTO BY THE AUTHOR

in picaresque narratives such as *Lazarillo de Tormes* and in Spanish society as a whole during this period. In Baldi's oeuvre, Coimbra is so large it merits two watercolors (figure 26),[75] as do other big cities such as Lisbon. The most curious facets of this part of Soller's itinerary are the sequence of his visit to Coimbra followed by Tomar (not the inverse as one would expect) and the speed of his travels between the two locales.

75 Magalotti, *Viaje de Cosme*, 2:LXI.

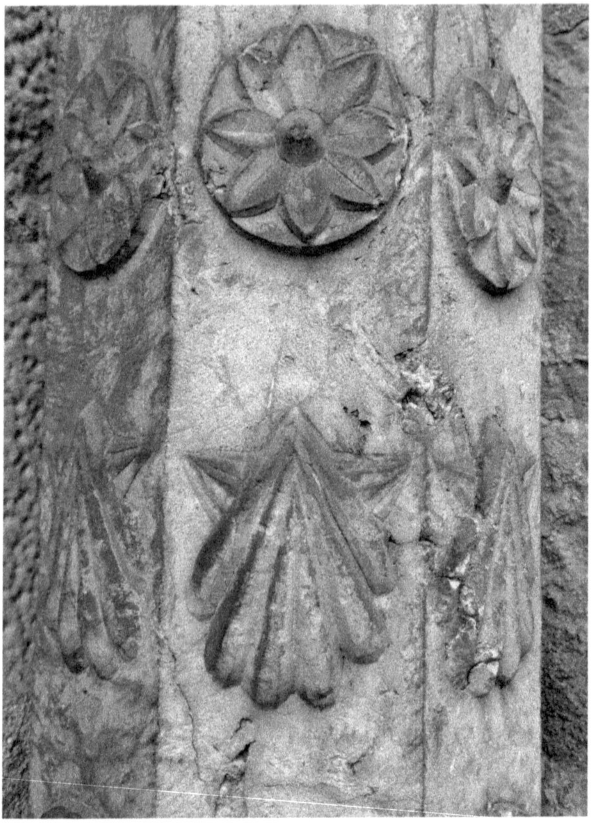

FIGURE 25 Detail of scallop shell symbolic of pilgrimage to Santiago de Compostela. Church of Santiago. Coimbra, Portugal. Twelfth century
PHOTO BY THE AUTHOR

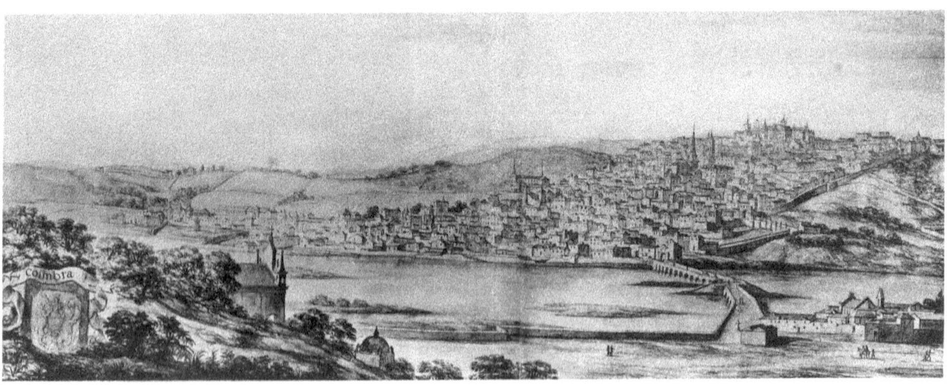

FIGURE 26 Coimbra, Portugal. 1669
PANORAMIC WATERCOLOR BY PIER MARIA BALDI

6 Tomar

On February 22, 1693, Soller abruptly switches directions from Coimbra in the north to arrive just a day later, on Feburary 23, 1693, in Tomar, which lies some 50 miles (80 kilometers) to the south. Most every pilgrim traveling on the Portuguese Way from Lisbon proceeds north because that is the general direction toward Santiago de Compostela. And most take longer than a day between the two locations. For instance, Cosimo III de' Medici takes two full days to travel from Tomar to Coimbra,[76] whereas Soller traverses the same distance in the span of a single day, if a long one. Cosimo III stayed in the Convento de Cristo in Tomar,[77] and he made three stops in between Tomar and Coimbra. (Pier Maria Baldi stopped to make sketches for his watercolors in the small towns of Estalagem de Gaita, Ansian, and Fonte Coberta.) Soller, on the other hand, barrels straight across the same distance (in the inverse direction) in half the amount of time.

In my experience, the terrain is mountainous and difficult. Even on horseback, the distance and topography would be extremely tough to cover in a single day. Soller would have to have been in a real hurry to travel so far over such a challenging landscape in such a short amount of time, riding at full gallop on any mount, especially during the short winter days of February. Soller also would have to have had a powerful reason to motivate him.

Remember that upon the inspection of the valuables in his knapsack, Soller has in his possession a cashbook dating to 1682 belonging to a merchant from Coimbra, one João Sánchez. Here is a description of the book and its contents:

> a quarto-sized, parchment-bound book with a label that reads, "1682. Cashbook of João Sánchez. Jesús, María, José." Inside, it is formatted as a journal of cash and transactions belonging to a Portuguese merchant from the city of Coimbra, foliated, the last leaf of which is numbered 92, each countersigned beside the folio number with the surname Menezes, on the folios of which there are different account records with different persons and merchandise that profess to be worth a large sum of maravedis, and within it many credit documents, letters, memoranda, and payment orders of different quantities, some of them fastened to the folios with pins.[78]

---

76 He travels from February 20 until the evening of February 22, 1669, Magalotti, *Viaje de Cosme*, 1:312–314.

77 Serrão, Vitor, "Portugal," 549.

78 2^r; "un libro de a medio pliego con su pergamino con un rótulo al principio que dice '1682

Has Soller robbed this man as Deputy Prosecutor Rodicio suspects? If so, then that begs the question as to what else might have been stolen along with the cashbook, including clothes and/or money.

Did Soller suddenly change directions to throw off his pursuers, who possibly tried to follow him north toward Santiago? After a gentle slope to the northeast from Lisbon to Coimbra, the line of Soller's route precipitously lurches downward to Tomar from north to south and then unexpectedly shoots off to the northwest from Tomar to Aveiro (figure 1). Such a triangular vector is highly unusual and might have been designed to throw any pursuers off his scent.

Soller tells the authorities in Ourense that he had purchased this cashbook in Santiago for the bargain price of six *cuartos* and that he was headed back to Coimbra to return the cashbook to the merchant (figure 1). Soller says he hopes to be given a reward of some new clothes from Señor Sánchez: "so that in exchange for his discovery the book's owner would give Soller some shirts or clothing to dress himself."[79] Old clothes were a typical "reward" (*galardón*) for servants, especially household servants, and there was a brisk trade in such clothing if we are to believe the social reality depicted in the picaresque novels and paintings of the period.[80] Soller is interested in clothing and clearly is in the market for disguises, as well, of which the cashbook itself may have been a part. It would not be surprising for Soller, amid his shape-shifting identities, to have impersonated a merchant at some point in his travels as part of a broader strategy to maintain freedom of movement within and between the cities and towns of Portugal and Spain.

In his accusations before the Chief Magistrate, Deputy Prosecutor Rodicio argues the following about Soller:

> And the cashbook with which he has been apprehended makes him guilty and makes a case for it having been stolen, not as he wishes to get out of in his confession, saying that he bought it for such a low price from another

---

años. Libro de *caixa* de João Sánchez. *Yesús, María, Josef*'. Y por adentro enuncia ser un libro de caja y asiento de un mercader portogués de la ciudad de Coimbra foliado, cuya última hoja tiene el número 92, rubricadas todas ellas junto a la foleatura con un apellido que dice 'Menezes', en cuyas hojas hay diferentes partidas de cuenta con diferentes sujetos y mercadurías que anuncian importar mucha suma de maravedíes, y dentro de él muchos papeles de crédito, cartas, misivas, y libramientos de diferentes cantidades, y algunos presos con alfileres en las hojas."

79 18^{v}; "para que por su hallazgo le diese algunas camisas o ropa para vestirse."

80 Quevedo, *The Grifter*, xxviii–xix. The aforementioned street urchin in Esteban Murillo's painting *The Young Beggar* (*El joven mendigo*), for example, graphically illustrates just how raggedy and recycled the clothes of the poor could be.

> pilgrim, whose nationality he does not say. Being, as it is written, from the city of Coimbra, this is forceful evidence that the abovementioned stole the cashbook. This is deduced from his safe conduct from Lisbon and letter of recommendation from the city of Lisbon, from which place he came to Coimbra, and from the endorsement of the religious administrators of said confraternity, as is known from their signatures on the backside of the credential.[81]

In the above passage at least, I find Rodicio's argument convincing. But the Deputy Prosecutor does not mention the most compelling piece of evidence of all: Soller's sudden change in direction from north to south on a northward journey coupled with the vast distance he covers over treacherous terrain in so short a time. Moreover, if Soller truly were intending to return to Coimbra as he suggests,[82] returning the way he had arrived, via Tui, would have been a much more direct route.

In another curiosity of his itinerary subsequent to Tomar and then Aveiro, Soller apparently never stopped in Porto, a large and important place. Perhaps this was to escape attention where the communication might have been better, i.e., where the authorities could have been alerted to the potentially illicit activities of Soller in Coimbra. Instead, Soller seems to have skipped over the major city of Porto to arrive at the tiny town of Moreira on March 9 (below).

But in Tomar, the Virgin over the main doorway of the sixteenth-century Church of the Misericórdia in Tomar is different from what Soller had seen so far. This place is named for Our Lady of Grace (Nossa Senhora da Graça), also referred to in Tomar as Our Lady of Prison (Nossa Senhora da Cadeia). The attribution of this Virgin as Our Lady of Prison is unique to this town, as far as I know.[83] A patron saint with such a purview over jails later would have come in handy for Soller.

---

81 20^{v}; "Y el libro de caja con que ha sido aprendido le culpa y arguye haber sido hurtado, no como se quiere librar en su confesión diciendo lo ha comprado por precio de tan poco dinero a otro peregrino que no dice que nación. Y siendo como es escrito en la ciudad de Coimbra, es indicio vehemente contra el susodicho haberlo hurtado. Se infiere del pasaporte de Lisboa y carta de recomendación de la ciudad de Lisboa, de cuyo lugar vino a Coimbra, y en el refrendo de los mayordomos de dicha cofradía, como se conoce de sus firmas a la vuelta del despacho."

82 4^{r}, 18^{v}.

83 Inside the blue-and-white tiled church is a panel showing the Eucharistic miracle of Saint Anthony. This notable painting is the sixteenth-century *Miracle of the Host*, attributed to Gregório Lopes. In this story, a donkey, after having been deprived of food for three days, chooses to kneel before the Eucharist instead of eating hay. By means of this miracle, Saint Anthony of Padua leads a previously skeptical man to believe in the power of the host to become transfigured into the body of Christ.

The creation of the Misericórdia of Tomar was the culmination of the Portuguese reforms of the fifteenth and sixteenth centuries to aid the sick and poor, as an inscription outside the church attests: "The Hospital substituted the Nossa Senhora da Graça Hospital (fifteenth century) as a result of Prince Henrique's unification of all the hospitals and hospices in the town." The Misericórdia became the primary entity responsible for providing social assistance in Tomar as it did elsewhere in Portugal.[84]

A descriptive document for the conservation and restoration of the Nossa Senhora da Graça sculpture from the Archive of the Misericórdia in Tomar dates the limestone sculpture of Our Lady of Grace to the thirteenth century and attributes it to the Cistercian order, one of whose members reportedly had a vision of this Virgin sheltering his Cistercian brothers under her protective mantle. This gesture was interpreted as a symbol of her grace, hence the moniker Nossa Senhora da Graça. In contrast to other manifestations of the Virgin of Mercy in which her mantle is outstretched to shield those whom she protects, the cape of Our Lady of Grace rests close to her shoulders (figure 27).[85]

The fifteenth-century hospital adjacent to this church was named for Nossa Senhora da Graça before being replaced by the Hospital of the Misericórdia during the latter part of the seventeenth century.[86] Given the signature on behalf of the Misericórdia of Tomar on the backside of Soller's pilgrim credential (figure 11b), the pilgrim likely visited this church and hospital. The front of

84 For more on how hospitals and structures established previously under Prince Henry the Navigator later were combined with those of the Misericórdia of Tomar, as well as for how the wealth of the Order of Christ was used to further the beneficent aims of the hospital and of the Misericórdia, see Bento, "Convento de Cristo," 52–54, 67–68.

85 Restoration document from the Technical Institute of Higher Learning (Escola Superior de Tecnologia) of Tomar called "Conservation and Restoration of Our Lady of Mercy" (*Conservação e restauro da Nossa Senhora da Mesericórdia*). As of June 2018, part of the Church of the Misericórdia in Tomar was being renovated, including a sixteenth-century oil-painted cloth and wooden flag of the Misericórdia by Simão de Abreu with a *Pietá* (*Senhora de Piedade con Jesus*) on one side and on the other a painting of Nossa Senhora da Misericórdia, her cloak protecting the clergy and nobility as in other representations of this Virgin (figures 17, 23). Two other contemporaneous paintings—one of Saint Dominic de Guzmán, possibly by Simão de Abreu, and the other of *The Miracle of the Host*, possibly by Gregório Lopes—had not been taken out of the church for restoration during my return site visit on June 22, 2018. Manuela Redol, archivist of the Misericórdia of Tomar, shared the restoration documents of all of these works with me.

86 Per an inscription over a hospital doorway, the nobleman Manuel Nunes da Costa left his estate to the Santa Casa de Misericórdia in Tomar, and the first stone of the current hospital was laid in 1672.

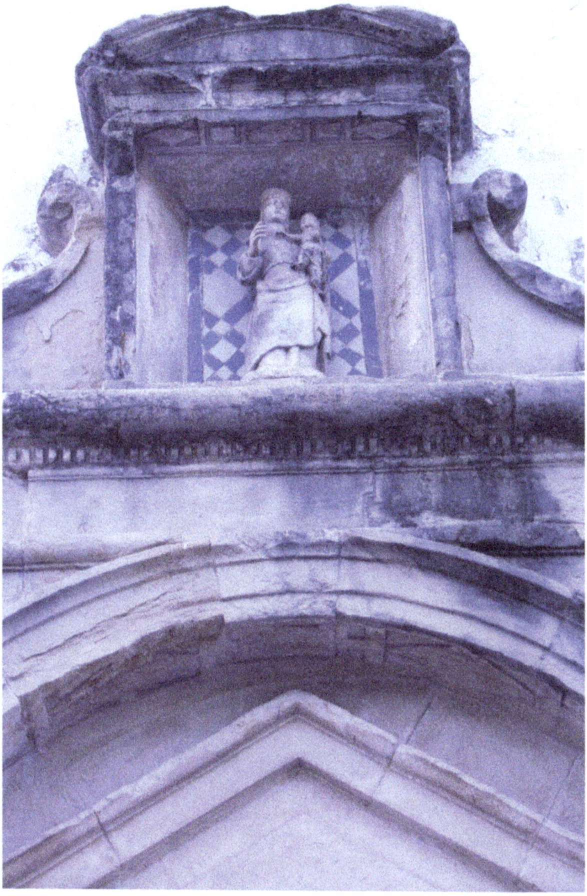

FIGURE 27 Statue of Our Lady of Grace, also known as Our Lady of the Chain or Our Lady of Mercy. Exterior of the main entrance to the Church of the Misericórdia. Tomar, Portugal. Thirteenth century
PHOTO BY THE AUTHOR

Soller's pilgrim credential has "Convent of Tomar" (Convento de Tomar) written in the upper right-hand corner (figure 11a), and so Soller also must have visited the Convent of Christ in Tomar, a major monastery that originated in the twelfth century as the headquarters of the Knights Templar, to then be taken over by the Order of Christ when the Templars were forced to disband in the fourteenth century. In the sixteenth century under Kings Manuel I and João III, the Convento was expanded and then provided hospitality to travelers. One of these new buildings includes the main cloister (figure 28). The Convento de Cristo functioned in tandem with the Misericórdia of Tomar, and the wealth of

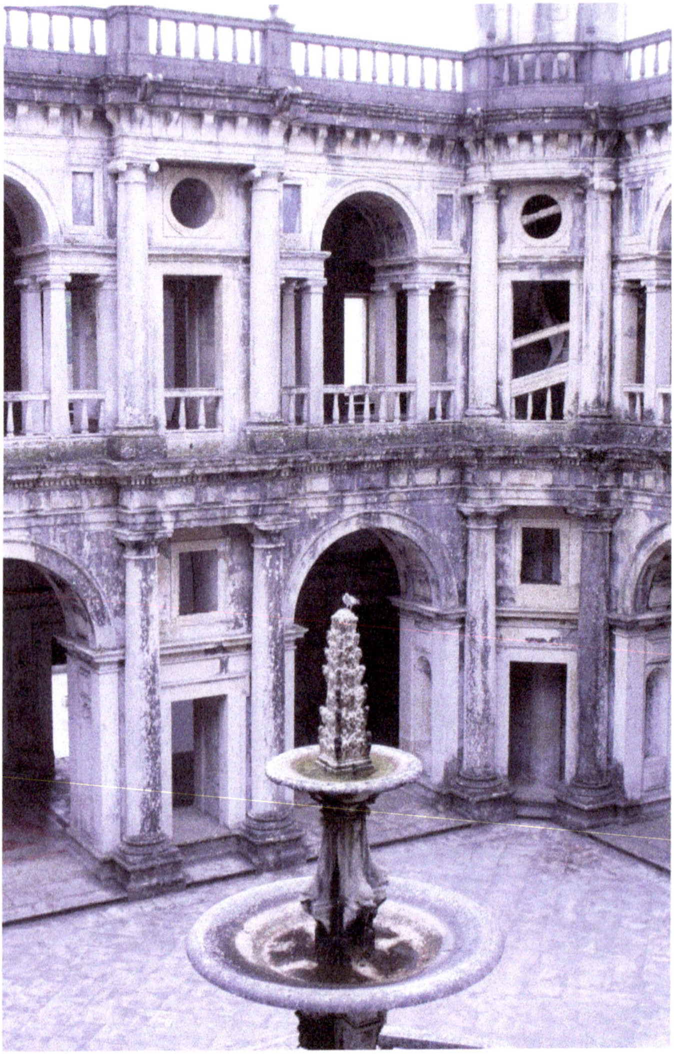

FIGURE 28 Main cloister, Convent of Christ in Tomar, Portugal. Sixteenth century
PHOTO BY THE AUTHOR

the Order of Christ was used to fund and to further the benevolent goals of the Misericórdia in Tomar.[87]

The Convento de Cristo had become a sprawling monastic complex of truly vast proportions by Soller's day. Exploring its ruins now, one notes how easy

87 Bento, "Convento de Cristo," 52–54.

it would have been for Soller to disappear into the myriad cloisters, corridors, and rooms therein. There would have been, for example, zones of the convent in which many and varied servants moved and other areas in which only known servants were seen, the former being perhaps the kitchens and the stables and the latter being the cells of the monks (although all of these places were thoroughly stratified, as well). In this convent, as elsewhere in his journey, there would have been room for Soller to adapt his identity to the exigencies of the moment in order to pass through unbothered.

7 Aveiro

Using a constellation of architects and artists who had worked on the Misericórdia's structures from Coimbra to Porto and elsewhere, the construction of the buildings in Santa Casa da Misericórdia de Aveiro took place over the course of the first half of the seventeenth century despite a variety of setbacks such as disagreements among the brothers. These structures included the hospital, serving one of its primary missions, to house the sick and poor (figure 29).[88] The patterned tile found inside the Church of the Misericórdia in Aveiro was representative of this institution's seventeenth-century chapter houses (figures 30 and 31).[89] Though further to the north, Aveiro is a coastal town with a population of roughly five percent of enslaved people, most of these of black-African descent. Soller's presence would not have been completely anomalous in Aveiro either.

8 Moreira

The monastery of Saint Salvador de Moreira stands out among all of the other religious houses established in the Middle Ages and located in the Maia region north of Porto, Portugal, for the deep influence it was able to project in its vicinity, especially the western strip of the province along the coast. This monastery's vast estate is acknowledged in fourteenth-century documents and was maintained throughout the following centuries.[90] Nothing remains today of the buildings built during this period.

88 Misericórdia de Aveiro, *A Arte na Misericórdia*, 17–20.

89 The exterior tiles on the façade, however, date to the nineteenth century, long after Soller's time.

90 Carvalho, *S. Salvador de Moreira*, 37, 76–77.

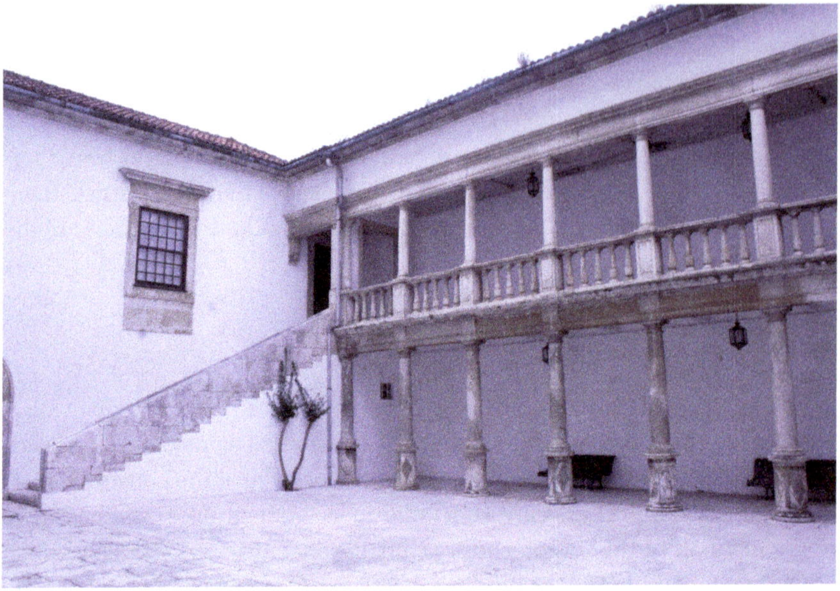

FIGURE 29 Original patio of the Misericórdia Hospital. Aveiro, Portugal. Early seventeenth century
PHOTO BY THE AUTHOR

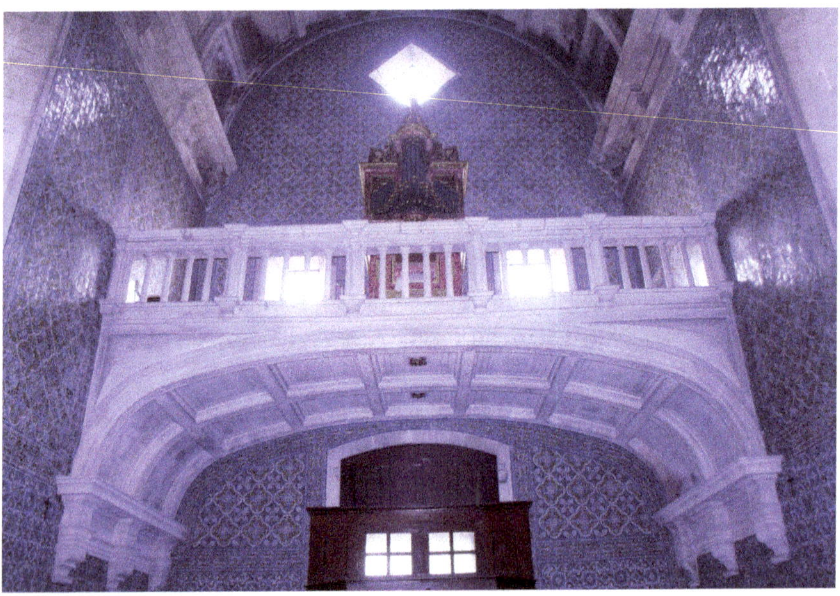

FIGURE 30 Patterned tile. Interior of the Church of the Misericórdia. Aveiro, Portugal. Seventeenth century
PHOTO BY THE AUTHOR

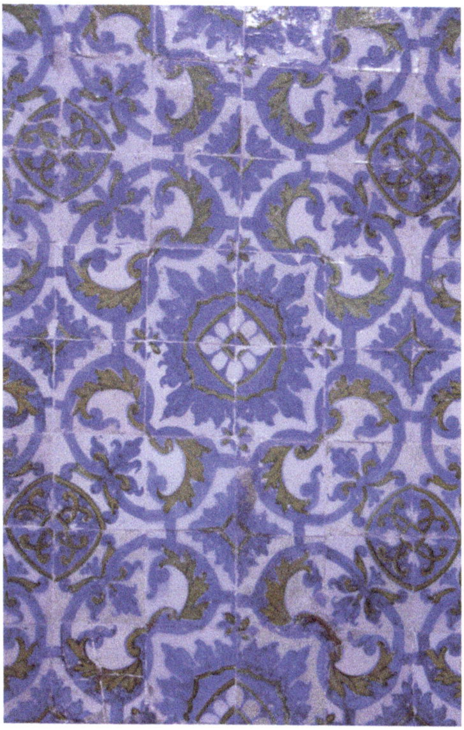

FIGURE 31
Close-up of patterned tile. Interior of the Church of the Misericórdia. Aveiro, Portugal. Seventeenth century
PHOTO BY THE AUTHOR

The whole structure of today's Monastery in Moreira—inside and out—did not begin to be built until 1695, but it is in same place as the one where Soller may have stayed. Magalotti mentions nothing about Moreira except that he passes through it.[91] From Baldi's watercolor, it appears that there is nothing much to the town of Moreira.[92]

9 Viana do Castelo

Viana do Castelo is a northwestern Portuguese coastal town lying along the beautiful Emerald Coast (Costa Verde). This place also is referred to as Viana da Foz do Lima or simply as Viana.[93] Soller's visit is on March 12, 1693.

Viana founded its chapter of the Misericórdia in the city center during the first half of the sixteenth century. It was instituted to help alleviate the city's

91 Magalotti, *Viaje de Cosme*, 1:326.
92 Magalotti, *Viaje de Cosme*, 2:LXV.
93 Cosimo III went to Viana do Castelo on February 25, 1669. Serrão, Vitor, "Portugal," 550.

chasm between rich and poor, the latter of whom consisted of hungry beggars, widows, and orphans.[94] King Manuel I signed the statutes of the Viana chapter on November 2, 1521, out of a desire to unite the new class of wealthy men in the form of the Viana chapter of the brotherhood by means of their performance of the Christian works of charity in order to save the poverty-stricken people in the city. Even so, there already were charity-granting institutions for pilgrims in the city given that it is situated along one of Portuguese pilgrim roads to Santiago de Compostela.[95] As with other chapters in Portugal, the charter of this chapter of the Misericórdia seeks to follow the fourteen acts of mercy, seven corporal and seven spiritual, giving emphasis to the former but never sacrificing the latter.[96] The positions of some new members of the Assembly of Viana included a clerk, cobbler, tailor, and barber,[97] likely destined to clothe the naked.

From approximately 1586–1589, the Viana chapter of the Misericórdia instituted a hospital at the main plaza,[98] known since medieval times as the Oven Plaza (Praça do Forno) and today as the Plaza of the Republic (Praça da República). The building is a unique exemplar inspired by Renaissance and mannerist architectural styles with Italian and Flemish influences.[99] The structure was finished in 1594[100] and today serves as the town hall.[101] The fountain in this plaza by João Lopes o Velho also dates from the 16th century, to 1554 (figure 32). The original Church of the Misericórdia of Viana is no longer extant since it was demolished in 1714.[102] Today's Church of the Misericórdia dates to later in the eighteenth century, after Soller's visit here.

Viana lies along a main pilgrimage route to Santiago in Galicia. One remaining culturally significant building is the first pilgrim's hospital, established in 1468, but completely remodeled in the sixteenth century. Once the hospital built by the Misericórdia was completed in the late sixteenth century, the previous structure became known as the Old Hospital, or Hospital Velho.[103]

---

94 Maciel, "Misericórdia de Viana," 25.
95 Maciel, "Misericórdia de Viana," 26.
96 Maciel, "Misericórdia de Viana," 27.
97 Maciel, "Misericórdia de Viana," 29.
98 Maciel, "Misericórdia de Viana," 31.
99 Maciel, "Misericórdia de Viana," 32.
100 Maciel, "Misericórdia de Viana," 33.
101 According to the technical coordinator of the Archive of Viana, Adriano Pinto, the façade and veranda facing the Praça do Forno of the Santa Casa in Viana date to 1582, and the lateral door and façade also date to the late sixteenth century. Private conversation, July 2014.
102 Lobo de Araújo, "Pasaportes de caridad," 18.
103 Historical marker outside the Hospital Velho in Viana.

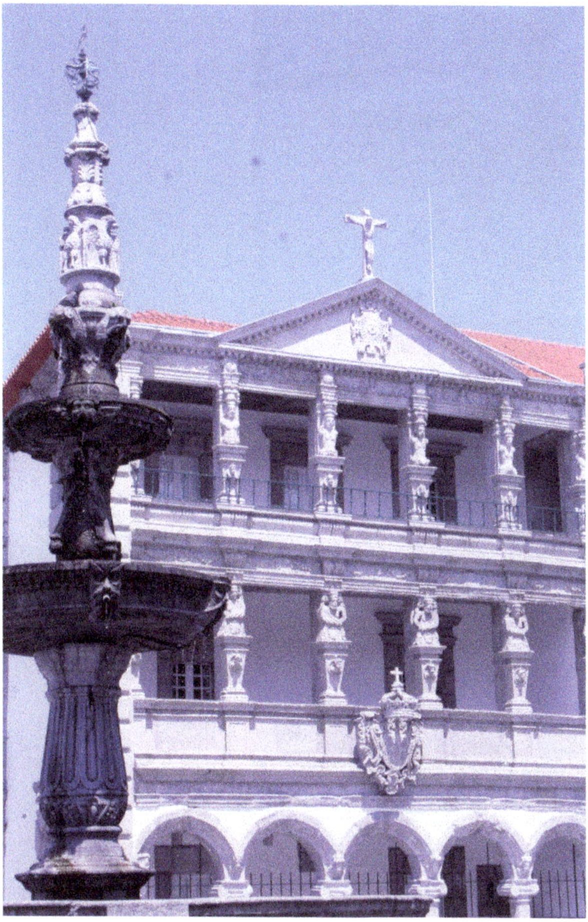

FIGURE 32 Former Hospital of the Misericórdia, circa 1589, with a Fountain by João Lopes o Velho, 1554. Viana do Castelo, Portugal. Sixteenth century
PHOTO BY THE AUTHOR

This was one of numerous hospitality centers within the same district in Viana and later in Soller's journey, in Caminha. In Soller's day, the Hospital Velho was named the Hospital of the Holy Savior (Hospital de São Salvador) for the seventeenth-century sculpture of the resurrected Christ called the Lord of the Resurrection (Señor da Ressurreição), located in the niche.[104] Although the

104 This sculpture was commissioned by the Portocarreiro family, whose family crest is located just below the niche in bas-relief.

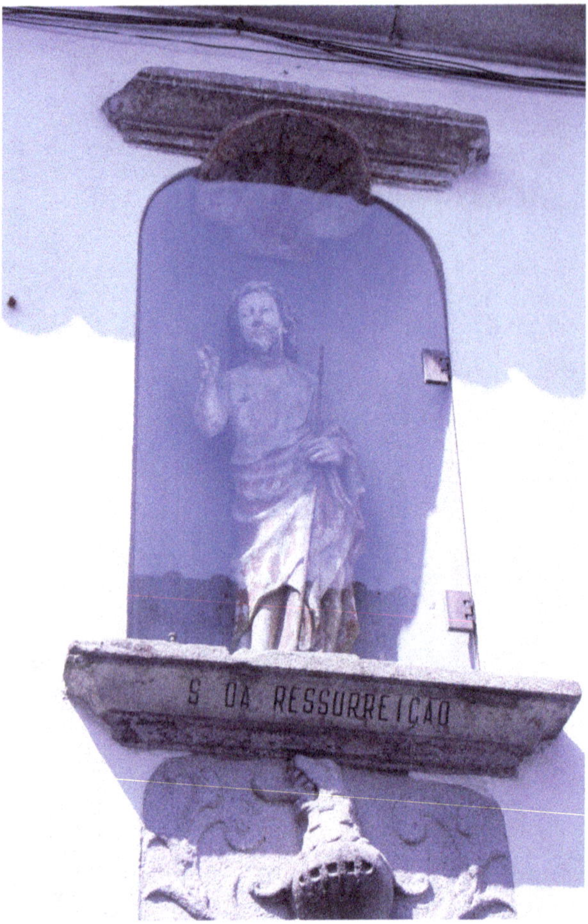

FIGURE 33 Lord of the Resurrection (Señor da Ressurreição). Niche of the façade of the Old Hospital (Hospital Velho), or Hospital de S. Salvador. Viana do Castelo, Portugal. Seventeenth century
PHOTO BY THE AUTHOR

inside has been completely reconfigured, what one sees here today is the façade restored to its original form.[105] Holding a staff and underneath a scallop shell, this sculpture represents the risen Christ as a pilgrim (figure 33).

The meaning of this sculpture has everything to do with hospitality, that foundational concept of pilgrimage. The visual reference here is to the biblical story of the road to Emmaus in the book of Luke, specifically as the narra-

105 Alpuim and Vasconcelos, *Casas de Viana Antiga*, 55–58; Abreu, *Viana do Castelo*, 34, 36.

tive concerns the hospitality provided to the risen Christ, who appears in the guise of a "stranger" to two disciples traveling along the road to Emmaus after the Resurrection.[106] In the Vulgate, Saint Jerome translates the Greek word for "stranger," *xenos* (ξένος), into the Latin as *hospes*, a word etymologically related to "hospitality." Each of these words for "stranger" can mean both "guest" and "host," as well. Moreover, in the Portuguese edition of the Bible (Difusora Bíblica), the word is rendered as "pilgrim" (*peregrino*), which can be seen as a testament to the cultural weight left by the Jacobean routes in Portugal.[107] Hence the portrayal of Christ, the Lord of the Resurrection, as a pilgrim in this sculpture. The whole point of the story, as understood by charity-providing Christian organizations from monasteries to the Misericórdia, is to take care of pilgrim-guests in need, whoever these may be, even and especially if they be unknown to the hosts personally. Any one of these peripatetic pilgrims could be Christ traveling in disguise as a stranger—Christ, whose holy presence was revealed to the disciples in the sacred context of hospitality: "they knew him in the breaking of the bread."[108] This sculpture embodies the Emmaus narrative, and the figure of Christ-as-pilgrim here symbolizes every passing wayfarer who sought lodging and provisions in the Old Hospital of Viana.

10 Caminha

As in Viana, there were a number of hospitals for pilgrims and the sick here in this picturesque town where the Minho (Miño in Spanish) River meets the Atlantic Ocean. Cosimo III de' Medici finished his visit in Caminha before going to Valença and crossing the Miño into the Spanish city of Tui.[109] Torres Villaroel also enters Spain from Portugal via Tui on his mid-eighteenth-century pilgrimage to Santiago.[110] Caminha was a common stopping point for pilgrims on the Portuguese Way to Santiago.

The Misericórdia of Caminha was founded in 1516 and built its church from 1551 to 1561. The sixteenth-century façade was remodeled roughly a century later in 1650. The date 1672 over a lateral doorway possibly indicates the date these façade renovations were completed. The main entrance, with its iconography pertaining to the Road to Santiago, was left intact and appears as it did in

106 Luke 24:13–35, in particular verse 18 (Douay-Rheims Catholic Bible).
107 Abreu, *Viana do Castelo*, 33.
108 Luke 24:35 (Douay-Rheims Catholic Bible).
109 Serrão, Vitor, "Portugal," 550.
110 Torres Villaroel, *Vida*, 166–167.

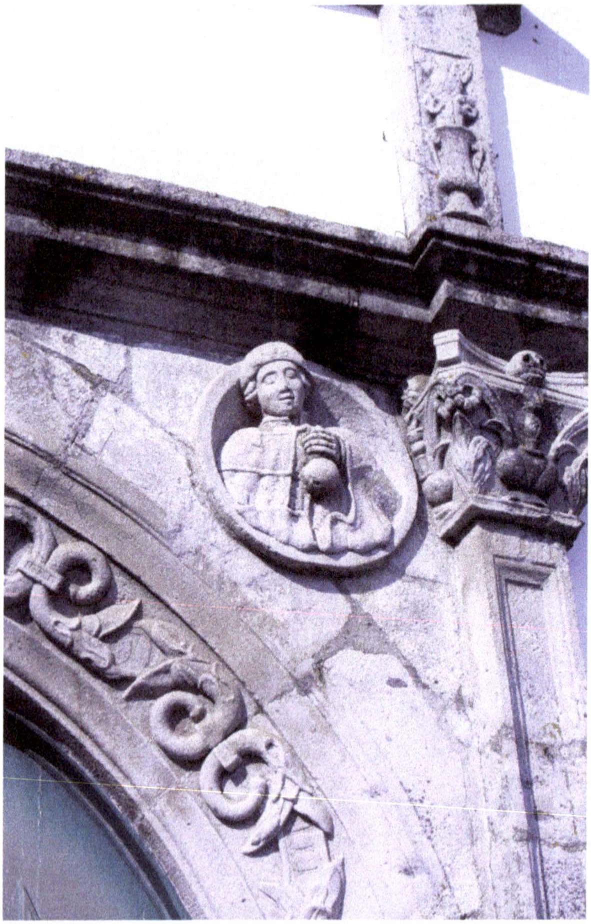

FIGURE 34 Close-up, bas-relief of a pilgrim to Santiago. Main entrance of the Church of the Misericórdia, Caminha, Portugal. Sixteenth–seventeenth century
PHOTO BY THE AUTHOR

Soller's day. The image of the pilgrim with his scallop-adorned hat and drinking gourd acts as a mirror and encouragement for the sojourners to Santiago passing through this doorway (figure 34).

While the Misericórdia Church is Soller's most likely stopping point in Caminha, two other important structures from his day also remain here. One is the Clock Tower, formerly one of three towers of a medieval castle adorned with a clock in 1610 (figure 35). Another is the fifteenth to sixteenth-century Fortress-Church built of granite, whose intricate sixteenth-century Mudéjar woodwork ceiling over the nave was carefully restored in the twentieth century

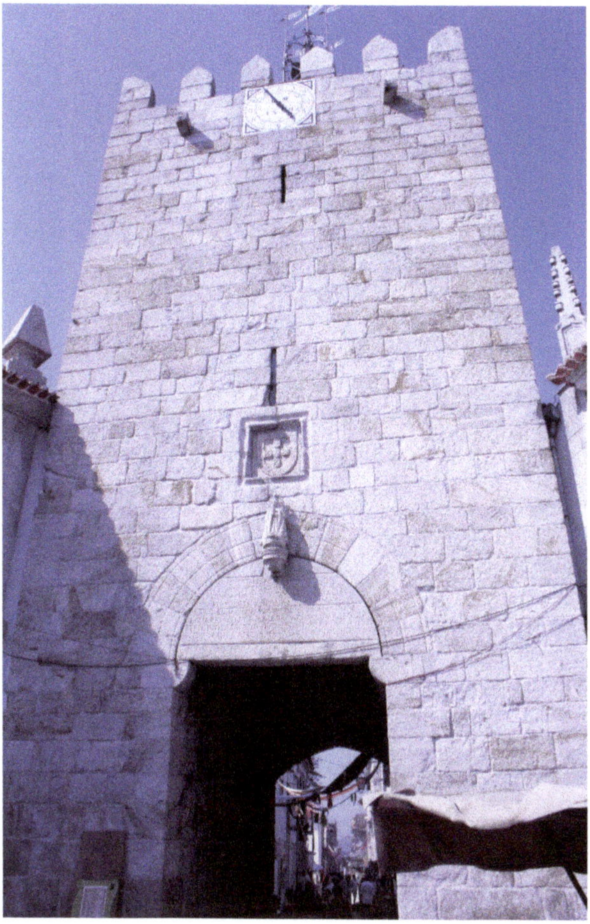

FIGURE 35 Clock Tower. Caminha, Portugal. Twelfth through seventeenth centuries
PHOTO BY THE AUTHOR

(figure 36). These architectural marvels are just a short distance downriver on the Minho from Soller's final stopover in Portugal, Valença do Minho.

11 Valença do Minho

Soller arrives to Valença do Minho (Valença for short) on March 14, 1693, five days before Holy Thursday of that year. His presence in Santiago is not confirmed until eleven days later on March 25, 1693, two days after Easter Sunday. Soller's projected route crosses valleys within the mountain range known as

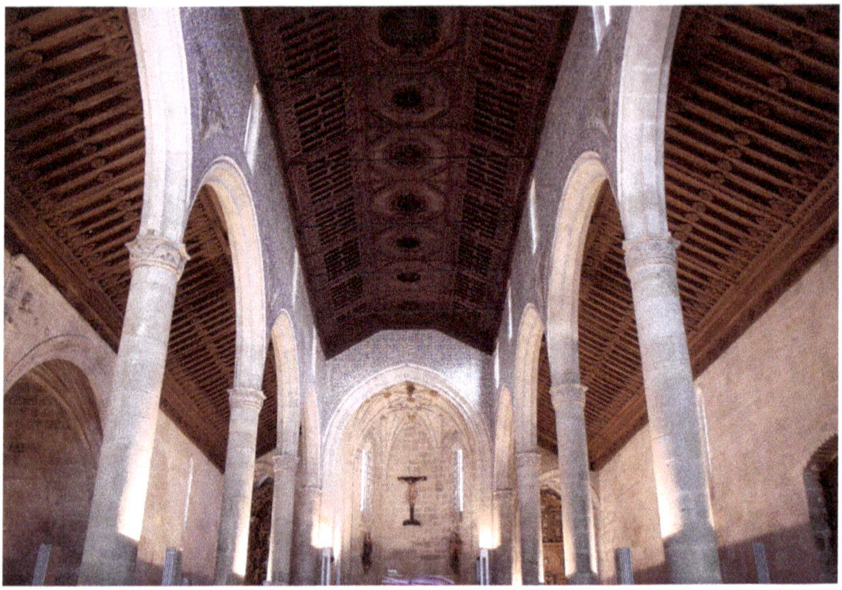

FIGURE 36 Mudéjar woodwork ceiling, Church of Caminha. Sixteenth century
PHOTO BY THE AUTHOR

the Galician Massif, which itself follows the natural fault lines in between, created by tectonic plates. As with most other pilgrims to Santiago in Valença, he crosses the Minho River here to the Spanish city of Tui. The Cathedral of Tui is clearly visible across the Minho River from the perspective of the complex of the Santa Casa de Misericórdia in Valença, as seen in Baldi's panoramic watercolor rendering (figure 37).[111]

We can reconstruct Soller's projected route from the itineraries of his contemporaries. For instance, after crossing the Minho River, Cosimo III de' Medici and his entourage take two days to travel from Tui to Santiago, from March 1–March 3, 1669, proceeding through the locales of Redondela, Pontevedra, and Padrón along the way.[112] Caldas is another town lying in between Pontevedra and Padrón through which Soller may have passed. This is what Soller's probable itinerary between Valença do Minho, Portugal, and Santiago de Compostela, Spain, would have looked like, although these locales are not listed in his credential or anywhere else in the case file.[113]

111 No extant structures of the Misericórdia from Soller's time remain in Valença.

112 Magalotti, *Viaje de Cosme*, 1:XXXI.

113 Despite a first-rate hospitality infrastructure, the autobiographical narrator of *Estebanillo González* does not have much to say about the city of Santiago except that there are too

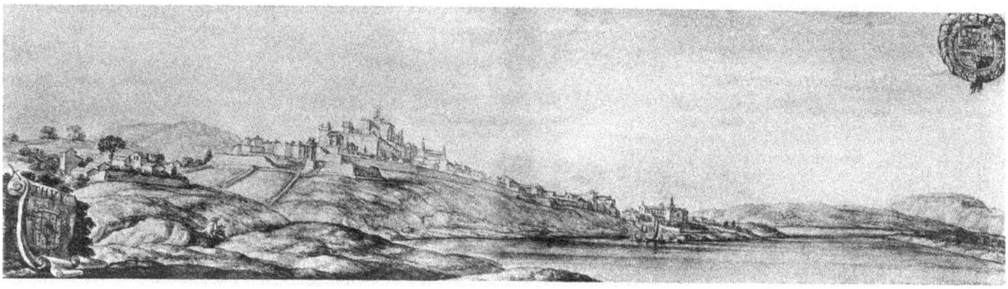

FIGURE 37 Tui, Spain, as seen from the direction of the Santa Casa de Misericórdia in Valença, Portugal. 1669
PANORAMIC WATERCOLOR BY PIER MARIA BALDI

12 Santiago de Compostela

Cosimo III de' Medici was one of the more famous pilgrims to Santiago and devotees of Saint James, and the Tuscan prince arrived in 1669, a little over two decades before Soller. The Archduke of Tuscany was not especially moved upon his initial arrival to the city. Magalotti, the chronicler in his retinue, described these initial impressions: "The city of Santiago is situated up high and surrounded by some places with higher mountains, which tower over the city. Small, ugly, and mostly built of wood; stone walls with towers interspersed, all of them covered in ivy and most of them in a state of ruin."[114] Miguel Taín Guzmán interprets this poor impression as a product of the blustery Atlantic storm that had settled into the area during the time of Cosimo III de' Medici's arrival to Santiago. All of the rain had muddied the path and made the way difficult. Baldi's painting alludes to these conditions (figure 38).[115] Baldi's depiction reveals a panoramic view of Santiago prior to the urbanization of the city from the perspective of the hill of Santa Susana.[116] The painting is done from

---

many pilgrims and too few who give alms there. This is the rationale Estebanillo provides for his return to the kingdom of Portugal via Pontevedra and Tui in Galicia until arriving to Valença do Minho and then on to Coimbra in Portugal, inverting the route Soller most likely takes from Portugal into Galicia. *Estebanillo González*, 176–178.

114 Magalotti, *Viaje de Cosme*, 333; "La Città di S. Jago è posta nell'alto, et è circondata da qualche parte da altri monti più alti, che la dominano. Piccola, brutta e per lo più fabbricata di legno; le mura sono di pietra tramezzate da torri, ma tutte recoperte d'ellera, e gran parte di esse en stato di rovinare." See also González Fernández, "Compostela en las crónicas," 235, García Iglesias, "Visita de Cosme III," 583; and Taín Guzmán, *La ciudad de Santiago*, 49.

115 Taín Guzmán, *La ciudad de Santiago*, 48.

116 García Iglesias, "Visita de Cosme III," 584.

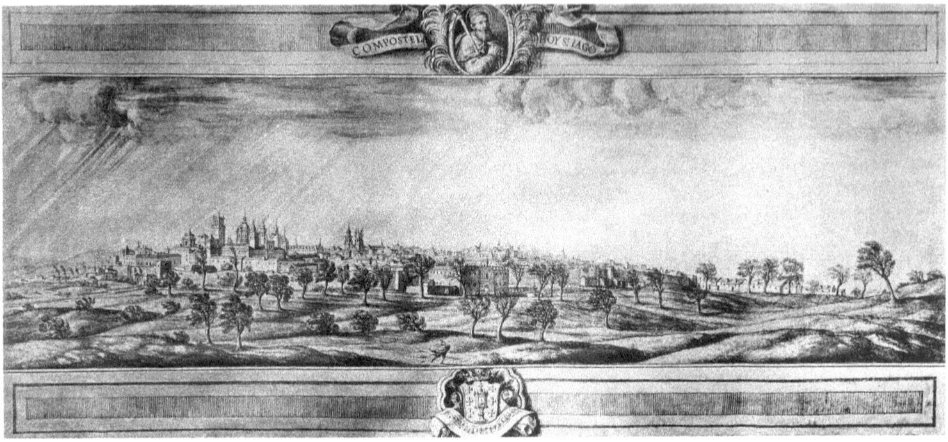

FIGURE 38 View from the west of Santiago de Compostela, Spain. 1669
PANORAMIC WATERCOLOR BY PIER MARIA BALDI

the combined perspective of multiple points along this hill, which lies to the west of the city.[117] This drawing depicts two juxtaposed worlds: one rural, illustrating the humble countryside immediately outside the city walls, including the Barrio do Hórreo in the far right of the image with its road departing for Ourense; one urban, that is, the city itself with its elegant towers foreshortened in the perspective of the drawing.[118] Despite Magalotti's poor impression of the city, Baldi's painting is the most valuable graphic representation of Santiago from the 1600s found to date.[119] Baldi painted the extremely wide angle topographic urban vista of the city of Santiago de Compostela on a wide-format, large, horizontal sheet measuring 1,555 mm × 580 mm, and did so with the goal of underscoring, despite Magalotti's disappointment with the city, the grandeur of the urban center set amid the countryside.[120] The presence of a scallop containing the Galician coat of arms underneath the scenery constitutes a reference to the pilgrimage to Saint James, a phenomenon that was extremely well-known in Florence, from where the Tuscan prince hailed.[121]

The city that this Florentine prince visits, as described by the members of his entourage, still was the capital of the kingdom of Galicia. A medieval walled city with tight streets and wooden houses, Santiago then was more medieval than

117 Taín Guzmán, *La ciudad de Santiago*, 46.
118 Costa Buján, "Evolución urbana," 59.
119 Taín Guzmán, *La ciudad de Santiago*, 15.
120 Taín Guzmán, *La ciudad de Santiago*, 45.
121 Taín Guzmán, *La ciudad de Santiago*, 47.

modern.[122] These features are confirmed by the watercolor and in the chronicles of the trip: "the city is densely populated behind old walls, with dwellings in very close quarters to one another, the majority built of wood, giving way to wide, wet, and dark streets that attracted the attention of the authors of the daily accounts [of Cosimo's travels]."[123]

Another such pilgrim and diarist was a different Italian, Domenico Laffi, an ordained parish priest who traveled on foot extensively, at least four times to Spain and once to the Holy Land during his lifetime in the seventeenth century.[124] James Hall, a translator and editor of the account of one of Laffi's journeys to Santiago, considers that "On matters of art and architecture he is informative and, on the whole, an accurate guide. His descriptions of buildings and monuments that are no longer standing, or of paintings and sculpture that have since been lost or destroyed, often provide useful information about the past that would otherwise have remained inaccessible to us."[125]

Laffi's description of the city is revealing. He notes the size of the city (small); the number of city gates (four); how many suburbs lie outside the walls (two, one to the east, the other to the west); the topography (on top of a hill); and the material used to build the surrounding walls (masonry). In particular, Laffi is charmed by the Franciscan monastery, which was Gothic during the time of Laffi's visit, soon to be rebuilt in Baroque fashion in the late seventeenth century during Soller's visit. Laffi additionally alludes to the tradition that asserts that this monastery was founded by Saint Francis himself following his legendary pilgrimage to Santiago in the thirteenth century.[126]

But the most important structure in Santiago de Compostela was then and is now this city's Cathedral. Magalotti notes the singular importance of the Cathedral of Compostela relative to the other churches there and offers a detailed description.[127] He additionally comments on the stone door of the western Obradoiro Plaza entrance to the Cathedral.[128]

The perspective of Baldi's watercolor is too far removed to see the Obradoiro doorway, but a drawing by José de Vega y Verdugo from 1656–1657 shows its

122 Taín Guzmán, *La ciudad de Santiago*, 11.

123 Taín Guzmán, *La ciudad de Santiago*, 48; "la ciudad se halla densamente poblada tras viejas murallas, con viviendas muy pegadas unas a otras, la mayoría construidas de madera, dando lugar a calles angostas, húmedas y oscuras que llamaron la atención de los autores de los diarios."

124 Laffi, *Journey*, 9.

125 Laffi, *Journey*, 10.

126 Laffi, *Journey* 174; Laffi, *Viaggio* 207–208.

127 Magalotti, *Viaje de Cosme*, 1:334–337; González Fernández, "Compostela en las crónicas," 237.

128 Magalotti, *Viaje de Cosme*, 1:334.

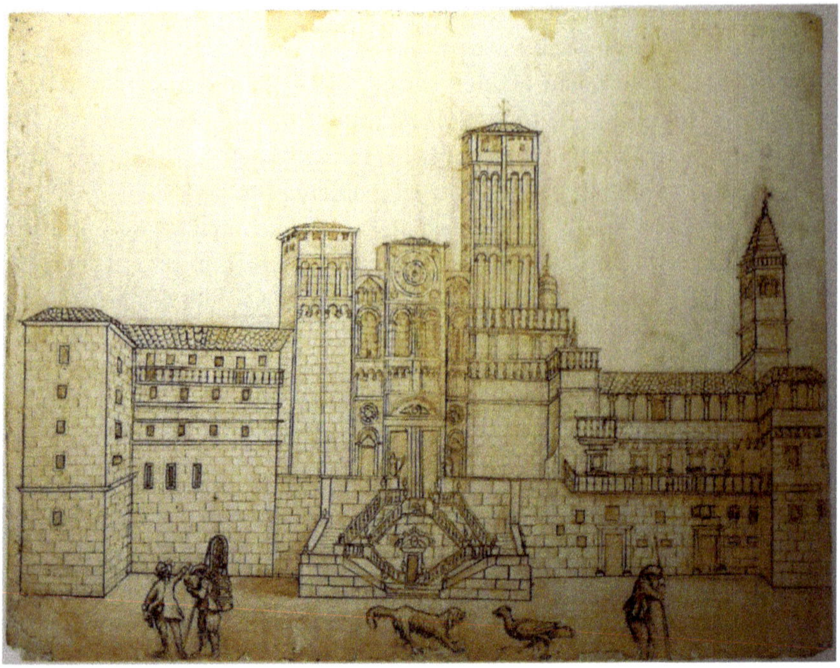

FIGURE 39 Western façade of the Cathedral of Compostela from the Plaza of the Obradoiro. Santiago de Compostela, Spain. 1656–1657
DRAWING BY JOSÉ DE VEGA Y VERDUGO

rectilinear-frame entrance (figure 39).[129] Pilgrims foreground the scene. The imposing baroque façade seen from this perspective today would not be built until after Laffi's visit and Magalotti's chronicle. In 1669, much of the original Romanesque basilica was still intact, specifically its three façades and some of the original towers.[130] Such was the appearance of the Cathedral façade facing the Obradoiro plaza in Soller's day.

Due to the levy known as the Voto de Santiago, Santiago de Compostela during the seventeenth century prospered in comparison with the rest of Spain and Galicia, which had widespread social problems and an ever-decreasing standard of living. Spain in general had fallen away from its former glory: "The level of decadence reached by the Spanish Empire and the rupture of its politico-economic system in the twilight of the rule of the House of Austria in Spain was palpable."[131] Everywhere there was abject poverty together with

129 García Iglesias, "Visita de Cosme III," 586.

130 Taín Guzmán, *La ciudad de Santiago*, 51.

131 Costa Buján, "Evolución urbana," 58; "La decadencia alcanzada por el Imperio español y

a decreasing population, not to mention the outright abandonment of agriculture, industry, and business.[132] In Santiago the population was in decline in large part due to the war of secession with Portugal, which did not conclude until the Treaty of Lisbon in 1668. As a result, the city council did not feel itself capable of fulfilling Carlos II's request of service of over 300 men from Santiago to A Coruña. And yet, such penury did not prevent the city from building such costly structures as the magnificent baroque façade of the Cathedral of Santiago de Compostela.[133]

13 The Hospital Real

The worn façade of the Hospital Real facing the Obradoiro Plaza, where I could not find a record of Soller's stay, underwent renovations after 1675, less than two decades before Soller's arrival. This facelift gave the Hospital Real the balconies it has now on this façade.[134] The Royal Hospital was founded by the Catholic Monarchs in 1499 to lodge pilgrims and heal the infirm.[135] Centuries later, Laffi would affirm its ability to hold a multitude of sick people whose beds were organized in the shape of a cross in order to allow all of the patients to listen to Mass from a chapel in the center. Laffi describes the Royal Hospital of the Catholic Monarchs as palatial both inside and out, and his contemporaries described it as the crown jewel of all of Christendom.[136] Regardless of whether or not they were sick, all pilgrims were allowed to stay three days in the Royal Hospital of the Catholic Monarchs, as Fernando and Isabel had intended.[137]

14 Mass in the Cathedral

Since there is no record of Soller having stayed in the pilgrim's hospital, we are left to work with the date on Soller's pilgrim's diploma: March 25, 1693, three days after Easter. Soller's stay in Santiago would seem to have overlapped with Easter Sunday, March 22, 1693. This service would have involved the arch-

---

la quiebra de su sistema político-económico en el ocaso del reinado de la Casa de Austria en España fue patente."

132 Costa Buján, "Evolución urbana," 58.
133 Costa Buján, "Evolución urbana," 62.
134 García Iglesias, "Visita de Cosme III," 596.
135 Taín Guzmán, *La ciudad de Santiago*, 53.
136 Laffi, *Journey*, 166–168; Laffi, *Viaggio*, 203.
137 Magalotti, *Viaje de Cosme*, 1:334.

bishop and church canons dressed in full pontifical regalia, as well as the swinging thurible (*botafumeiro*) casting the smoke of burning incense across the transept and whole cathedral, as still occurs today.

Domenico Laffi's description of High Mass in the Cathedral offers some insight into what an Easter service would have looked like in Soller's time.:

> I truly believe there is no other church, except St Peter's at Rome, where they organize it so well as they do here. First the archbishop entered, wearing full pontificals, including the pallium, as is worn by the Pope himself. Apart from the Pope, the pallium may be worn by no one else except the archbishop of Compostella. This dignity was conferred on him by Paschal in 1104. Behind the archbishop who, as I said, was in pontificals with mitre and pastoral staff, came the canons. They are known here by the courtesy title of cardinal, a dignity also conferred by the Pope. They too were wearing pontificals with a bishop's mitre. There were nine canons, all dressed the same way.
>
> When the solemn feast of High Mass has been celebrated by the archbishop, the canons then take turns to officiate, day by day. They stand beneath the baldachin, arrayed in their vestments, which are in every way different from the archbishop's, each one taking his turn throughout the week until they reach the beginning again. One cannot speak too highly of the grace and solemnity they habitually bring to performing the Offices in this church.
>
> Before the high altar is a great thurible in the shape of a large lamp, attached by a rope to the ceiling at the very top of the dome. It is lowered when they put in the incense and light it. Then they draw it to one side, to such a height that only a few can still reach it, and then they give it a push. It swings from one door to the other, that is, from south to north, along the arms of the cross. Because of its size and speed it makes a great wind. The burning incense and other odours produce a thick, fragrant smoke, which permeates the whole church.[138]

138 Laffi, *Journey*, 171–172; Laffi, *Viaggio*, 205–206; "Veramente non credo che doppo San Pietro di Roma, si trovi chiesa così bene officiata come questa. Esce l'Arcivescovo vestito alla ponteficale, col palio medesimo che porta il Pontefice. Questo palio, eccetto il Pontefice, non lol puol portar alcuno, fuori che l'Arcivescovo di Compostella, dignità concessagli da Pasquale secondo, l'anno 1104. Dietro all'Arcivescovo, vestito come dissi alla ponteficale, con mitra in testa e pastorale, seguitano li signori canonici, chiamati col titolo di Cardinali, dignità concessali parimente dal Pontefice, tutti vestiti ancor essi in habito ponteficale, con mitre in testa da Vescovi e tutti vestiti ad un modo e sono al numero di nove canonici. Questi, doppo la festa solenne, dove l'Arcivescovo canta la messa grande, seguitano poi

Cosimo III's chroniclers also comment on the botafumeiro.[139]

In Soller's time, confessors always attended masses in the Cathedral in order to tend to pilgrims, who would receive their sealed pilgrim's diploma after communion, which served as an exhortation for the Christian faithful to offer these Jacobean pilgrims charity on their journey home.[140] In response to the myriad abuses along the hospitality routes, the *compostela* was a crucial form of verification of need for such aid, which could take the form of food and lodging in the homes of individuals, or in hospices specifically for pilgrims. Nonetheless, to Deputy Prosecutor Rodicio, Soller's diploma is a meaningless forgery due to its description of the pilgrim as a "Priest of the Indies."

Laffi's description of obtaining the pilgrim's diploma in Santiago involves him attending Mass first and then proceeding to acquire his *compostela*. His companions and he visited relics associated with the saint near the altar of Santiago, where Laffi obtained his indulgence for the completion of his pilgrimage.[141] Starting in 1666, the Holy Eucharist began to be administered in the Chapel of the King of France to all pilgrims who came to visit the holy sepulcher of the Apostle James the Greater, which ran on the donations these pilgrims offer for the expenses of this chapel.[142] Laffi noted just how impressive this Chapel of the King of France is, and additionally describes its location right behind the altar of Santiago (figure 40). Laffi also points out that this is where pilgrims are issued their *compostelas*, which must be purchased.[143] This is the very chapel in which Soller obtains his pilgrim's diploma.

Soller's *compostela* mentions the Chapel of the King of France, which is so named for the endowment Louis XI provided this chapel in 1447, when he

---

uno per uno, la settimana a cantar la messa grande, stando ancor'essi sotto al baldachino con apparati da Vescovo, ma differente ogni cosa da gli apparati dell Arcivescovo e così, di mano en mano, seguitando per tutta la settimana, fino che ritormano da capo, veramente non si può dire la polizia e gravità che usano in officiare questa chiesa.

Avanti l'altar maggiore vi è un gran turibolo fatto a guisa d'una gran lanpada il quale, con una corda, è attaccato al volto della tribuna maggiore e questo calano a basso quando vogliono mettervi dentro il fuoco e l'incenso e poi lo tirano su fino a quell'altezza che alcuno non li possi arrivare e poi gli danno la spinta. Questo, pigliando l'onda, va da una porta all'altra, cioè dalla porta d'oriente a quella d'occidente, che sono le sopradette porte delli due bracci della croce, onde, per la sua grandezza e velocità, fa un gran vento e per il fuoco e l'incenso e altri odori che vi sono dentro, fa un gran fumo odorifero, quale profuma tutta la chiesa."

139 García Iglesias, "Visita de Cosme III," 593.
140 García Iglesias, "Visita de Cosme III," 587.
141 Laffi, *Journey*, 179; Laffi, *Viaggio*, 212.
142 García Iglesias, "Visita de Cosme III," 593.
143 Laffi, *Journey*, 164; Laffi, *Viaggio*, 202.

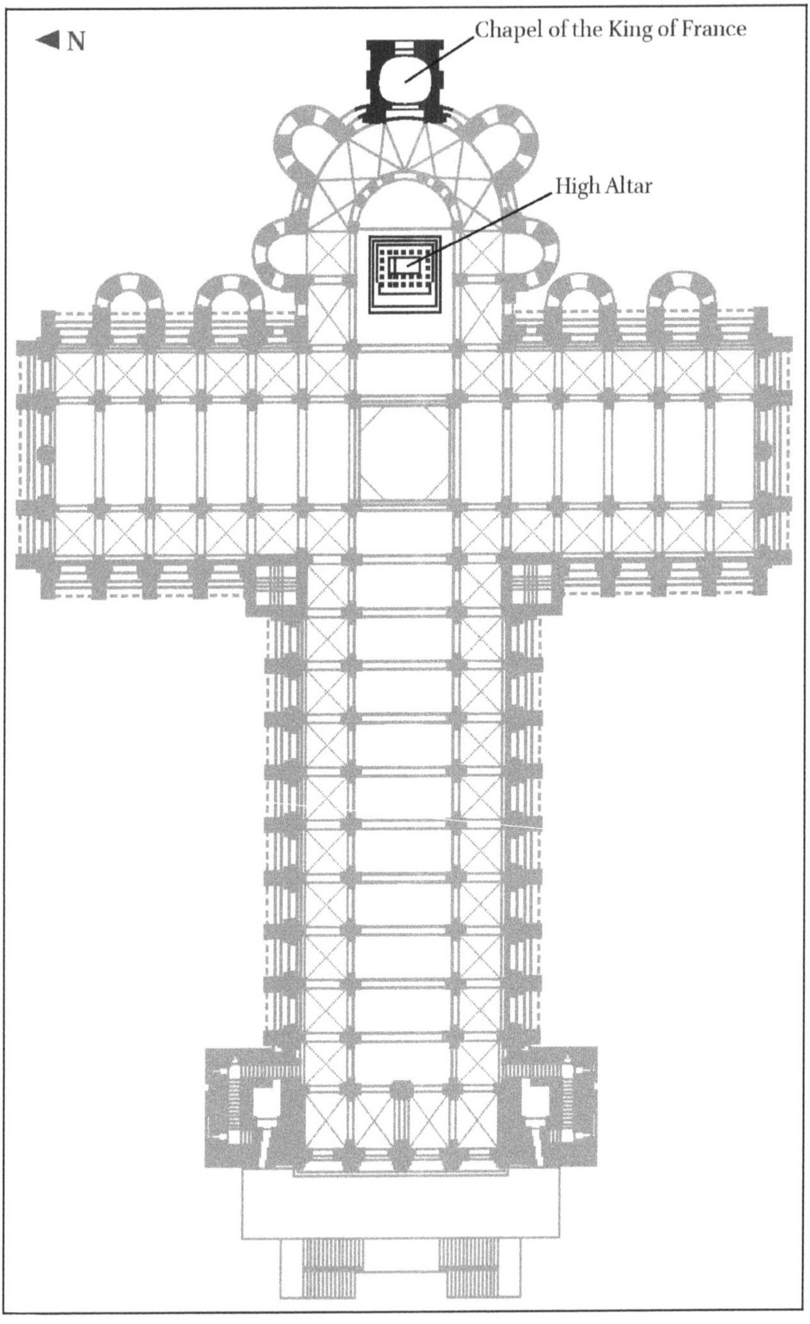

FIGURE 40 Vertically oriented bird's-eye view of the Cathedral of Santiago de Compostela, Spain
PLAN BY THE UNIVERSITY OF WISCONSIN–MADISON CARTOGRAPHY LAB

was heir-apparent to the French throne. This income provided for three chaplains, who were to offer Mass daily inside the chapel.[144] To this day, arriving French pilgrims continue, appropriately enough, to stake out this chapel for their daily Masses in French. This place, where pilgrim diplomas once were distributed, is where the three Catalan priest-pilgrims testify that Soller also is a priest.

Soller mentions that he traveled from Portugal to the kingdom of Galicia to make a pilgrimage to the "Apostle Santiago"[145] in Compostela and to the "Holy Christ"[146] statue in the Cathedral of Ourense. As Caroline Walker Bynum notes, pilgrims "went to Santiago not because a peasant had a vision of St. James but in order to kiss James's head,"[147] or rather to kiss the head of the thirteenth-century polychromatic sculpture of James in the main altar of the Cathedral there; the stone likeness served as a stand-in for the saint's relics themselves. Bynum mentions this detail to provide one example among many of "objects that conferred and conveyed sacrality in medieval Christianity."[148] The tactile encounter with the sacred is paramount in pilgrimage. In the seventeenth century, pilgrims began to hug this medieval statuesque likeness of Saint James, a ritual that still is maintained today. But this practice scandalized Cosimo III's chroniclers because pilgrims would place their hats on his head in order to free their arms for the embrace, and the accounts alternately regard the ritual as a ridiculous superstition and sincere devotion.[149] The ornate canopy over this statue already was in place by the time of Soller's visit, and the statue already sat atop the main altarpiece (figure 41).

Domingo de Andrade was a great architect and master (*maestro mayor*) of the Cathedral.[150] He designed the baroque clock tower of the Cathedral, as well as the magnificent gilded baldachin with its numerous sculptures covering the medieval statue of the Apostle Santiago (not to mention that of the Santo Cristo in Ourense). Laffi notes that the body of James the Greater purportedly lies beneath the high altar of the Cathedral. This ornamental canopy above the altar was completed by 1673.[151]

---

144 Fernández Sánchez and Freire Barreiro, *Guía de Santiago*, 149. Louis XI additionally gave an incense-burner in the shape of a fortress worth a thousand ducats, as well as two large bells.

145 18r; "apóstol Santiago."

146 18r; "Santo Cristo."

147 Bynum, *Christian Materiality*, 278.

148 Bynum, *Christian Materiality*, 278.

149 Magalotti, *Viaje de Cosme*, 1:334; González Fernández, "Compostela en las crónicas," 238.

150 Taín Guzmán, *La ciudad de Santiago*, 11.

151 Laffi, *Journey*, 164; Laffi, *Viaggio*, 202.

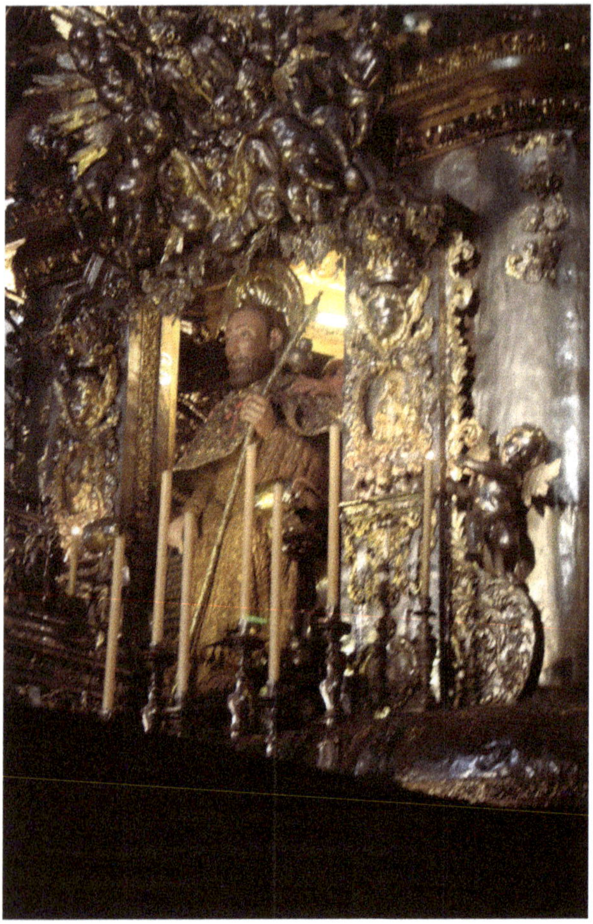

FIGURE 41 Detail of the High Altar of the Cathedral of Santiago de Compostela featuring polychromatic medieval statue of Saint James. Santiago de Compostela, Spain. Thirteenth-century statue, seventeenth-century altar
PHOTO BY THE AUTHOR

Behind the statue there were short ladders for people to climb in order to give the traditional hug to Saint James.[152] Magalotti comments that pilgrims were not content to give one or even a few hugs but rather hugged the statue of Saint James all over his body—neck, back, waist—as many as fifteen times

152 Magalotti, *Viaje de Cosme*, 1:334; García Iglesias, "Visita de Cosme III," 586, 590–591.

with "ridiculous and superstitious piety."[153] Domenico Laffi is one of these pilgrims who hugged the statue of St. James: "Then we went behind the altar and climbed a few steps, where we could embrace the apostle's image ... Pilgrims put their cape on the statue and their hat on its head while they embrace it, and then stay a few moments."[154] This ritual embrace has persisted over the centuries from Soller's time through today.

15 Ourense

Ourense is located to the south of the banks of the river Minho. Just before reaching Ourense, the waters of the Minho are joined by those of the Sil River, whose headwaters begin in Castilla y León immediately to the south of the southern border of Asturias. By this point the Minho has created a six-kilometer wide, asymmetrical river valley that serves as a natural depression for the convergence of the diagonal crossroads that connect southeastern Galicia. Such accessibility is surely a factor in determining the eventual development of this city in this location.[155]

The Romans built the city's expansive stone bridge over the Minho River in the first centuries after Christ, during the rule of Emperor Trajan (98–117 AD), though it was possibly even earlier, around the time of Christ under the Emperor Augustus (27 BC–14 AD). Its original ten arches were rebuilt from the thirteenth through the seventeenth centuries, and today it has seven. The central arch measures 41.8 yards (38.2 meters) high above the waters of the Minho, while the bridge itself measures 227.8 yards (208.3 meters) between buttresses.[156] The base of the supports are what remain of the original Roman construction (figure 42). The pilgrimage road coming from Santiago, the Silver Way (Vía de la Plata), also known as the Mozarabic Route (Ruta Mozárabe, so named for Spain's Christianized Arab Muslims), crosses this bridge to Ourense.

---

153 Magalotti, *Viaje de Cosme*, 1:334; "ridicola, et superstiziosa pietà."

154 Laffi, *Journey*, 163; Laffi, *Viaggio*, 202; "Poi andammo doppo l'altare di detto Santo, salendo alcuni scalini per abracciare la di lui imagine ... A questa statua li pellegrini mettono mantelline al collo e li capelli in testa, abbracciando detta statua, stanno qui fermi per alquanto spatio."

155 Somoza Medina, *As Lagoas*, 27.

156 Historical marker. The greatest of this bridge's ten arches then measured 156 geometric feet wide and a 135 geometric feet high from the top of the arch to its base. The geometric foot was a unit used in Spanish military engineering from the Renaissance through the nineteenth century, when the articles about Ourense were published by the anonymous P.F.G. y C., "España pintoresca." See also Navarro Loidi and Merino Saenz, "Military Engineering."

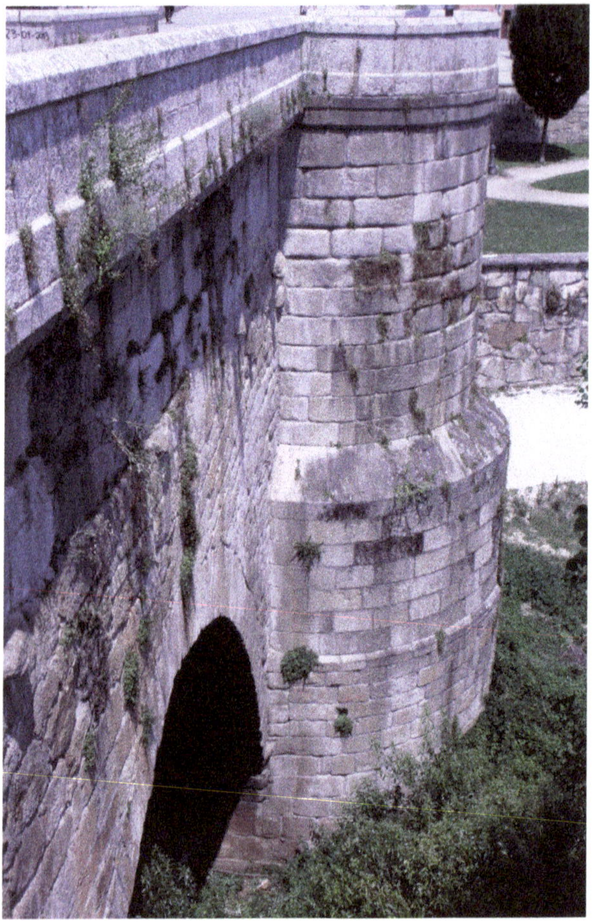

FIGURE 42 Base of original portion of Roman Bridge. Ourense, Spain. First centuries after Christ
PHOTO BY THE AUTHOR

The geomorphological depression that made Ourense a hub of this network of roads additionally gave rise to the geothermal waters that spring forth just a short distance from the Río Barbaña in the heart of Ourense before this river joins the Miño. The city is surrounded by mountain ranges, and abounds with hot springs (*aquae calidae*), commonly referred to as Burgas. Travelers noted these boiling springs, including Fernando Colón (Christopher Columbus's son), who in 1520 describes the Burgas as a sort of river flowing through the middle of a plaza in Ourense.[157] The stonemason Pedro de la Vega

157 Somoza Medina, *Ourense*, 66.

finished the fountains of las Burgas by 1584.[158] Today these thermal waters flow from public fountains renovated in the eighteenth century[159] and are channeled through pools in the Plaza Burgas. For centuries, residents have gathered hot water here for domestic use, just as they have kneaded bread here. And they have washed their clothes and rinsed their slaughtered animals directly in the hot fountains. People would use the cold fountains as drinking water.[160] To this day, locals gather hot water for a variety of household uses, and they drink from the cold fountains. I can attest from personal experience that both residents and visitors continue to soak in these hot springs, as well as in those that arise on the banks of the Miño. The pilgrimage route to Santiago passes right alongside these Burgas.

All of these thermal waters have been an attraction for their therapeutic properties since Roman times.[161] Magalotti lists Ourense as one of the five major cities of Galicia[162] and notes that here "there are springs of hot water for medicinal use."[163] As impressed as he is with the Burgas, Ambrosio de Morales is not fully convinced of their healing properties, suggesting that in the summertime, the thermal waters overheat the city and cause the epidemics that occurred in his time.[164] While the city does get extremely hot in summer, this phenomenon is more likely a bowl effect caused by the city being surrounded by mountains, which trap the heat.

The fictional 17th-century picaresque traveler Estebanillo González makes his way to Ourense and notes very real parts of the city such as its famous fountains. Estebanillo's well-versed pilgrim partners explain to him that "there pilgrims of all stripes would wash their bodies and in Santiago their souls."[165] Indeed, in history, as well, pilgrims to Santiago took relief in these very fountains and washed their underwear here.[166] The function of allowing Santiago pilgrims to cleanse themselves is similar to that of them washing their bodies and clothing in Lavacolla before arriving in Santiago along the French Way (Camino Francés).

---

158 Gallego Domínguez, *A cidade de Ourense* 132–133.

159 No extant drawings or paintings of the fountains seem to be extant prior to 1842.

160 Morales, *Viage*, 150–151; Barriocanal López, *O camiño real*, 313, 315.

161 Barriocanal López, *O camiño real*, 313.

162 Magalotti, *Viaje de Cosme*, 337.

163 Magalotti, *Viaje de Cosme*, 1:338; "sono sorgenti d'acqua calda per uso medinicale."

164 Morales, *Viage*, 150–151.

165 *Estebanillo González*, 175; "allí los peregrinos de toda broza lavaban los cuerpos y en Santiago las almas."

166 Barriocanal López, *O camiño real*, 315.

Such ritual ablutions are not limited to the pilgrimage to Santiago de Compostela or even to Christianity and in fact are commonly performed by Muslims before entering any mosque in the Islamic world. Although the fountains were completed by the time of his visit and were already a major attraction, Soller does not mention the Burgas. This may be because the trajectory of his journey proceeds from Santiago to Ourense and not vice versa, thereby obviating the need for him to clean himself before coming face-to-face with the remains of the Apostle Santiago.

Due in no small part to these mineral springs, the site was a pilgrimage center even before its imperial takeover by the Romans. In fact, the initial Roman encampment began in part as cluster of merchants with their hostels, taverns, stores, shops, and stands catering to the needs of these early pilgrims seeking restoration and healing. Ourense's strategic location at a natural crossroads midway along the course of the Miño River additionally favored the city's Romanization.[167]

Ourense is significant for eventually becoming an episcopal see at least by the late sixth century. The first known bishop, Witimer, attended the Council of Lugo in the year 571. Ourense truly began to gain ascendancy when Teresa of Portugal renewed Ourense's status as a city and as the seat of the bishop's authority when she granted episcopal jurisdiction to bishop Diego de Velasco and his successors in 1122. It was around this time that construction began on the new Cathedral of San Martiño, converting what was a Suevi fortress into a bishop's palace. Ambrosio de Morales describes how Emperor Alfonso VII of León first granted the privilege of ruling over Ourense to the Bishop in 1131, and that the King's successors renewed the privilege for the Bishop in subsequent decades.[168]

Bishop Don Lorenzo finished the Cathedral and the palace in 1218, and he began construction on a bridge to encourage the arrival of pilgrims. Bishop Lorenzo is responsible for the Portal of Paradise (Pórtico do Paraíso) at the western entrance of the Cathedral, basically a copy of Master Mateo's Portal of Glory in the Santiago Cathedral, and a beautiful one at that.[169] In the Middle Ages, Ourense's relationship to other cities in the Galician urban network was solidified. Laws governing pilgrimage centers between Santiago and Ourense were consolidated, and locales in and around Ourense tended to prosper due to the city's status as an episcopal see.[170]

---

167 Barriocanal López, *O camiño real*, 299.

168 Morales, *Viage*, 147.

169 Somoza Medina, *As Lagoas*, 28–29, 31–34; Barriocanal López, *O camiño real*, 303.

170 Somoza Medina, *As Lagoas* 36.

Ourense's cathedral was finished around 1230 under the Spanish rule of Fernando III, "the Saint" (el Santo). Construction had begun in the latter part of the thirteenth century under Bishop Don Pedro Seguín (1157–1169) and was mostly completed in the first half of the thirteenth century under Bishop Don Lorenzo (1218–1248). The structure was initially designed as a cathedral-fortress but has undergone so many restorations, renovations, and expansions that its architectural logic is rather incoherent.[171] The anonymous P.F.G. y C., writing in 1847, considers the Cathedral of Ourense to be "a parody of the majority of churches of this type that were built during the twelfth and thirteenth centuries, an era of splendor and perfection."[172]

With the exception of the Portal of Christ at the northern transept entrance, the exterior is lacking in ornamentation and decoration relative to other cathedrals built during the same period in Burgos, León, and Seville. The view of the main entrance on the western end, though striking, is virtually completely obstructed by the elevated structures built immediately across the narrow Street of the Shops (Rúa das Tendas) in front of the cathedral, making this portal difficult to view except by those who specifically seek it out. Nonetheless, as the main church of the city, the Cathedral of Ourense became the epicenter of the city's religious life.

16 Holy Christ of Ourense

Of particular note is the Chapel of the Holy Christ (Santo Cristo), with its "infinite adornments, statues, and high reliefs, alluding to the Passion of the Lord, which fill up even the smallest of spaces," according to one nineteenth-century writer.[173] This particular sculpture of the Holy Christ was highly revered and attracted pilgrims from throughout Galicia and Portugal, including Soller. Even

171 Gallego Domínguez, *A cidade de Ourense*, 175. There is an intriguing Gothic statue of a seated Santiago-as-Knight (Armacaballeros) in the trumeau (*parteluz*) of the Portal of Paradise (Pórtico do Paraíso) of the Cathedral of Ourense, but this sculpture was not placed here until 1857, so that Soller could not have seen it. Yzquierdo Perrín, *La Catedral de Ourense*, 60; Barriocanal López, *O camiño real*, 321.

172 P.F.G. y C., "España pintoresca," 50; "una parodia de la mayor parte de los templos de este género que fueron construidos durante los siglos XII y XIII, época de lustre y perfección."

173 P.F.G. y C., "España pintoresca," 50; "los infinitos adornos, estatuas y altos relieves, alusivos a la pasión del Señor, que llenan hasta el menor espacio." As was the case with other chapels in Ourense, the Chapel of the Santo Cristo was maintained financially through income obtained from eleven houses and from eight fiscal exemptions. Somoza Medina, *As Lagoas*, 38.

as it had been a source of devotion since medieval times, the Chapel of the Santo Cristo became a requisite stop for nearly every Santiago pilgrim during the seventeenth century, as well. Popes granted major indulgences for those who came to prostrate themselves at the feet of the Holy Christ of Ourense, and the Santo Cristo's miracles were of great renown.[174] No wonder: according to legend, the main sculpture of the Santo Cristo was found in a box at sea and then brought to the cathedral in the fourteenth century.

This type of miracle-story is associated with similar sculptures in Burgos and Palencia. It is the bishop of Ourense, Vasco Pérez (de) Mariño who purportedly brought this sculpture of the Santo Cristo to this city's cathedral from Finisterre.[175] This bishop died in 1343, and so he would have had to have made his donation of the image to the Cathedral of Ourense sometime in advance of that date.[176] After Pérez de Mariño brought this sacred icon from Finisterre to Ourense in the fourteenth century, he built a chapel to house it in the Cathedral and ordered that he himself be buried there. Today the remains of this former bishop lie directly across the northern transept of said chapel.[177]

The chapel of the Santo Cristo underwent major reforms in the seventeenth century. The grill still setting apart the chapel of the Santo Cristo at the main entrance of the Cathedral was placed there in 1606. Pedro de Arén led the expansion of the chapel in 1674. Domingo de Andrade, the architect of the canopy covering the statue of Saint James in the main chapel of the Cathedral of Santiago, designed and had completed the canopy covering the Chapel of the Santo Cristo in the Ourense Cathedral by 1679.[178]

The Holy Christ image in Ourense is fairly graphic in its depiction of the Passion (figure 43). The Santo Cristo's arms are among the most realistic elements of the statue, while the open mouth contributes to the sensation that Christ has died. The figure measures two meters high.[179]

The Santo Cristo sculptures in the Burgos Cathedral and the convent of Saint Claire in Palencia are similarly lifelike. The pathos all of these images of the Man of Sorrows evoked, especially among pilgrims, along with the materials used gave rise to the legends surrounding them: that their hair and nails would grow; that they sweated and even bled; and that the sculptures really were

174 Barriocanal López, *O camiño real*, 303, 321–322.
175 Martínez Martínez, "El Santo Cristo," 212, 212n16, 239.
176 Martínez Martínez, "El Santo Cristo," 239; Barriocanal López, *O camiño real*, 322.
177 P.J.G. y C., "España pintoresca," 58.
178 Somoza Medina, *Ourense*, 63; Barriocanal López, *O camiño real*, 318, 321–322; Yzquierdo Perrín, *La Catedral de Ourense*, 150.
179 Yquierdo Perrín, *La Catedral de Ourense*, 150.

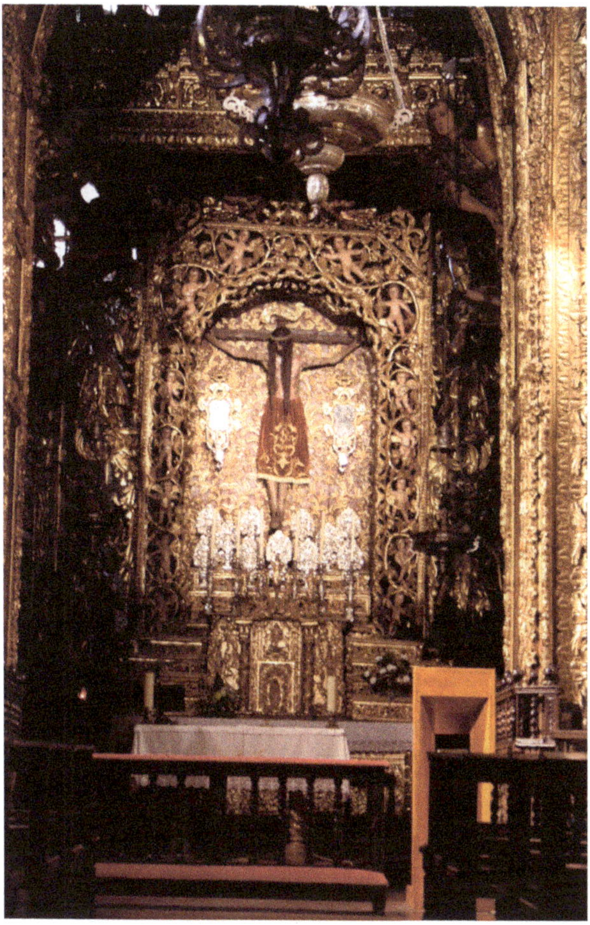

FIGURE 43 Statue of the Santo Cristo of Ourense, Spain. Fourteenth-century sculpture, seventeenth-century altar
PHOTO BY THE AUTHOR

mummies (of whom, it is not clear).[180] It may be difficult to understand how this last interpretation came to be since the mummification of Christ's body is irreconcilable with Christian articles of faith surrounding the Resurrection—"He is not here, for he is risen, as he said."[181]—and the Ascension—"And the Lord Jesus, after he had spoken to them, was taken up into heaven, and sit-

180 Martínez Martínez, "El Santo Cristo," 212.
181 Matthew 28:6 (Douay-Rheims Catholic Bible).

teth on the right hand of God."[182] And yet there is a logic explaining how these sculptures can be understood in this way despite the theological questions: "Altarpieces and devotional statues conflated depictions of Christ or the saints with the real presence of the consecrated wafer or relic. Distinctions between living and dead, body and thing, presence and mimesis, part and whole, animate and inanimate, tended to blur; all of creation could convey and reveal God."[183] In other words, through the use of such evocative materials as animal skin in the form of parchment to represent human skin on the statue, these objects of devotion were not merely realistic representations; they had the capacity to come alive, in a sense to be living, as *animate* objects.[184]

The hair and nails of the Holy Christ Sculpture were believed to be human, and the skin so soft as to be human-like.[185] In reality, these elaborate Spanish sculptures of Christ are constructed with hidden joint articulation and linen or parchment lining.[186] People claimed that this statue had to be shaved and to have its nails cut once a week. In the period leading up to the seventeenth century, much of Christian society still believed in the mystical power of physical matter, and devotional sculptures such as the Santo Cristo of Ourense called attention to the stuff of which they are made: "Depictions of Christ's body as a charter on which nails or a flail write in blood ink *are* what they depict when the charter is drawn on real skin—that is, parchment."[187] Images capable of transformations such as the Santo Cristo growing hair transcended their material nature by signaling beyond themselves to the extraordinary, to the divine.[188] People believed the Santo Cristo statues to be miraculous and sang songs about them.[189]

Many of these legends arose among the numerous pilgrims the Santo Cristo statues attracted internationally from the fourteenth through the eighteenth centuries, from France to the New World.[190] The fame of the statue in Burgos along the French Way (Camino Francés) was especially widespread since the pilgrimage to Santiago allowed these tales to circulate and promote the cult of this statue among pilgrims. Signage explaining the provenance of the image

182 Mark 16:19 (Douay-Rheims Catholic Bible).
183 Bynum, *Christian Materiality*, 267.
184 Bynum, *Christian Materiality*, 25, 282.
185 Martínez Martínez, "El Santo Cristo," 217n43.
186 Martínez Martínez, "El Santo Cristo," 237.
187 Bynum, *Christian Materiality*, 25.
188 Bynum, *Christian Materiality*, 29.
189 Laffi, *Journey*, 140.
190 Martínez Martínez, "El Santo Cristo," 212–214, 221–222, 225–226. Her observations mainly apply to the Santo Cristo of Burgos.

was posted in multiple foreign languages, from Greek to Portuguese, for these devotees, many of whom carried a pictorial reproduction of the statue on their person.[191] The seventeenth-century Italian pilgrim Domenico Laffi described the Holy Christ of Burgos in dramatic terms: "Indeed, this holy image would move the very stones to compassion, were they capable of feeling. It is so well made and has such a mournful expression that when people set eyes on it, it draws tears of pity. One cannot deny that this is the true and real likeness of Christ, so lacerated by the scourge that his human aspect is lost."[192]

Soller claims to journey to Ourense on pilgrimage to the Holy Christ of this city. Ambrosio de Morales describes this sculpture based on his visit to Ourense in the mid-eighteenth century. He describes it as famous, as the cause of great devotion, and as appearing on an altar in the transept in a luxurious chapel. Moreover, Morales compares the Santo Cristo of Ourense to that of Burgos: "truly the face is extremely devout, with a countenance of great severity and restraint."[193] The appearance of the effigy in Morales's day is much the same as it was in Soller's day, just as it is today.

The Gothic statue of the Santo Cristo in Ourense also was believed to transfer its holiness and power to those in its presence by virtue of the sheer corporeality, or materiality of the statue. Beyond the realism (with skin so soft it appears to be human) and associations with the miraculous (having been found in a box at sea) of this Gothic image and other Holy Christ sculptures like it—such as in the monastery of the Poor Clares of Palencia and in the Cathedral of Burgos—the "insistent materiality" of the statue is palpable, particularly in the naturalness of its human hair and in the parchment layered over the articulated parts of the sculpted wood. It is not so much that this statue was thought to be lifelike as much as it was believed in a sense to be living, as in the sculpture's purported ability to grow hair and fingernails, to sweat, and to bleed. As Bynum says about other similar material objects, this image along with the other examples "do more than comment on, refer to, provide signs of, or gesture toward the divine. They lift matter toward God and reveal God through matter … [T]hey disclose, not merely signify, a power that lies beyond."[194]

---

191 Martínez Martínez, "El Santo Cristo," 230, 232.

192 Laffi, *Journey* 137; Laffi, *Viaggio*, 181; "In vero questa santa imagine moverebbe a compassione sino le pietre, se fossero capaci d'affetto, e è fatto tanto bene e sta in atto tanto compassionevole, che, quando lo scoprono, cava le lagrime per pietà, onde bisogna confessare che questo sia il vero e reale ritratto di Christo quando dai flagelli stracciato, perduto haveva ogni sembiante humano."

193 Morales, *Viage*, 150; "verdaderamente el rostro es devotisimo con semblante de gran severidad, y mesura."

194 Bynum, *Christian Materiality*, 35.

Beyond the period Bynum describes, which includes the fourteenth and fifteenth centuries, there still was a significant contingent in the population during the seventeenth century who believed in the power channeled in these representations, not just that they pointed toward God but also that the images themselves in some sense were embodiments of the divine. The James statue in the main altar of the Cathedral of Compostela and the Holy Christ of Ourense are two such sculptures. José Soller could have been attempting to capitalize on these popular beliefs in his own defense, and he could have been a devout believer in the power of the images themselves. Regardless, Soller would need all the help he could get defending himself in Ourense.

CHAPTER 6

On Trial, under Sentence, and in Absentia

> If there is any jurisprudence in which the door may be open to abuse, to every subterfuge, it is, incontrovertibly, that of Spain.
>
> JUAN FRANCISCO PEYRON[1]

∵

The map of Ourense during the seventeenth century essentially was the same as that during the medieval period except the urban core became denser over time, leading to the disappearance of intramural vegetable gardens. The population remained fairly constant, as well, due to: various plagues, epidemics, famines, and poor harvests; the closure of foreign markets to the exportation of wine; and the high tributes collected to pay for the numerous wars of the Spanish Crown from the sixteenth into the eighteenth centuries. The excessive fiscal pressure coupled with climactic irregularities produced an undernourished and disease-ridden population, all of which combined to create a vicious circle of famine–plague–famine.[2]

The population of Ourense oscillated between as few as 1,700 at low points such as the beginning of the sixteenth century and as many as 3,750 inhabitants during growth periods such as the mid-seventeenth century. At this time the rural populace was far healthier than were city dwellers due to the rapid spread of disease, which caused mass mortality in the urban centers. There was economic growth in the sixteenth century and stagnation in the seventeenth and

1 Peyron, *Ensayos sobre España*, 423; "Si hay alguna jurisprudencia en donde la puerta esté abierta a abuso, a todos los subterfugios, es, sin contradicción, la de España." Peyron was a French diplomat who wrote essays based on his late-eighteenth-century travels through Spain. His criticism comes from a section on jurisprudence and the courts and is consistent with his denunciation of the corruption and of the perversion of justice pervading the Spanish legal system. A differently worded version of the passage is quoted in Guillamón Álvarez and Pérez Hervas, "Los forzados de galeras," 75. Cf. Ortego Gil, "La pena de muerte," 170. In any event, Peyron's attitude is consistent with Enlightenment opinions on Old-Regime justice during the post-Beccaria reform period.

2 Somoza Medina, *Ourense*, 66. As we have seen in the previous chapter, Ambrosio de Morales connected the hot summers of Ourense with these epidemics. Morales, *Viage*, 150–151.

 | DOI:10.1163/9789004422704_007

eighteenth centuries. As discussed earlier (part 1, chapter 2), during the latter period, the city became a profiteering venture for the upper echelon of society, while the lower social classes paid more than their fair share. The economy remained stagnant as a result. The underclass relied upon alms and charity to survive.[3] Soller, who, as a pilgrim at least, really was in this bottom social category in his reliance upon the hospitality network, was attempting to empower himself if not rise significantly toward the top of the social hierarchy through his use of the priestly disguise.

1 Fish Market Plaza

Period maps and documents show that in Soller's day, the Fish Market Plaza (Plazuela de la Pescadería),[4] where the barbers' tents in the Soller case are located, would have been on what today is Barreira Street (Rúa Barreira), right around the corner from Ourense's Town Hall (Casas Consistoriales),[5] south-by-southwest of this building's façade, approximately where the fruit and bread market now stands near Rúa Barreira, no. 9. In the seventeenth century, this street was called Fontiña, which is listed as Fontaíña in the manuscript and is where fountains have been excavated in various archeological interventions.[6] The Fish Market moved from place to place over the centuries but still was housed in an earthen structure at this same location by the mid-eighteenth century.[7] Fontaíña Street was renamed Cervantes Street in 1850,[8] and the seg-

3 Somoza Medina, *As Lagoas*, 38; Somoza Medina, *Ourense*, 55–58, 62–63, 65–66; Somoza Medina, *Historia de Ourense*, 42, 57.

4 Rodrigo Méndez Silva notes in 1675 that market days are the seventh and eighth of each month. Somoza Medina, *Ourense*, 66–67. Soller's presence in Ourense is not confirmed until the fourteenth of April, 1693.

5 Gallego Domínguez, *A cidade de Ourense*, 136. A structure for city hall was urgently needed since the council had no place of its own to convene prior to the construction of the Casas Consistoriales in the sixteenth century, The architect and sculptor Francisco de Castro Canseco, from the city of Melide in Galicia, was commissioned to rebuild the Casas Consistoriales in 1697. Gallego Domínguez, *A cidade de Ourense*, 136. This is why the Town Hall in use during Soller's day no longer remains.

6 Rodríguez Cao, "Excavación arqueolóxica," 118; García Valdeiras, "Intervencións arqueolóxicas," 163, 182–183. Fontaíña refers to a rather insignificant fountain. In 1584, Attorney General Antonio de Puga denounced as unsanitary a fountain in this area, the Fonte do Rosal, and ordered the residents of Fontaíña Street and Ferrería Street to clean it at their own expense. Gallego Domínguez, *A cidade de Ourense*, 154.

7 Gallego Domínguez, *A cidade de Ourense* 133.

8 Gallego Domínguez, *A cidade de Ourense* 77. In 1850, the city council changed the name of

ment of the same street south of Rúa Barreira still retains the name Rúa Cervantes. While Soller's barber works out of the stores at the Fish Market Plaza on Fontaíña Street, his tailor is just down the road along the same street (figure 44).

2 The Aira Gate

The city during the Old Regime continued its growth along the north–south longitudinal axis that the Camino Real followed to connect Castile with southern Galicia. Roads became streets (*rúas*), as in the case of the Corredoira, and new dwellings constructed at either end made the urban scene more dense.[9] At the southernmost end of the city, the Aira Gate (Porta da Aira in Galician; Puerta de Aira in the Spanish of the manuscript), heading for Castile, had two towers, one on either side, while the Corredoira Gate (Porta de la Corredoira) in the north of the city (leading to Santiago) was a crenellated gate.[10] Also on the northern side of the city was the Vilar Gate (Porta do Vilar), which made its way to the old Roman bridge (Ponte Vella). Once across the river, the road split into two paths, one toward the coast and the other to Santiago.[11] The Porta da Aira was the main entrance to the city for those headed from Castile, or in Soller's case, toward Castile via Seixalbo along the very rough Royal Road (Camino Real).[12] In 1585, the City Council asked the King for 6,000 ducats to

---

the street from Fontaíña to Cervantes along with a series of other nomenclature modifications due to the perception that the older names were "ridiculous and unlikeable" (*ridícula y contraria al gusto*). Gallego Domínguez, *A cidade de Ourense*, 77.

9 Somoza Medina, *Ourense*, 65.

10 Gallego Domínguez, "Torres," 249–250. A thirteenth-century hostel serving the poor and pilgrims lies just beyond the Corredoira gate to the north of the city. Near this same location, a Dominican monastic church was established in the seventeenth century, which, together with the establishment of a Jesuit church to the northeast of the city, encouraged the growth of the city toward the Miño River. The Dominican and Jesuit churches were founded with donations from Spanish émigrés to the New World (*indianos*) from Peru (Potosí). The Church of Santo Domingo was inaugurated in 1666, although the Dominican brothers had been present since 1634. Somoza Medina, *Ourense*, 64; Barriocanal López, *O camiño real*, 305. These donations underscore the connection between the New World and Ourense, the relevance being that Soller claiming to hail from Hispaniola would not make him any sort of outlier during the seventeenth century, at least in terms of geography. The question becomes, however, whether a mixed-race man claiming to be from the Americas would make him more suspicious or less so to local law enforcement.

11 Somoza Medina, *Historia de Ourense*, 45.

12 This road was so rocky that it was difficult to travel by horse or on foot. Even after restoration work in the seventeenth century, it was still considered dangerous to traverse in the year 1692, the year before Soller took this route. Barriocanal López, *O camiño real*, 33–38.

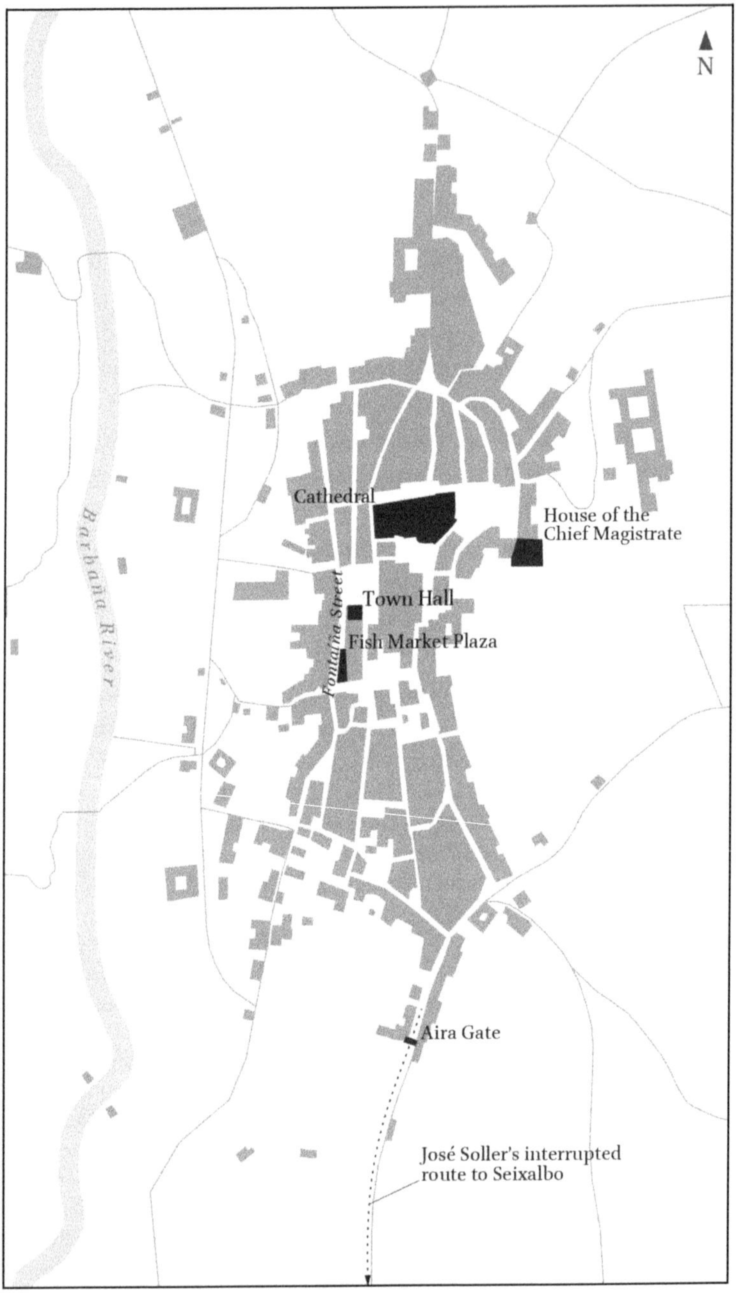

FIGURE 44 Map of Ourense circa 1693, illustrating key places associated with Soller's case and pilgrimage
MAP BY THE UNIVERSITY OF WISCONSIN–MADISON CARTOGRAPHY LAB

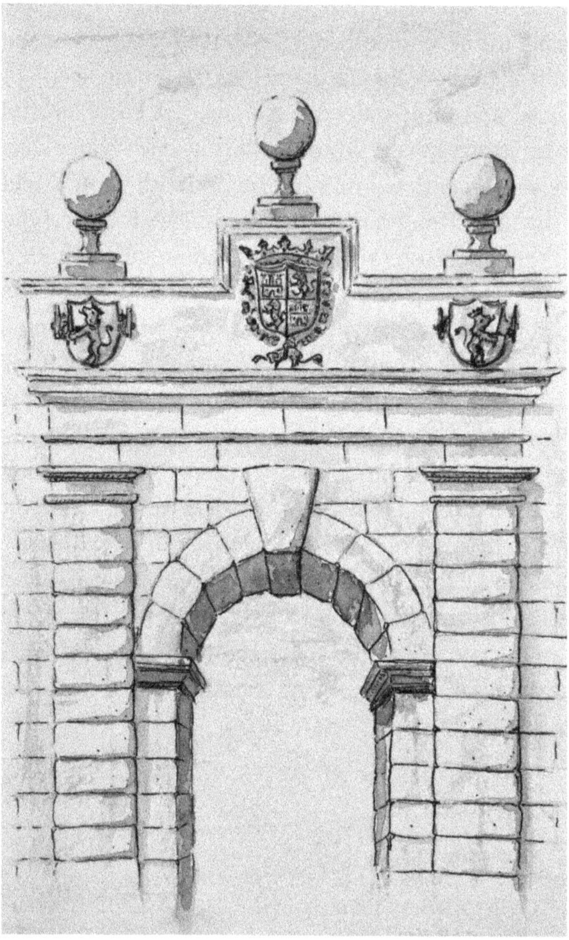

FIGURE 45 Reconstruction of the Aira Gate. Ourense, Spain. Seventeenth century
Note: This drawing is based on the rendering of the Aira Gate in Gallego Domínguez, "Torres," 267.
WATERCOLOR SKETCH BY CLINTON LARISCY

renovate and beautify this gate, explaining at the time that it was made merely of mortar and had been constructed to quarantine for recurrences of plague.[13]

Ourense could not afford complete city walls and for its defense relied instead on the numerous towers atop the major buildings associated with the Church: the Cathedral, the Bishop's Palace, the Church of Santa María, the

13 Gallego Domínguez, "Torres," 265; Barriocanal López, *O camiño real*, 300.

Church of the Trinity. These religious structures themselves were built like fortresses.[14] City gates during the seventeenth century served much the same purpose as during the medieval period, that is, to enclose the city, to keep out pestilence in times of plague, and to help defend the city. The Porta da Aira was totally rebuilt by stonemasonry master Antonio Martínez de Araque during the first quarter of the seventeenth century in 1616 under the Lord Chief Magistrate of Ourense at the time, Don Francisco de Verástegui, Esquire, who previously had completed the new Hospital de San Lorenzo in 1614.[15] In 1675, Rodrigo Méndez Silva describes the hospital as of a high quality.[16] Scholars today know from a descriptive plan of the Porta da Aira signed by Martínez de Araque and Verástegui that above the arch, this gate bore the coat-of-arms of Castilla y León, topped by a crown and above a sheepskin,[17] which represents the Order of the Golden Fleece (figure 45).

The Porta de Aira is the only one of Ourense's original city gates of which any ruins remain.[18] Only a fragment of a pilaster of this gate can be found on what today is the Rúa Xulio Prieto Nespereira (at the edge of the historic district where the street meets the Rúa Lugo), on the main road out of town headed to Castile (figure 44). This gate is some three and a half kilometers (or a little over two miles), about a 40-minute walk from the extramural village of Seixalbo, toward which Soller was traveling before being apprehended. It would be a rocky road, both literally and figuratively.

3 Town Hall

The old Town Hall (Casas Consistoriales), located in the exact spot of the current one that replaced it, is where Soller and the tailor are initially indicted (figure 44): "the Lord Chief Magistrate ordered his officials to return said José Soller to the jail and to secure him in shackles and chains, and that said tailor appear in the patio of the Town Hall for the outcome that should be approved."[19] There

14 Somoza Medina, *Historia de Ourense*, 40.
15 Gallego Domínguez, "Torres," 266–267, 268n109; Somoza Medina, *Ourense*, 63; Barriocanal López, *O camiño real*, 300.
16 Somoza Medina, *Ourense*, 66.
17 Gallego Domínguez, "Torres" 267, 278; see in particular the artist's rendering reconstructed from this description on 267. See also Barriocanal López, *O camiño real*, 300.
18 Somoza Medina, *Ourense*, 63; Barriocanal López, *O camiño real*, 300.
19 5^{r}; "el Señor Corregidor mandó a sus ministros volviesen a la cárcel a dicho Josef Soller y le asegurasen en las prisiones, y que el dicho sastre compareciese en los patios de las Casas Consistoriales para el efecto que hubiese lugar."

is no record of any sort of town hall in Ourense until the sixteenth century,[20] when the Chief Magistrate begins to take charge of the urban development of the city center with a broad array of projects such as maintaining and beautifying the city gates, the planting of trees, and the like.[21] The first recorded formal session of the City Council in its own building is January 14, 1519. Built in the late-Gothic style that was commonly used in sixteenth-century Ourense, the new structure was built on the Plaza del Campo, essentially the Plaza Mayor of Ourense in which the monthly and annual festivals and fairs took place.[22] This town hall was completely replaced once in 1697 and then again in 1881. The City Council meets to this day in the nineteenth-century structure, located in the same spot.

The first Town Hall building, however, is the one Soller would have known. This first structure was in a state of serious decay by February of 1689, such that the roof and hallway where the town gathered for festive functions were verging on ruins and the stairwells usable only with great difficulty. In February through August of 1693, the stairwells were replaced, and the interior wooden hallways and exterior wrought-iron promenade were renovated. These half-measures were fingers in the dike, so to speak, staving off the inevitable reconstruction five years later.[23] The town hall Soller experienced not only was the first one built but also was virtually in a state of collapse by the time of his arrival.

4 The Royal Jail

In Ourense during the Old Regime, jails were an inherent consequence of penalties and crimes in the criminal and civil jurisdiction held by the King and in his stead, the lords of the jurisdiction. Jails had prisoners in their custody, often on trial without even having been sentenced, in what today might be called "preventative prison." Jails were tiny structures that did not meet the most minimal modern standards of security, much less of hygiene.[24] The low level of security would have been a contributing factor to the frequent escapes cited in the reforms of the Royal Tribunal of Galicia in the following century.

20 Gallego Domínguez, "Casas Consistoriales," 107.

21 Somoza Medina, *Ourense*, 63.

22 Gallego Domínguez, "Casas Consistoriales," 109. For a history of this first building, see Rodríguez González, *A Casa do Concello*, 11–42.

23 Gallego Domínguez, "Casas Consistoriales," 110–111, 114; Rodríguez González, *A Casa do Concello*, 41.

24 Justo Martín, "A cárcere de Ourense," 195.

The maintenance of prisoners was not a priority:

> In the early modern era jails were places of detention for persons awaiting trial or decisions on their appeals, a procedure that usually lasted several years. During that time no provisions were made for their upkeep, and if prisoners could not afford to purchase food and other necessities of life from wardens and jailers, then it was expected they would be supported by relatives and friends. Failing this, inmates supported themselves by begging and with alms donated by religious and charitable institutions, but the funds collected in this manner were hardly enough to sustain life. Many poor and destitute prisoners died of starvation.[25]

These conditions explain why visiting prisoners of course is one of the seven Corporal Works of Mercy, an obligation the Misericórdia brotherhood took seriously.[26] Given that Soller appears to have been both poor and from elsewhere, we can see how impoverished his conditions truly must have been while he was in jail. His continual complaints regarding his nudity and suffering may not be an exaggeration at all.

Jails tended to be at ground level and attached to the great monasteries or houses of powerful lords. Some were located in towers or forts.[27] For a long time, the city of Ourense had had a variety of jails to serve the various jurisdictions under the bishops, laypeople, the Church, the City Council, and so forth. These jails did not begin to have their own buildings until the sixteenth century.[28]

Once the Chief Magistrate (Corregidor) arrived in 1571, the battles over jurisdiction, including jails, began. The struggle ended in an agreement with the King's Representative in 1628 in which the bishops abandoned their claim to any jurisdiction over the city, including the jail for laypersons.[29] The royal jail was established at the start of the sixteenth century as a distinct entity from the jail of the City Council (Consello). Upon the arrival of the Corregidor in 1571, the royal jail was assigned to the jurisdiction of this magistrate and eventually was combined with that of the Consello. The Royal Jail wound up being housed

25 Pike, *Penal Servitude*, 16. See Copete on how the salaries of jailers and wardens were paid by the prisoners. "L'assistance aux prisonniers," 28–29.

26 See Copete on these conditions and the both the spiritual and material assistance provided to prisoners in southern Spain by a variety of Catholic orders during the early modern period. "L'assistance aux prisonniers."

27 Justo Martín, "A cárcere de Ourense," 195.

28 Gallego Domínguez, *A cidade de Ourense*, 138.

29 Gallego Domínguez, *A cidade de Ourense* 140.

in a tower attached to his residence, the Tower of the Chief Magistrate (Torre del Corregidor).[30] Soller was held in this very tower.

5 The King in Question

The King in question is the invalid Carlos II, cruelly nicknamed "the Bewitched" (el Hechizado) by his political enemies.[31] Historians virtually unanimously attribute the infirmity of this monarch, the last of the Hapsburg line, to generations of inbreeding. His illness most likely was excessively weak bones due to a deficiency of or an inability to metabolize vitamin D, called rickets (or rachitism), a condition that can lead to bow legs, a hunched spine, and a swollen spleen among other manifestations. It is also believed Carlos II suffered from a chromosomal disorder known today as Klinefelter's syndrome. The King additionally was slow and deficient intellectually. Carlos II was incapable of producing an heir, probably due to sterility (though possibly because he was a true intersexual, or hermaphrodite, at least according to one study),[32] and suffered from a variety of maladies throughout his life, which lasted until thirty-nine years of age. The King fell gravely ill in the spring of 1693, right during the time of the Soller trial. Moreover, the bedeviled king additionally was extremely indecisive, so much so that he never governed in any real sense. He is widely considered to have been an incompetent monarch in over his head at a critical juncture in the history of the Spanish Hapsburg Empire.[33] This on top of Carlos II's many other deficiencies leads to the conclusion that the King, though invoked as "His Majesty" throughout the proceedings, was not directly involved in any meaningful way with this or any such case.

In other words, the King's relationship to Soller's criminal proceedings was indirect. Although ultimate authority rested with the sovereignty of the Monarch, regular royal justice under the Hapsburg regime coexisted alongside competing jurisdictions, many of them in rivalry with one another.[34] The law in the seventeenth-century Spanish empire was more exhortative than mandatory,

30 Gallego Domínguez, *A cidade de Ourense* 142. Gallego Domínguez and Fariña Busto, "Casas Reales," 203–204.

31 Henry Kamen synthesizes the existing research in order to illustrate just how exaggerated and distorted were the politically motivated rumors of Carlos II's demon possession. Kamen, "El rey hechizado," 321–350.

32 Kamen, "El rey hechizado," 249–250.

33 Ribot García, "España de Carlos II," 63–66.

34 Bádenas Zamora, "Consideraciones," 521.

more a set of suggestions than a list of penalties: "when faced with the breaking of rules, the king did not punish, threat, or use angry words. He brought the matter to his council and listened to what the 'fiscal' (the representative of his interests in the council) had to say … The king constituted a soft political system, where the use of force was minimal and the logic far more complex than that of authority in itself."[35] It is the Lord Chief Magistrate who imparts justice in the name of the King in the in the city and region under his jurisdiction, Ourense.

6 The Lord Chief Magistrate

Whereas the King symbolizes the "font of justice" (*fons jurisdictionis*), the Chief Magistrate embodies the "long hand of the King" (*longa manu regis*),[36] much like today's sheriffs or police chiefs personify the proverbial "long arm of the law." In an inverted image of Foucault's modern panopticon penitentiary, that seeing-eye prison in which an invisible authority may surveil multiple bodies at any given moment, the Corregidor is an extension of "the body of the king, … with the force that he himself deploys or transmits to some few others."[37] This judicial authority is referred to as "Your Grace" (Vuestra Merced) and as "Lord Chief Magistrate" (Señor Corregidor) in the trial proceedings.

The Corregidor represented royal authority in the municipality to which he was assigned and additionally presided over town councils. This type of magistrate was the main tool the Hapsburg monarchs used to govern Castilian towns as the authority of first instance for civil and criminal trials.[38] The Corregidor was not supposed to be a jurist but could be an attorney, as the magistrate presiding over Soller's case, the aforementioned Lord Don Juan Antonio Covillas, seems to have been since there is no deputy there in court interpreting the law on Covillas's behalf. The Corregidor was a municipal justice, and as such, he mostly worked with municipal office holders. These magistrates "had wide discretionary power in this period to increase or decrease penalties."[39]

Chief magistrates took the place of the justices of the medieval court system in the process of unification under the absolutist administration of the Catholic

35 Herzog, "Spanish Monarchy," 161.
36 Morelli, "Pueblos, alcaldes y municipios," 40, 42.
37 Foucault, *Discipline and Punish*, 208; Foucault, *Surveiller et punir*, 210; "Le corps du roi, … avec la force que lui-même déploie ou qu' il transmet à quelques-uns."
38 Heras Santos, *La justicia penal*, 60–61.
39 Pike, *Penal Servitude*, 8.

Monarchs, which lasted until the end of the Hapsburg dynasty. This transition took place once the bishops of Ourense lost power in their struggle against the City Council (Consello), which was comprised of family members from a few select lineages among the nobility whose sole objective became to perpetuate their own power. In other words, it was an oligarchy. Most councilors were appointed by the King. While they theoretically served on the Consello as representatives of the people, in reality their positions wound up being sold to the highest bidder. Beneath this upper echelon consisting of the Corregidor, the members of the Consello, and the Attorney, there was an additional bureaucratic layer that included deputies, bailiffs, clerks, judicial secretaries, majordomos, overseers, doctors, masters of trade (i.e., carpenters), and managers (i.e., jailers), all on the administrative payroll. As discussed earlier (part 1, chapter 2), this extensive apparatus placed a great fiscal burden on the common laborer, as none of the members of the aforementioned oligarchy or their dependents paid any taxes whatsoever. Neither did any members of the nobility or the clergy for that matter.[40]

The neighborhood of Cima de Vila, known today as the Praza do Correxidor, is where tensions finally erupted between the bishop and members of the City Council at the beginning of the thirteenth century. The allies of Pedro Yáñez de Nóboa (also written as Novoa) pursued members of the Consello to a Franciscan monastery, in which holy place the councilmen sought refuge. The bishop's men attacked and killed them nonetheless, along with several monks, before the structure burned to the ground. The head governor (*adiantado maior*) of Galicia excommunicated Yáñez de Nóboa, forcing him to rebuild the monastery of San Francisco, which now lies on the outskirts of the city. This episode epitomizes the extent to which the bishop did not want to share power with the City Council, whose members among the nobility jealously clung to their privilege and authority. In fact, the presence of the bishops seemed to restrain the economic growth of the city.[41]

The influence of the Consello grew, and by 1427 the Council had instituted regulations governing commerce, health, prisoners, weights and measures,

40 Gallego Domínguez, *A cidade de Ourense*, 18; Somoza Medina, *Ourense*, 59–60; Somoza Medina, *Historia de Ourense*, 56–57.

41 Somoza Medina, *As Lagoas*, 34; Somoza Medina, *Historia de Ourense*, 40. Tensions and confrontations between the Bishop and *Consello* had previously come into bold relief in the mid-thirteenth century under the reign of Alfonso X, when the City Council declared fealty directly to the King and denied any homage whatsoever to the bishop. This situation required the intervention of Alfonso "the Wise" (el Sabio) in 1259, when he presented a compromise to both sides in his court in Toledo. Somoza Medina, *Historia de Ourense*, 38–39.

stores, and the imposition of fines. The City Council also ruled over the lands held in common, known as *terras de "man común"* in Galician and *montes vecinales en mano común* in Castilian, meaning that they are not owned by an individual but rather by the collective group of citizens (*vecinos*). These citizens acquired this land politically over the centuries, largely in the river valleys of the Miño and Barbaña in the vicinity of Ourense, and shared it to graze their cattle, chop firewood, and the like.[42] This custom is descended from Germanic law and is in use to this day in Galicia (preface).

In the early modern era, jurisdictional control passed from the Bishop to the Chief Magistrate.[43] King Felipe II tried to resolve the struggle between the two figures in 1586, when he removed the bishops from power and installed the Corregidor as his official representative. The episcopal prelates, however, continued to demand their customary privileges. This led to the dispute over the corral (*preito do curral*), an area that led into the main plaza of the city, the Praza do Campo, and therefore was of vital importance to the city. The then-bishop tried to hem in all his possessions—the Cathedral, Bishop's Palace, and so on—by filling in the *curral* with houses. The Concello protested vehemently because such an act would severely damage business by completely choking off a key artery to the fish market, meat market, and fountains. The eventual compromise reached in 1603 was that the prelate would relinquish part of this territory for the creation of a permanent street, today's Rúa Bispo Carrascosa, in exchange of the Council renouncing its claim to any other part of the *curral*.[44] The ongoing contentious relationship between the bishop and city council finally was resolved in 1628, when, in an agreement with King Felipe IV, Bishop Juan Venido stopped complaining over his loss of jurisdiction in exchange for parishes containing the most profitable sanctuaries in the province, including the Abbey of Saint Mary of Holy Waters (Santa Mariña de Aguas Santas).

By the end of the fifteenth century, the Catholic Monarchs previously had institutionalized the figure of the Corregidor as the true delegate of their government. Not only did the Chief Magistrate serve as the monarch's chief representative in the city, but he also ruled, issued sentences, enforced agreements, directed urban development, all while leading the City Council, which had as many as thirty-nine councilors by the end of the seventeenth century. Many of these competencies and priorities were outlined in the the guidelines (*capítulos*) King Fernando and Queen Isabel prescribed to the office of Corregidor.

---

42 Somoza Medina, *As Lagoas*, 35.
43 Somoza Medina, *Ourense*, 55.
44 Somoza Medina, *Ourense* 59; Somoza Medina, *Historia de Ourense*, 54–55.

The position was reserved for those born outside the city, and Chief Magistrates were reappointed every three years.[45] Through the end of Hapsburg-era Castile, the Corregidor remained the "chief example" (*caso paradigmático*) of the concentration of royal powers to balance local ones within a single entity or figure.[46]

Located in the present-day plaza of the Corregidor, the House of the Chief Magistrate (Casa do Corregidor), known alternatively as the Royal Residences at the City Summit (Casas Reais de Cimadevila) or simply as the Royal Residences (Casas Reales), became the official residence of the Chief Magistrate in the time of the Catholic Monarchs. The structure went through various stages of renovation and ruin until it was definitively demolished in 1988 amid the general indifference of Ourense's residents. The Casa do Corregidor occupied the southeastern corner of the Plaza do Corregidor (figure 44). This structure's façade had a projecting balcony underneath the coat-of-arms of the Catholic Monarchs that still adorns the new structure built in place of this residence. The Casa do Corregidor also had an inner courtyard similar to that of other Renaissance structures in the city,[47] as well as Gothic windows (figure 46).[48] The coat-of-arms bearing the symbols of the Catholic Monarchs is topped by a single-headed Eagle of St. John the Evangelist, a favorite in the heraldry of Queen Isabel and therefore indicative of a time during her reign with Fernando (figure 47). (In contrast, the two heads of the bicephalous eagle from later Hapsburg royal crests each face outward, one toward either end of the Spanish empire.) By this same logic, the inscription of the House of the Corregidor, dated 1626, would appear to post-date the coat-of-arms (figure 48). The Royal Jail in which Soller is held was attached to the Magistrate's residence here.

Oddly, the Corregidor absolves Soller of the crime he was accused of (impersonation) and instead finds that he is a vagabond, or "vagrant" (*vagamundo*), and sentences him as such. The abrupt switch is at least partly explained by the wide judicial discretion held by this municipal justice, which often worked in favor of the defendant, and also by the utilitarian needs of the Crown. The Magistrate condemns Soller to two years "without salary at the oars of His Majestey's galleys."[49] The sentence is less severe than capital punishment and yet still is one of the more brutal forms of slavery in continental Europe during

45 Asensjo González, "El Corregidor," 99–100; Somoza Medina, *As Lagoas*, 38; Somoza Medina, *Ourense*, 58–59; Somoza Medina, *Historia de Ourense*, 54–56.

46 Bermejo Cabrero, *Poder político*, 98, 375.

47 Gallego Domínguez, *A cidade de Ourense*, 134; Somoza Medina, *Historia de Ourense*, 55.

48 Gallego Domínguez and Fariña Busto, "Casas Reales," 209.

49 32^{r}; "en las galeras de Su Majestad a remo y sin sueldo."

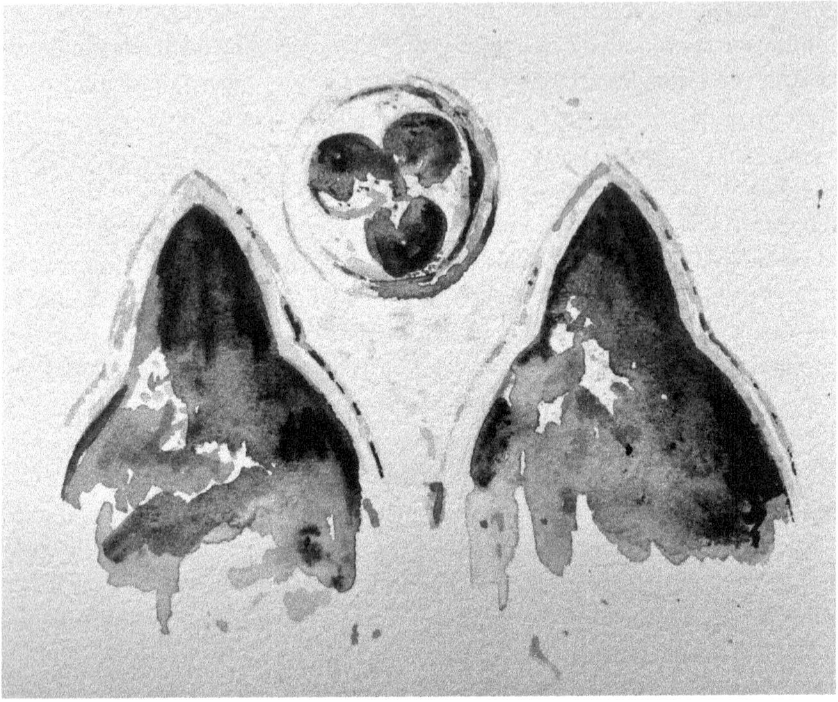

FIGURE 46 Detail of Gothic windows in the House of the Chief Magistrate. Ourense, Spain. Late sixteenth century
Note: This drawing is based on a detail in a photograph taken prior to the demolition of this residence. Gallego Domínguez and Fariña Busto, "Casas Reales," 209.
WATERCOLOR SKETCH BY CLINTON LARISCY

that time. The punishment actually did lead to death for many.[50] Soller does not appear in any other document from the city of Ourense that I could locate.[51]

7 Mulatto Vagabonds

Soller's vagrancy conviction is no huge surprise in part because these sentences were very common, especially for non-whites. In New Spain during the colonial

50 Capital punishment typically was reserved for: high treason (*lèse majesté*) against the Crown; crimes against the faith; homicide; homosexuality and bestiality; and some financial crimes. López Gómez, *Real Audiencia*, 1:252. Since Soller ostensibly is a Christian, he does not seem to have committed a crime against the faith.

51 For example, the proceedings (*actas municipales*) for the *Consello* are missing for the entire century between 1609 and 1709. And while there is a book of decisions (see *Libro de Acuerdos*) for each of the years 1693 and 1694, Soller does not appear within its pages.

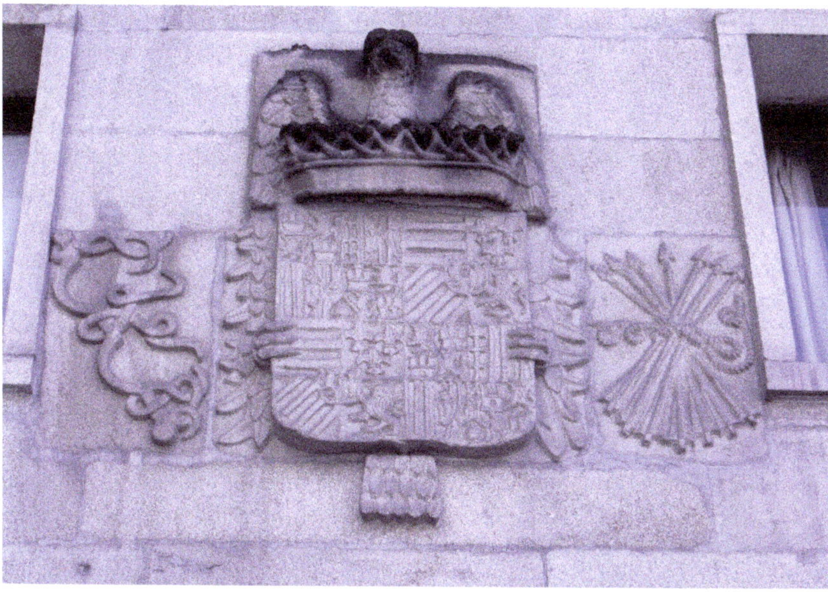

FIGURE 47 Coat of arms recovered from the Casa do Corregidor. Ourense, Spain. Late fifteenth, early sixteenth century
PHOTO BY THE AUTHOR

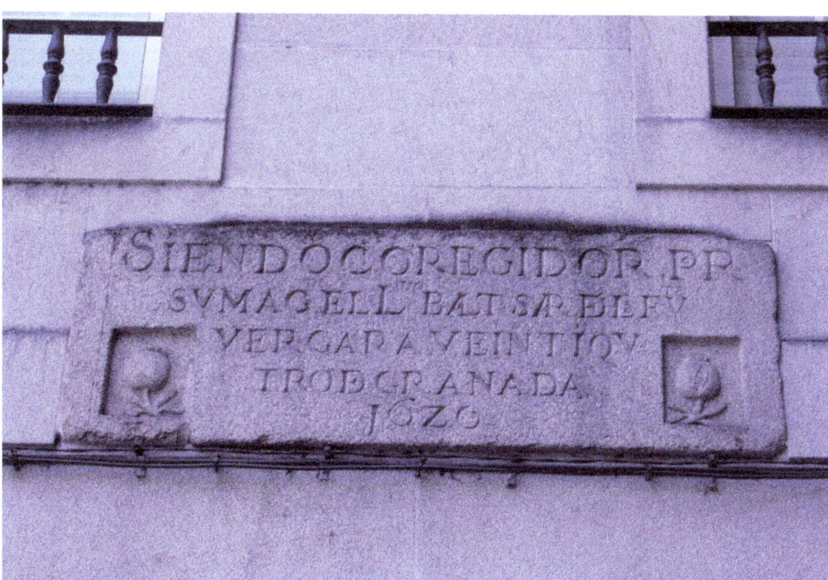

FIGURE 48 Stone inscription recovered from the House of the Corregidor. Ourense, Spain. 1626
PHOTO BY THE AUTHOR

period, for example, "individuals of mixed ancestry—predominantly mestizos and mulatos—were regularly perceived to be listless, wastrels, or vagabonds. This depiction centered on the Spanish belief that such persons were not tied to family and existed in a nebulous space unbounded by Spanish ideals of kinship and family life."[52] Mulattos and mestizos were not even included in a late-sixteenth-century ecclesiastical census because they were believed to be vagabonds in no fixed place.[53]

A law from New Spain (Mexico) dating to the early seventeenth century[54] commands the following:

> That blacks and mulattos not gather in numbers greater than three anywhere, in public or in secret, neither day nor night, whether under the auspices of confraternities or by other means, under penalty of two hundred lashes to each one of those who should be found in said meetings. And may the priors, vicars, and ecclesiastical superiors not allow it. And may all the mulattos and free blacks who may be in this city without a profession consent to serve known masters, where they should be occupied and free from the harmful situations caused by them walking around in the Republic idle and vagrant.[55]

This law is interesting for at least a few reasons. First, it lumps mulattos and blacks together under a single category. Second, it views them both as potentially dangerous when organized together in any type of meeting (*junta*). Third, the law associates blacks and mulattos with vagrancy, which itself is presented as a danger to the realm. In other words, the statute encapsulates the viewpoint of the authorities toward people of black-African descent in the seventeenth century Spanish Empire as a whole. While laws in other Spanish kingdoms proscribe vagabonds and idleness (Cuzco, May 18, 1654; Pamplona, 1662), some to the point of punishing by expulsion (Mallorca, 1612; Valencia, May 8, 1619), this law directly addresses the question of blackness in relation to vagabondage.

---

52 Schwaller, "Mestizos and Mulatos," 716.

53 Schwaller, "Mestizos and Mulatos," 717.

54 *Ordinance and Judgment Agreed upon April 2, 1612. Law 83* (*Ordenanza y Auto acordado el 2 de Abril de 1612. LXXXIII*), 73 (fol. 2).

55 Beleña, *Recopilación sumaria*, 73; "Que los Negros y Mulatos no se junten en más número de tres en ninguna parte pública ni secreta, de dia ni de noche, á título de Cofradias, ó en otra manera, só pena de doscientos azotes á cada uno de los que se hallaren en dichas juntas. Y los Priores, Vicarios y Superiores de los Conventos no lo consientan. Y todos los Mulatos y Negros libres que hubiera en esta Ciudad sin oficio propio, asienten á servir con amos conocidos, donde se entretengan y escusen los daños que se causan de andar en la República ociosos y vagamundos."

These observations beg a critical question: is there a possibility of racialized sentencing in the Soller case? In other words, was he given a harsher sentence by virtue of his blended ethnicity? It is possible. Sweet observes, "A quick survey of those banished to the galleys seems to confirm … that blacks were punished disproportionately … Among the Portuguese only, blacks represented one-quarter of those condemned to galley labor … Most of the black galley laborers were convicted for carrying illegal weapons, usually knives. Others had run away from their masters and were living as 'vagabonds' before being arrested."[56] "Vagabond" is a label authorities like to use when they cannot prove someone who is black also is a fugitive slave, someone like Soller. And a much higher percentage of people of black-African descent are sent to the galleys than are in the population as a whole.

The Deputy Prosecutor certainly employs ethnic stereotypes and may himself be prejudiced against people of color, but such negative traits do not constitute race-based sentencing in and of themselves. In relation to Soller, the Deputy Prosecutor maligns Soller's "idleness" (*ociosidad*) as the "beginning of the ruin of men."[57] Soller's sentence to row at the King's galleys for two years unpaid is at the lower end in the range of penalties for vagabonds during the period and would not seem to be based on his race. Even so, Soller's ethnicity certainly did not help his case.

A white vagabond not prosecuted for his wanderings is Diego de Torres Villarroel. As an elite person of European descent, Torres Villaroel can get away with being a vagrant (*vago*) more easily than can Soller: "I lived vagrant and idle from one town to another, waiting the verdict of the judges and the mercy of the king to restore my citizenship, but my bad luck delayed any relief."[58] Torres Villaroel says that he lived three years in this way, noting especially the deprivation, poverty, and sickness that brought him to the brink of death.[59] Despite his exile, Torres Villaroel wanders freely.

Soller also is not helped by his status as a pilgrim, another group commonly associated with vagabonds. For example, Sebastián de Covarrubias presents an extended definition of wandering (*vagar*) and the long history of legislation against vagabonds:

---

56 Sweet, "African Lisbon," 241–242.

57 29^{r}; "principio a la ruina de los hombres."

58 Torres Villaroel, *Vida*, 161; "Vago y ocioso de uno en otro pueblo vivía yo, esperando en el examen de los jueces y en la piedad del rey la restitución a mi patria, pero mi mala suerte me retardaba los alivios."

59 *Vida*, 162–163.

> Vagabond, he who wanders idle or goes wandering everywhere. There are laws against vagabonds throughout the kingdom, and in every republic these [laws] are well orchestrated because these [vagabonds] are very harmful. And if they [vagabonds] do not have anything to eat, they must pilfer or steal it; this is why Draco, in his cruel laws, condemned them [vagabonds] to death. Moderating this penalty, Solomon declared them to be vile. Our laws force them to work or exile them, and sometimes, finding them to be guilty, either whip them or send them to the galleys. This [vagabondage] is a plague that spreads a lot in kings' courts and in large and populous towns, and for this reason the criminal justices make a great effort to rid the Republic of these bad people. *Bagamundo*, see above, and note that although it may be equivalent to vagabond, some attribute its etymology to certain pilgrims who tend to come from France to Spain, officially to visit the body of Lord Santiago and other sanctuaries; and in olden times a lot of them came from a city in France called Bagamún, which today we call Tornay; and from there they were called *bagamundos*. Better that they should be called vagabonds, from *vagor, aris*.[60]

The wood-cut illustration selected for this entry in Covarrubias is of two rough-looking Santiago pilgrims.[61] A similar association between false pilgrims and vagabonds seems to be at work in the minds of the authorities in the Soller case.[62]

In the sixteenth-century legal code of Felipe II, as we have seen, foreign pilgrims are not to beg alms more than four leagues from their main route. Should

60 Covarrubias, *Tesoro*, 1506; "Vagamundo, el que se anda ocioso o vagando por todas partes. Contra los vagamundos hay leyes del reino, y en todas las repúblicas bien concertadas las tienen, porque estos son muy perjudiciales, y si no tienen de qué comer lo han de hurtar o robar; y por eso Dracón, en sus leyes sangrientas, los condenó a muerte. Solón, moderando esta pena los declaró por infames. Nuestras leyes los compelen a trabajar o los destierran, y a veces, hallando en ellos culpas, o los azotan o los echan a galeras. Esta es una plaga que cunde mucho en las cortes de los reyes y en los lugares grandes y populosos y a esta causa los jueces criminales hacen gran diligencia en limpiar la república desta mala gente. Bagamundo, *vide supra*, y nota que aunque sea lo mesmo que vagamundo le dan algunos origen de ciertos peregrinos que suelen venir de Francia a España, con título de visitar el cuerpo de señor Santiago y otros santuarios; y en tiempos atrás acudieron muchos de una ciudad de Francia dicha Bagamún, que hoy llamamos Tornay; y de allí se dijeron bagamundos. Mejor se dirían vagabundos, de *vagor, aris*."

61 Covarrubias, *Tesoro*, 1506.

62 In Torres Villarroel's eighteenth-century musings, as well, pilgrims (*peregrinos*) and vagabonds (*vagos*) are repeatedly treated as virtual equivalents. Torres Villaroel, *Vida*, 270.

Spaniards wear the pilgrim's habit or foreigners be found without the appropriate dimissory letters (*dimisorias*), they will be found guilty of idle wandering and suffer the penalties assigned to vagabonds in Spain.[63] Not in possession of such *dimisorias*, Soller legally is guilty of being a vagabond. His sentence to row unpaid at the King's galleys is in keeping with the Spanish code of penalties for idle wanderers.

8 Galley Slavery

The sentence Soller received could have been much worse. First of all, he could have been sentenced to hard labor in the mines of Almadén, Spain, which was a principal source of mercury shipped to the New World until the nineteenth century. Conditions were so toxic there that miners regularly contracted mercury poisoning and died as a result. Those sentenced to the mines envied the good fortune of those sent to row at oars of the King's galleys. By the same token, in 1701, several galley oarsmen actually refused to have their sentences reduced by two years and commuted to the mines of Almadén because they knew doing so would be a literal death sentence.[64]

Recommended penalties tended to far outweigh any presumed crime and to be based on the repressive criteria of the Crown, which is another way of saying that sentences were intended to punish and had neither a corrective nor a rehabilitative purpose (a modern approach to punishment, in any case). Seemingly arbitrary legal norms were entangled in a confusing morass: theft and robbery were addressed with the same blunt justice as homicide and murder; bestiality the same as high treason.[65] Soller's penalty might be considered a product of this "legal indeterminacy" (*indeterminación legal*)[66] in which Castilian laws were bendable to the whims of judges, who actively participated in both civil and criminal proceedings via the inquisitorial (i.e., investigative) procedure and who did not have to justify their sentences.[67] Under such legislative guidelines, it seems improbable that Soller's sentence would have been based on ethnicity, but the ruling surely was based on class since members of the nobility or clergy could not be sentenced to the galleys or any other type of forced servitude.

---

63 Felipe II, "Romeros y peregrinos," 199.
64 Heras Santos, "Ejemplaridad, paternalismo y utilitarismo," 195, 206.
65 Guillamón Álvarez and Pérez Hervas, "Los forzados de galeras," 65.
66 Guillamón Álvarez and Pérez Hervas, "Los forzados de galeras," 66.
67 Villalba Pérez, *La administración de justicia*, 25.

The nature of punishment in Old Regime Spain was similar to that which existed elsewhere on the European continent at the time. The courts followed the type of common law known as *ius commune*, which ascribed specific punishments to crimes. This jurisprudence was a hybrid Roman-canon law adapted for the needs of continental Europe from the twelfth through the seventeenth centuries. The civil component incorporated the sixth-century legal code of the Emperor Justinian with jurists' readings of this post classic-period Roman law. These interpretations formed the effective legislation of the continental European realms. Whereas Roman law laid out an example for the actions of the model citizen, canon law set forth a guide for the behavior of a good Christian. *Ius commune* aligned with the interests of monarchs who sought to neutralize subversion and gave them a mechanism for autocratic control over their kingdoms.[68]

There were limits, however, inasmuch as early-modern Castilian kings had to build consensus through consulting their councils in matters that touched all involved (*quod omnes tangit*), but even this practice of consultation was prescribed by *ius commune* and ultimately served to consolidate the interests and power of the Crown.[69] Nonetheless, the more the Spanish monarchs' influence waned over the decadent seventeenth century, the more difficult it became for them to garner the necessary support from the Castilian commonwealth. The Crown's effectiveness was directly tied to its ability to administer justice for the greater good of society.[70] In a paradox of royal power, "Adherence to the rule of law as the foundation of justice made the monarch respected and more capable of guiding political affairs; 'tyranny' led to ineffectual royal government, which increasingly characterized seventeenth-century Hapsburg rule."[71]

On the Iberian Peninsula and Balearic Islands, *ius commune* had formed an integral part of Portuguese law since the fifteenth century, on through the Manueline period, straight up until the 1769 Enlightenment Law of Good Reason (Lei da Bõa Razão).[72] This European Common Law was firmly in effect in seventeenth-century Mallorcan jurisprudence, as well.[73] From the beginning, *ius commune* was assimilated into Spanish law and adapted to suit the needs of Castilian society. Its procedures and prescriptions are contained and described

68 Martínez Martínez, Faustino, "*Ius commune, Utrumque ius*," 373–374, 380–381.
69 González-Varas Ibáñez, "El *ius commune* y la convocatoria de concilios," 163–164.
70 Owens, *"By My Absolute Royal Authority"*, 213, 231.
71 Owens, *"By My Absolute Royal Authority"*, 242.
72 Domingues, "Códices medievais de *ius commune* em Portugal," 743.
73 Planas Roselló, "La recepción del *ius commune*," 582.

in such foundational legal texts as the *Royal Code* (*Fuero Real*) and the *Seven Divisions* (*Siete Partidas*) among others in the Castilian legal canon.[74]

Because by the early modern period many jurists considered the prescribed punishments too harsh, they began applying "arbitrary punishments" which in this case were *not* considered arbitrary in a bad, but in a good sense, because they were less harsh than the punishments ascribed by law (legal doctrine). Hence magistrates had a tendency to give a lesser, more lenient penalty than prescribed[75] and considered whether or not clemency should intervene. (This situation only changes in the post-Beccaria[76] reform period in the eighteenth-century, when judicial free decision, or discretion, gains a negative connotation for being arbitrary.) And so "lower justices enjoyed judicial discretion, but it was always a measured and very restricted discretion that cannot be equated in any way with the arbitrariness about which so many have written without any basis."[77] Similarly, although it sounds plausible that galley service was a means to an end as it supplied free labor, the justification given in the Old Regime was that it replaced death, a much worse penalty, often ascribed by law. Indeed, Hapsburg authorities would commute a convicted felon's death sentence to galley servitude as a form of pardon.[78]

At the same time, the monarchy began to see the prison population in a more utilitarian way as it became increasingly centralized.[79] The Spanish state began to employ prisoners in a whole host of challenging and undesirable environments, including in mines, arsenals, galleys, and so on: "The practice of sending convicts to row began under Fernando and Isabel at the end of the fifteenth century, and these *forzados* gradually replaced the free oarsmen over the course of the sixteenth ... [B]y the late sixteenth century penal servitude in the galleys had become the usual fate for convicted commoners."[80] By the middle of the reign of Felipe II of Spain, many if not most of these galley oarsmen consisted of gypsies and vagabonds given the increasing pressure to more

74 Pérez Martín, *El derecho procesal*, 44.

75 Heras Santos, *La justicia penal*, 212–213; Ortego Gil, "El arbitrio," 140, 142, 147.

76 Martínez Martínez, "*Ius commune, Utrumque ius*," 372–373; Cesare de Bonasana, the Marquis of Beccaria, was an eighteenth-century Enlightenment reformer whose treatise on crime and punishment lambasted what he viewed as the barbarity of the justice system under the Old Regime.

77 Ortego Gil, "El arbitrio," 219; "los jueces inferiores gozaron de arbitrio, pero siempre fue un arbitrio reglado y muy restringido que no puede equipararse, en modo alguno, con la arbitrariedad de la que tantos han escrito sin ningún fundamento."

78 Heras Santos, *La justicia penal*, 49.

79 Pike, *Penal Servitude*, 4.

80 Phillips, *Slavery*, 30.

strictly enforce the laws against this peripatetic population.[81] Legislation and religious charity had failed to solve the social problems of vagabondage and pauperism by the seventeenth century, a reality that precipitated increasingly harsh responses from the Hapsburg regime against vagabonds,[82] especially given the increasing association between these idle wanderers and thieves.[83]

Spanish monarchs from the time of Felipe II were counseled to eliminate vagabonds from society and to call upon marginalized groups such as these to serve the Hapsburg state. After all, those who feigned poverty cast doubt upon the legitimacy of the true poor; that is, the bad example set by vagrants marked both the false poor and true poor as potential delinquents. Authorities hardly distinguished licensed beggars from those who impersonated the poor such as vagabonds, and associated all of them with criminality. By the reign of Felipe III, most social reformers no longer held any sway over the Hapsburg rulers. At the same time, these monarchs needed men for the galleys as much as anything. From the time of Felipe III onward, perceived delinquents and convicted criminals were increasingly forced into service in the King's wars.[84]

Soller's sentence to the galleys fit in with the broader pattern for his time and place, especially given his conviction of being a vagabond. As we have noted, this crime fell well within the range of punishable offenses, and the amount of time sentenced was at the lowest end of the range of possibilities: "In 1552 the penalty for vagabondage was increased to four years on the galleys for the first offense, eight for the second, and life for the third. This legislation defined vagabonds as gypsies, foreign tinkers, and healthy mendicant poor."[85] This Toledo decree sentenced all unlicensed beggars to the galleys as an attempt to exert some measure of civil control over vagabonds.[86] In newer regulations from Book 12 of the *New and Very New Compilation* (*Nueva y Novísima Recopilación*), anybody and everybody—from moriscos to gypsies; from ruffians to slaves; from bigamists to blasphemers, including those labeled vagabonds (*vagos*) such as Soller—was sentenced to the galleys. Sentencing periods varied from a minimum of two years to a maximum of ten years, the latter of which (according to a royal decree of August 10, 1653) was considered

81 Thompson, "A Map of Crime," 245; Sánchez Gómez, *Delincuencia y seguridad*, 179.
82 Cruz, *Discourses of Poverty*, 62.
83 Heras Santos, *La justicia penal*, 305.
84 Cruz, *Discourses of Poverty*, 65–68, 116.
85 Pike, *Penal Servitude*, 6–7.
86 Cruz, *Discourses of Poverty*, 29.

perpetual galley slavery since it was completed in permanent exile.[87] Consider the following exchange from the episode of the galley slaves in *Don Quijote*:

> "What crimes can he have committed," said don Quixote, "if they have only have gotten him put into the galleys?"
> "He's going for ten years," replied the guard, "which is the same as what they call CIVIL DEATH."[88]

Galley service is comparable to exile inasmuch as the latter has represented "civil death" (*mors civilis*), which means death as a citizen, at least since the medieval legal code of Alfonso X. And again, the death penalty was much more severe.

This is why there is a warning attached to Soller's sentence via a violation (*quebrantamiento*) clause admonishing him not to contravene his sentence at the oars "on penalty of death by hanging."[89] Violation clauses typically were used to warn offenders not to repeat the offense or else suffer a far more severe punishment the second time. They also served to lighten the sentence, as a way not to impose the standard penalty established by the law without completely absolving the defendant of the accusation.[90] In this fashion, judges had the discretion to soften the harshness of criminal law.[91] In Soller's case, the violation clause applies not to a repeat offense but rather to his sentence at the galleys, meaning that if he does not serve the two years completely, he will be executed.

Deputy Prosecutor Rodicio fervently advocates for Soller to receive the death penalty, but this outcome does not seem to have ever taken place. Had such a sentence been handed down, the practical enforcement of it may have been the same in any case. For example, a Royal Decree (Pragmática) of October 13, 1639, reaffirms two decrees from the century prior by explicitly recommending that whenever possible, a death penalty sentence be commuted to service in the King's galleys.[92] Carlos I of Spain (Carlos V of the Holy Roman Empire) issued the first of these earlier decrees in Madrid on January 31, 1530, when the nature of the death penalty shifted away from vengeance and intimidation to

---

87 Guillamón Álvarez and Pérez Hervas, "Los forzados de galeras," 64.
88 Cervantes, *Don Quixote*, 161. Cervantes, *Don Quijote*, 1:276; "—¿Qué delitos puede tener—dijo Don Quijote—, si no han merecido más pena que echalle a las galeras? / —Va por diez años—replicó la guarda—, que es como muerte civil."
89 32^r; "pena de muerte de horca."
90 Ortego Gil, "Apercibimientos penales," 16.
91 Ortego Gil, "Apercibimientos penales," 18.
92 Ortego Gil, "La pena de muerte," 147–148.

a utilitarian pragmatism in keeping with the interests of the Crown.[93] Capital punishment could effectively become a civil death in lieu of a physical one, as some of those convicted were sentenced to the galleys in perpetuity or permanent exile.[94] The commutation of the death penalty to galley slavery was largely a by-product of the insatiable needs of the Hapsburg kings for manned labor on their ships, and convicts wound up forming a majority of Spanish galley oarsmen in the Mediterranean theater of war.[95] The marked increase in the substitution of forced labor for the death penalty, and for the terms of these sentences to be continually extended, demonstrates how utilitarian the penal system had become in the seventeenth century.[96]

Compared to sixteenth-century sentences for vagabonds, it might seem that Soller got off extremely easy, but galley oarsmen often were detained for their forced service well beyond the chronological limits of their sentences: "The illegal retention of prisoners after the completion of their sentences was one of the worst abuses of the galleys, and it continued for three centuries. Men were retained beyond their terms because the King needed their services."[97] The demand of the Spanish Crown due to its near-constant war against the Islamic empire in the Mediterranean outstripped the supply of rowers: "Free oarsmen almost disappeared from the Spanish galleys by the end of the sixteenth century, and in the seventeenth century those rowers who bore that title were convict oarsmen or *forzados* who had completed their sentences and were being retained illegally because of the critical shortage of rowers."[98] At 40-some-odd years of age, Soller is at the upper end of the average age range of those sentenced to the galleys, which was anywhere from seventeen to fifty years old.[99] The situation was so acute by the latter part of the seventeenth century, that any sentence to the galleys, whether in a term of years or perpetual servitude, was a sentence for life.[100]

So it is understandable why Soller would have wanted to flee galley slavery, as conditions were so horrid that they often led to death, and perhaps death would be preferable. In any event, "work on the galleys was so hard that very few survived."[101] The French knight François Cocardon, captured by Algerian corsairs,

93 Guillamón Álvarez and Pérez Hervas, "Los forzados de galeras," 63.
94 Ortego Gil, "La pena de muerte," 151.
95 Heras Santos, *La justicia penal*, 316, 326.
96 Heras Santos, "Los galeotes," 289.
97 Pike, *Penal Servitude*, 14.
98 Pike, *Penal Servitude*, 4.
99 Guillamón Álvarez and Pérez Hervas, "Los forzados de galeras," 64–65.
100 Pike, *Penal Servitude*, 14.
101 Bravo Rodríguez, "Matrimonio," 165; "el trabajo en las galeras era tan duro que muy pocos sobrevivían."

said that he knew no man, no matter how bad his crimes, who possibly could deserve the punishment of being a galley oarsman, under which conditions one is a slave. Another of Cocardon's observations is that the galley slaves are forced to relieve themselves right there on rowing bench, which compares unfavorably to being held in prison, where at least one has a bucket to go in and a lid to trap the stench. The oarsmen's diet consisted of hardtack, essentially unleavened wheat bread cooked twice to stop the process of fermentation, so hard it had to be dipped in water, the one other option on the menu. The chronicler of Carlos V, Brother (Fray) Antonio de Guevara, commented about the galley oarsmen—tongue firmly planted in cheek—that it was their great privilege to eat this hardtack, so long as it was worm-eaten, covered in spider webs, and moldy, and to not ask for clear, cool, and clean water but rather only turbid, hot, swamp water. While this sad state of affairs may have been the case for many galley slaves, in reality they also got a pot of beans and a bowl of soup made from the bits of leftover hardtack.[102] And yet even these meager rations were reduced due to shortages of both flour and beans at the end of the seventeenth century.[103]

Another facet of the life of the galley oarsman was being continually splashed by the stinging waves. While they could cover themselves at night with canvas tarps, the galley slaves could not do so while rowing during the day. The sea-water on their backs left a salty residue that caused their skin to burn. The rowing itself required considerable strength: "The arms were not the only members that were exercised. The handling of the oar required a continual back-and-forth of the whole body. One had to stand up and sit down continually, moving forward and backward in this fashion, without stopping."[104] Cocardon describes the experience as a process of continually dying that destroyed the oarsmen's muscles and bodies so completely that they hardly felt any pain. Unsurprisingly, people got sick, wounded, or were killed, often by pirates who boarded the ship. In the event of shipwreck, the galley oarsmen drowned because they were chained and nailed to the rowing bench: "What made the galleys so feared in the popular consciousness was the loss of freedom that they represented—particularly the practice of chaining men to their benches and

102 Heras Santos, "Los galeotes," 294–296.

103 Pike, *Penal Servitude*, 22.

104 Heras Santos, "Los galeotes," 296; "Los brazos no eran los únicos miembros que se ejercitaban. El manejo del remo requería un ajetreo continuo de todo el cuerpo. Había que levantarse y sentarse continuamente, avanzar adelante y hacia atrás; y así continuamente, sin parar."

the uncertainty of release."[105] The mortality rate of the galley slaves rose from an already high thirteen percent in the sixteenth century to as much as seventeen percent of oarsmen in the eighteenth century who died before being discharged.[106]

In the *Trials of Persiles and Sigismunda*, there are two newly freed galley slaves who, next to the heavy chains they recently have shed, narrate their misadventures to the pilgrims via a small painting shown and described to the travelers. As the "freed captive" (*libre cautivo*) puts it:

> This ship, which you see reduced in size here because the picture requires it, is a small galley with twenty-two benches whose master and captain is the Turk standing on the center runway between the two lines of oarsmen; he's holding in his hand an arm he's cut from the Christian you see over there in order to use it as a whip and lash for the other Christians tied to the benches. He's afraid he'll be overtaken by these four galleys you see here, which are chasing and closing in on him. That first captive on the first bench, whose face is stained by the blood that has stuck to it from the blows with the dead arm, is I myself, who acted as the stroke on this galley, and the other man next to me is my companion here, who isn't so bloody because he'd been beaten less.[107]

This fictionalized account—though clearly an exaggeration—represents at least some shade of the truth behind the historical reality of the sheer brutality of galley enslavement.

The demand was so great for galley rowers that "it became standard practice to take convicted offenders who were awaiting the outcome of their appeals in jails to serve during the interim (*en depósito*) on the galleys. Although the legality of this practice was questionable, it was deemed necessary in view of the

---

105 Pike, *Penal Servitude*, 17.

106 Heras Santos, "Los galeotes," 296–297.

107 Cervantes, *Trials of Persiles*, 251. Cervantes, *Persiles y Segismunda*, 332; "es una galeota de veintidós bancos, cuyo dueño y capitán es el turco que en la crujía va en pie, con un brazo en la mano, que cortó a aquel cristiano que allí veis, para que le sirva de rebenque y azote a los demás cristianos que van amarrados a sus bancos, temeroso no le alcancen estas cuatro galeras que aquí veis, que le van entrando y dando caza. Aquel cautivo primero del primer banco, cuyo rostro le desfigura la sangre que se le ha pegado de los golpes del brazo muerto, soy yo, que servía de espalder en esta galeota, y el otro que está junto a mí, es este mi compañero, no tan sangriento porque fue menos apaleado."

long delays involved in the appeals system."[108] Such delays gave prisoners time to escape. To avoid this problem or others, "Convicted criminals sentenced to the galleys were sent by their local justices to the central prisons (*depósitos de rematados a galeras*) of their respective judicial areas (Toledo, Soria, Valladolid, Seville, Granada). When enough of them were gathered (not less than twelve), they were chained together and manacled and marched overland under heavy guard until they reached the galleys."[109] Such chained prisoners are closely related to those forced to serve (*forzados*) seen above in the episode of the galley slaves (*galeotes*) in *Don Quijote*. These *forzados* are "'men sentenced by the king and forced to row in his galleys ... [T]hese are people who, because of their crimes, are sentenced to serve the king in galleys, by force'" in Sancho Panza's formulation.[110] Valladolid would have been the closest central prison to Ourense.

When I spoke about Soller's case with prisoners in Alabama, most were convinced that this convicted vagabond was sent to the galleys immediately and then unjustly tried in absentia. Such is these felons' confidence (or lack thereof) in the justice system of this formerly Spanish jurisdiction.[111] Nonetheless, I have found no direct evidence that Soller was sent forcibly to Valladolid or anywhere else in one of the chain gangs or that he was forced to serve his sentence prior to learning the outcome of his appeal. Moreover, Carlos II himself intervened at the end of the seventeenth century to command municipal justices to send appellants directly to the jails of the Royal Chancery in lieu of allowing the abusive enforcement of their sentences pending appeal.[112]

Several regulations in place at the time stipulated that such prisoners did not have to report for duty until their sentences were upheld on appeal, thus buying them all the time they needed to escape from such a harsh fate. It became extremely common for defendants sentenced to the galleys to break free from their jail cells.[113] And remember, nearly three-quarters of all convicts in Haps-

108 Pike, *Penal Servitude*, 7.

109 Pike, *Penal Servitude*, 18.

110 Cervantes, *Don Quixote*, 156. Cervantes, *Don Quijote*, 1:270; "gente forzada del rey, que va a las galeras ... [E]s gente que por sus delitos va condenada a servir al rey en las galeras, de por fuerza." There were two main types of galley slaves: *arráeces*, who "were held as slaves permanently" and those "sentenced to the galleys after having been convicted of a crime" but who never again attained their freedom. Phillips, *Slavery*, 31.

111 Author talk to (and conversation with) prisoners in the Donaldson Correctional Facility in Bessemer, Alabama on May 10, 2016.

112 Heras Santos, *La justicia penal*, 313.

113 Guillamón Álvarez and Pérez Hervas, "Los forzados de galeras," 64.

burg Spain never even served their sentences because they had escaped.[114] Soller may have been one of these who never reached the galleys; after all, he was tried "in absentia" (*en rebeldía*), literally "in rebellion," possibly for having made a jailbreak.

9 Absent and in Rebellion

Circumstances in Galician jails were such that there were frequent escapes. The situation was so dire by the eighteenth century in the court system of this kingdom that most criminal defendants were absent from trial, escaped from prison, or both. Flights from jail were the norm. The proximity to Portugal made such escapes fairly easy and common.[115] This was doubly the case for Ourense, as close as it is to thoroughfares leading to Braga or especially Chaves in Portugal,[116] as close as it was to the free haven for vagabonds known as Couto Mixto (figure 1 and part 1, chapters 2 and 7) on the border of Spain and Portugal—roughly 35 miles (56 km), or 70 percent of the distance Soller traversed in a single day between Coimbra and Tomar, Portugal.

Regarding any possible jailbreak, we might bear in mind the Magistrate's sentence for Soller's vagabondage: "I should sentence and do sentence him to serve in His Majesty's galley ships for two years, rowing without pay. Having begun to fulfill them, he may not violate them, on penalty of death by hanging."[117] Had Soller already begun to serve out this sentence prior to his appeal, then the defendant would not have been able to appear in the appeals trial in A Coruña due to the inflexible nature of this violation clause. The sentence was issued September 5, 1693. The appeal is filed just over a month later on October 13 of the same year.[118] At any rate, October 13, 1693, is the earliest date mentioned in the appeal. Clearly there would have been time for Soller to have begun his sentence. There is no indication, however, that Soller did in fact begin to row in the galley ships of His Majesty, Carlos II.

The primary indication that Soller did *not* begin to serve out his sentence would be the term used for Soller's absence during his appeal: "in absentia,"

---

114 Heras Santos, *La justicia penal*, 39.

115 Ortega Costa 23, 27; López Gómez, *Real Audiencia*, 1:255–256; López Gómez, "Sala del Crimen," 318.

116 Somoza Medina, *Historia de Ourense*, 45.

117 31[v]; "le debo de condenar y condeno a que sirva en las galeras de Su Majestad por dos años al remo y sin sueldo. Y habiendo empezado a cumplirlos, no los quebrante, pena de muerte de horca."

118 33[v].

or *en rebeldía*, literally "in rebellion." The basic idea of *en rebeldía* is that "the defendant has the duty to respond, to show up in person at the trial. This idea has been the unchanging basis of civil proceedings at every moment [in legal history]. Without this concept, the administration of justice and judicial protection are impossible."[119] Soller's is a criminal and not a civil proceeding, which is why such would have been all the more the case for him. A judgment rendered *en rebeldía* is a manifestation and consequence of being held in contempt (*contumacia*) of court. In Germanic law, a sentence issued *en rebeldía* applies only to the one against whom it is ordered,[120] and the situation is not so different in Spanish law.

Covarrubias describes *rebeldía* as a "legal term" for "when the one who is summoned and ordered to appear in court does not appear."[121] The *Dictionary of the Authorities* (*Diccionario de Autoridades*) gives a similar meaning: "In the legal realm it is understood as the defendant's or the plaintiff's neglect or delay in responding or appearing at trial in the period of the summons or order to appear given by the judge."[122] If one is judged *en rebeldía*, this means that one is not present, in other words, that one ignores the judge's formal subpoena.

Even in the case that Soller had not been moved from Ourense to A Coruña for the appeal, which would be extremely rare, he at least would have been represented by a lawyer and would have presented a written response to the prosecutor. This is especially the case since the Lords Governor and Judges "ordered to notify the opposing party"[123] that the King's Representative had introduced his response to Soller's appeal. But there is no response from Soller's side. It would appear that José Soller had escaped from jail by this time.

Soller should have been present at his own appeal and was not. *Rebeldía* is the failure to proceed judicially and refers not only to the absence of the party but also to that of his lawyer or other legal representative.[124] Both Soller and his public defender (*procurador de pobres*) fail to appear for the appeal. In other

---

119 Wach, *Conferencias*, 170; "para el demandado existe el deber de responder, de apersonarse en el proceso. Esta idea ha sido la base invariable del procedimiento civil en todos los tiempos. Sin ella, la administración de justicia y la protección jurídica son imposibles."

120 Wach, *Conferencias*, 216.

121 Covarrubias, *Tesoro*, 1396; "término forense, cuando no comparece el que está citado y llamado."

122 Real Academia Española, *Diccionario* 3:507; "En lo forense se toma por la omisión y tardanza en responder, o comparecer en juicio el reo u actor, en el término de la citación o llamamiento hecho por el Juez." Such is the case in Germanic law, as well. Wach, *Conferencias*, 174.

123 33^{v}; "mandaron dar *treslado* a la contraria."

124 Wach, *Conferencias*, 174.

words, in cases such as that of Soller, he would have been compelled to appear in court had he still been in jail or anywhere in custody.

Usually, *en rebeldía* sentences are reserved until such time as the accused is apprehended. However, Soller fails to appear in the courtroom (*sala*) of the Royal Appellate Court (Real Audiencia), and moreover, no sentence ever is given.[125] The fact is, Soller's sentence on appeal no longer exists. We do not know what was decided in A Coruña in the Real Audiencia or why the initial appeal was decided "in disagreement" (*en discordia*) among the justices involved. This appellate court and other *audiencias* tended to keep books where the judges recorded their individual votes (*libros de votos*), but these books were kept secret. This particular one from Galicia may not have survived.

In the appeal, Soller's perceived status as a fugitive and his perceived flight receive a great deal of attention.[126] Could this be because Soller had broken free of jail? On the very next folio, Court Clerk Montes is described as "absent" (*ausente*),[127] a term that easily could have been applicable to Soller, as well, had it been so simple a matter as Soller having been absent for reasons beyond his control.

It was not unusual for absentee criminal defendants in this time and place to be prosecuted and sentenced despite their having fled. In fact, over 55% of those sentenced in The Hall of Mayors of the Royal Household and Court (Sala de Alcaldes de Casa y Corte) had fled in 1693, the same year as that of Soller's original and only definitive sentence. This and other superior courts and royal councils could and did regularly proceed with delivering in absentia verdicts and sentences in the early-modern Spanish kingdoms.[128] No known judgment, however, is rendered in Soller's appeal.

Continuing the proceedings despite the absence of one of the parties is not completely anathema to contemporary legal practices in the United States:

125 The register of the Royal Appellate Court's *Rulings* (*Sentencias*) comprising decisions for 1694 does not contain any sentence whatsoever for Soller. In fact, only two sentences at all are preserved for 1694. In this court's *Petitions* (*Pedimentos*) file, there is nothing at all for the year 1694. Nothing from 1693 appears in either file bundle.

126 33^{r}.

127 34^{r}.

128 Heras Santos, *La justicia penal*, 54, 188. For Alberto Montoro Ballesteros, the absence of one of the parties does not constitute an excuse for allowing the administration of justice to be thwarted. Montoro Ballesteros, *Conflicto social*, 86. Sergio Cotta argues that a judgment rendered against an absent defendant is not so much a ruling against a man as it is against a thing (his crime). Regardless of the evidence, due to the absence of the accused during the proceedings judgments rendered in contempt (*en contumacia*) for being in absentia (*en rebeldía*) are always false and imperfect. Cotta, *Itinerarios humanos*, 39.

> In a criminal case, if the defendant's absence (failure to appear) is shown to be willful and intentional (or if by his or her behavior the defendant has been excluded from the courtroom), the court can proceed with a trial without the defendant being present and a verdict can be lawfully returned. In most jurisdictions a criminal defendant may not be sentenced in absentia, however. When the defendant fails to appear at trial, generally speaking an arrest warrant will issue, and the proceedings are stayed pending the arrest or return of the defendant. It would be unheard of for the case to proceed to trial if it was not already set to go forward.[129]

Undergirding this reluctance to proceed unless absolutely necessary lies the assumption that in absentia sentences are inherently flawed.

Such thinking eventually additionally took hold in modern constitutional Spanish law, in which sentences rendered *en rebeldía* are invalidated by the absence of the defendant. Such in absentia proceedings are considered contrary to the individual right of the accused to be present. This means that under article 841 in the Spanish Criminal Trial Law (Ley de Enjuiciamiento Criminal) of 1882, no defendant can be convicted in absentia. However, articles 9 and 10 of the law of December 2, 1963, from the Court of Public Order (Tribunal de Orden Público) in Madrid do allow a verdict and sentence to be rendered to an absent defendant.[130] No such vacillation existed in seventeenth-century Spanish law. Individuals could be and were sentenced in absentia on a regular basis. The distinct judicial perspectives on this issue are at least in part a result of the difference between inquisitorial and adversarial law, between presumption of guilt and presumption of innocence.

There are a number of proceedings contemporaneous with those of Soller in which the trials continued in the absence of one of the parties, usually the defendant. One such sentence *en rebeldía* was pronounced in 1688 against one Juan Carrasco, the mulatto slave of an abusive land-grant holder (*encomendero*), Captain Don Diego Eugenio Saenz de Rojas in Nueva Andalucía, the province immediately to the east of the province of Venezuela and to the north of Guyana, north of the Orinoco River. Carrasco himself reportedly had harmed the native indentured servants on the estate and did not appear in court with his master. He nonetheless was sentenced *en rebeldía* to 200 lashes of the whip while being tethered to the pillory. Importantly, Carrasco was sentenced not only for his own injurious behavior toward the King's vassals, the Indians, but

129 Communication via email from Benjamin L. McGowan, Esquire. October 30, 2014.
130 Morón, *Reflexiones*, 11.

also for his disobedience in failing to appear himself.[131] This sentence surely was intended to be enforced once Carrasco was apprehended.

In the mid-seventeenth century, a Senior Magistrate (Alcalde Mayor) of the Royal Appellate Court (Real Audiencia) of Galicia, Antonio Coelho, whose rank was just below that of Judge (Oidor) and who had as his primary objective the prosecution of all criminal cases in the entire kingdom of Galicia, prosecuted Jerónimo de Montero and Francisco Jimeno, who had allowed presumed assassins into their home and who fled once they heard Coelho was coming for them. The departure of Montero and Jimeno did not stop Coelho from prosecuting them in absentia after they had escaped. Their absence did not prevent them from being condemned to death, losing half their belongings, and being fined 500 ducats.[132]

In an anomaly among the realms of Spain, proceedings held *en rebeldía* were forbidden in Mallorca until 1625, when Felipe IV tried to introduce trials similar to those held in most other Spanish kingdoms. Despite a good deal of controversy and resistance among Aragon's institutions and estates, which led to the suspension of much of Felipe IV's order imposing in-absentia rulings, a variety of measures ensured that justice would be served to those who had fled: the absentee defendant was presumed guilty; it was assured that corporal punishment would be administered once the defendant was captured; and it was inadmissible for a defendant convicted *en rebeldía* to appeal a fine beyond a year and a day from the date of a guilty sentence. Under Bourbon Monarch Felipe V in the first part of the eighteenth century, the law governing in absentia proceedings was fully in line with that of the other kingdoms in Spain.[133] All of the preceding assumes absentee defendants have fled.

Take the case of Francesc García, leader of the peasant revolt of 1693 in the Spanish kingdom of Valencia and convicted *en rebeldía* in 1694. This fugitive never was captured.[134] In this example from Carlos II's reign, one of the two leaders of the rebellion in Valencia is judged in absentia because he cannot be captured, in other words, because he has escaped: "Francesc García was judged in absentia and sentenced to die in January of 1694, although they never did capture him."[135] There is a strong parallel with Soller's situation here. This *en*

131 Prato-Perelli, *Las encomiendas*, 1:282, 3:219.

132 Blázquez Miguel, *Yecla*, 416.

133 Planas Roselló, "El proceso penal," 119–120.

134 Molas Ribalta et al., *La transición*, 200.

135 Ribot García, "España de Carlos II," 200; "Francesc García fue juzgado en rebeldía y condenado a muerte en enero de 1694, aunque jamás lograron capturarle." Rodríguez Flores

rebeldía sentencing even transpires in 1694, the very same year that Soller's appeal is "adjourned in disagreement among the magistrates."[136]

The King's Representative certainly believes the Chief Magistrate's sentence is insufficiently rigorous, which is why he responds so vigorously to the appeal. He uses the word "lenient" (*begnina*)[137] to describe what he perceives as the Chief Magistrate's permissiveness. In seventeenth-century Galicia, however, actual capital punishment tended to be reserved for the most serious crimes only, such as those involving homicide, high treason, forging money, et cetera.[138] Also, the Real Audiencia overturned lower court rulings imposing the death penalty more than this Royal Appellate Court imposed the death penalty upon appeal.[139] In fact, in all of the seventeenth century, the data indicates that the death penalty was imposed only 1.7% of the time by the Real Audiencia. And importantly, the vast majority of those sentenced to die had to be judged *en rebeldía* because they were absent for having fled to nearby Portugal.[140] This statistic is specific to Galicia. In this kingdom, therefore, it apparently was not uncommon for convicted criminals to flee justice. Though not sentenced to die (being a vagabond was not supposed to be an offense punishable by death anyway),[141] Soller nonetheless seems to have been one of these fugitives since he, too, was judged at the appellate level *en rebelión*.

---

describes sixteenth-, seventeenth-, and eighteenth-century legal cases in which a family member begs pardon for a defendant convicted *en rebeldía* who remains absent. Some of these cases use both terms, *rebelión* and *ausencia*, together, implying a distinction in meaning. *El perdón real*, 96, 96n9. In other words, the defendants were convicted of having fled both the proceedings and the verdict.

136 Cov. 1; "visto en la discordia." At the appeals level, there had to be at least three judges voting in agreement for the appeal to be decided. López Gómez, *Real Audiencia*, 1:227. This principle is the precedent for article 262 of the current Spanish constitution, which breaks a tie vote via the Court of Disagreement (Sala de Discordia) which produces new hearings with additional judges, totaling an odd number, until a majority decision is reached. Santaolalla López, "El voto de calidad," 204, 204n7. There were only two out of three votes in agreement in the Soller case, which is why the decision is described as in disagreement (*discordia*).

137 33^{r}.

138 Cuello Calón, "Contribución al estudio," 14–19; Ortego Gil, "La pena de muerte," 152.

139 Ortego Gil, "La pena de muerte," 152.

140 Ortega Gil, "La pena de muerte" 154, 167.

141 Death penalty decisions could be appealed to the Chancery (*Chancillería*) of Valladolid, which effectively was the Supreme Court of Spain until 1834. López Gómez, *Real Audiencia*, 1:228. Had the King's Representative been successful in getting the death penalty assigned to Soller, the latter would have been able to appeal the decision to the highest court in the land. My search of the online archives of the *Chancillería* of Valladolid, however, did not produce any case with Soller's name.

By the time of Soller's appeal to the Royal Appellate Court of Galicia in A Coruña, this elusive man of color has disappeared from the text, from the trial, and apparently from the custody of the Chief Magistrate, whose house in Ourense was attached to the jail tower where Soller was held. By this point in the story, Soller is judged *en rebeldía*, when he clearly should have been present at trial to answer charges and easily could have been compelled to appear in court—had he still been a prisoner. It appears that by the end of the legal case, our José Soller has made a jailbreak.

10 The Appeal

In Castilian law, making an appeal required permission, and this decision, like so many others, was left to the discretion of the municipal trial justices.[142] It always was the convicted felon who requested these licenses. The right of the Crown's vassals to appeal what they perceived to be unjust or unreasonable sentences was established in principle in the thirteenth-century legal code of Alfonso X and became codified Castilian law by the middle of the following century.[143] Royal subjects could appeal the first-instance rulings of the municipal justice to the relevant appellate authority, including the Royal Appellate Court and others among the Monarch's tribunals.[144] Moreover, entering an appeal not only was guaranteed to Soller as a right but also would have been fairly easy for him to do: "a litigant had only to justify it in terms of natural law, stating that the inherent justice of his case had been ignored or denied by the presiding magistrate."[145] This is why the royal courts became clogged with appeals and why convicted felons so often used the appeal to delay the effective date of their trial-court sentences. Usage of the appeal-as-delay tactic was especially popular among those defendants sentenced to the galleys, who constituted a full eighty percent of all prisoners being held in the sixteenth- and seventeenth-century Crown of Castile.[146]

It therefore seems logical to surmise that Soller appealed his conviction (arguing that he was a pilgrim, not a vagabond) and that the King's Representative (*fiscal*) responded, this response being the document we currently have. That is, it seems we are missing a first part, which included first the permission

---

142 Heras Santos, *La justicia penal*, 185.
143 Kagan, *Lawsuits and Litigants*, 47.
144 López Díaz, "La administración de la justicia señorial," 566–567, 587.
145 Kagan, *Lawsuits and Litigants*, 48.
146 Heras Santos, *La justicia penal*, 276–280.

to appeal and then Soller's appeal. In other words, because there is no license to enter an appeal, it is clear that something is missing, and this would seem to include not only the license but also Soller's initial appeal. The text itself lends to such a conclusion, as the *fiscal* argues that these proceedings "come on appeal."[147] It is clear, regardless of the appeal, that Soller neither was fully what he alleged—a pilgrim barber herbalist from Santo Domingo somehow associated with the Count of Alayos who tried to smooth his travels by giving the impression he was a cleric—nor was he necessarily what the representatives of the Crown alleged—that he was a worthless vagabond, fugitive slave, and criminal. It is, however, clear that he was not an upstanding, firmly rooted, and gainfully employed citizen resident (*vecino*) anywhere. It would appear that the King's Representative then takes advantage of this opportunity to request a harsher punishment.

The various parties to the case include the *fiscal*, the lawyers, and the accused, who did not know which judge would decide his case, much less the order of actions this judge would take. The Real Audiencia had various member courts at the territorial level within Galicia. This tribunal judged all cases, whether criminal or civil, within five leagues of A Coruña, where it was headquartered, and all appeals from the entire kingdom of Galicia.[148] Soller's case is an appeal since Ourense, where the initial trial took place, is far more than five leagues' distance (roughly 12 miles or 18 km) away from A Coruña.[149] Once again, the purpose of the Royal Appellate Court was not to protect the weak but rather to preserve the established order and to safeguard the system of privileges belonging to the Old Regime.[150]

One might presume that Soller's case was an entirely civil affair and therefore would not have passed through ecclesiastical courts and that this is why all the records are from civil authorities. However, the Royal Appellate Court of Galicia appears to have handled ecclesiastical cases, as well. In fact, there effectively was a turf war between the Royal Appellate Court of Galicia and the

---

147 33^r; "vienen por apelación."

148 López Gómez, *Real Audiencia*, 1:224–225.

149 The Royal Tribunal was situated in A Coruña and not Santiago de Compostela to move it outside the jurisdiction and beyond the sphere of influence of the Archbishop of Santiago. López Gómez, *Real Audiencia*, 1:676.

150 One facet of such hegemony is the imposition of Castilian Spanish and the exclusion of Galician as the official language of these trial documents. López Gómez, *Real Audiencia*, 2:1391–1392. And yet there are traces of Galician and Portuguese throughout the text that cannot be erased and which could not be suppressed. See the Linguistic Variants index (part 3).

Inquisition in this region. Others may presume the involvement of the Spanish Inquisition in cases such as Soller's, but this scenario is far from reality.

There was huge anti-Inquisition sentiment in early-modern Galicia: in part due to the abuses of the Holy Office's bureaucrats; partially as portion of the aftermath the horrible plague of 1598; and due as well to the open territorial battle between the Royal Appellate Court of Galicia, allied with the Church and local authorities, and the Spanish Inquisition. Local bishops handled matters of heterodoxy quite well on their own in their view, and the atmosphere could not have been more hostile between the two entities. The Inquisition was mostly inactive in Galicia after 1650 and was basically defunct here after 1678.[151] The Royal Appellate Court had a strong aversion to the Inquisition and its interference within its jurisdiction.[152]

11 Jurisdiction

It was a crime in jurisdictions belonging to the Inquisition to pretend to be a priest, and yet in the eighteenth century, this practice was not uncommon given that in so doing, one fairly easily could earn a living giving spiritual counsel and advice to one's neighbor.[153] This reality was equally true during the seventeenth century in Spain and Portugal. As early as the fifteenth century, it was considered licit to cloak or conceal, that is, to dissimulate, so long as such an action was not intended to harm another; at the same time to pretend, to simulate, generally was considered to be deception or trickery and therefore unacceptable. By the seventeenth century, it was a baroque commonplace to state that that rulers who do not dissimulate do not know how to govern.[154]

As discussed earlier (part 1, chapter 4), one seventeenth-century Mexican figure in New Spain who passed himself off as a priest successfully for an extended period of time is Martín Garatuza. In an auto-da-fé in 1648, Garatuza, who had led Mass in the Cathedral of Mexico City several times, received 200 lashes for his mockery of justice and of the Inquisition in New Spain.[155] Back in old Spain, while the Inquisition did not have jurisdiction in lands covered by the Royal

151 López Gómez, *Real Audiencia*, 1:444, 447.

152 The rivalry between the Dominicans and Franciscans had something to do with the conflict, which may account for why the latter maintained the Archive of the Real Audiencia. López Gómez, *Real Audiencia*, 2:1406–1407.

153 Torquemada, *La Inquisición*, 184.

154 Carrasco Manchado, "'Simular' y 'disimular,'" 343–345, 352.

155 Cordero y Torres, "Martín Garatuza," 271.

Appellate Court of Galicia, the fears of exactly this type of passing and ridicule of the law can be seen in Soller's trial proceedings. For instance, the concept of "public vengeance" (*vindicta pública*)[156] figures prominently in the arguments of Deputy Prosecutor Rodicio, who wishes to make an example of Soller for the betterment of society.

A sentence from the Inquisition for impersonating a priest could be far worse than what Garatuza received from the Holy Office in Mexico, and especially than what Soller received from the Chief Magistrate in Ourense, Spain. For impersonating a priest, the Spanish Inquisition condemned Benito Ferrer in 1624 to be burned alive at the Fuencarral Gate in the north of Madrid.[157] As we just have seen, the Inquisition hardly operated in seventeenth-century Galicia, where the Royal Appellate Court ruled supreme at the regional level.

Regardless, although it is true that the Inquisition could have persecuted (and did persecute) someone who impersonated a priest (because it would be heretical, and heresy was under the jurisdiction of the Inquisition), from the way this process was managed it is clear that impersonation was a means to argue that the suspect was a vagabond and that he was trying to conceal his true nature. That is, whoever denounced, prosecuted, and sentenced Soller was not interested in his religious beliefs, which is what the Inquisition would be charged with, but with social order, which is what the royal courts were about. Jurisdiction matters.

12 Caveats

Even though the two held separate jurisdictions, one might make an analogy between how the case files of the Royal Appellate Court of Galicia and those of the Inquisition should be interpreted. Consider Stuart Schwartz's observation on the trepidation required when evaluating the archives of the Inquisition:

> [I]t would be naïve to think that these archives are ... unproblematic, and they must always be used with caution. The very conditions under which testimony was gathered, including the disparity of power between the individual and the Church, the shadow of an omnipresent implicit threat of torture, the unequal dialogue between the learned inquisitors and their often unlettered prisoners, and the multiple strategies of

156 20ʳ, 27ʳ.

157 Rincón García, "La Plaza Mayor española," 277.

> accused, accusers, and witnesses, complicate the use of these records. Confessions were not necessarily expressions of true belief, nor were charges and accusations free of other motivations. Often the value of the records lies as much in what they reveal about the mental frameworks of inquisitors and accused as it does in the veracity of a specific charge of a defense.[158]

Confessions in the trials at the level of the Royal Appellate Court of Galicia likewise were elicited by means of torture, depending in large measure on the physical strength and psychological composure of the criminal suspect.[159] At the appellate level, torture was considered "a fundamental element in establishing the defendant's confession. Physical and psychological torture [were] practiced in an atmosphere of terror and aggression, and without any guarantee for the accused, and without any responsibility on the part of the magistrates in the event of injury or harm."[160] Above any moral or ethical concerns, the authorities viewed torture and violence as an efficient political tool essential to the inquisitorial method.[161] However, the trial described here happened in front of the Corregidor of Ourense, not the Audiencia.

Torture was applied by both the Inquisition and the regular courts because the best proof was considered to be a confession. Torture was a recognized part of the procedure. As a result, if Soller had been tortured by the Corregidor, we would have known: it always forms part of the proceedings and is documented in them (the fact that he was tortured, the confession under torture, and the confirmation of it after torture, et cetera). The chances that the Audiencia would have tortured him are zero not only because Soller was absent but because it rarely did in cases of appeal, in which proofs normally would not be submitted.

It is not just the Inquisition's records that give one pause in this regard. Virtually any colonial and imperial record, including the case files of the Royal Appellate Court of Galicia, must be considered in light of its intention and practices:

158 Schwartz, *All Can Be Saved*, 9.

159 López Gómez, *Real Audiencia*, 1:251.

160 López Gómez, *Real Audiencia*, 1:251; "un elemento fundamental en establecer la confesión del reo. Torturas físicas y psíquicas, practicadas en un clima de terror y agresividad, y sin ninguna garantía para el acusado, y sin la responsibilidad alguna para los jueces en caso de lesiones o daño."

161 López Gómez, *Real Audiencia*, 1:251.

> Early modern state power was tenuous, shallow, and weak. Terms like "conquest" and "slavery," with all their latent and explicit references to European dominance over Indians and Africans, can obscure as much as they illuminate. They are abstractions reinforced by a historiography that relies upon the paperwork left behind by lay and clerical European settlers and imperial bureaucracies. Extant archives register the everyday operations of the various local and state powers and therefore register their aspirations of mastery and sovereignty rather than the complicated and endlessly negotiated on-the-ground realities of life in the Americas.[162]

This legal case is just such a document, the Royal Appellate Court of Galicia just such an imperial bureaucracy.

Labels such as "slave" in this context can be misleading. In other words, even though Soller "seems to be a slave"[163] to the Chief Magistrate and a "fugitive slave"[164] to the Deputy Prosecutor and to the King's Representative in the trial proceedings, this does not mean Soller actually was a runaway slave, not by any means. Such comments are more akin to the rhetorical strategies of the conquistadors. As conveyed in Laila Lalami's fictionalized perspective of the historical slave Estebanillo, a member of the Pánfilo de Narváez expedition to Florida, begun in 1527: "How strange, I remember thinking, how utterly strange were the ways of the Castilians—just by saying that something was so, they believed that it was. I know now that these conquerors, like many others before them, and no doubt like others after, gave speeches not to voice the truth, but to create it."[165] The Soller case and other such records must be considered in light of this troubling difference—between what the prosecuting authorities wish to impart as true in the historical record versus what the average defendant's everyday reality truly was.[166] This legal case reveals the authorities' desire for mastery more than their actual power over José Soller.

---

162 Cañizares-Esguerra, Childs, and Sidbury, *Black Urban Atlantic*, 7.
163 1^{r}; "parece ser esclavo."
164 24^{r}; "esclavo fugitivo." 33^{r}; "esclavo fugetivo."
165 Lalami, *The Moor's Account*, 10.
166 Cañizares-Esguerra, Childs, and Sidbury, *Black Urban Atlantic*, 16.

13 End of Story?

As if borrowed from the post-modern pages of Jorge Luis Borges or Julio Cortázar, not only does Soller disappear from the text by its end, but also the case itself vanishes within the actual folios of the dossier. In the Royal Appellate Court of Galicia, sentences were dated and kept separately in their own file series, *Rulings* (*Sentencias*).[167] This could explain the disappearance of the Soller case at its end: the documents relating to the sentencing phase and all that preceded it were preserved independently of the record relating to the appeal. In the final folio of the criminal proceedings, the case cannot be located. The Lord Weekly Justice (Semanero) was in charge of preserving the proceedings.[168] Yet the case record, at least the appeal portion, escaped momentarily from the study of the first Court Clerk, Don Juan de Montes, Esquire, before the Semanero could safeguard or transfer the archives to a new court clerk. Despite a thorough search of absent Court Clerk Montes's study, "The referred-to one, entitled *His Majesty's Representative with Said José Soller*, could not be found," states the text;[169] yet found it was, since the original documents form part of what we have. Once the trial moves to A Coruña,[170] Soller has gone absent (*en rebeldía*), Court Clerk Montes disappears, and the case itself vanishes at its very ending.

167 López Gómez, *Real Audiencia*, 1:252.

168 López Gómez, *Real Audiencia*, 1:229.

169 fol. 37^{v}; "no se pudo hallar al referido intitulado por *El fiscal de Su Majestad con dicho Joseph Soller*."

170 33^{r}–37^{v}.

CHAPTER 7

Into Thin Air

And their eyes were opened, and they knew him: and he vanished out of their sight.

Gospel of Luke[1]

Despite the case file's initial disappearance, these trial proceedings eventually make their way into the Archive of the Kingdom of Galicia. But to where did Soller disappear beyond the court document folios? According to the appeal, he is gone elsewhere by October 13, 1693, and he remains absent in 1694. Might Soller have headed to distant Rome, as his diploma attests his intention to be? Or maybe he went back to Coimbra, Portugal, where he told the authorities in Ourense he had intended to go? Did Soller perhaps seek asylum in the nearby refuge for vagabonds called Couto Mixto (figure 1 and part 1, chapter 2)? Could he possibly be the same José Soller who captained a packet boat from Cádiz, Spain to Veracruz, New Spain? Although there is no way to know for certain where Soller went after being sentenced to the King's galley ships, two of these possibilities are worth exploring in a tentative, measured manner.

1 Couto Mixto

Had it maintained its autonomy and not been divided in the border treaty of September 29, 1864, between Spain and Portugal, Couto Mixto today might have acquired a status similar to that of the principality of Andorra, which borders France and Spain along the Pyrenees, as well as a set of privileges that the region no longer maintains, including the right to asylum.[2] Rather than a fully independent micro-state, however, Couto Mixto was a unique political borderland that for centuries resisted colonization by any one nation.[3] Locals

1 Luke 24:31 (Douay-Rheims Catholic Bible).
2 Hernández Figueiredo, "Apuntes," 232.
3 Paül and Trillo-Santamaría, "La construcción literaria," 291, 293.

 | DOI:10.1163/9789004422704_008

claimed the citizenship rights of Portuguese or Spanish natives without any clear national designation.[4] In the nineteenth century, Couto Mixto wanted to be recognized as another Andorra, but both the Spanish and Portuguese governments refused with good reason.

The name Couto Mixto literally translates to "mixed domain" or "combined fief," meaning that the area depended on two lords, although another way of putting it might be "In-between Land." Indeed, this separate space was ambiguous not only in terms of its dueling seigneurial allegiances but also according to the hybrid condition of its national sovereignty.[5] Despite its poor soil and remote location, the right to asylum and various other privileges meant that Couto Mixto was overpopulated until the territory's dissolution in the nineteenth century.[6] Outlaws and others considered this singular space to be a virtual utopia. The political immunity that this In-between Land afforded refugees and fugitives would have been particularly useful for Soller in the event of a prison escape.

Until the nineteenth century, different households—even adjacent houses —within this border region could claim different loyalties. Locals were the subjects of two different lords—one a count, the other a duke—and two crowns—Portugal and Spain: "members of both communities lived and 'mixed' together,"[7] and they were confused with one another, as sovereignty was determined by the identity of each head of household. Since this selection did not depend upon geography, houses claiming loyalties to either kingdom were sprinkled throughout the three villages of Couto Mixto, forming "islands of jurisdiction in a sea of unclear land."[8]

The three towns towns located in the former Couto Mixto occupy an isolated valley in the mountains. Meaus (now part of Spain) is the closest one of these to the city of Ourense. Meaus is about a 35 mile (56 km) walk from Ourense and is located within the same province. This distance should take less than thirteen hours to walk and could be covered in a day and a half to two days on foot.

Religiously, this autonomous border region historically belonged to the Diocese of Ourense, and even after the treaty of 1864, towns across the national border that had been Portuguese for over fifty years continued to belong religiously to the Diocese of Ourense.[9] This situation conveys not only the region's cultural

4 Herzog, *Frontiers of Possession*, 221.
5 García Álvarez and Puente Lozano, "Las Comisiones Mixtas," 91.
6 Paül and Trillo-Santamaría, "Discussing the Couto Mixto," 57–58.
7 Herzog, *Frontiers of Possession*, 225.
8 Herzog, *Frontiers of Possession*, 226.
9 Hernández Figueiredo, "Apuntes," 234, 236.

closeness but also its geographic proximity to the city of Ourense where Soller was held. Of course the Galician province of Ourense directly borders Portugal.[10] Moreover, Couto Mixto—like the province of Ourense as a whole—is a relatively unsettled space in which establishments are known only by tradition, not by clear markers, since residents created them without the consent of any outside polity.[11]

The privileges of this region were numerous and significant: "there were no taxes, customs or compulsory cultivation requirements (even in the feudal years), nor were there military drafts. The rights of asylum and free choice of nationality (Portuguese, Galician/Spanish, or no nationality) were guaranteed."[12] In a practice descended from medieval frontier culture, people could buy and sell their goods duty-free in Couto Mixto.[13] The liberality of this In-between Land's policies meant that in later years it would be the brunt of criticism labelling the region a sanctuary for corruption, illegality, contraband and vagabondage.[14] Spain and Portugal both perceived Couto as a dangerous place, leading to its eventual dissolution.[15] The ambiguous status of this "mixed" jurisdiction, one that did not belong completely to either Portugal or Spain, was perceived to have "transformed their territory into a safe haven for outlaws,"[16] several of whom most assuredly were vagabonds.

10 Some authors deemed dual status of Couto to be noteworthy in the mid-nineteenth century, and the dual allegiance of the towns in Couto Mixto are documented in several eighteenth-century documents. The destruction of the territory's archive, however, eliminated the history of how this area came to serve jointly two separate crowns simultaneously. The earliest documentary evidence of Couto Mixto comes from the sixteenth century. Paül and Trillo-Santamaría, "Discussing the Couto Mixto," 62.

11 García Álvarez and Puente Lozano, "Las Comisiones Mixtas," 75–76.

12 Paül and Trillo-Santamaría, "Discussing the Couto Mixto," 64.

13 Barros, "La frontera medieval," 32. Apart from some uprisings in border towns during the sixteenth century, we unfortunately cannot know much about the history of Couto Mixto due to the destruction of this area's archive in the Spanish war of Independence from France in the nineteenth century. Hernández Figueiredo, "Apuntes," 232–233. These records were burned in 1809. Paül and Trillo-Santamaría, "Discussing the Couto Mixto," 58.

14 García Álvarez and Puente Lozano, "Las Comisiones Mixtas," 78; García Álvarez and Puente Lozano, "La frontera hispano-portuguesa," 768.

15 Paül and Trillo-Santamaría, "Discussing the Couto Mixto," 65.

16 Herzog, *Frontiers of Possession*, 230.

2 Ship Captain

A more distant possibility—distant in terms of geography, chronology, and probability—is that this same José Soller Chivo eventually became the elderly captain of a ship from Spain to New Spain. The only other mention of any José Soller I have been able to find in the archives is a ship captain named José Soller, who appears in the manifest and registry of a voyage to New Spain in 1742, *Registry of Departures to New Spain*, "Agustín Domingo de Arechaga, Chief Officer and Agent of the French Packet Boat 'San Juan Bautista,' Its Captain José Soller, with Mercury-bearing Ships."[17] The documents therein chronicle the permissions and licenses obtained for the French packet boat San Juan Bautista and its accompanying fleet to ship 60 tons or 600,000 kilograms of mercury (*seiscientos quintales de azogue*) along with copious quantities of wine and vinegar, wax, olives and olive oil, saffron, cinnamon, et cetera, from Cádiz, Sanlúcar de Barrameda, and Sevilla, Spain, to Veracruz, Mexico (New Spain). The ship departed on April 12, 1742, and as quicksilver was used to amalgamate actual silver mined in Mexico (and also in the Andes),[18] the packet boat was supposed to bring back silver among other goods on the return voyage.

It is not likely that this José Soller would be the same as the one from the criminal proceedings. That said, it is true that there were mulatto and black ship captains at this time, and barbers had long experience as resident healers on trans-oceanic voyages. Soller's self-proclaimed profession of "herbalist barber" (*barbero arbolario*)[19]—a more socially permissible "profession" (*oficio*) for him to have than "the status and rank of priest"[20]—helps explain how he could have come to acquire seafaring experience. The dominant perception was that the most menial jobs belonged to those of black African descent. As it turns out, Soller's stated profession of barber came to be dominated in his day by people of color, including mulattos, many of whom were former slaves.[21]

17 *Registros de ida a Nueva España*. "Agustín Domingo de Arechaga, maestre y apoderado del paquebote francés 'San Juan Bautista', su capitán José Soller, con azogues." The description: "Number 10. In the Year 1742. Part 2 of four parts" (*Número 10.-Año de 1742.-4 ramos ... Ramo 2*).

18 Mercury was shipped to the Americas, usually inside of leather bags, for this purpose. Quicksilver later was discovered in Peru, but Almadén, Spain (and Idrija, now in Slovenia) continued to be one of the main sources of mercury until Mexican Independence. Julie Orr via Luana Duggan, e-mail correspondence, March 29, 2019.

19 18^{r}.

20 1^{v}; "el estado y dignidad de sacerdote."

21 Soares, "African Barbeiros," 218.

In Rio de Janeiro, barbers (*barbeiros*) were a cross between "healers, blood letters, and hairdressers" who obtained for themselves a certain degree of independence: "As slaves for hire, barbeiros were frequently sent as surgeons on ships, visiting ports in Africa and India."[22] Barbers took the place of surgeons on transatlantic voyages, and healers were used in their stead if a barber was unavailable. The Royal Medical College licensed barbers, while healers practiced informally.[23] The reference to Soller as an "herbalist barber" might be akin to him being called a barber-healer, that is, an unlicensed barber.

During the seventeenth century, it is unlikely that Soller would have performed surgical procedures as a barber in the Atlantic world of the various national empires given that "barbers came to be regarded as unfit to perform bleedings or small surgeries."[24] It was at this time that barbers began to be required to obtain a license and additionally to work in the maritime industry, especially aboard slave-bearing ships.[25]

To the best of my knowledge, there is no evidence Soller had such a license. And yet whereas barbers were mostly white in preceding centuries, "During the seventeenth century, the proportion of black barbeiros (meaning slaves) increased substantially."[26] In other words, the transition in this occupation from free whites to enslaved people of color in the transatlantic world took place during Soller's day. Moreover, the maritime connections between Africa and Brazil brought a number of sailors and black-African voyagers to Lisbon.[27] In Soller's day, these individuals of color added their number to the expanding population of port workers, stevedores, and maritime tradesmen, among others. Most of these people of African background in the trans-Atlantic ports had been forced to arrive "either directly or indirectly by the transatlantic slave trade."[28] There were slaves who worked in a variety of ship-faring capacities in Portugal, including as interpreters on ships heading to Africa: "Back in Portugal, black slaves often operated the ferries on the major rivers,"[29] waterways such as the Tagus, which Soller knew. Some enslaved black-Africans piloted ships. These black ship captains generated their own "counterculture" in the seafaring community.[30] Having a person of color as the ship captain is an inversion

22 Cañizares-Esguerra, Childs, and Sidbury, *Black Urban Atlantic*, 11.
23 Soares, "African Barbeiros," 216–217.
24 Soares, "African Barbeiros," 209.
25 Soares, "African Barbeiros," 209.
26 Soares, "African Barbeiros," 210.
27 Sweet, "African Lisbon" 246.
28 Cañizares-Esguerra, Childs, and Sidbury, *Black Urban Atlantic*, 3–4.
29 Phillips, *Slavery*, 110.
30 Dawson, "Enslaved Ship Pilots," 166.

of the usual racialized power structure in society, and this was all the more true when these ship captains additionally were slaves.[31]

In the criminal proceedings against him, Soller invokes the Admiral of Castile (Almirante de Castilla) after being sentenced to the galleys, saying that he will appeal to this higher authority.[32] Soller gives the impression of knowing that the Admiral is the most powerful figure in the court at the time. It perhaps is relevant that the function of an admiral is to command an armada and to represent his sovereign out on the open ocean. Soller's allusion to this maritime authority toward the end of his case brackets his previous mention of traveling by ship "in the company of" another nobleman, the count of Alayos, on his way from Hispaniola to the Iberian Peninsula.

One of Carlos II's most loyal allies throughout his reign was the Almirante de Castilla. This nobleman figures time and again in the history of Carlos II's reign, and by 1695, the Admiral of Castile seems to have been the most powerful figure in the political circles of the court.[33] The eleventh and last Admiral of Castile and the third generation in his family to serve in this capacity, don Juan Tomás Enríquez de Cabrera represented the King as the "Prince on the Sea" (Príncipe en la mar) from 1691, upon his father's death, until the end of the Hapsburg dynasty a decade later.[34] Enríquez de Cabrera was so powerful that he was widely deemed the King's favorite in the court and additionally served as Carlos II's chief stableman, or constable (*conde de establo*).[35] The power of this individual and his titles is what Soller seems to realize already by 1693, when he stakes his claim to justice by threatening to appeal his sentence to none other than this very admiral of Castile. What Soller is telling indirectly the Chief Magistrate, the King's Representative, and any other royal delegate may be "You think *you* represent the King? I will show you who represents the King."

Both the Conde de Alayos and especially the Admiral of Castile are associated directly with overseas travel, as is Soller. This point is one of the few shreds of evidence making it remotely plausible that he be the same person as the José Soller listed as the captain of the mercury-bearing ship listed in the Archive of the Indies. But the odds are that this José Soller is different from the "mulatto pilgrim" accused of impersonating a priest and other crimes in 1693 Galicia.

31 Dawson, "Enslaved Ship Pilots," 168–169.
32 32^{v}.
33 Ribot García, "España de Carlos II," 129.
34 Fernández Duro, *El último almirante*, 3.
35 Fernández Duro, *El último almirante*, 48.

Based on his estimated age range in the legal case (anywhere from 40 to 46 depending on the varying testimony of the trial), Soller would be somewhere between 89 and 95 years of age by the time of becoming a ship captain. (Talk about an old man and the sea.) Though elderly and possibly frail, such an age is still within the realm of possibility, however remotely: "Nothing evidences the creoles' easy integration into the mainland society better than the number who survived into old age ... Before the end of the century, numbers of black people lived long enough to see their grandchildren."[36] Grandchildren, sure, but great-grandchildren? This prospect seems more dubious.

Moreover, there is no indication of his second surname, Chivo. Next, having examined every reference to Soller in this set of documents, I can attest that there is no mention of his ethnicity, not even in a descriptive manner. Finally, it seems that Soller is a Hispanization of a French surname: not only is the packet boat of French origin, but so is its Captain, "Joseph Sollard,"[37] rendered elsewhere as "Sollar" (once) or "Soller" (everywhere else).[38]

Quicksilver, also called mercury, was shipped to the Americas to extract silver and gold. The element is used in mining because it easily forms amalgams with precious metals such as gold and silver. When the mixture is heated, however, only the gold or silver remains because the mercury evaporates into thin air—as does Soller. The José Soller of this ship is unlikely to be the same one as the man of the trial documents, be he the pilgrim, the mulatto, or the would-be priest from the New World. All the same, José Soller Chivo is mercurial to the bitter end.

---

36 Berlin, "Creole to African," 267n55.

37 *Registro*, 4^r–4^v.

38 The document with "Joseph Sollard" bears the Second Seal, meaning it is of greater official importance than those with the Fourth Seal, which includes every other sealed document in the registry.

PART 2

His Majesty's Representative versus José Soller, Mulatto Pilgrim, for Impersonating a Priest and Other Crimes: *Edition and Translation*

Note on the Translation

The translation of Soller's legal case involved multiple stages. First, I rendered early modern Castilian, Portuguese, and Latin into what might be best considered an English variety of legalese, but any readable text needs to be more accessible than jargon. My next step was to convert the case from legalese to a more readable form of English while maintaining the integrity of the legal text and official travel documents. Many of these terms required extensive research to translate appropriately in different contexts. Because the Spanish legal system of the Old Regime is so fundamentally different in basis and practice from the modern United States system and even from that of Spain today, many of the terms for officers of the court and stages in the process simply do not have exact equivalents, and require some explanation of my choices.

I have chosen "His Majesty's Representative" as the most all-encompassing translation of *el fiscal de Su Majestad*. Although there would be good reason to translate *fiscal* as "prosecutor," the two terms are not quite equivalent. A *fiscal* was a representative of royal interests, not only or even mainly a prosecutor. He was, for example, the one giving opinion as a royal magistrate regarding how to decide matters (*vista fiscal*), especially those dealing with financial, that is to say, fiscal concerns.

In some instances, a single term can produce a variety of meanings. Among the best examples of these is *auto*, a noun that by itself can mean "decision," "judicial decree," "ruling," "decree," "edict," "proceedings," "court record," "indictment," or "charge." Yet words in Castilian Spanish other than *auto* often more precisely represent some of these concepts in English: *sentencia* for "decision"; *acusación* as "charge"; and *sumaria* for "indictment." In this legal case, *auto* is best translated in the singular as "ruling" and in the plural as "proceedings." When combined with other terms, *auto* has other implications: *auto de oficio* can mean a "judgment" or "official decision"; an *auto de prueba* is an "order to produce evidence"; and an *auto de publicación* is an "order to publish."

Another good example of the complexity of the translation process involves *escribano*, which I interpret as "judicial secretary": he who writes the *autos*, the declarations of witnesses, et cetera.[1] Other translation options considered for this term were "notary public," "scribe," "court clerk," "notary," and "scrivener."

1 Heras Santos, *La justicia penal*, 172.

 DOI:10.1163/9789004422704_009

An *escribano de número* is "one of a certain number of notaries public, before whom only certain deeds can be executed"[2] or who is assigned to and works in a city[3] (in other words, a fully-fledged notary public), which I translate as "full notary." Meanwhile, I understand the phrases *escribano relator* (including *relator* by itself) and *escribano recetor* (for *receptor* in modern Spanish), which both refer to the same individual, to have as their closest equivalent in modern American English "head court clerk," i.e., he who manages flow of cases to the other court clerks in the various courtrooms (*salas*) of the Royal Appellate Court (Real Audiencia) of Galicia and who handles the fines and payments coming into the court.

A particularly challenging term is *visto*, which usually means the legal actors have studied the precedents, heard the testimonies, or read the documents and are ready to make a decision. The term is used to expedite the proceedings, almost as if to say, "Enough. Let us move on already." As a masculine noun, *visto* means a "hearing" (of a case), and as a past participle of *ver* it can mean "heard" (by a judge), "seen" (by a defendant, witness, et cetera), and even "adjourned." All of these meanings of *visto* are employed in the manuscript, and the usage varies according to context. Add to this complexity a constellation of phrases with the related lexeme *vista*: the feminine singular noun itself in this case means "consideration"; *en vista de* is best understood as "in light of" or "in consideration of"; *dar vista de* is translated as "to consider"; while *tomar vista* is "to inspect, see, have access" (to a file).

Transcribing and then translating *cividade* requires precision. There are several possible meanings of *cividade*, an Old Portuguese form deriving from the Latin *civitas* (specifically its ablative singular declension, *civitate*) that evolved to *cidade* in modern Portuguese. Though uncommon, *cividade* is attested to in a variety of place names in Portugal, including the Cividade parish in Braga. And while *cividade* can mean "citizenship," "citizenry," or "community"—the last meaning of which is retained in the Celtic settlements of Cividade Bagunte and Cividade Terroso, as well as in the street named rua da Cividade (on which road lies an inn named the Cividade Villa) in Povóa de Varzim—the word also can mean "city," "capital," or "walled settlement," especially when the city is understood to include its associated territory. In the context of this manuscript, however, the best translation of *cividade* in the phrase *cividade del Perú* is "kingdom," especially considering that Perú here can be understood to represent all of the Hispanic New World. Hence the translation "from the kingdom of Perú"

2 Velázquez de la Cadena, *New Pronouncing Dictionary*, 292.
3 Busto Duthurburu, "Los escribanos," 162.

would mean simply that Soller hails from Hispano-America, more specifically the Island of Hispaniola, referred to as the Island of Santo Domingo throughout the case file.

Other instances in the Castilian required getting beyond a literal translation. In the case of the formulaic *lo mandó*, my hunch was that "he so ordered" would make a better translation than the literal "he ordered it." It was helpful to find confirmation of this instinct in a reputable translation.[4] I researched the best interpretation of specific legal concepts such as *vindicta pública*, which can be understood as "atonement for crime as an example"[5] (meaning that the punishment is intended as a lesson for the benefit of society) and which is more simply translated as "public vengeance."[6] In a final example, the phrase *en rebeldía* literally means "in rebellion," which carries some truthfulness in the case of Soller. However, the legal term "in absentia" is the most straightforward and accurate phrase. The section entitled "On Trial, under Sentence, and in Absentia" (part 1, chapter 6) addresses the powerful implications of the term *en rebeldía* that go beyond translation.

---

4 *Doña Teresa de Aguilera*, 157v.

5 Velázquez de la Cadena, *New Pronouncing Dictionary*, 658.

6 Garrone, *Diccionario Jurídico*, 4:786.

Editorial Norms

The editorial norms as applied to the legal case in Castilian Spanish (part 2) seek to respect and maintain any phonetic difference of this late seventeenth-century text with contemporary Castilian and Portuguese while modernizing the orthography, or in the case of the Latin travel documents, simply regularizing the writing. These criteria hew closely to established norms applied to major literary works written in seventeenth-century Spanish. Of particular value are the criteria used by the PROLOPE research group in their editions of the dramatic works (*comedias*) of Spanish playwright Lope de Vega, as well as those of the Golden Age Research Group (Grupo de Investigación Siglo de Oro, known as GRISO), as articulated in Ignacio Arellano's volume *Editar a Calderón*, on editing the works of the Shakespeare of Spain, Pedro Calderón de la Barca. A concise summation of the PROLOPE norms follows here: "The text is edited in the closest way to current orthographic norms, but those peculiarities that could register a phonetic pronunciation different from the modern one are respected. In this way, only the characters of the base text that could have phonetic value are maintained. Neither can linguistic peculiarities of a morphological or syntactic character be modernized."[1] Arellano likewise proposes to bring up to date only that spelling in the text which does not have phonetic value: "Pronunciation is the limit: we are referring to, then, strictly a graphic modernization."[2] Put another way, in following these norms, my edition modernizes variant spellings of the same word to render that word more recognizable so long as there is no phonetic difference in such a representation.

Such an approach means, for example, that the edited text converts *reproduzgo* to *reproduzco* since the *c* in the latter can become a sonorous glottal stop (as is the *g* in the former) through assimilation with the *z*. Modernizing in this way avoids overly complicated readings as would be the case if an editor, for instance, were to leave all the duplicative forms of *s* (*ss*) and *t* (*tt*), which have no phonetic value, and were not to modernize other graphemes without phonetic value, such as *x* with a phonetic value of /*x*/ and the Latinate

1 PROLOPE, *La edición del teatro*, 26; "Se edita el texto en la forma más próxima a la norma gráfica actual, pero se respetan aquellas particularidades que pueden cifrar una realización fonética distinta de la moderna. Así pues, se mantienen únicamente las grafías del texto base que puedan tener valor fónico. Tampoco pueden modernizarse peculiaridades lingüísticas de carácter morfológico o sintáctico."

2 Arellano, *Editar a Calderón*, 37; "La fonética es el límite: nos estamos, pues, refiriendo a la modernización estrictamente gráfica."

 | DOI:10.1163/9789004422704_010

ph for *f*. Without modernizing the orthographic norms, the title of the case would appear as *Josseph SSoller Chivo, peregrino mulatto, por finxirsse sazerdotte y ottras cossas*. This approach would not produce a very readable edition, especially if maintained over the course of the entire case.

These norms would have been more conservative had this been a text in medieval Spanish, which would have meant a difference of pronunciation between *finxirse* and *fingirse*, *sazerdote* and *sacerdote*. But by the early modern period these phonetic differences had disappeared despite the persistence of orthographic variation dating from the time of Alfonso X of Castile (1221–1284).[3] While I of course make an exception for the Latin in the travel documents and that quoted in Castilian text containing *Josephum* and *Joseph*, it is not phonetically different from the early modern Spanish to render a much more readable title: *Josef Soller, peregrino mulato, por fingirse sacerdote y otras cosas*.

In accordance with this approach, I modernize the punctuation and accentuation while additionally preserving orthographic variance that would reflect a phonetic difference, however minimal,[4] for forms of which textual witnesses can be found. Oscillation among consonant clusters is maintained, for example, in the *t* / *ct* pattern with *otubre* versus *Doctor*, *respecto*, *efecto*, *defecto*, *vindicta*, and *aspecto*. And while there is no alternation in the cluster *c* / *cc* (before *i* and *e*) in the manuscript, I maintain *jurisdición* in the edited text. An example of variation in the consonantal cluster *n* / *gn* includes *inorancia* / *ignorancia*.

Vocalic oscillation also is maintained except in the case of *y hiço*, which I modernize to *e hizo* per contemporary pronunciation norms in order to facilitate reading. This means that this edition does not modernize *barbero y arbolario* to *barbero y herbolario* or *barbero arbolario* to *barbero herbolario* since *arbolario* existed and was used as both a noun and adjective and because changing it would mean changing the pronunciation. In this vein, I do not correct the metathesis in *perjuicio* either. *Audencia* is retained as a monophthong variant of its more standard dipthong counterpart, *Audiencia*, and the edition additionally maintains a host of other vocalically alternating forms, including *pedido* / *pidido*, *delito* / *dilito*, and *confesión* / *confisión*. A complete and organized listing of both consonantal and vocalic alternation within words and morphemes can be found in part 3, Linguistic Variants.

---

3 Real Academia, *Ortografía*, 25–32, especially 30.

4 PROLOPE, *La edición del teatro*, 26–28.

The edition expands all scribal abbreviations without comment or indication. The abbreviations I have added myself are *fol.* and *fols.* for "folio" and "folios," *cub.* for *cubierta*, and *cov.* for "cover" in the English translation. The manuscript originally is foliated through folio 7^v beginning with the first folio and not including the two covers. The rest of the case was not numbered initially. Now, however, it has modern numeration written in pencil beginning from the first cover. The edition's folio numeration follows this modern foliation. This edition does not spell out all numbers in long form unless these are written out as such in the manuscript.

Contractions with *que* and *de* are expanded according to modern usage. Because of synaloepha, this strategy facilitates the identification of words without altering pronunciation.[5] In this manuscript, these include: *desta* → *de esta*; *del* → *de él*; *della* → *de ella*; *dellos* → *de ellos*; *dellas* → *de ellas*; *questa* → *que está*; and *dello* → *de ello*. Likewise, I separate combined words into their modern counterparts with contemporary word spacing: i.e., *conanimo* → *con ánimo*; *deprofanar* → *de profanar*. To facilitate recognition, the edition combines separated words into their modern form: i.e., by uniting *de clare* into the single word *declare*; *de Ben* into *Debén*, *Mariña Mansa* into *Mariñamansa*, and *la fuente Eyña* into *la Fontaíña* (see also part 3, Proper Names in the Dossier); as well as *por que* into *porque* when the meaning is "because." By the same token, the preposition *de* followed immediately by the definite article *el* is contracted into the modern *del*.

Modern capitalization and punctuation are incorporated into the edited text, including accent marks, diereses, commas, periods, et cetera. Punctuation norms for Spanish and English are followed according to each language. For example, in the Castilian Spanish text, periods and commas are placed outside close quotation marks, while in the English translation, these fall inside the same. The various titles used in the title page, on the two manuscript covers, with the safe-conduct, and for the appeal are capitalized according to the contemporary norms of each language, italicized, and placed in small caps font. The edition incorporates modern word spacing, as well.

Titles of nobility are capitalized only inasmuch as they take the place of a proper name. In the manuscript, this capitalization is not necessary with *licenciado* or *señor licenciado* since this title is followed by a proper name in every instance. Capitalization is necessary, however, with *Señor Corregidor* since this title is a formal means of address that substitutes for a proper name. Whereas *corregidor* left uncapitalized follows the name of the individual and/or pre-

5 PROLOPE, *La edición del teatro*, 32.

cedes the place name (i.e., "corregidor de esta ciudad"), terms such as *Su Majestad, Vuestra Merced, Su Merced, Señores Gobernador y Oidores, Señores Gobernador y Alcaldes Mayores*, and *Señor Cardenal* are capitalized in this edition since they are not referred to by name or named specifically.

In the edition, the foliation is indicated within the inside margin of the edition's pages. A vertical line (|) in the body of the text marks page breaks in the original manuscript. Blank folios are indicated in the body of the text by an additional vertical line immediately followed in the margin by the subsequent folio. Since the case is a prose document, there is no need to maintain line breaks as they appear in the manuscript. One exception is text with numbered calculations at the end of a line, as in the Amount of Court Costs (*Tasa de costas*) section.[6] Hyphenated words spanning the end of one line and the start of the next line are written as a single word without any indication of line breaks or the scribal hyphenation. Stamped text is described in Case Notes but not repeated on every folio: i.e., *Para despachos de oficio, dos maravedíes.* Ellipses in between *cruces desperationis* (†...†) are put in the place of the few instances of illegible text, which are located principally in the Portuguese credential (fols. 8^r–8^v).

Page breaks occurring in the middle of a word hyphenated by a scribe are inserted into the space immediately following such a word. Text that is underlined and written to the margin as a form of summary heading in the manuscript is moved in this critical edition above the paragraph it heads and if underlined, is placed in italicized text. One exception is the bar beneath the addends and over the sum in court cost calculations,[7] which is left untouched. Handwritten text filling in Soller's printed travel documents also is italicized, whereas the printed text is not (unless already italicized in print). Signatures bearing the added flourish of a Spanish rubric are italicized, as well, and are aligned with the side of the folio in which they appear in the case file. Rubrics without signatures are not indicated in the text of the edition itself but rather are cited in the Case Notes section (part 3). The text in the edition is justified to that margin in which it is found in the trial proceedings.

I correct apparent scribal errors by replacing them with the correct form: i.e., by providing *sitio* for the manuscript's "sito [*sic*]." All such corrected lapses of the judicial secretary appear in Scribal Errors. The edition additionally supplies in square brackets text that is missing from the manuscript, i.e., *habiéndole* [*afeitado*] *la barba, Otra* [*notificación*] *a Josef Soller, Viana* [*do Castelo*], and

6 17^v.

7 17^v.

Valença [*do Minho*]. No other comment is made, as the inclusion of the square brackets makes it clear this is an editorial intervention. Where the judicial secretary makes a self-correction such as a strikethrough and then elaborates on which part of the text is valid and which is not, I simply follow his instructions and eliminate the invalid text along with the scribal explanation of the self-correction. The same is true for scribal insertions. All examples of such changes are contained in part 3, Case Notes.

Words that hail from Galician or Portuguese are not Castilianized, even as these appear alongside their Castilian counterparts. The term *caija* is a Galicianized or Portuguese-influenced version of *caja*, stemming from *caixa*. I update *caija* to *caixa* in the edited text. These borrowed words are italicized per the PROLOPE norms.[8] A complete and categorized listing is found in part 3, Linguistic Variants.

Modernization in the Castilian Text

– The archaic use of *x* is modernized to *j* in front of a, o, and u, and to *g* before the vowels *e* or *i*. Meanwhile, *g* and *j* are employed according to modern norms.

finxirse / finjirse, finxiendo → *fingirse, fingiendo*
correxidor → *corregidor*

caxa → *caja*
oxa, oxas → *hoja, hojas*

alaxas → *alhajas*
alforxas → *alforjas*

muger → *mujer*
viage, biaxe → *viaje*

– With the exception of Meneçes → Menezes, in which case I opted for the Portuguese variant since the name identifies individuals from Portugal in the manuscript (see Proper Names in the Dossier), the letters *ç* and *z* are modernized to *c* before the vowels *e* and *i* and to *z* in front of *a*, *o*, and *u*.

8 PROLOPE, *La edición del teatro*, 27–28.

alçaquello, alçacuello → *alzacuello*
pobreça → *pobreza*

saçerdote, sazerdotte → *sacerdote*
carçel, carzel → *cárcel*

calçon, calçones → *calzón, calzones*
mestiço → *mestizo*

plaçuela → *Plazuela*

-zion as suffix → *-ción* as suffix
i.e., *ynclinazion* → *inclinación*

ziudad, çiudad → *ciudad*
prozedimiento → *procedimiento*

– The letters *b*, *v*, and *u* also are regularized in accordance with modern usage.

bagante, bagamundo → *vagante, vagabundo*
vayeta → *bayeta*
varberos → *barberos*
fugetibo, fugitibo → *fugetivo, fugitivo*
avito, havito → *hábito*
cavello → *cabello*

– This modernization takes place whether *v* or *u* have consonantal or vocalic value.

barva → *barba*
vno → *uno*

– The letter *n* becomes *m* before *p* or *b*.

onbre → *hombre*
hanbre → *hambre*

enplasto → *emplasto*
Conpostela → *Compostela*

– In the same way *m* is modernized to *n* before *f*.

comfesion → *confesión*

– The edition likewise normalizes the letters *i* and *y* according to their respective vocalic or semi-vocalic value, as in the following cases.

io → *yo*
Ytalia → *Italia*
Yglesia → *Iglesia*
ynterrogatorio → *interrogatorio*
ley → *leí* (first person preterite singular of *leer*)
lei, leies → *ley, leyes* (the sustantive)
ysla → *isla*

– The edition also modernizes the letters *c* and *q*. In the Latin text of the safe-conduct and *compostelana*, however, the morphemes *qua* and *quo* are left unchanged.

quello → *cuello*
quenta → *cuenta*

quonsortes → *consortes*
quontra → *contra*

– In instances where the silent letter *h* would appear in modern Castilian, this letter is provided.

abito, avito, havito → *hábito*
oxa, oxas → *hoja, hojas*
onbre → *hombre*
urtado → *hurtado*

– The letter *h* is removed from where it would not appear in modern Castilian, except in the case of *hedad* in this text, a high-frequency lexeme, along with *harriero* in the seventeenth century.[9] The probable aspiration of the initial *h* in the case of *hedad*, which makes fifteen appearances in this manuscript,

9 Hidalgo, "El español de América," 79.

is the rationale behind leaving it untouched in the text. Compare to *horden* (→ *orden*), which alternates with *orden* in the MS and appears to have no phonetic value in this instance.[10]

theniente → *teniente*
hordinario → *ordinario*
hordenes → *órdenes*
christiano/a → *cristiano/a*
but
hedad = *hedad*

- The letters *rr* and *r* as an intervocalic multiple vibrant are normalized to *rr* in this edition.

- Cacographies in which the letters *z*, *ç*, or *c* these should be *s*—or vicecersa—are regularized.

fizcal → *fiscal*
inocensia, *inoçensia* → *inocencia*
mestiso → *mestizo*
riso → *rizo*

Latin Travel Documents

- I regularize the capitalization.

- The edition also normalizes the consonantal and vocalic *v* and *u*.

Ciuidade → *cividade*[11]
Georgivs → *Georgius*
Vniversis → *Universis*
Hyacinthvs → *Hiacinthus*
Svarez → *Suárez*
vt → *ut*
vnici → *unici*

10 Blake, "Sound Change," 55.

11 *Cividade* is an archaic Portuguese form of *cidade* deriving from the Latin *civitas*, specifically its ablative singular declension, *civitate*. See Note on the Translation.

- I alter the vocalic and semi-vocalic *j* to *i*.

  hujusmodi → huiusmodi
  ejusque → eiusque
  auxilij → auxilii
  Dominjs → Dominis
  patrocinij → patrocinii
  Febuarij → Febuarii

- And the edition converts the vocalic *y* to *i*.

  Ullysipone → Ullisipone
  Hyacinthvs → Hiacinthus

- I modify the grapheme *i*, when this character represents the palatal consonant, to *j* and retain *j* as such when it conforms to modern usage.

  Iacobi → Jacobi
  Jacobus / Jacobus
  justis / justis

- The edition regularizes the Latin graphemes.

  & → et
  long s (*ſ*) → s
  Æ, œ → AE, ae

- But I keep ss.

  ss / ss

- The edition expands the following Latin abbreviations.

  SS. D.N. = *Sanctissimus Dominus Noster*
  dictæ S. sedis = dictae Sanctae Sedis
  Doctor D. = Doctor Divinitatis
  S. *IACOBI = Sancti Jacobi*
  &c. = et cetera

Portuguese Credential, or Carta de Guia

- I modernize the graphemes.

  & → *e*
  long s (*ſ*) → *s*

- The edition leaves *ç* alone in the Portuguese since this is still an active grapheme.

  Valença
  favoreção
  Gonçalo

- I normalize the vocalic *y* to *i*.

  vay → *vai*
  foy → *foi*
  muyta → *muita*
  Guya → *Guia*

- The edition renders double *l* (*ll*) as *l*.

  esmollas → *esmolas*
  ell → *el* (an archaic variant of the Portuguese masculine singular definite article *o*)

- I modernize the accentuation.

  Vossas Mercés → *Vossas Mercês*
  mez → *mês* (The pronunciation of *mês* would not differ from that of the archaic *mez* due to the sonorization of the *s* assimilated with the *d* of *de* that follows in *mês de*.)

- The edition updates cacographies involving *z* and *s*:

  mez → *mês*
  Misericordia, Misericordias, Mizericordia → *Misericórdia, Misericórdias*

- As with the Castilian text, I modernize the capitalization and punctuation, including the capitalization of titles that substitute for proper names such

as *Vossas Mercês*, *Provedor*, *Irmaõs*, *Provedor*, and *Mesa*, as well as proper names, including *Misericórdia*.

- The edition preserves the oscillation of *n* / *nn*.

  annos / *anos* (see part 3, Linguistic Variants)

- I also maintain the vocalic oscillation.

  niste / *neste* (see Linguistic Variants).

- The edition separates contractions according to modern usage.

  desta → *de esta*

- I leave *favoreçao* as a valid archaic Portuguese form that is a counterpart to the modern *favorecido* and which is retained due to its different pronunciation.

El Oficio de la Justicia y el fiscal de Su Majestad en este reino con Josef Soller Chivo, peregrino mulato, sobre fingirse sacerdote y otras cosas

El fiscal de Su Majestad contra José Soller, peregrino mulato, por fingirse sacerdote y otros delitos

Real Audiencia
Legajo 26339 / 13

The Justice Office and His Majesty's Representative in This Kingdom with Joseph Soller Chivo, Mulatto Pilgrim, Concerning His Impersonation of a Priest and Other Matters

His Majesty's Representative versus José Soller, Mulatto Pilgrim, for Impersonating a Priest and Other Crimes

Royal Appellate Court
File 26339 / 13

Visto en 13 de noviembre de 1693. Señores León, Riaño, y Alvarado. cub. 1
Visto en la discordia.

Número 20
Siglo 17
Figueroa

El Oficio de la Justicia y el fiscal de Su Majestad en este reino con Josef Soller Chivo, peregrino mulato, sobre fingirse sacerdote y otras cosas

Auto de oficio en 14 de abril de 1693

Relator Montes, y por su ausencia Relator Balboa

Sentencia, 2 años de galeras

Un alzacuello de bayeta.
Dos cuellos.
Un par de mangas y fundas de bayeta.
Un par de calzones de bayeta negra sin forro.
Un pedazo de bayeta negra cosa de una vara.
Un libro de medio pliego con su pergamino con rótulo que dice "*1682*.
Libro de *caixa* de João Sánchez. Jesús, María, Josef," que por adentro denota ser libro de un mercader portugués de Coimbra, foliado, y la última hoja tiene el número 92, rubricadas todas ellas junto a la foliatura, y su apellido, que dice "Menezes."
Más un despacho de Santiago firmado de don Jacinto Suárez de marzo de 93 que dice "don Josephum Soler, sacerdotem indianum." | cub. 2

Seglar *Señor Corregidor* *anno 1693*

Auto y procedimiento de oficio contra Josef Soller, peregrino mulato, y consortes sobre fingirse sacerdote y otras cosas

Escribano Antonio Pérez | 1r

Para despachos de oficio, dos maravedíes

Sello cuarto. Año de mil y seiscientos y noventa y tres

Auto de oficio contra un peregrino mulato

En la ciudad de Orense, a catorce días del mes de abril de mil y seiscientos y noventa y tres años, por ante mí, escribano. El señor licenciado don Juan Antonio Covillas, corregidor de esta ciudad y su tierra por Su Majestad, dijo que ahora se le ha dado noticia se halla en esta ciudad un

cov. 1 Adjourned on November 13, 1693. Lords León, Riaño, and Alvarado. Adjourned in disagreement among the magistrates.

The Justice Office and His Majesty's Representative in This Kingdom with Joseph Soller Chivo, Mulatto Pilgrim, Concerning His Impersonation of a Priest and Other Matters

Number 2
17th Century
Figueroa

A flannel clerical neckband.
Two collars.
A pair of flannel sleeves and covers.
A pair of unlined, black flannel pants.
A piece of black flannel measuring about a rod.
A quarto-sized book bound in parchment with a label that reads, "1682. Cashbook of João Sánchez. Jesús, María, José," which is foliated and inside shown to belong to a Portuguese merchant from Coimbra. The last sheet is numbered 92, with every sheet countersigned with his last name, which reads, "Menezes," next to the page numbering.
Plus a diploma from Santiago signed by Don Jacinto Suárez in March of
cov. 2 '93, which reads, "Don Joseph Soller, Priest of the Indies." |

Judgment on April 14, 1693

Court Clerk Montes, and by his absence, Court Clerk Balboa

Sentence, 2 years at the galleys

Layman *Lord Chief Magistrate* *Year 1693*

Judgment and Proceedings against Joseph Soller, Mulatto Pilgrim, and Consorts, concerning His Impersonation of a Priest and Other Matters

1r *Judicial Secretary Antonio Pérez* |

For legal offices, two maravedis

Fourth Seal. The Year One Thousand Six-Hundred Ninety-Three

Judgment against a Mulatto Pilgrim

In the city of Ourense on the 14th day of the month of April of the year 1693, before me, the judicial secretary. Lord Don Juan Antonio Covillas, Esquire, Chief Magistrate of this city and its territory for His Majesty, said that he recently has been notified that a mulatto pilgrim who seems to

peregrino mulato que parece ser esclavo y que hoy día *fingiendo ser sacerdote se abrió e hizo corona de tal sin traer* cuello ni otra insignia alguna que manifieste serlo más de dicha corona y que anda en público con ella, manifestándola sin recato alguno. Y para que se averigüe lo que hay en esta relación y se pueda pasar al castigo de semejante delito cometido en vituperio del santo sacerdocio, mandó Su Merced hacer este auto de oficio y cabeza de proceso contra el susodicho y más que resultaren culpados. Y que primero y ante todas cosas se asegure la persona del susodicho en la cárcel real de esta ciudad y se le tome su declaración en orden a si es sacerdote o no, registrándole para ello a mayor abundamiento los papeles que tuviere para, en vista de todo, proveer lo que sea de justicia, para lo cual da comisión en forma a Bernardo de Pando, su alguacil ordinario. Y por este auto así lo mandó y firmó.

licenciado Covillas

Ante mí,
Antonio Pérez

Prisión

En la ciudad de Orense a los dichos catorce de abril de mil y seiscientos y noventa y tres años, Bernardo de Pando, alguacil ordinario de esta ciudad, en ejecución y cumplimiento del auto de arriba buscó por esta ciudad al sujeto peregrino que contiene dicho auto. Y habiendo hallado noticias se había escapado de ella y enderezado su viaje por la calle de la Puerta de Aira y camino que va al lugar de Sexalbo, le fue siguiendo hasta el sitio del crucero de Mariñamansa en donde preguntando a unos muchachos dijeron | que una mujer les había dicho como en la viña de 1v
Berjano y de Pedro Debén que están allí inmediatas se había entrado había poco rato un hombre moreno con unas alforjas y un bastón de peregrino. Y habiendo pasado a su reconocimiento asistido de Gregorio de Castro, Matías Sueyro, herradores, Miguel de Albor, barbero, se halló a dicho peregrino recogido, espulgándose medio desnudo en una casa vieja de la viña de dicho Pedro Debén, con su corona abierta al parecer de hoy día como si fuera la de un sacerdote. Y habiéndole aprehendido y asegurado se le preguntó si era sacerdote o no y qué motivo tenía para haber abierto dicha corona. Respondió *no era sacerdote, que la corona* la había abierto para poner *en ella un emplasto por achaques que padecía* y que su

Corona. Dice no es sacerdote.

be a slave is found in this city and that today, *impersonating a priest, he had himself a tonsure cut and shaved without wearing* a clerical collar or any other insignia showing him to be a priest apart from said tonsure, and that he is walking around in public, shamelessly displaying it. In order to find out what is in this report and so that such a crime committed in offense of the holy priesthood be liable to due punishment, His Grace commissioned this judgment and summary trial against the aforementioned person and others who should turn out to be guilty. First and foremost, may the aforementioned person be secured in the royal jail of this city and have his affidavit taken in order to determine whether or not he is a priest, and furthermore, making a record for this purpose of the documents that he should have in order to administer, in consideration of everything, what may be just, for which purpose the Chief Magistrate authorizes Bernardo de Pando, his bailiff. For this ruling he so ordered, and signed.

Covillas, Esquire

Before me,
Antonio Pérez

Arrest

In the city of Ourense on said 14th of April of the year 1693, Bernardo de Pando, bailiff of this city, in execution and fulfillment of the indictment above, searched this city for the pilgrim subject that said indictment contains, and having found news that he had escaped from the city and directed his journey through the street of the Aira Gate and the road that goes to the town of Seixalbo, the bailiff went following him to the site of
1v the Mariñamansa intersection, where, asking some boys, they said | that a woman had told them how in the Berjano vineyard and that of Pedro Debén, which are right there, a dark-skinned man with some knapsacks and a pilgrim's staff had entered a short time ago. Having identified him with the assistance of Gregorio de Castro and Matías Sueyro, blacksmiths, and Miguel de Albor, barber, said pilgrim was found delousing himself half-naked, holed up in an old house in the vineyard of said Pedro Debén, with his tonsure apparently having been shaved today as if it were that of a priest. Having apprehended and secured him, he was asked whether or not he was a priest and what motive he had for having shaved said tonsure. He responded that *he was not a priest*, that he had shaved *the tonsure* to apply *on it a poultice for the maladies from which he suffered*, and that his

Tonsure. He says he is not a priest.

oficio era de barbero. Y en vista de lo referido le hizo traer asido a la cárcel de esta ciudad, en donde protesta pasar al reconocimiento de las alhajas que trae en dicha alforja. Y para que todo lo referido conste, lo mandó así poner por deligencia y firmó con mí, el escribano, que de todo ello doy fe.

Ante mí,
Antonio Pérez

Declaración

En dicha ciudad de Orense, dicho día, mes y año dichos, dicho Bernardo de Pando, alguacil ordinario de ella, estando a la puerta de la cárcel real antes de entrar en ella para saber si el susodicho es sacerdote o no y resolver la parte donde se ha de poner preso el dicho peregrino, mestizo al parecer por la cara, color, y pelo de él, tomó y recibió juramento, que lo hizo en debida forma por Dios nuestro Señor y una señal de cruz en su mano derecha. Prometió de decir verdad. Y habiéndole preguntado cómo
Que es de la isla de Santo Domingo, aunque antes dijo era de Italia.
se llama y donde es natural y si es sacerdote o no y si trae papeles que acrediten su estado, *dijo: que él se llama Josef Soller, mestizo cristiano católico que cree firmemente en la ley* de Dios; y que es de la isla de Santo Domingo, *aunque antes había dicho era de Italia o Nápoles*; y que su estado era de peregrino que había venido en romería al apóstol Santiago, de donde venía; y su oficio era de barbero pero no tenía el estado y dignidad de
Corona por achaques
sacerdote ni órdenes mayores ni menores, ni tampoco sabía latín, que sólo era un pobre barbero; que la corona la había abierto por achaques que padecía y ser estilo de su tierra. Y esto dijo y declaró debajo dicho juramento, en que se afirmó y ratificó. No lo firmó porque dijo no saber ni
No sabe leer.
tampoco leer, según así lo confesó, de que yo, el escribano, doy fe, y que
46 es de hedad de cuarenta | y seis años poco más o menos. Firmolo dicho 2r
ministro con mí, el escribano, que de todo ello doy fe.

Alhajas que hayó en las alforjas

Ante mí,
Antonio Pérez

profession was that of a barber. In light of the abovementioned matter, he was restrained and brought to this city's jail, where the bailiff insists on identifying the objects that Soller carries in said knapsack. And so that the abovementioned matter be documented, the bailiff ordered it put on the record in this fashion. He signed with me, the judicial secretary, to all of which I attest.

Before me,
Antonio Pérez

Affidavit

In said city of Ourense on said day, month, and year, the aforementioned Bernardo de Pando, its bailiff, being at the gate of the royal jail before entering into it in order to learn whether or not the abovementioned is a priest and to resolve the matter as to where to place said pilgrim as a prisoner, apparently of mixed race judging by his face, color, and hair. He took and received an oath, which he did formally by God, Our Father, and the sign of the cross in his right hand. He promised to tell the truth. Having asked him his name, where he is from, whether or not he is a priest, and whether he carries documents that prove his status, *he said: that his name is José Soller, mixed-race-Catholic-Christian who believes firmly in the law* of God and who is from the island of Santo Domingo, *although previously he had said he was from Italy or Naples*; that his status was that of a pilgrim who had arrived on pilgrimage to the Apostle Santiago, from where he was coming; that his profession was that of barber but that he did not have the status and rank of priest, neither major nor minor orders (neither did he know Latin); that he only was a poor barber who had shaved the tonsure for ailments from which he suffered and for being the fashion of his country. This he said and swore under said oath, which he confirmed and upheld. He did not sign because he said he did not know how or how to read, as he confessed it in this fashion, to which I,
2r the judicial secretary, attest, and that he is forty-six | years old more or less. Said official so signed with me, the judicial secretary, to all of which I attest.

That he is from the island of Santo Domingo, although he previously said he was from Italy.

Tonsure for ailments

Does not know how to read.

46

Valuables that were found in his knapsacks.

Before me,
Antonio Pérez

Reconocimiento de las alhajas de la alforja

Y luego incontinenti dicho Bernardo de Pando, asistido de mí, escribano, y a presencia de dicho Josef Soller, peregrino, pasó al reconocimiento de las alhajas que trae en las alforjas que se le cogieron al susodicho. Y a presencia de muchas personas se hallaron en ellas las alhajas siguientes: un alzacuello de sacerdote nuevo de *baeta* de Palencia negra; dos cuellos de paño blanco de clérigo; un par de mangas o fundas de la misma *baeta*; un par de calzones del mismo género sin forro, todo nuevo; y un pedazo de *baeta* negra del mismo género como cosa de una vara; un libro de a medio pliego con su pergamino con un rótulo al principio que dice "1682 años.
Libro de *Caja*
Libro de *caixa* de João Sánchez. *Yesús, María, Josef.*" Y por adentro enuncia ser un libro de caja y asiento de un mercader portogués de la ciudad de Coimbra foliado, cuya última hoja tiene el número 92, rubricadas todas ellas junto a la foleatura con un apellido que dice "Menezes," en cuyas hojas hay diferentes partidas de cuenta con diferentes sujetos y mercadurías que anuncian importar mucha suma de maravedíes, y dentro de él muchos papeles de crédito, cartas, misivas, y libramientos de diferentes cantidades, y algunos presos con alfileres en las hojas. Más se halló en dicha alforja: una cartera de hoja de lata; y dentro de ella algunos papeles y despachos de pasaporte en orden a la perigrinación de Josef Soller; y entre ellos *un despacho de Santiago en latín de letra de molde con la hechura del apóstol Santiago firmado del Doctor don Jacinto Suárez, su fecha en Com-*
En 25 de marzo de 93
postela a veinte y cinco de marzo de este presente año; *y en un* blanco de dicho despacho de letra de mano entre dos renglones de molde hay un rótulo que dice así, "*Don Josephum Soler, Sacerdotem Indianum.*" Y en vista de dicho despacho se pasó al reconocimiento de los demás pasar si en ellos se hallaba relación de que el susodicho fuese sacerdote mediante lo menciona serlo el despacho referido de la ciudad de Santiago. En los cuales no se halló fuese tal sacerdote. Todo lo cual se halló en dichas alforjas en donde se volvió a recoger con dicho libro para dar cuenta de ello y manifestarlo al Señor Corregidor. Y habiéndole preguntado dicho ministro al susodicho | que respecto tenía declarado no ser sacerdote ni 2v
constaba serlo por los despachos que traía, exceto el de Santiago, dijese a
Que los barberos de su tierra se vestían con el hábito de sacerdotes.
qué propósito había mandado hacer el alzacuello de *baeta*, traía los cuellos de eclesiástico, y quien le había dado la *baeta*, a lo cual *respondió el susodicho que los barberos en su tierra traían aquella insinia como los clérigos, y que por eso lo había mandado hacer* en esta ciudad de tres varas de

Inspection of the Valuables in the Knapsack

Immediately, the aforementioned Bernardo de Pando, with the assistance of myself, judicial secretary, and in the presence of said José Soller, pilgrim, proceeded to the inspection of the valuables that the abovementioned carries in the knapsacks seized from him, and in the presence of many people, the following valuables were found: a new clerical neckband made from black Palencia flannel; two white priest's collars made of white cloth; a pair of sleeves or covers made from the same flannel; a pair of unlined pants of the same type, completely new; a piece of black flannel of the same type, about a rod in length; a quarto-sized, parchment-bound book with a label that reads, "1682. Cashbook of João Sánchez. Jesús, María, José." Inside, it is formatted as a journal of cash and transactions belonging to a Portuguese merchant from the city of Coimbra, foliated, the last leaf of which is numbered 92, each countersigned beside the folio number with the surname Menezes, on the folios of which there are different account records with different persons and merchandise that profess to be worth a large sum of maravedis, and within it many credit documents, letters, memoranda, and payment orders of different quantities, some of them fastened to the folios with pins. More was found in said knapsack: a tin-plate wallet, inside it some passport documents and certificates having to do with the pilgrimage of José Soller, among them *a printed diploma from Santiago in Latin with the printed image of the Apostle Santiago, signed by Doctor Don Jacinto Suárez, dated in Compostela on the 25th of March of this present year. On a* blank line of said diploma, handwritten between two lines of print, there is an inscription that reads as follows: *Don Joseph Soller, Priest of the Indies.* In light of said diploma, the other documents were inspected to determine if any an account was found that the abovementioned should be a priest, as the specified diploma from the city of Santiago mentions him being one. Among these documents he was not found to have been a priest. Everything that was found in said knapsacks was gathered and returned with said book in order to take account of it and show it to the Lord Chief Magistrate. Said official, having asked the abovementioned | about his claim that he was not a priest, nor was he documented as being one by the certificates he carried (except for the one from Santiago), to state for which purpose he had made the flannel clerical neckband, carried the priest's collars, and who had given him the flannel, to which *the abovementioned responded that the barbers in his country wore the same regalia as priests and that this is why in this city he had ordered it to be made* from three rods of Palencia flannel, which he

Cashbook

On the 25th of March of '93

2v

That the barbers from his country don the habit of priests.

baeta de Palencia que había comprado a seis reales y medio la vara. Y en vista de todo lo referido, dicho ministro le puso preso en la cárcel y entregó por tal a Antonio dos Santos, carcelero. Y protestó dar cuenta de todo ello al Señor Corregidor y manifestarle todas las alhajas para que en su vista provea lo que fuere servido. Y para [que] todo ello conste, lo mandó poner por deligencia, que firmó, estando a todo ello presentes por testigos Andrés Pérez, Gregorio de Castro y Matías Sueyro, herradores vecinos de esta ciudad, e yo, escribano, que [de] todo ello da fe.

Ante mí,
Antonio Pérez

Auto

Depósito en poder del escribano.

En la ciudad de Orense a los dichos catorce días del mes de abril de mil y seiscientos y noventa y tres años, el señor licenciado don Juan Antonio Covillas, corregidor de esta ciudad y su tierra por Su Majestad, habiendo visto estos autos y reconocido las alhajas, libro, y papeles de cartera, dijo que mandaba y mandó que el dicho libro de caja con los papeles que están dentro de él y los de la cartera los resguarde y tenga en su poder el presente escribano cerrados y en custodia para el seguro del dueño de dicho libro. Y las más alhajas se ponga en depósito | por el alguacil ordinario, 3r
para que se le da comisión en forma. Y en cuanto a la prosecución de esta causa protesta Su Merced hacer las deligencias necesarias. Y por este auto así lo mandó y firmó.

licenciado Covillas

Ante mí,
Antonio Pérez

Orense y abril, 14 de 1693

Tengo en mi poder el libro de caja y cartera de papeles que refieren estos autos, lo firmo.

Antonio Pérez

had bought for six-and-a-half reals per rod. In light of all of the aforementioned, said official imprisoned him and entrusted him as a prisoner to Antonio dos Santos, Warden, and he insisted on accounting for everything to the Lord Chief Magistrate and on showing him all the valuables so that he may provide what might be of use. For all of that to be documented, he ordered it put in writing, which he signed, being present as witnesses to all that Andrés Pérez, Gregorio de Castro, and Matías Sueyro, resident blacksmiths of this city, and I, the judicial secretary, who attests to all of that matter.

Before me,
Antonio Pérez

Ruling

In the city of Ourense on said 14th day of the month of April of the year 1693, Lord Don Juan Antonio Covillas, Esquire, Chief Magistrate of this city and its territory for His Majesty, having heard these proceedings and inspected the valuables, book, and wallet-documents, said that he would order and ordered that said cashbook with the documents that are inside it and those of the wallet be protected and for the present judicial secretary to have them in his possession, sealed and in custody for the security of the owner of said book, and that the other valuables be placed under
3r custody | by the bailiff, for which he is authorized. As far as carrying out this case, His Grace insists on completing the necessary procedures. By this ruling he so ordered, and signed.

Deposit in possession of the judicial secretary.

Covillas, Esquire

Before me,
Antonio Pérez

Ourense and April 14, 1693

I have in my possession the cashbook and wallet of documents to which these proceedings refer. I so sign.

Antonio Pérez

Depósito de las alhajas

Depósito de los bienes

En Orense, dicho día, Bernardo de Pando, alguacil ordinario de esta ciudad en cumplimiento del auto de arriba, entregó y puso en depósito en manos y poder de Domingos Sánchez, vecino de esta ciudad, un alzacuello, unas mangas, y un par de calzones de *baeta* de Palencia negra y un pedazo de *baeta* del mismo género de hasta una vara con poca diferencia, todo ello recogido en unas alforjas viejas. Y le apercibió tenga dichos bienes en su poder a ley de depósito, sin acudir con ellos a ninguna persona sin orden del Señor Corregidor. Y visto por el susodicho [Sánchez], acetó dicho depósito en la forma que se le manda y se obligó de dar cuenta de dicha ropa cada y cuando que le sea pedida, pena de pagarlo de sus bienes. No firmó por no saber. Hízolo dicho ministro, siendo testigos Francisco y Andrés Pérez e yo, el escribano, que de ello doy fe.

Ante mí,
Antonio Pérez | 3v

Declaración del reo

En la ciudad de Orense y dentro de la cárcel real de ella, a quince días del mes de abril de mil y seiscientos y noventa y tres años, el señor don Juan Antonio Covillas Venero, corregidor de esta ciudad y su tierra por Su Majestad, por ante mí, escribano, tomó y recibió juramento del reo contenido en estos autos, que lo hizo en debida forma por Dios nuestro Señor y una señal de cruz. Prometió de decir verdad y luego le hizo las preguntas siguientes. Preguntado diga cómo se llama, dónde es natural, qué oficio tiene, si es casado o soltero o qué estado tiene y a qué viene a esta tierra, dijo: se llama José Soller Chivo, natural de la isla de Santo Domingo en el Perú de Indias, de donde salió habrá diez y seis años; y vino en compañía del conde de Alayos; y asistió mucho tiempo en Madrid y otras partes; y que su oficio *es de barbero* y arbolario; y no tiene ni ha tenido otro estado ni ejercicio; *ni sabe leer ni escribir*; y que tiene de hedad cuarenta y dos o cuarenta y cuatro años poco más o menos porque no trae la fe de bautismo; y que a esta tierra vino desde la Villa de Zafra en romería

Que hay 16 años que salió de su tierra

Deposit of the Valuables

In Ourense on said day, Bernardo de Pando, bailiff of this city, in fulfillment of the above ruling, turned in and placed under custody and in the hands and possession of Domingos Sánchez, resident of this city: one clerical collar, some sleeves, a pair of black Palencia flannel pants, and a piece of flannel of the same type measuring up to almost exactly a rod, all of it contained in some old knapsacks. He was admonished to keep said goods in his possession under custody law, without approaching anyone with them absent an order from the Lord Chief Magistrate. Seen by the abovementioned [Sánchez], he accepted said deposit in the manner he is ordered, and he was obliged to take account of said clothing when and where he should be asked, under penalty of paying for it from his own possessions. He did not sign because he doesn't know how. Said minister did sign, being witnesses Francisco and Andrés Pérez, and I, the judicial secretary, to all of which I attest.

Deposit of the goods

Before me,
3v *Antonio Pérez* |

The Prisoner's *Affidavit*

In the city of Ourense and inside its royal jail, on the 15th day of the month of April of the year 1693, Lord Don Juan Antonio Covillas Venero, Chief Magistrate of this city and its territory for His Majesty, before me, the judicial secretary, took and received the oath of the prisoner contained in these proceedings, which he did formally by God Our Lord and a sign of the cross. He promised to tell the truth, and right then and there he was asked the following questions. Asked to tell his name, where he is from, what profession he has, whether he is married or single, or to which estate he belongs and for what purpose he comes to this country, he said: his name is José Soller Chivo, native to the island of Santo Domingo in Perú of the Indies, from where he left going on sixteen years ago; that he came in the company of the Count of Alayos; that for a long time he was present in Madrid and other parts; that his profession *is that of barber* and herbalist; that he does not have nor has he had any other estate or practice; that *he does not know either how to read or to write*; that he is more or less forty-two or forty-four years of age, because he does not carry his baptismal certificate; and that he came to this country from the villa of Zafra on

That he left his country 16 years ago

al apostol Santiago, como constará de sus papeles, que están reconocidos. Y responde.

Preguntado, pues dice que no es sacerdote ni tiene órdenes algunas, ni sabe leer ni escribir, diga por qué dispuso que en el despacho que se le dio se le escribiese que era sacerdote de las Indias. Diga verdad. Dijo que como había de pasar al reino de Francia y otras partes y haberle ya preso algunas

Causa de fingirse sacerdote

veces con el pretesto de que era esclavo, para andar con libertad y que no le volviese a suceder lo mesmo, pidió se le escribiese era sacerdote, asegurándolo así. Y la causa de haberlo logrado fue porque a pedimento suyo unos sacerdotes peregrinos catalanes aseguraron en la ciudad de Santiago

En Orense hízose la corona. alzacuello

que el que declara era también sacerdote. Y en vista de ello, se lo escribieron así en el despacho. Y en conformidad de ello en esta ciudad anteayer, abrió la corona de sacerdote y mandó hacer un alzacuello de tal para dos cuellos que tenía y lograr con este hábito pasar libre y que no le prendiesen por esclavo según la fisonomía de su rostro moreno y *cabelo* rizo como lo habían hecho en otras ocasiones. Y que lo referido no lo hizo con ánimo de profanar el estado eclesiástico, sí sólo por la causa que lleva referido. Y responde. Preguntado diga qué barbero le hizo la corona y qué sastre le hizo el alzacuello, mangas y calzón de *baeta* negra que contienen estos autos, dijo que no conoce a uno ni a otro. Sí, sólo conocerá las casas y los
sujetos | si se le da lugar a ello. Y responde. Preguntado diga quién le ha 4r
dado un libro de caja al parecer de un mercader portogués, vecino de la

Libro. Que compró el libro en Santiago por 6 cuartos

ciudad de Coimbra, reino de Portugal, y si ha estado en algún tiempo en dicha ciudad, dijo: que dicho libro lo compró en la ciudad de Santiago a un peregrino, no sabe de qué nación; y le dio seis cuartos por él, pero que no sabe de quién es; y compró con ánimo de saber de quién era para entregárselo y que le diese algún hallazgo, para lo cual estaba determinado pasarse por el reino de Portogal, por cuyo reino vino también a éste y a esta ciudad a visitar el Santo Cristo. Y esto dijo ser la verdad so cargo del juramento que fecho tiene, en que se afirmó y ratificó. No firmó porque dijo no saber, y por ahora Su Merced suspendió esta deligencia con

pilgrimage to the Apostle Santiago, as will be manifest in his documents, which have been inspected. He responds.

Reason for impersonating a priest

He made the tonsure in Ourense.

Clerical collar

Asked to tell why he determined to have written in the diploma he received that he was a priest of the Indies since he says he is not a priest, does not have any orders whatsoever, and knows neither how to read nor how to write. Tell the truth. He said: that as he had passed through the kingdom of France and other parts and had been imprisoned already several times under the pretext that he was a slave, in order to walk freely and so that the same thing should not happen to him again, he asked for it to be written that he was a priest, assuring his freedom in this fashion; that the reason for his having carried it out was because at his request, some Catalan pilgrim-priests claimed that he who is testifying also was a priest, and considering all of that, they wrote it for him in this fashion on the diploma; that in acceptance of that apparent fact in this city the day-before-yesterday, he shaved the priest's tonsure and commissioned that a clerical neckband be cut for two priest's collars that he had, with this clerical habit to manage to move freely so that they should not apprehend him as a slave according to the physiognomy of his dark-skinned face and curly hair, as they had done on other occasions; and that he did not do the abovementioned with the intention to desecrate the clergy but rather only for the reason that he produces above. He responds. Asked to tell which barber made him the tonsure and which tailor made him the clerical collar, sleeves, and black flannel pants that these proceedings contain, he said that he does not know one from the other but rather that he will
4r recognize the dwellings and the individuals | if he is allowed to for that purpose. He responds. Asked to tell who gave him the cashbook apparently belonging to a Portuguese merchant, resident of the city of Coimbra, kingdom of Portugal, and whether he has been in said city at some time, he said: that he bought said book in the city of Santiago from a pilgrim, he does not know of which nationality; that he gave him six *cuartos* for it, but he does not know whose it is; and that he bought it with the intention of finding out whose it was in order to turn it in to him and to be given some finder's reward, for which purpose he was determined to pass through the kingdom of Portugal, through which kingdom he also came to this one and to this city in order to visit the Holy Christ. This he said to be the truth under obligation of the oath that he took, which he confirmed and upheld. He did not sign his name because he said he does not know how. For now, His Grace suspends this procedure with the inten-

Book. That he bought the book in Santiago for 6 *cuartos*

protestación de proseguir en las que sean necesarias, y lo firmó con mí, escribano, de que doy fe.

Covillas

Ante mí,
Antonio Pérez

Auto

En la ciudad de Orense a los dichos quince días del mes de abril de mil y seiscientos y noventa y tres años, el Señor Corregidor, en vista de la declaración de arriba, y que por ella no consta quiénes fueron los barbero y sastre que hicieron la corona y alzacuello, mangas y calzón que refieren los autos al dicho Josef Soller, para justificarlo, mandó Su Merced que al susodicho se le saque de la cárcel y se lleve a las tiendas de barberos y sastres de esta ciudad para que reconozca las dónde se le hizo la corona | 4v
y ropa, como también los maestros u oficiales que intervinieron en ello, para en su vista proveer justicia. Y por este auto así lo mandó y firmó.

Covillas

Ante mí,
Antonio Pérez

Reconocimiento de las tiendas. *Barbero y sastre*

En la ciudad de Orense a los dichos quince días del mes de abril de mil y seiscientos y noventa y tres años, el señor licenciado don Juan Antonio de Covillas, corregidor de esta ciudad y su tierra por Su Majestad, asistido de mí, el escribano, y de sus ministros, hizo sacar de la cárcel al dicho Josef Soller, contenido en estos autos. Y en conformidad del auto de arriba, lo hizo enderezar y llevar por sus ministros a la Plazuela de la Pescadería, donde los barberos tienen sus tiendas. Y habiendo llegado a ella, le mandó reconociese la tienda donde se le había abierto la corona. Y en vista de ello, immediatamente se enderezó sin tropiezo y con todo conocimiento a la tienda de Antonio Forneiro, maestro barbero, en donde no se halló persona alguna, por cuya razón dicho Señor Corregidor mandó a dicho Josef Soller declare el sujeto que le abrió la corona en dicha tienda y qué señales tenía, para venir en su conocimiento. El cual dijo que el barbero

tion of continuing the ones that may be necessary. He signed with me, the judicial secretary, to which I attest.

Covillas

Before me,
Antonio Pérez

Ruling

In the city of Ourense on said 15th day of the month of April of the year 1693, the Lord Chief Magistrate, considering the above affidavit and that it is not clear from that who the barber and tailor were who shaved the tonsure and made the clerical collar, sleeves, and pants to which the proceedings refer for José Soller, in order to rectify it, His Grace ordered that Soller be removed from the jail and be taken to the shops of the barbers and tailors of this city so that he may inspect those where he was given a
4v tonsure | and clothing, as he also may the tradesmen and skilled workers who took part in the matter, in order, in his consideration, to administer justice. By means of this ruling he so ordered, and signed.

Covillas

Before me,
Antonio Pérez

Identification of the Shops. *Barber and Tailor*

In the city of Ourense on said 15th day of the month of April of the year 1693, Lord Don Juan Antonio de Covillas, Esquire, Chief Magistrate of this city and its territory for His Majesty, with the assistance of myself, the judicial secretary, and of his officials, had said José Soller, contained in these proceedings, removed from jail, and in accordance with the above ruling, had him directed and taken by his ministers to the Fish Market Plaza, where the barbers have their shops. Having arrived at the Plaza, he ordered that Soller identify the shop where he had his tonsure shaved. Considering the matter, he immediately directed himself without stopping and with full knowledge to the shop of Antonio Forneiro, master barber, where not a single person was found, for which reason said Lord Chief Magistrate ordered said José Soller to describe the individual who shaved his tonsure in said shop and what features he had in order to be able to recognize him. Soller said that the barber who had shaved him and

que le había afeitado y abierto | la corona en dicha tienda era un sujeto bajo de cuerpo, moreno de rostro y el cabello rizo y negro. Y habiéndose hecho pregunta qué sujeto sería y qué oficiales había en aquella tienda, se halló noticia que los oficiales que asistían en ella eran Antonio de Castro y Antonio Siabal, y que este último era quien había barbeado y abierto la corona al dicho Josef Soller. Y hecho todo lo referido, Su Merced mandó al susodicho se encaminase a la casa o tienda del sastre que le había hecho el alzacuello, mangas, y calzón, el cual se enderezó a la calle de la Fontaíña, y en ella a la casa de Pedro Castro, sastre, el cual estaba trabajando a la puerta de su casa. Y visto y reconocido por dicho Josef Soller, dijo al Señor Corregidor que aquel maestro era el que le había hecho la ropa y alzacuello que refieren los autos, y en ello estaba cierto por conocerle muy bien. Y visto por el dicho Pedro de Castro, sastre, dijo que era verdad le había hecho a aquel hombre un alzacuello, mangas y calzón de bayeta, y así lo confesó, de que yo, el escribano doy fe. Y en vista de ello, el Señor Corregidor mandó a sus ministros volviesen a la cárcel a dicho Josef Soller y le asegurasen en las prisiones, y que el dicho sastre compareciese en los patios de las Casas Consistoriales para el efecto que hubiese lugar. Y habiéndose ejecutado así y dado orden se buscase al dicho Antonio de Siabal, en virtud de ello, compareció ante el Señor Corregidor. Y siendo preguntado, declaró inmediatamente era verdad había hecho la corona al sujeto por quien se le preguntaba, pero lo había ejecutado así por haberle dicho era sacerdote y traer ya señal de corona, que a saber lo contrario no lo hubiera hecho. Y para que todo lo referido conste, Su Merced lo mandó así poner por deligencia y firmó con mí, el escribano, que de todo ello doy fe. 5r

licenciado Covillas

Ante mí,
Antonio Pérez

Auto de prisión

Y luego incontinenti dicho Señor Corregidor, en vista de la declaración | y deligencia antecedente hecha por los dichos Antonio González y Pedro de Castro, dijo que mandaba y mandó que los susodichos sean puestos 5v

5r shaved | his tonsure in said shop was an individual short in stature, dark-skinned in the face, and with a black and curly head of hair. Having asked which individual it would be and which skilled workers were in that shop, it was discovered that the skilled workers who helped in the shop were Antonio de Castro and Antonio Siabal, and that it was the latter who had cut and shaved the tonsure of said José Soller. The aforementioned matter being completed, His Grace sent the abovementioned to show the way to the house or shop of the tailor who had made him the clerical collar, sleeves, and pants. Soller directed himself to Fontaíña Street, and on it to the house of Pedro Castro, tailor, who was working at the doorway of his house. Seen and recognized by said José Soller, he said to the Lord Chief Magistrate that it was that master tailor who had made him the clothing and clerical collar to which the proceedings refer, and in this matter he was certain in having recognized him very well. Seen by said Pedro de Castro, tailor, he said that it was true that he had made for Soller a clerical collar, sleeves, and flannel pants. So he confessed, to which I, the judicial secretary, attest. Considering the matter, the Lord Chief Magistrate ordered his officials to return said José Soller to the jail and to secure him in shackles and chains, and that said tailor appear in the patio of the Town Hall for the outcome that should be approved. Having in this fashion carried out and given the order to search for said Antonio de Siabal, he appeared before the Lord Chief Magistrate as a result. Being questioned, he immediately stated it was true he had made the tonsure for the individual about whom he was being asked but that he had carried it out in this fashion on account of Soller having told Siabal that Soller was a priest and for already bearing the mark of the tonsure, which, had Siabal known otherwise, he would not have given. So that the abovementioned matter be documented, His Grace ordered that a written record be made in this fashion. He signed with me, the judicial secretary, to all of which I attest.

licenciado Covillas

Before me,
Antonio Pérez

Prison Ruling

Immediately, said Lord Chief Magistrate, considering the previous affi-
5v davit | and record made by said Antonio González and Pedro de Castro, said that he would order and ordered that the abovementioned persons

presos en la cárcel real de esta ciudad para tomarles sus declaraciones y pasar a lo que haya lugar de derecho. Y por este su auto así lo mandó y firmó.

licenciado Covillas

Ante mí,
Antonio Pérez

Declaración de Antonio González Siabal

En la ciudad de Orense y dentro de la cárcel real de ella, a los dichos quince días del mes de abril de mil y seiscientos y noventa y tres años, el señor licenciado don Juan Antonio Covillas, corregidor de esta ciudad y su tierra por Su Majestad, asistido de mí, escribano, vino a dicha cárcel para efecto de tomar la declaración a Antonio González Siabal, barbero, vecino de esta ciudad, del cual tomó y recibió juramento, que lo hizo en debida forma por Dios nuestro Señor y una señal de cruz. Prometió de decir verdad y luego le hizo las preguntas siguientes. Preguntado diga si sabe que como tal barbero está obligado a no hacer coronas de órdenes mayores ni menores a ninguna persona forastera que no sea muy conocida y que por su hábito y noticias se le pueda hacer, diga verdad. Dijo que inora lo que se le pregunta. Y responde. Preguntado si es verdad que el día trece pasado de este presente mes llegó a su tienda un hombre peregrino, forastero moreno, al parecer mestizo y esclavo, sin traer hábito ni insinias clericales, al cual habiéndole [afeitado] la barba, le hizo y abrió una corona del tamaño de las de los sacerdotes, diga verdad. Dijo que la es de que el susodicho llegó a dicha tienda para afeitarse y habiéndole limpiado la cara, le dijo al que declara le hiciese también la corona. Y haciendo juicio era sacerdote por verle traía señal de corona en la cabeza, le respondió que aún se reconocía que no era necesario señalársela más, a que | dijo 6r no la había limpiado desde Lisboa. Y con esta instancia es verdad le hizo dicha corona por el cerco y señal que traía, y le pagó cuatro cuartos por su trabajo. Y esto dijo ser la verdad so cargo del juramento que fecho tiene, en que se afirmó y ratificó y lo firmó, y que es de hedad de treinta y tres años. Firmolo el Señor Corregidor con mí, escribano, de que doy fe.

Que traía señal de corona

licenciado Covillas *Antonio González*

Ante mí,
Antonio Pérez

be held prisoner in the royal jail of this city in order to take their affidavits and proceed to what may be lawfully approved. By this his ruling he so ordered it, and he signed.

Covillas, Esquire

Before me,
Antonio Pérez

Affidavit of Antonio González Siabal

In the city of Ourense and within its royal jail, on the 15th day of the month of April of the year 1693, Lord Don Juan Antonio Covillas, Esquire, Chief Magistrate of this city and its territory for His Majesty, with the assistance of myself, judicial secretary, came to said jail for the purpose of taking the affidavit of Antonio González Siabal, barber, resident of this city from whom he took and received an oath, which he did formally by God, Our Father, and a sign of the cross. He promised to tell the truth, and then he asked him the following questions. Asked to tell whether he knows that as a barber, he is obligated to not give tonsures of the major or minor orders to any outsider who is not very well known and who by his habit and news can be known to him. Tell the truth. He said that he is unaware of what he is being asked. He responds. Asked if it is true that on the previous 13th day of the present month, a dark-skinned male pilgrim-outsider, apparently of mixed-race and a slave, not wearing any habit or priestly regalia, having shaved his beard for him, he made and shaved him a tonsure of the size of those of priests. Tell the truth. He said that it is true that the abovementioned arrived to said shop for a shave. Having shaved his face, Soller asked he who is testifying to make him a tonsure, as well. Judging he was a priest by seeing that he bore the outline of the tonsure on his head, González Siabal responded to him that it still was distinguishable, that it
6r was not necessary to show it to him anymore, to which | Soller replied he had not shaved it since Lisbon. In this case, it is true that González Siabal made said tonsure because of the outline and mark that he Soller bore, and he paid him four *cuartos* for his work. This he said to be the truth under obligation of the oath he has sworn, which he confirmed, upheld, and so signed, and that he is thirty-three years old. The Lord Chief Magistrate so signed with myself, the judicial secretary, to which I attest.

That he already bore the mark of a tonsure

Covillas, Esquire

Antonio González
Before me,
Antonio Pérez

Declaración de Pedro de Castro

Dentro de dicha cárcel, dicho día, mes y año dichos, dicho Señor Corregidor, prosiguiendo la averiguación de esta causa para el castigo de culpados, tomó y recibió juramento de Pedro de Castro, *xastre*, vecino de esta ciudad, preso en dicha cárcel, el cual lo hizo en debida forma por Dios nuestro Señor y una señal de cruz, prometió de decir verdad. Y luego le hizo las preguntas siguientes. Preguntado si es verdad que el día trece pasado de este presente mes llegó a su casa peregrino forastero moreno, mestizo, llamado Josef Soller, sin insinia alguna de sacerdote, el cual le entregó al que declara un poco de *baeta* negra para que le hiciese un alzacuello de eclesiástico, unas mangas o fundas y un calzón, diga verdad. Dijo que la es lo que se le pregunta, pero que dicha ropa y alzacuello se la hizo creyendo era sacerdote mediante le ha visto corona de tal, aunque no llevaba otra insignia. Y después de hecha la obra, le pagó su trabajo, sin que en el que declara hubiese habido culpa alguna respecto haber dicho era clérigo, y como tal traía la corona. Y esto dijo ser la verdad so cargo del juramento que fecho tiene, en que se afirmó y ratificó. No firmó porque dijo no saber, y que es de hedad de veinte y ocho años poco más o menos. | 6v
Firmolo el Señor Corregidor con mí, el escribano, que de todo ello doy fe.

licenciado Covillas

Ante mí,
Antonio Pérez

Auto

En la ciudad de Orense dicho día, mes y año dichos, el señor licenciado don Juan Antonio Covillas, corregidor de esta ciudad y su tierra por Su Majestad, habiendo visto todos estos autos, dijo que para más justificación de esta causa mandaba y mandó que el presente escribano ponga a continuación de este auto los pasaportes y papeles que se hallaron al dicho Josef Soller, recogidos en la cartera que refieren los autos, en que se incluye el despacho que parece se le dio en la ciudad de Santiago, firmado

Affidavit of Pedro de Castro

Within said jail on said day, month, and year, said Lord Chief Magistrate, continuing the inquiry of this case for the punishment of the guilty, took and received the oath of Pedro de Castro, tailor, resident of this city, prisoner in said jail, which he did formally by God, Our Father, and a sign of the cross. He promised to tell the truth, and then he was asked the following questions. Asked if it is true that on the previous 13th day of this present month, a dark-skinned, mixed-race pilgrim-outsider named José Soller arrived at his house without any priestly regalia, who delivered to him who testifies a little bit of black flannel for him to make him a clerical collar, some sleeves or covers, and a pair of pants. Tell the truth. He said that it is true what he is being asked but that he made said clothing and clerical collar for him believing he was a priest by means of having seen his tonsure, although he did not wear any other regalia. After the task was completed, he paid him for his work without there having had been any blame on the part of him who testifies, considering that Soller said he was a priest and as such, wore the tonsure. This he said to be the truth under obligation of the oath he has made, which he confirmed and upheld. He did not sign because he said he did not know how, and that he is twenty-
6v eight years old more or less. | The Lord Chief Magistrate signed with me, the judicial secretary, to all of which I attest.

Covillas, Esquire

Before me,
Antonio Pérez

Ruling

In the city of Ourense on said day, month, and year, Lord Don Juan Antonio Covillas, Esquire, Chief Magistrate of this city and its territory for His Majesty, having heard all these proceedings, said that for further proof in this case he would order and did order that the present judicial secretary place following this ruling the passports and documents that were found on said José Soller, gathered in the wallet to which the proceedings refer, among which is included the diploma that he seems to have been given in the city of Santiago, signed by Doctor Don Jacinto Suárez, in which it

del Doctor don Jacinto Suárez, en que se hace mención que el susodicho es sacerdote indiano. Y por este auto así lo mandó y firmó.

licenciado Covillas

Ante mí,
Antonio Pérez | 7r

[salvi conductus]

Georgius Cornelius

Dei, et apostolicae sedis gratia Archiepiscopus Rhodiensis, Sanctissimi Domini nostri Papae, praelatus domesticus, et assistens, eiusque, et dictae Sanctae Sedis in Portugallia, et Algarbiorum regnis, atque dominiis cum potestate legati de Latere nuntius.

Universis, et singulis praesentes nostras salvi conductus litteras visuris, lecturis, seu legi audituris, salutem in Domino sempiternam. Cum dilectus in Christo *Joseph Soller, indianus del cividade de Perú,* exponi fecerit, quod justis de causis eum moventibus, et praecipuè devotionis gratiâ *ad Jacobum in Compostella, et postea Romam* se conferre intendat, nobisque propterea humiliter supplicari fecerit, ut eum nostris litteris concomitari dignaremur. Nos considerantes altissimo pergratum esse Peregrinis favere, huiusmodi supplicationibus inclinati, omnes, et singulos principes, comites, barones, militiarum duces, magistratus civitatum, et oppidorum, capitaneos, milites, alios quoscunque, ad quos latorem praesentium divertere contigerit, rogamus, atque in Domino hortamur, ut eidem liberum aditum, et transitum tam in eundo, quàm redeundo permittant, et concedant, nec patiantur damno vel injuria à quoquam vexari, sed omni benignitatis, auxilii, et patrocinii argumentum eidem praestare dignentur, mercedem ab omnipotenti Deo, benefactorum remuneratore, et vicissitudinem officiorum ad occasiones quascunque parem à nobis accepturi. In quorum fidem, et cetera. Ullyssipone die 4 mensis *Februarii* 1693.

Gratis ubique. *Dominus Archepiscopus Rhodiensis*

Legis ferendarum. *Joannes Andreas Rinaldarum, secretario* || 7v 8r

Provida niste Convento de Tomar,
23 de fevereiro, de 693
†...†

refers to the abovementioned being a priest from the Indies. By this ruling he so ordered, and signed.

Covillas, Esquire

Before me,
7r *Antonio Pérez* |

GIORGIO CORNARO [safe-conduct]

THE ARCHBISHOP OF RHODES, BY THE GRACE OF GOD AND OF THE APOSTOLIC SEE, domestic prelate in residence to His Holiness our Lord Pope and for him NUNCIO and Legate at Large with full authority of said Holy See to the Lords of Portugal and the Algarves.

To one and all who may see, read or hear read these our present letters of safe conduct, enduring greetings in the Lord. As our beloved in Christ *Joseph Soller, Spanish subject of the Indies from the kingdom of Perú*, made known with lawful motive on his journey *to Santiago de Compostela, and subsequently to Rome*, and especially moved by devotion, requested be conferred up him, and thereafter humbly beseeched us that we might deem him worthy of our accompanying documentation. As we consider it pleasing to the Most High to aid pilgrims and to be favorably inclined to those who petition in this way, we beg and, in the name of God, exhort princes, counts, barons, military commanders, city and town officials, captains, soldiers, and whoever else to whom the present letters may broadly pertain, that they allow him the same free approach and travel in going as in returning, and that they not allow such persons to suffer harm or injury or to be harassed anywhere but rather offer them the same support of kindness, aid, and shelter in disputes, counting on recompense from Almighty God, rewarder of good works, that the vicissitudes of permissions and whatever happenstance be accounted as granted to us. In witness whereof, et cetera. In Lisbon on the *4th* day of the month of *February*, 1693.

Free of charge everywhere. *The Lord Archbishop of Rhodes*

7v 8r *To be lawfully administered.* *João André Rinaldo, secretary* | |

Furnished in this Monastery of Tomar
February 23, 1693
†...†

[carta de guia] O PROVEDOR e Irmaõs da Mesa da Misericórdia da cidade de Lisboa fazemos saber aos Provedores e Irmaõs da Mesa das Misericórdias a que esta nossa carta de guia for apresentada que de esta cidade vai *Josef Soller para Valença* [*do Minho*] com cavalgadura.

E por nos constar de sua muita pobreza e necessidade, foi provido com as esmolas de esta Santa Casa pelo que pedimos a Vossas Mercês que indo el seu caminho direito, favoreçaõ com suas esmolas para ajuda de passar seu caminho. Escrita na Mesa, a os 11 dias do mês de *fevereiro* de 1693 annos.

Fernan de Soiza Castelbranco
Coitinho e Menezes
Luis de Mello
Nuno da Silva Seller
Vasco Anfeiar de Menezes
Antonio Correa da †…†on

Provida na Mesa de Santarém
en 17 de fevereiro de 693 anos.
Antonio †…† Velho

Provida na Misericórdia de Tomar
en 23 de fevereiro 693

†…† †…† †…† †…†

Provido neste mosteiro
de Moreira em 9 de março
de 1693
†…†

Provida nesta Misericórdia de
Viana [*do Castelo*] *em 12 março*
de 1693.
Andre da Costa do †…†, Provedor

Provido nesta Misericórdia
de Valença [*do Minho*], *em 14 de*
março de 1693.
†…† Gonçalo Teisera Coelho. | |

Jo†…† da Silveira
†…†
Antonio Brabo da Silva

Miguel Manesca
Manoel Nunes | 8v

Provida nesta a Misericórdia
da Vila da Golegã, dozoito de
fevereiro de 693.
José Sebastião Ravello †…†

Provido nesta Misericórdia de
Coimbra, 22 de fevereiro de 1693.
Bernardo P†…†

Provido nesta Misericórdia
de Aveiro en 28 de fevereiro
de 1693 e pedió y
†…† †…† †…†.

Provida †…† Santa T†…††…†
fevereiro 23, 1693 †…†.

Provido nesta Misericórdia de
Caminha, 13 de março 1693 anos.
†…† Almeida Leiva

9r–v
10r

THE DIRECTOR and brothers of the Assembly of Misericórdia make known to the directors and brothers of the Assembly of Misericórdias that according to this, our conferred credential, *Joseph Soller* is traveling on horseback *to Valença do Minho*. [pilgrim's credential]

And his great poverty and need being known to us, he was provided with the alms of this Holy House, through which we ask Your Graces that, virtuously undertaking his travels, he be provided with your charity to help him continue his journey. Written in the Assembly on the *11th* day of the month of *February* of the year 1693.

Fernan de Soiza Castelbranco
Coitinho e Menezes
Luis de Mello
Nuno da Silva Seller
Vasco Anfeiar de Menezes
8v *Antonio Correa da †...†on.*

Furnished in the Assembly of Santarém on the 17th of February, 1693.
Antonio †...† Velho

Furnished in the Misericórdia of Tomar on the 23rd of February, 1693.

†...† †...† †...† †...†

Furnished in this monastery of Moreira on the 9th of March of 1693.
†...†

Furnished in this Misericórdia of Viana do Castelo on the 12th of March, 1693.
Andre da Costa do †...†, Director

Furnished in this Misericórdia of Valença do Minho, on the 14th of March of 1693.
9r–v *†...† Gonçalo Teisera Coelho.* | |
10r

Jo†...† da Silveira
†...†
Antonio Brabo da Silva

Miguel Manesca
Manoel Nunes |

Furnished to the Misericórdia of the town of Golegã the eighteenth of February of 1693.
José Sebastião Ravello †...†

Furnished in this Misericórdia of Coimbra the 22nd of February of 1693.
Bernardo P†...†

Solicited and furnished in this Misericórdia of Aveiro on the 28th of February of 1693 and
†...††...† †...†

Furnished †...† Santa T†...††...†
February 23, 1693 †...†.

Furnished in this Misericórdia of Caminha, the 13th of March, 1693.
†...† Almeida Leiva

[compostela] Doctor Dominus Hiacinthus Suárez, Cardinalis Maior, Dignitas, et Canonicus huius Metropolitanae et Apostolicae Ecclesiae Compostellanae, necnon Administrator Capellae Christianissimi Francorum Regis, ibi constitutae ut ex toto terrarum Orbe Christi fidelibus intimo devotionis affectu seu voti ad implendi gratia limina Apostoli nostri ac Hispaniarum unici et singularis patroni et tutelaris, Sancti Jacobi. Visitantibus Sacramentaliter sub veniatur, omnibus et singulis praesentes litteras inspecturis notum, facio *Don Josephum Soler, Sacerdotem Indianum*, huius sacratissimi templi limina visitasse confessumque, et absolutum eucharisticum Domini corpus sumpsisse. In quorum fidem praesens confero testimonium meo nomine subscriptum, et sigillo eiusdem Sanctae Ecclesiae munitum. Datum Compostellae, die *25*, mensis *martii*, anno *1693*.

Doctor Hiacinthus Suárez || 10v 11r

Pedro de Castro, *xastre*, vecino de esta ciudad, preso en la cárcel real de ella por decir había compuesto un alzacuello a un forastero que venía en traje de clérigo, de que estoy sin culpa, suplico a Vuestra Merced se sirva mandarme tomar mi confesión y dar vista de los autos para decir de mí justicia, que pido con costas y para ello, etcétera.

Soutullo | 11v

Tómesele su confesión. Cométese con comisión en forma al presente escribano de la causa. Lo decretó el señor licenciado don Juan Antonio Covillas, corregidor de esta ciudad y su tierra por Su Majestad, en Orense a diez y seis de abril de mil y seiscientos y noventa y tres años.

licenciado Covillas

Ante mí,
Antonio Pérez

Confesión

En la ciudad de Orense, a diez y seis días del mes de abril de mil y seiscientos y noventa y tres años, yo, escribano, en conformidad del auto de arriba tomé y recibí juramento de un reo preso en dicha cárcel, el cual lo hizo

DOCTOR DON JACINTO SUÁREZ, Senior Cardinal, Dignitary and Canon of this Metropolitan and Apostolic Church of Compostela, and also the Administrator of the Chapel of his most Christian Majesty of France, to which see are constituted from all lands of the Earth for the faithful in Christ moved by profound devotion or by vow for garnering grace at the thresholds of our Apostle of all Spain, its unique and special patron and protector, SAINT JAMES, who should come sacramentally to those visitors, let it be known to one and all who inspect these present letters that I confirm that *Don Joseph Soller, Priest of the Indies*, has visited the thresholds of this sacred temple, made confession, and once absolved, received the Eucharistic body of Christ. In faith of which I confer this diploma signed in my name below, and validated with the seal of the same holy church. Dated in Compostela, the *25th* day of the month of *March* in the year *1693*. [pilgrim's diploma]

10v
11r *Doctor Jacinto Suárez* | |

I, Pedro de Castro, tailor, resident of this city, imprisoned in its royal jail for stating I had fabricated a clerical collar for an outsider who arrived in priest's attire, for which I am without guilt, beseech Your Grace deem just to offer to receive my confession and to consider the proceedings in order to ensure justice on my behalf, which I request with costs and for that purpose, et cetera.

11v *Soutullo* |

May his confession be received, and may the present judicial secretary of the case be authorized for this purpose. Lord Don Juan Antonio Covillas, Esquire, Chief Magistrate of this city and its territory for His Majesty, so ruled in Ourense on the 16th of April of the year 1693.

Covillas, Esquire

Before me,
Antonio Pérez

Confession

In the city of Ourense on the sixteenth day of the month of April of the year 1693, I, the judicial secretary, in acceptance of the above ruling, took and received the oath of a prisoner imprisoned in said jail, which he made

por Dios nuestro Señor y una señal de cruz, prometió de decir la verdad. Y luego le hizo las preguntas siguientes. Preguntado diga cómo se llama, dónde es vecino, qué hedad y oficio tiene, dijo se llama Pedro de Castro, vecino de esta ciudad, y tiene de hedad veinte y ocho años poco más o menos y su oficio es de *xastre*. Y responde. Preguntado si es verdad que: los días pasados llegó a su casa un peregrino mulato llamado Josef Soller, sin llevar insinia alguna que manifestase ser eclesiástico; y le entregó al confesante un poco de *baeta* negra para que le hiciese un alzacuello de clérigo, unas mangas y un par de calzones; y le hizo dicha ropa. Diga verdad. Dijo que afirmándose en lo que ya tiene declarado, vuelve a decir es verdad que el sujeto que se le pregunta le mandó hacer dicha ropa, y el alzacuello se lo hizo creyendo era sacerdote respecto le ha visto corona de tal, que a saber que no lo era no se lo hubiera hecho. Y responde. Fuéronle hechas otras preguntas y repreguntas al caso tocantes, a que dijo se afirma en lo que lleva dicho por ser así la verdad, so cargo del juramento que fecho tiene en que se afirmó y ratificó. No lo firmó por no saber, de todo ello, yo, escribano, doy fe.

Ante mí,
Antonio Pérez | 12r

Antonio González Siabal, barbero, vecino de esta ciudad, preso en la cárcel real de esta ciudad por decir había hecho la barba y corona a un forastero que venía en traje de clérigo, de que estoy sin culpa, suplico a Vuestra Merced se sirva mandarme tomar mi confesión y dar vista de los autos para decir de mí justicia, que pido con costas, y para ello, etcétera.

Soutullo | 12v

Tómesele su confesión. Cométese con comisión en forma al presente escribano de la causa. Lo declaró el señor licenciado don Juan Antonio Covillas, corregidor de esta ciudad y su tierra por Su Majestad, en Orense a diez y seis de abril de mil y seiscientos y noventa y tres años.

licenciado Covillas

Ante mí,
Antonio Pérez

by God, Our Father, and a sign of the cross. He promised to tell the truth, and then he was asked the following questions. Asked to state his name, where he resides, how old he is and what his occupation is, he said: his name is Pedro de Castro, resident of this city; he is 28 years old more or less; and his profession is that of tailor. He responds. Asked if it is true that in the preceding days: a mulatto pilgrim named José Soller arrived to his house without bearing any regalia showing that he was a priest; handed the confessant a little bit of black flannel to have him fabricate a priest's collar, some sleeves, and a pair of pants; and that he made him said clothes. Tell the truth. He said that, upholding what he already has testified, he repeats that it is true that the individual about whom he is being questioned commissioned said clothing, and he made the clerical collar for him believing he was a priest based on having seen his tonsure, which had he known otherwise, he would not have made it for him. He responds. He was asked and asked again other questions pertinent to the case, to which he said he maintained what he has previously said on account of it being the truth, under obligation of the oath that he has taken, which he confirmed and upheld. He did not sign because he doesn't know how, to all of which I, the judicial secretary, attest.

Before me,
12^r *Antonio Pérez* |

I, Antonio González Siabal, barber, resident of this city, imprisoned in the royal jail of this city for stating I had shaved the beard and tonsure of an outsider who arrived in a priest's outfit, for which I am without guilt, beseech Your Grace deem just to offer to receive my confession and consider the proceedings in order to ensure justice on my behalf, which I request with costs and for that purpose, et cetera.

12^v *Soutullo* |

May his confession be received. May the present judicial secretary of the case be authorized for this purpose. Lord Don Juan Antonio Covillas, Esquire, Chief Magistrate of this city and its territory for His Majesty, so ruled in Ourense on the 16th of April of the year 1693.

Covillas, Esquire

Before me,
Antonio Pérez

En la ciudad de Orense a los dichos diez y seis días del mes de abril de mil y seiscientos y noventa y tres años, yo, escribano, en conformidad del auto de arriba, vine a dicha cárcel para efecto de tomar la confesión a un reo preso en ella, del cual tomé y recibí juramento, que lo hizo en debida forma por Dios nuestro Señor y una señal de cruz. Prometió de decir verdad, y luego le hice las preguntas siguientes. Preguntado diga cómo se llama, dónde es vecino, qué hedad y oficio tiene, dijo se llama Antonio González Siabal, vecino de esta ciudad, y que es de hedad de treinta y tres años poco más o menos y su oficio es de barbero. Y responde. Preguntado diga si es verdad que los días pasados llegó a [su] tienda un peregrino mulato llamado Josef Soller, sin insinia de eclesiástico por donde pudiese conocer fuese sacerdote, y le pidió le hiciese la barba y corona de tal, y con efecto pasó a hacérsela. Diga verdad. Dijo que la es que el susodicho fue a su tienda al efecto referido, y habiéndole afeitado, le dijo le hiciese también la corona, que era sacerdote. Dijo le había dicho lo era Juan Bautista,
Que ya traía señal de corona
vecino de esta ciudad, y así por esta razón como por haberle reconocido la cabeza y hallado en ella el cerco de corona de sacerdote y haber dicho no la había limpiado desde la ciudad de Lisboa, haciendo juicio era tal sacerdote, es verdad | se la limpió. Y por ello le dio cuatro cuartos según 13r
ya lo tiene declarado, en que se afirma y ratifica. Y responde. Preguntado si es verdad que el dicho peregrino no traía hábito ni cuello de eclesiástico ni otra insinia alguna que lo manifestase, antes sí por su fisonomía, rostro moreno y cabello rizo, pudo hacer juicio era esclavo y no sacerdote. Diga verdad. Dijo que no hizo mucho reparo en las insinias, sí sólo en el cerco de la corona, y que es verdad no traía cuello ni hábito sacerdotal. Y reconoció era moreno de cara y rizo de pelo. Y responde. Fuéronle hechas otras preguntas y repreguntas al caso tocantes, a que dijo se afirma en lo que tiene dicho por ser así la verdad, en que se afirma y ratifica. Y lo firmó con mí, el presente escribano, que de todo ello doy fe.

Antonio González

Ante mí,
Antonio Pérez | | 13v 14r

In the city of Ourense on said sixteenth day of the month of April of the year 1693, I, the judicial secretary, in acceptance of the above ruling, came to said jail for the purpose of receiving the confession of a prisoner detained there, from whom I took and received an oath, which he made formally by God, Our Father, and a sign of the cross. He promised to tell the truth, and then I asked him the following questions. Asked to state his name, where he resides, his age, and his profession, he said: he is named Antonio González Siabal, resident of this city; that he is thirty-three years old more or less; and his profession is that of a barber. He responds. Asked to state if it is true that: in recent days, a mulatto pilgrim named José Soller arrived at his shop without clerical regalia by which he could have been known to be a priest; asked him to shave his beard and tonsure; and with that intention, he went on to shave it for him. Tell the truth. He said it was true that the abovementioned went to his shop for said purpose, and having shaved him, he asked him to shave his tonsure, as well, because he was a priest. He said Juan Bautista, resident of this city, had told him he was a priest and that in this fashion and for this reason, as well as for having inspected his head and found on it the outline of a priest's tonsure and for having said he had not shaved it since the city of Lisbon, judging he was
13r such a priest, it is true | that he shaved it. For that purpose he gave him four *cuartos* according to what he already has testified, which he confirms and upholds. He responds. Asked if it is true that said pilgrim was not wearing either the habit or the collar of a priest, or any other regalia that would show him to be one, but rather by his physiognomy, dark-skinned face, and curly head of hair, he could have determined he was a slave and not a priest. Tell the truth. He said that: he did not pay much attention to the regalia but rather only to the outline of the tonsure; that it is true that he was not wearing either the collar or the habit of a priest; and that he recognized that he was dark-skinned in the face and curly in the hair. He responds. He was asked and asked again other questions pertinent to the case, to which he said he maintains what he already has said on account of it being the truth, which he confirms and upholds. And he so signed with me, the present judicial secretary, to all of which I attest.

That he already bore the visible sign of a tonsure

Antonio González

Before me,
13v
14r *Antonio Pérez* | |

Pedro de Castro, *xastre*, vecino de esta ciudad, preso en la cárcel real de ella por decir compuse un alzacuello a un forastero que venía en traje de sacerdote, de que estoy sin culpa y mi confesión tomada, y la verdad del caso es lo que ella contiene, por lo cual y que soy un pobre, a Vuestra Merced suplico se sirva mandarme soltar libremente de dicha prisión, no procediendo más contra mí en dicha causa, respecto mi inocencia que consta de los autos. Y para ello, desde luego, concluyo a difinitiva. Y en todo espero recibir merced con justicia, que pido, y para ello, etcétera.

Soutullo | 14v

Autos. Lo decretó el señor licenciado don Juan Antonio Covillas, corregidor de esta ciudad y su tierra por Su Majestad, en Orense a diez y siete de abril de mil y seiscientos y noventa y tres años.

Juan Antonio Covillas

Ante mí,
Antonio Pérez

Vistos estos autos por el señor licenciado don Juan Antonio Covillas, corregidor de esta ciudad y su tierra por Su Majestad, en Orense a diez y siete de abril de mil y seiscientos y noventa y tres años, dijo que mandaba y mandó que fiando a esta parte Pedro, digo Antonio González Siabal, barbero, su compañero en esta causa, de estar a derecho en ella, pagar juzgado y sentenciado, vaya suelto de la prisión, apercibido si de este procedimiento resultare más culpa, para pagar y cumplir lo que Su Merced determinare. Y pagando las costas causadas hasta ahora, se libre el mandamiento de soltura, y lo firmó.

licenciado Covillas

Ante mí,
Antonio Pérez

Notificación y fianza

En la ciudad de Orense y dentro de la cárcel real de ella, a diez y siete días del mes de abril de mil y seiscientos y noventa y tres años, yo, escribano, hice saber y notifiqué el auto de arriba a Pedro de Castro, *xastre*, vecino de esta ciudad, preso en dicha cárcel. Y por él entendido, dijo lo obedece

I, Pedro de Castro, tailor, resident of this city, imprisoned in its royal jail for stating I made a clerical collar for an outsider who arrived in the outfit of a priest, for which I am without guilt and my confession received, and the truth of the matter is what it contains, for this reason and because I am a poor person, beseech Your Grace deem just to request that I be released freely from said prison, not proceeding further against me in said case, considering my innocence which is recorded in the proceedings. For that purpose, of course I conclude definitively. In all matters, I hope to receive grace with justice, which I request, and for that purpose, et cetera.

14v *Soutullo* |

Proceedings. Lord Don Juan Antonio Covillas, Esquire, Chief Magistrate of this city and its territory for His Majesty, so ruled in Ourense on the 17th of April of the year 1693.

Juan Antonio Covillas

Before me,
Antonio Pérez

Lord Don Juan Antonio Covillas, Esquire, Chief Magistrate of this city and its territory for His Majesty, in Ourense on the 17th of April of the year 1693, having heard these proceedings, said that he would order and ordered that, vouching in this matter for Pedro, I mean Antonio González Siabal, barber, his partner in this case, being compliant in it, judged and sentenced to pay, be released from prison, being forewarned that if these proceedings should result in further offense, to pay and to obey what His Grace should order. Paying the costs incurred up to now, may the release order be dispatched. He so signed.

Covillas, Esquire

Before me,
Antonio Pérez

Notice and Bail Bond

In the city of Ourense and inside its royal jail, on the 17th day of the month of April of the year 1693, I, the judicial secretary, informed and notified Pedro de Castro, tailor, resident of this city, imprisoned in said jail, of the above ruling. Understood by him, he said he obeys it and consents, and

y consiente. Y en su cumplimiento se obliga en debida forma y a sus bienes muebles y raíces habidos y por haber | de estar a derecho y justicia en 15r
esta causa y pagar todo lo en que fuere juzgado y sentenciado en ella por el Señor Corregidor, atendiendo a su leve culpa, pena de ser compelido a ello por todo rigor de derecho. Y pagará las costas y daños que se causaren, y a mayor abundamiento, en conformidad del auto antecedente del Señor Corregidor, da por su fiador, deudor y principal pagador a Antonio González Siabal, barbero, vecino de esta ciudad, también preso en dicha cárcel, el cual, que está presente, dijo lo aceta. Y haciendo de deuda y caso ajeno suyo propio y entendiendo lo que en esto aventura, con renunciación de la ley del engaño, dijo se obligaba y obligó en forma con su persona y bienes muebles y raíces habidos y por haber de que el susodicho estará a derecho y justicia en esta causa. Y pagará toda la cantidad en que fuere condenado y sentenciado en ella por el Señor Corregidor en la forma que va obligado, y en defecto, el otorgante, como tal su fiador, deudor y principal pagador que por tal se constituye, lo cumplirá y pagará de sus bienes. Y a ello quiere y consiente ser compelido y pagará las costas y daños que se causaren. Y para la guarda, cumplimiento y ejecución de ello ambas partes, cada una por lo que le toca, dan todo su poder cumplido y se someten a las justicias seglares de Su Majestad y de su fuero y jurisdición que de ellos puedan conocer conforme a derecho para que así se lo hagan guardar y cumplir como si esta carta y su contenido fuera sentencia difinitiva de juez competente pasada en cosa juzgada, cerca de lo cual renunciaron todas leyes, fueros y derechos de su favor, la general y derechos de ella. Y otorgaron obligación y fianza en bastante forma. Y la firmó el dicho Antonio González y por que el dicho Pedro de Castro dijo no saber, de su ruego lo firmó un testigo de los presentes, que lo fueron a todo ello Andrés Pérez, Antonio dos Santos, alcaide, y Facundo Álvarez, vecinos de esta ciudad, e yo, escribano, que de todo ello doy fe y de que conozco a los otorgantes.

Antonio González

Como testigo y a ruego,
Andrés Pérez
Ante mí,
Antonio Pérez || 15v 16r

in fulfillment of it he is formally obliged and by his personal property and
15r real estate acquired and yet to be acquired | to be in compliance and law-abiding in this case and to pay all that should be judged and sentenced in it by the Lord Chief Magistrate, accepting his mild guilt, under penalty of being compelled to that matter by the full force of law. He will pay the costs and damages that should be incurred, and moreover, in agreement with the preceding ruling by the Lord Chief Magistrate, he presents Antonio González Siabal, barber, resident of this city, also imprisoned in said jail, as his guarantor, debtor, and principal payor, who, being present, said he accepts it. Making of the debt and matter of another his own and understanding what is risked in this matter, in renunciation of the law of deceit, he said he would commit and committed formally with his person, personal property, and real estate acquired and yet to be acquired that the abovementioned will be in compliance and law-abiding in this case, and he will pay the full amount to which he should be penalized and sentenced in it by the Lord Chief Magistrate in the manner in which it is obliged. In its absence, the signing party, who as such is become his guarantor, debtor, and principal payor, will fulfill it and will pay from his possessions. For that purpose he wishes and consents to be compelled, and he will pay the costs and damages that should be incurred. For the protection, fulfillment, and execution of that matter, both parties, each one according to what affects him, give all of their full power, and they submit themselves to the secular judicial processes of His Majesty and of his authority and jurisdiction, that from them they may understand according to law so that in this fashion, they protect and fulfill it as if this document and its contents were the final decision of a proper judge passed into law, in pursuit of which they renounced all laws, privileges, and rights in their favor, the general law and its rights. They rather formally transferred a promissory note and bail. Said Antonio González so signed. Because said Pedro de Castro said he did not know how, upon his request, a witness so signed among those present, among whom were there for all of the matter Andrés Pérez, Antonio dos Santos, warden, and Facundo Álvarez, residents of this city, and I, the judicial secretary, to all of which I attest, and that I know the parties who sign and execute this public instrument.

Antonio González

As a witness and signed upon request,
Andrés Pérez

15v Before me,
16r *Antonio Pérez* | |

Antonio González Siabal, barbero, vecino de esta ciudad, preso en la cárcel real de ella por decir he refrendado la corona y hecho la barba a un forastero que venía en traje de sacerdote, de que estoy sin culpa y mi confesión tomada. Y la verdad del caso es lo que ella contiene, por lo cual y que soy un pobre suplico a Vuestra Merced se sirva mandarme soltar libremente de dicha prisión, no procediendo más contra mí en dicha causa respecto mi inocencia, que consta de los autos. Y para ello concluyo a difinitiva. Y en todo espero recibir merced con justicia, que pido, y para ello, etcétera.

Soutullo | 16v

Júntese a los autos y se traigan. Lo decretó el señor licenciado don Juan Antonio Covillas, corregidor de esta ciudad y su tierra por Su Majestad, en Orense a diez y siete de abril de mil y seiscientos y noventa y tres años.

Juan Antonio Covillas

Ante mí,
Antonio Pérez

Auto

Vistos estos autos por el señor licenciado don Juan Antonio Covillas, corregidor de esta ciudad por Su Majestad, en Orense a diez y siete de abril de mil y seiscientos y noventa y tres años, dijo que mandaba y mandó que fiando a esta parte Pedro de Castro, sastre, su compañero en esta causa, de estar a derecho en ella, pagar juzgado y sentenciado, vaya suelto de la prisión, apercibido si de este procedimiento resultare más culpa para pagar y cumplir lo que Su Merced determinare, y pagando las costas causadas hasta ahora, se le libre el mandamiento de soltura. Y lo firmó.

licenciado Covillas

Ante mí,
Antonio Pérez

I, Antonio González Siabal, barber, resident of this city, imprisoned in its royal jail for stating I have redone the tonsure and shaved the beard of an outsider who was arriving in the outfit of a priest, for which I am without guilt and my confession taken, and the truth of the case is that which it contains, for which reason and because I am a poor person, beseech that Your Grace deem just to order me freely released from said prison, not proceeding further against me in said case, considering my innocence, which is recorded in the proceedings. For that purpose, of course I conclude definitively. In all matters, I hope to receive grace with justice, which I request, and for that purpose, et cetera.

16v *Soutullo* |

May the proceedings be gathered and brought. So ruled Lord Don Juan Antonio Covillas, Esquire, Chief Magistrate of this city and its territory for His Majesty, in Ourense on the 17th of April of the year 1693.

Juan Antonio Covillas

Before me,
Antonio Pérez

Ruling

These proceedings having been heard by Lord Don Juan Antonio Covillas, Esquire, Chief Magistrate of this city for His Majesty, in Ourense, on the 17th of April of the year 1693, he said that he would order and ordered, vouching in this matter for Pedro de Castro, barber, González Siabal's partner in this case, being compliant in it, judged and sentenced to pay, that Castro be released from prison, being forewarned that if these proceedings result in further offense, to pay and to obey what His Grace should order. Paying the costs incurred up to now, may the release order be dispatched. He so signed.

Covillas, Esquire

Before me,
Antonio Pérez

Notificación y fianza

En la ciudad de Orense y dentro de la cárcel real de ella, a diez y siete días del mes de abril de mil y seiscientos y noventa y tres años, yo, escribano, notifiqué el auto de arriba a Antonio González Siabal, barbero, vecino de esta ciudad, preso en dicha cárcel. Y por él entendido, dijo lo obedece y consiente. | Y en su cumplimiento, se obliga en forma con su persona y 17r
bienes muebles y raíces habidos y por haber de estar a derecho y justicia en esta causa y pagar todo lo en que fuere juzgado y sentenciado en ella por el Señor Corregidor, atendiendo a su leve culpa, pena de ser compelido a ello por todo rigor. Y pagará todas las costas y daños que se causaren. Y a mayor abundamiento, en conformidad del auto antecedente del Señor Corregidor, da por su fiador, deudor y principal pagador a Pedro de Castro, *xastre*, vecino de esta ciudad, también preso en dicha cárcel, el cual, que está presente, dijo lo aceta. Y haciendo de deuda y caso ajeno suyo propio y entendiendo lo que en esto aventura, con renunciación de la ley del engaño, dijo salía y salió por fiador, deudor y principal pagador del dicho Antonio González Siabal, y se constituyó por tal en esta causa. Y se obligó en forma con su persona y bienes muebles y raíces habidos y por haber de que el susodicho estará a derecho y justicia en ella. Y pagará toda la cantidad en que fuere juzgado y sentenciado por el Señor Corregidor u otro juez competente. Y en defecto, el otorgante, como tal su fiador, deudor y principal pagador lo pagará de sus bienes con las costas y *danos* que se causaren, a que consiente ser compelido y apremiado por todo rigor. En cuya conformidad ambas partes para la guarda, cumplimiento y ejecución de ello dan todo su poder cumplido y se someten a las justicias seglares de Su Majestad, de su fuero y jurisdición, que de ellos puedan y deban conocer conforme a derecho para que así se lo hagan guardar y cumplir como si esta escritura y lo en ella contenido fuera sentencia difinitiva de juez competente pasada en cosa juzgada. Cerca de lo cual renunciaron todas leyes, fueros y derechos de su favor, la general y derechos de ella. Y otorgaron obligación y fianza en bastante forma. Y la firmó el dicho Antonio González. Y porque el dicho Pedro de Castro dijo no saber, de su ruego lo firmó un testigo de los presentes, que lo fueron a todo ello Andrés

Notice and Bail Bond

In the city of Ourense and inside its royal jail, on the 17th day of the month of April of the year 1693, I, the judicial secretary, informed and notified Pedro de Castro, tailor, resident of this city, imprisoned in said jail, of the
17r above ruling, and understood by him, he said he obeys it and consents. | In fulfillment of it, he is formally obliged and by his personal property and real estate acquired and yet to be acquired to be in compliance and law-abiding in this case and to pay all that should be judged and sentenced in it by the Lord Chief Magistrate, accepting his mild guilt, under penalty of being compelled to do so by the full force of law. He will pay the costs and damages that should be incurred, and moreover, in agreement with the preceding ruling by the Lord Chief Magistrate, he presents Pedro de Castro, tailor, resident of this city, also imprisoned in said jail, who being present, said he accepts it. Making his own the debt and case of another, and understanding what is risked in this matter, in renunciation of the law of deceit, he said he would vouch and vouched for said Antonio González Siabal as the guarantor, debtor, and principal payor. He appointed himself as such in this case, and he formally committed himself with his person, personal property, and real estate, acquired and yet to be acquired, that the abovementioned will be in compliance and law-abiding in this case. He will pay the full amount to which he should be penalized and sentenced by the Lord Chief Magistrate or another proper judge. If not, the signing party, as such his guarantor, debtor, and principal payor, will pay from his possessions the costs and damages that should be incurred, to which he consents to be urged and compelled with full force. In agreement of which, both parties, for the protection, fulfillment, and execution of that matter, give all of their full power and they submit themselves to the secular laws of His Majesty and of his authority and jurisdiction, that from them they may and ought to understand according to law so that in this fashion they protect and fulfill it as if this document and its contents were the final judgment of a proper judge passed into law, in pursuit of which they renounced all laws, privileges, and rights in their favor, the general law and its rights. They rather formally transferred a promissory note and bail. Said Antonio González so signed. Because said Pedro de Castro said he did not know how, upon his request a witness so signed among those present, among whom were there for all of it Andrés Pérez,

Pérez, Facundo Álvarez y Antonio dos Santos, alcaide de dicha cárcel, e yo, escribano, que de todo ello doy fe y de que conozco a los otorgantes.

Antonio González

Como testigo y a ruego,
Andrés Pérez
Ante mí,
Antonio Pérez | 17v

Tasa de costas

En la ciudad de Orense a los dichos diez y siete días del mes de abril de mil y seiscientos y noventa y tres años, el señor licenciado don Juan Antonio Covillas, corregidor de esta ciudad y su tierra por Su Majestad, por ante mí, escribano, hizo la tasa de costas de todos estos autos para que las paguen por mitad los dichos Antonio González y Pedro de Castro en la manera siguiente. Para Su Merced de todos derechos hasta esta tasa

inclusive quince reales:	015.
Para el presente escribano hasta esta tasa, veinte y siete:	027 reales.
Para Bernardo de Pando, alguacil ordinario, por la prisión y más deligencias que hizo:	006.
Y en esta forma hizo Su Merced dicha tasa y la firmó, de que doy fe.	*48*

licenciado Covillas

Ante mí,
Antonio Pérez

Pagaron treinta reales, deben lo demás.

Auto

En la ciudad de Orense a 20 días del mes de abril de mil y seiscientos y noventa y tres años, el señor | licenciado don Juan Antonio Covillas, corregidor de esta ciudad y su tierra por Su Majestad, en vista de estos autos dijo que mandaba y mandó que el presente escribano tome la confesión 18r

Facundo Álvarez, and Antonio dos Santos, warden of said jail, and I, the judicial secretary, to all of which I attest, and that I know the parties who sign and execute this public instrument.

Antonio González

As a witness and signed upon request,
Andrés Pérez
Before me,
17v *Antonio Pérez* |

Amount of Court Costs

In the city of Ourense on said 17th day of the month of April of the year 1693, Lord Don Juan Antonio Covillas, Esquire, Chief Magistrate of this city and its territory for His Majesty, before me, the judicial secretary, calculated the amount of court costs for all these proceedings so that said Antonio González and Pedro de Castro split them in the following manner. For His Grace, by all rights up to this amount,

including fifteen reals:	015.
For the present judicial secretary up to this amount, twenty-seven:	027 reals.
For Bernardo de Pando, bailiff, for the prison and other duties he executed:	006.
In this fashion His Grace calculated said amount.	*48*

He so signed, to which I attest.

licenciado Covillas

Before me,
Antonio Pérez

They paid thirty reals; they owe the rest.

Ruling

In the city of Ourense on the 20th day of the month of April of the year
18r 1693, Lord | Don Juan Antonio Covillas, Esquire, Chief Magistrate of this city and its territory for His Majesty, in consideration of these proceedings, said that he would order and ordered that the present judicial secretary receive the confession of José Soller Chivo, that for that purpose

a Josef Soller Chivo, que para ello se le da comisión en forma y hecho. Se dé vista y traslado de todos estos autos al teniente promotor fiscal. Y lo firmó.

licenciado Covillas

Ante mí,
Antonio Pérez

Confesión

En la ciudad de Orense y dentro de la cárcel real de ella a veinte y un días del mes de abril de mil y seiscientos y noventa y tres años, yo, escribano, en cumplimiento del auto de arriba, vine a dicha cárcel para efecto de tomar la confesión a un reo preso en ella, del cual tomé y recibí juramento, que lo hizo en debida forma por Dios nuestro Señor y una señal de cruz. Prometió de decir verdad, y luego le hizo las preguntas siguientes. Preguntado cómo se llama, dónde es vecino, qué hedad y oficio tiene, dijo: se llama Josef Soller Chivo, natural de la isla de Santo Domingo en el Perú; y que su oficio es de barbero arbolario; y que vino a esta tierra peregrinando en romería al apóstol Santiago y al Santo Cristo de esta ciudad; y que su hedad [es de] cuarenta y dos o cuarenta y cuatro años poco más o menos. Y responde. Preguntado pues dice es barbero, diga si es verdad que los días pasados, | fingiendo ser sacerdote, hizo que un barbero le abriese 18v
corona de tal, como con efecto lo hizo, y mandó hacer un alzacuello de *baeta* negra que se le halló con dos cuellos en las alforjas. Diga en todo verdad. Dijo que afirmándose y ratificándose en lo que antes de ahora tiene declarado por ante el Señor Corregidor y del presente escribano, vuelve a decir que es verdad que por haberle sucedido en su peregrinación haberle preso algunas veces por decir era esclavo, dispuso ponerse de clérigo para pasar libre y sin embarazo por todas partes. Para lo cual, hallándose en la ciudad de Santiago, pidió a dos o tres sacerdotes estranjeros declarasen ante el Señor Cardenal de los pasaportes que también lo era el confesante para que se le escribiese así en el despacho que se le diese. Y así se ejecutó. Y llegando a esta ciudad, mandó abrir la corona y hacer el alzacuello diciendo era clérigo por lograr hacer su viaje libremente con hábito de sacerdote, que este fue el motivo y no otro alguno. Ni jamás ha tenido ánimo de profanar el estado de sacerdote porque como católico, es muy temeroso de Dios. Y responde. Preguntado diga si es verdad se le halló en sus alforjas un libro de caja y de cuenta y razón de un mercader llamado Juan Sánchez, vecino de la ciudad de Coimbra, reino

he is given formal and actual authorization. May all these proceedings be delivered and communicated to the Deputy Prosecutor. He so signed.

Covillas, Esquire

Before me,
Antonio Pérez

Confession

In the city of Ourense and within its royal jail on the 21st day of the month of April of the year 1693, I, the judicial secretary, in fulfillment of the above ruling, came to said jail with the intention of receiving confession from a prisoner detained there, from whom I took and received an oath, which he made formally by God, Our Father, and a sign of the cross. He promised to tell the truth, and then was asked the following questions. Asked his name, where he resides, how old he is and what profession he has, he said: his name is José Soller Chivo, native to the island of Santo Domingo in Perú; that his profession is that of an herbalist barber; that he came to this country journeying on pilgrimage to the Apostle Santiago and to the Holy Christ of this city; and that he is forty-two or forty-four years old, more or less. He responds. Asked since he says he is a barber, tell whether
18v it is true that in recent days, | impersonating a priest, he had a barber give him a tonsure, as with that intention he did it, and he commissioned a clerical neckband of black flannel, which was found in his knapsacks with two collars. Tell the whole truth. He said that confirming and upholding what he previously has testified before the Lord Chief Magistrate and the present judicial secretary, he repeats that it is true that on account of him having been imprisoned sometimes while on pilgrimage for being presumed to be a slave, he set out to dress as a priest to pass everywhere freely and unencumbered, for which purpose, finding himself in the city of Santiago, he asked two or three foreign priests to testify before the diploma-granting Senior Cardinal that the confessant also was a priest so that it would be so written on the diploma that was given to him. It was executed in this fashion. Arriving to this city, he ordered a tonsure shaved and a clerical collar made, saying he was a priest in order to complete his journey freely in the priest's habit, that this was his motive and none other. Neither has he ever harbored an intention to desecrate the priestly caste because as a Catholic, he is very fearful of God. He responds. Asked to tell whether it is true that a cashbook and accounting ledger belonging to a businessman named Juan Sánchez, resident of the city of Coimbra, king-

de Portogal, y dónde hubo dicho libro, dijo que hallándose en dicha ciudad de Santiago con otros peregrinos de diferentes partes, uno de ellos, que no sabe de donde era, traía dicho libro y se lo vendió al confesante por seis cuartos. Y él lo compró con ánimo de pasarse por Portogal, preguntar por el dueño de dicho libro y entregárselo para que por su hallazgo le diese algunas camisas o ropa para vestirse. Y que en esta razón no hubo otra cosa. Y responde. Fuéronle hechas otras preguntas y repreguntas al caso tocantes, a que dijo que todo lo que lleva dicho en esta confesión y en la declaración hecha antes de ahora es la verdad, so cargo del juramento que fecho tiene, en que se afirmó y ratificó. No lo firmó porque dijo no saber leer ni escribir. De todo ello yo, el escribano, doy fe.

Ante mí, 19r–v
Antonio Pérez || 20r

Juan del Rodicio, teniente de promotor fiscal de esta ciudad, por lo que incumbe a la vindicta pública con la cual se castiguen culpados, ante Vuestra Merced en la mejor forma que de derecho lugar haya, me querello criminalmente. Acuso y pido entero cumplimiento de justicia de Josef Soller, peregrino mulato, y de las más personas que comprehendidas fueren en el dilito y caso de que abajo se hará mención, a las cuales y a cada uno de ellos les pongo acusación en toda forma. Y haciendo del caso verdadera relación, digo que el sobredicho, menospreciando el estado sacerdotal, siendo mulato, que se conoce de su aspecto, se fingió sacerdote, acreditando esta maldad con las vestiduras e insignias de tal, obligando que se le abriese corona para engañar a las personas con quien comunicase, y por este medio cargar su conciencia pidiendo limosna para misas. Y aún se puede inferir de este hecho que hombre tan depravado intentara en alguna aldea hacer sacrificio no obstante de la ignorancia que confiesa tener en leer y escribir, lo cual le agrava más el delito y el engaño y cautela porque persuadió al Doctor don Jacinto Suárez, cardenal en la Santa Iglesia de Santiago, de quien trae certificación de haber cumplido con su romería. Y en él le declara por sacerdote para acreditar con esto su mala intención, de que se infiere por el engaño en este despacho cometido ser también supuestos y fingidos los demás [papeles] con que quiere acreditar su pobreza y romería. Los cuales desvanece. La per-

dom of Portugal, where he came into possession of said book, were found in his knapsacks, he said that finding himself in said city of Santiago with other pilgrims from different parts, one of them, he does not know where he was from, was carrying said book and sold it to the confessant for six *cuartos*. Soller bought it with the intention of passing through Portugal, of asking for the owner of said book, and of turning it in to him so that in exchange for his discovery the book's owner would give Soller some shirts or clothing to dress himself, and that there was not anything else to this motive. He responds. Other questions relevant to the matter were asked and asked again to him, to which he said that all of which he stated previously in this confession and in his prior affidavit is the truth, under obligation of the oath he has taken, which he confirmed and upheld. He did not sign because he said he did not know how to read or write. To all of which I, the judicial secretary, attest.

Before me,
19r–v *Antonio Pérez* | |
20r

I, Juan del Rodicio, Deputy Prosecutor of this city, inasmuch as it is the responsibility of public vengeance by which the guilty may be punished, file a criminal claim before Your Grace in the best way so that it may be lawfully approved. I accuse and seek complete fulfillment of justice for José Soller, mulatto pilgrim, and for the other people who were rounded up in the crime and case of which mention will be made below, whom, each one of them, I formally accuse in full. Making a true statement on the matter, I say that the abovementioned, offending the priestly caste, being a mulatto, which is known from his appearance, impersonated a priest, enabling this wickedness with the vestments and regalia of the clergy, obliging that he be given a tonsure in order to deceive those with whom he should communicate, and to burden his conscience by this means, soliciting donations for mass. It even can be inferred from this act that such a depraved man would try to preach in some town despite the ignorance he confesses to have of reading and writing, which further aggravates the crime and the deceit and cunning, because he persuaded Doctor Don Jacinto Suárez, cardinal in the Holy Church of Santiago, from whom he brings certification of having fulfilled his pilgrimage. In his diploma, it claims him to be a priest in order to enable with this his evil intention, from which it is inferred from the deceit committed in this diploma that the rest of the documents with which he wishes to authenticate his poverty and pilgrimage also are false and forged. It annuls them. Reason

sona, que cuando no sea esclavo, se persuade la razón ser fugitivo de lugar a lugar. Y se infiere por lo vario de su confesón y delaraciones en que no da domicilio, mudándolo de Indias a Italia, y esta equivocación le declara | 20v
por vagante. Y el libro de caja con que ha sido aprendido le culpa y arguye haber sido hurtado, no como se quiere librar en su confesión diciendo lo ha comprado por precio de tan poco dinero a otro peregrino que no dice [de] qué nación. Y siendo como es escrito en la ciudad de Coimbra, es indicio vehemente contra el susodicho haberlo hurtado. Se infiere del pasaporte de Lisboa y carta de recomendación de la ciudad de Lisboa, de cuyo lugar vino a Coimbra, y en el refrendo de los mayordomos de dicha cofradía, como se conoce de sus firmas a la vuelta del despacho. Cuyas causas y cosas consideradas arguyen tan graves y atroces delitos que a la vista parece no hallar pena y castigo igual con que satisfacerlos y su vida ser poca para la paga de un desacato con que quiso el acusado sin licencia y órdenes alterar la disposición de la Iglesia. Por cuyo delito, sin los más declarados, merece pena de muerte para que, hallando en él digno castigo, sirva a otros de ejemplo para defensa de la religión cristiana en que temerosamente debemos vivir. A Vuestra Merced suplico se sirva declararlo así con los más pronunciamientos necesarios al cumplimiento de justicia, que pido con costas. Y con la jura debida reproduzco la demanda, etcétera.

Joan del Rodicio *Joan Suares de Pardiñas*

Traslado a Josef Soller y a Baltasar de Lisasueta en su nombre, como Procurador de Pobres. Lo decretó el señor licenciado don Juan Antonio Covillas, corregidor de esta ciudad y su tierra por Su Majestad, en Orense a dos de abril, digo mayo, de mil y seiscientos y noventa y tres años.

licenciado Covillas

Ante mí,
Antonio Pérez | 21r

Josef Soller, natural de la isla de Santo Domingo, reino del Perú, preso en la cárcel real con orden de Vuestra Merced por decir me finjo sacerdote sin serlo, digo que Vuestra Merced se ha de servir darme soltura libremente

persuades that the person, even if he is not a slave, is a fugitive from place to place. This is inferred from the inconsistency of his confession and affidavits in which he does not provide a domicile, switching it from the
20v Indies to Italy, and this equivocation gives him away | as a vagrant. And the cashbook with which he has been apprehended makes him guilty and makes a case for it having been stolen, not as he wishes to get out of in his confession, saying that he bought it for such a low price from another pilgrim, whose nationality he does not say. Being, as it is written, from the city of Coimbra, this is forceful evidence that the abovementioned stole the cashbook. This is deduced from his safe conduct from Lisbon and letter of recommendation from the city of Lisbon, from which place he came to Coimbra, and from the endorsement of the religious administrators of said confraternity, as is known from their signatures on the backside of the credential. These reasons and matters considered make a case for such grave and atrocious crimes that upon consideration, there seem not to be found a penalty and punishment equal to the task of satisfying them, and his life to be little repayment for the disregard with which the accused, without license or orders, tried to alter the disposition of the Church. For this crime, without considering the others stated previously, he deserves the death penalty, so that finding in it just punishment, it may serve as an example to others for the defense of the Christian religion, in which we should live fearfully. May Your Grace deem just to proclaim it so with the further pronouncements necessary to the fulfillment of justice, which I ask for with costs. With the proper oath, I am making a copy of the lawsuit, et cetera.

Joan del Rodicio *Joan Suares de Pardiñas*

Communicated to José Soller and to Baltasar de Lisasueta in his name, as the public defender. So ruled Lord Don Juan Antonio Covillas, Esquire, Chief Magistrate of this city and its territory for His Majesty, in Ourense on the 2nd of April, I mean May, of the year 1693.

Covillas, Esquire

Before me,
21r *Antonio Pérez* |

I, José Soller, native of the island of Santo Domingo, kingdom of Perú, imprisoned in the royal jail at the order of Your Grace for impersonating a priest without being one, declare that Your Grace must grant the favor

por lo que resulta de los autos y de mi confisión, en que me afirmo que es la verdad desnuda y sin fingimiento, sin que en mí hubiese malicia: sí, traza para pasar libre mi romería por los peligros de tan larga viaje. En cuya atención suplico a Vuestra Merced se sirva declarar como tengo pidido, usando de piedad por mi sencillez única, pobreza, y larga perigrinación y prisión. Pido justicia y piadosa merced, etcétera.

Lisasueta

Traslado al teniente promotor fiscal, y con lo que dijere o no, se traigan los autos. Lo decretó el señor licenciado don Juan Antonio Covillas Venero, corregidor de esta ciudad y su tierra por Su Majestad, en Orense a cuatro de mayo de mil y seiscientos y noventa y tres años.

licenciado Covillas

Notificación

En Orense dicho día, yo, escribano, hice saber y notifiqué el decreto de arriba al teniente promotor fiscal. Y por él entendido, dio | que afirmán- 21v
dose en lo que tiene dicho y, se aparta del *treslado* y pide se lleven los autos al Señor Provisor para que dé el de prueba. Esto respondió, de que doy fe.

Antonio Pérez

Auto de prueba

En la ciudad de Orense a seis días del mes de mayo de mil y seiscientos y noventa y tres años, el señor licenciado don Juan Antonio Covillas, corregidor de esta ciudad y su tierra por Su Majestad, habiendo visto estos autos, dijo que recibía y recibió este negocio y causa a prueba con término
6 días. de seis días comunes y con todos cargos de publicación, conclusión y citación para sentencia. Y por este auto así lo mandó y firmó.

licenciado Covillas

Ante mí,
Antonio Pérez

of releasing me freely on account of what results from the proceedings and my confession, which I uphold, which is the naked truth and without pretense, without there being in me any malice: yes, it does contrive for me to pass freely on pilgrimage amid the dangers of such a long journey. In awareness of which, I beseech Your Grace to deem just to proclaim as I have requested, taking pity on my uncommon simplicity, poverty, long pilgrimage, and prison. I ask for justice and for merciful pardon, et cetera.

Lisasueta

Be it communicated to the Deputy Prosecutor, and regardless of what he should say, bring the proceedings. So ruled Lord Don Juan Antonio Covillas Venero, Esquire, Chief Magistrate of this city and its territory for His Majesty, in Ourense on the 14th of May of the year 1693.

Covillas, Esquire

Notice

In Ourense on said day, I, the judicial secretary, informed and notified the
21v Deputy Prosecutor of the above order, and understood by him, he offered |
that, upholding what he has said there, he desists from the notification and asks that the proceedings be brought to the Lord Ecclesiastical Judge so that he may give the order to produce evidence. This he responded, to which I attest.

Antonio Pérez

Order to Produce Evidence

In the city of Ourense on the 6th day of the month of May in the year 1693, Lord Don Juan Antonio Covillas, Esquire, Chief Magistrate of this city and its territory for His Majesty, having heard these proceedings, said that he would receive and received this declaration and case on trial at the conclusion of six business days, and with all charges for public announcement, resolution, and subpoena for sentencing. He so ordered it by means of this ruling, and signed. 6 days

Covillas, Esquire

Before me,
Antonio Pérez

Notificación

En la ciudad de Orense a trece días del mes de mayo de mil y seiscientos y noventa y tres años, yo, escribano, notifiqué el auto de arriba a Josef Soller, preso en la cárcel, que dijo se aparta del auto de prueba y su término, da los testigos por ratificados y concluye a difinitiva. Pide misericordia al Señor Corregidor para que le mande soltar, que padece mucha necesidad. Esto respondió, de que doy fe.

Ante mí,
Antonio Pérez | 22r

Joan del Rodicio, teniente de promotor fiscal de esta ciudad, en la causa criminal que trato con Josef Soller, peregrino, por fingirse eclesiástico y lo más que contienen los autos, digo que en su vista contradigo la conclusión por el sobredicho a difinitiva. Y se debe proceder y sustanciar esta causa con todos términos sin conclusión antes de pasar los legales para que con ellos pueda merecer la pena el dicho Josef Soller. Se debe hacer por lo siguiente: y porque la sumaria hecha en cualquiera causa sólo mira a la prisión de persona y no a la justificación plena del dilito para asegurarla; y así en sumaria la de posesión de testigos no puede perjudicarle ni por sus dichos merecer el debido castigo hasta que se hallen ratificados en toda forma; y porque además de lo dicho siendo causa criminal, como lo es la intentada contra dicho acusado, y por ella merecer pena corporal, no se puede admitir en este caso la conclusión por el público y particular interés que ocasiona el perjuicio que de dicha conclusión se me puede ocasionar. Por lo cual la contradigo y pido prorrogación de más término, en el cual ofrezco dar mi interrogatorio para que el escribano de la causa ratifique mis testigos por ser todo de justicia, que pido con costas, etcétera.

Joan del Rodicio *Joan Suares de Pardiñas* | 22v

Hágase saber a Josef Soller y a su procurador hagan la deligencia que le convenga, y a esta parte se le prorrogan ocho días de más término, común a ambas partes. Lo decretó el señor licenciado don Alonso Guerrero, canó-

Notice

In the city of Ourense on the 13th day of the month of May in the year 1693, I, the judicial secretary, gave notice of the above ruling to José Soller, imprisoned in the jail, who said that he desists from the order to produce evidence and from the evidentiary period. He upholds his witnesses and definitively concludes. He requests clemency from the Lord Chief Magistrate so that he may be freed, for he is enduring great hardship. This he responded, to which I attest.

Before me,
22r *Antonio Pérez* |

I, Joan del Rodicio, this city's Deputy Prosecutor, in the criminal case that I address with José Soller, pilgrim, for impersonating a priest and the rest that the proceedings contain, say that in their consideration, I permanently contradict the conclusion by the abovementioned. This case should proceed and be conducted with every stipulation without conclusion before the legal ones occur, so that with them, said José Soller might be able to deserve punishment. This should be done for the following: because the indictment made in whichever case only considers a person's imprisonment and not the full justification of the crime used to hold him; so in the indictment, that of possession of witnesses cannot harm him or what they have said cause him to deserve due punishment until they have been found upheld in every way; because in addition to the aforementioned being a criminal trial, which the attempt against said defendant is, for which he deserves corporal punishment, the public's conclusion, and the extraordinary advantage that is put at risk by the harm which from said conclusion could be risked to me, cannot be admitted in this case. For which reason, I contradict it and request a postponement of a greater period during which I offer to present my interrogation so that the judicial secretary of the case may uphold my witnesses as being completely fair, which I request with costs, et cetera.

22v *Joan del Rodicio* *Joan Suares de Pardiñas* |

Inform José Soller and his lawyer to make the report that may be to his advantage. This party is granted a postponement of eight additional days, common to both parties. So ordered Lord Don Alonso Guerrero, Esquire,

nigo, digo don Juan Antonio Covillas, corregidor de esta ciudad y su tierra por Su Majestad, en Orense a cinco de junio de mil y seiscientos y noventa y tres años.

licenciado Covillas

Ante mí,
Antonio Pérez

En la ciudad de Orense a seis días del mes de junio de mil y seiscientos y noventa y tres años, yo, escribano, notifiqué el decreto de arriba a Baltasar de Lisasueta, procurador de Josef Soller, que dijo que afirmándose en la confesión de su parte y en lo que tiene alegado, vuelve a dar los testigos por ratificados. Apártase del término de prueba y concluye a difinitiva. Pide se lleven los autos para su determinación. Esto respondió, de que doy fe.

Ante mí,
Antonio Pérez

Otra [notificación] a Josef Soller

En la ciudad de Orense y dentro de la cárcel real de ella a los dichos seis días del mes de junio de mil y seiscientos y noventa y tres años, yo, escribano, notifiqué el decreto de arriba a Josef Soller, peregrino, | preso en 23r
dicha cárcel. Y por él entendido, dijo se aparta del término de prueba, da los testigos de la sumaria por ratificados y concluye a difinitiva. Y respecto de que su causa consiste lo más en su declaración que tiene hecho, por donde declara su delito hecho con la sencillez que tiene expresado en dos declaraciones, desde luego se afirma y ratifica en ellas por no tener otra cosa que decir. Y pide y suplica al Señor Corregidor que atendiendo a su larga prisión y mucha necesidad que está padeciendo en esta cárcel con la hambre, se sirva, usando con él de benignidad, mandarle soltar de la prisión. Esto respondió, de que doy fe.

Ante mí,
Antonio Pérez | | 23v 24r

Por las preguntas siguientes, y cada una de ellas, serán examinados y preguntados los testigos que fueren presentados por Joan del Rodicio,

Canon, I mean Don Juan Antonio Covillas, Chief Magistrate of this city and its territory for His Majesty, in Ourense on the 5th of June of the year 1693.

Covillas, Esquire

Before me,
Antonio Pérez

In the city of Ourense and within its royal jail on said 6th day of the month of June of the year 1693, I, the judicial secretary, informed Baltasar de Lisasueta, attorney for José Soller, of the above ruling. He said that upholding his confession and regarding what is alleged, he once again upholds his witnesses. He desists from the evidentiary period and definitively concludes. He asks that these proceedings be decided. This he responded, to which I attest.

Before me,
Antonio Pérez

Another Notice to José Soller

In the city of Ourense and within its royal jail, on said 6th day of the month of June of the year 1693, I gave notice of the above ruling to José
23r Soller, pilgrim, | imprisoned in said jail, and understood by him, he said that he desists from the evidentiary period, that he upholds his witnesses from the indictment, and that he definitively concludes. Considering that his case consists primarily of the affidavit he has made, in which he claims to have committed his crime with the simplicity he has expressed in two affidavits, of course he confirms and upholds them on account of not having anything else to say. He beseeches the Lord Magistrate, accepting as time served his long imprisonment and the great need that he suffers from hunger in this jail, to deem just to order him released from jail. This he responded, to which I attest.

23v Before me,
24r *Antonio Pérez* | |

Each one of the following questions will be explored and asked to the witnesses whom should be presented by Joan del Rodicio, Deputy Prosecutor

teniente de promotor fiscal en la causa criminal que trata con Josef Soller, peregrino, por fingirse clérigo y otras cosas, etcéra.

1. Primeramente por el conocimiento de las partes, noticia de esta causa, hedad y más generales de la ley, digan, etcétera.

2. Si saben que dicho Josef Soller, su aspecto personal y forma es de mulato, de que se infiere ser esclavo fugitivo, menos que no acredite lo contrario con papeles, y más cuando es de reino estraño, etcétera.

3. Si saben que dicho Josef Soller ha sido aprehendido por uno de los ministros de justicia de esta ciudad en traje y hábito de sacerdote, fingiéndose de tal para engañar, y solicitó el que se le [pregunta] abriese corona con la cual andaba públicamente sin traer licencia ni despachos para ello, etcétera.

4. Si saben que todo lo arriba dicho es la verdad, pública voz y fama.

Joan del Rodicio *Joan Suares de Pardiñas* | 24v

Juan del Rodicio, teniente promotor fiscal de esta ciudad, en la causa con Josef Soller sobre fingirse sacerdote, que está recibido a prueba delante Vuestra Merced, con la jura necesaria, hago presentación de este interrogatorio de preguntas para hacer mi probanza y ratificar los testigos de la sumaria. Suplico a Vuestra Merced lo haya por presentado y mande se me reciba a su tenor, cometiéndola con comisión en forma al presente escribano de la causa por ser así de justicia, que pido, y para ello, etcétera.

Joan Suares de Pardiñas *Joan de Rodicio*

Por presentada con el interrogatorio de preguntas. Admítese cuanto pertinente y hasta parte citada la contraria se le reciba la probanza que ofrece a su tenor, la cual se comete con comisión en forma al presente escribano de la causa. Lo decretó el señor licenciado don Juan Antonio Covillas Venero, corregidor de esta ciudad y su tierra por Su Majestad, en Orense a cuatro días del mes de julio de mil y seiscientos y noventa y tres años.

licenciado Covillas

Ante mí,
Antonio Pérez

in the criminal case having to do with José Soller, pilgrim, for impersonating a priest and other matters, et cetera.

1. First, as to their familiarity with the parties, news of this case, age, and additional general legal questions, et cetera.
2. If they know that said José Soller's personal appearance and figure are that of a mulatto, from which he is inferred to be a fugitive slave, unless he should prove the contrary with documents, and more so when he is from a foreign kingdom, et cetera.
3. If they know that José Soller has been apprehended by one of the officials of justice of this city in the outfit and habit of a priest, impersonating such a personage in order to deceive, and he asked that he being questioned shave him a tonsure with which he walked around publicly without carrying a license or documents for that purpose, et cetera.
4. If they know that all of the abovementioned is the truth and common knowledge.

24v *Joan del Rodicio* *Joan Suares de Pardiñas* |

Joan del Rodicio, this city's Deputy Prosecutor, in the case with José Soller regarding his impersonation of a priest, which is admitted as evidence before Your Grace, which with the necessary oath, I submit this list of questions in order to make my inquiry and uphold the witnesses of the indictment. I beseech Your Grace to set it on record and that its content be admitted to me, authorizing the present judicial secretary of the case, as is fair, which I ask for and for that purpose, et cetera.

Joan del Rodicio *Joan Suares de Pardiñas*

The list of questions is set on record. Please allow all pertinent information, even that the aforementioned opposing party be administered the inquiry and its proffered content, for which purpose the present judicial secretary of the case is authorized. So ruled the Lord Don Juan Antonio Covillas Venero, Esquire, Chief Magistrate of this city and its territory for His Majesty, in Ourense on the fourth day of July of the year 1693.

Covillas, Esquire

Before me,
Antonio Pérez

Citación a Josef Soller

En la ciudad de Orense a cuatro días del mes de julio y seiscientos y
noventa y tres años, yo, el escribano, cité con el auto de arriba a Josef
Soller, preso en la cárcel real de esta ciudad para | si por su procurador se 25r
quiere hallar presente al ver presentar, jurar y reconocer los testigos que
por parte del teniente promotor fiscal fueren presentados en la probanza
que pretende hacer en esta causa, lo haga. Y le hice saber cómo ha de
pasar por delante mí, el escribano, desde mañana cinco del corriente en
adelante, sobre que le hice citación en bastante forma. Y por él entendido,
dijo que afirmándose, como se afirma y ratifica en lo que tiene dicho y
declarado en sus declaraciones y respuestas que tiene hecho ante el Señor
Corregidor, dice que no tiene deligencia alguna que hacer, mediante tiene
confesado su culpa y la inorancia de haberla cometido. Y así suplica al
Señor Corregidor se sirva usar con él de benignidad, mandándole soltar
de la prisión en que se halla ha tanto tiempo, padeciendo mucha nece-
sidad en tiempo tan apurado. Esto respondió. Y no firmó porque dijo no
saber. De todo ello yo, el escribano, doy fe.

Ante mí,
Antonio Pérez

Presentación y juramento de dos testigos

En la ciudad de Orense ha cinco días del mes de julio de mil y seiscientos y
noventa y tres años, ante mí, escribano, el dicho Juan de Rodicio, teniente
promotor fiscal, para prueba y justificación de lo contenido en su inte-
rrogatorio de preguntas, presentó por testigos a Antonio González Siabal,
barbero, y a Pedro de Castro, *xastre*, vecinos de esta ciudad, de los cuales y
de cada uno de ellos tomé y recibí juramento, que lo hizo en debida forma
por Dios nuestro Señor y una señal de cruz. Prometieron de decir verdad
de lo que supieren | y les fuere preguntado. De todo ello yo, el escribano, 25v
doy fe.

Ante mí,
Antonio Pérez

Subpoena to José Soller

In the city of Ourense on the 4th day of the month of July and the year 1693, I, the judicial secretary, subpoenaed José Soller, imprisoned in the
25r royal jail of this city, with the above ruling so that | if through his attorney he wishes to be present to see the introduction, administration of the oath, and examination of the witnesses, who on the side of the Deputy Prosecutor should be introduced in the inquiry that he wishes to conduct in this case, may Soller do so. I informed him how it must proceed before me, the judicial secretary, beginning tomorrow, the 5th of the current month forward, about which I rather formally issued him the subpoena. Understood by him, he said that maintaining his responses, since he confirms and upholds what he has stated and testified in his affidavits and answers given before the Lord Chief Magistrate, he says, through having confessed his crime and the ignorance of having committed it, he does not have any report to make. So he beseeches the Lord Chief Magistrate to deem just to treat him with kindness, ordering him released from the jail where he has been for such a long time, suffering great need in such a harrowing moment. This he responded. He did not sign because he said he did not know how. To all of which I, the judicial secretary, attest.

Before me,
Antonio Pérez

Introduction and Oath of Two Witnesses

In the city of Ourense on the 5th day of the month of July of the year 1693, before me, the judicial secretary, said Juan de Rodicio, Deputy Prosecutor, for evidence and justification of that contained in his list of questions, introduced as witnesses Antonio González Siabal, barber, and Pedro de Castro, tailor, residents of this city, from whom and from each one of them I took and received an oath, which he formally made by God, Our Father, and a sign of the cross. They promised to tell the truth of what they should
25v know | and should be asked. To all of which I, the judicial secretary, attest.

Before me,
Antonio Pérez

Testigo

El dicho y declaración del dicho Antonio González Siabal, barbero, vecino de esta ciudad, presentado por el dicho teniente promotor fiscal, el cual después de haber jurado, según se requiere de derecho, y siendo examinado por mí, escribano, al tenor de dicho interrogatorio de preguntas, depuso a cada una de ellas lo siguiente:

1ª A la primera, dijo el testigo que conoce a la parte que le presenta y a Josef Soller, mulato, desde que se prendió en esta ciudad, pero no de antes. Y tiene noticia de esta causa. Y responde.

Generales Preguntado por su hedad y más generales de la ley, dijo que es de hedad de treinta y tres años poco más o menos, y que no le tocan generales algunas. Y responde.

2ª A la segunda pregunta del dicho interrogatorio, dijo el testigo que en razón de lo que ella contiene, ha hecho su declaración antes de ahora por delante el Señor Corregidor y del presente escribano, en la cual firmó su nombre y declaró todo lo que sabía en esta causa, que pide se le muestre y lea para reconocer si es la misma y si tiene alguna cosa que quitar, añadir o enmendar. Y habiéndola buscado en los autos y halládola al folio cinco vuelta, que fenece al folio seis, la leí y enseñé al testigo de manera que pudo entender su contenido, | que por él entendido, dijo que la declara- 26r
ción es la misma que hizo en la ocasión referida, y por suya la reconoce con su firma que tiene a la postre, y en ella está escrito todo lo que ha declarado. Y siendo necesario de nuevo, lo vuelve a decir y ha aquí por repetido su contenido. Y en ello se afirma y ratifica, y que no tiene ninguna cosa que quitar, añadir ni emendar. Y responde.

3ª A la tercera, dijo el testigo que se refiere a lo que lleva dicho en su primera declaración. Y responde.

4ª A la cuarta última pregunta, dijo el testigo que todo lo que lleva dicho y declarado es la verdad so cargo del juramento que tiene fecho, en que se afirmó y ratificó y lo firmó con mí, el escribano, que de todo ello doy fe.

Antonio González

Ante mí,
Antonio Pérez

Witness

The statement and affidavit of said Antonio González Siabal, barber, resident of this city, presented by the aforementioned Deputy Prosecutor, who after having sworn an oath as is required by law and being examined by me, the judicial secretary, with the content of said list of questions, testified to each one of them the following:

1st To the first, he said that he knows the party who appears before him and José Soller, mulatto, since he was apprehended in this city but not from before, and that he has been notified of this case. He responds.

Asked his age and further general legal questions, he said that he is thirty-three years old, more or less, and that no other general questions are pertinent to him. He responds. General Questions

2nd To the second question of said list of questions, the witness said that due to what it contains, he has given his previous affidavit before the Lord Chief Magistrate and the present judicial secretary, in which he signed his name and testified all that he knew in this case. He asks that the affidavit be shown and read to him in order to recognize whether it is the same one and whether he has anything to remove, add, or amend. Having looked for it in the proceedings and having found it beginning on folio 5v and ending on folio 6, I read it and showed the witness so that he could understand its
26r content, | which, understood by him, he said: that the affidavit is the same that he made on the referred-to occasion; he recognizes it as his own by his signature at the end; in it is written all that he has testified; and being necessary, he again repeats and approves the repetition of its content. He confirms and upholds it, and has nothing to remove, add, or amend. He responds.

3rd To the third question, the witness said that he refers to what he has said in his first affidavit. He responds.

4th To the fourth and final question, the witness said that all he has said and testified is the truth, under burden of the oath he has sworn, which he confirms and upholds. He so signed with me, the judicial secretary, to all of which I attest.

Antonio González

Before me,
Antonio Pérez

Testigo

El dicho y declaración del dicho Pedro de Castro, *xastre*, vecino de esta ciudad, presentado por el dicho teniente promotor fiscal para más prueba y justificación de lo contenido en sus preguntas, el cual testigo, después de haber jurado, según se requiere de derecho, ante mí, escribano, y siendo examinado por dichas preguntas, depuso a cada una de ellas lo siguiente:

1ª A la primera pregunta, dijo el testigo que conoce al promotor fiscal que le presenta y al dicho Josef Soller desde el tiempo que está preso y no de antes. Y tiene noticia de esta causa. Y responde. | 26v

Generales Preguntado por su hedad y más generales de la ley, dijo es de hedad de veinte y ocho años poco más o menos, y que no le tocan generales algunas. Y responde.

2ª A la segunda pregunta del dicho interrogatorio, dijo el testigo que en razón de lo que ella contiene, hizo una declaración antes de ahora por delante del Señor Corregidor y del presente escribano en donde declaró todo su contenido y lo que sabía sobre esta causa, que pide que le busquen los autos y lea para reconocer si es la misma y si en ella está escrito todo lo que ha declarado y si tiene alguna cosa que quitar, añadir o enmendar en ella. Y habiéndola buscado y halládola al folio seis de la sumaria, la leí y declaré al testigo. Y por él entendido, dijo que dicha declaración es la misma que hizo en la ocasión referida y en ella está escrito todo lo que ha declarado. Y siendo necesario de nuevo, lo vuelve a decir y declarar y ha aquí por repetido su contenido. Y en ello se afirma y ratifica, y que no tiene ninguna cosa que quitar, añadir ni emendar en ella. Y responde.

3ª A la tercera, dijo el testigo se refiere en lo que lleva dicho. Y responde.

4ª A la cuarta última, dijo el testigo que todo lo que lleva dicho y declarado es la verdad so cargo del juramento que fecho tiene, en que se afirmó y ratificó. No firmó por no saber. De todo ello yo, escribano, doy fe.

Ante mí,
Antonio Pérez | 27r

Witness

The statement and affidavit of said Pedro de Castro, tailor, resident of this city, presented by the aforementioned Deputy Prosecutor for further evidence and justification of the matter contained in the questions, to which the witness, after having sworn an oath, as is required by law, before me, the judicial secretary, and being examined by said questions, testified to each one of them the following:

1st In response to the first question, the witness said that he knows the Deputy Prosecutor who appears before him and the aforementioned Joseph Soller since the time he has been imprisoned and not from before,
26v and that he has news of this case. He responds. |

Asked his age and other general legal questions, he said that he is twenty-eight years old more or less, and that other general questions are not pertinent to him. He responds. General Questions

2nd To the second question of said interrogation, the witness said that due to what it contains, he gave a previous affidavit before the Lord Chief Magistrate and the present judicial secretary, in which he stated all its content and what he knows about this case, which he asks them to search for in the proceedings and that it be read to recognize whether it is the same one and if in it is written all that he has testified and whether he has something in it to remove, add, or amend. Having searched for and found it on folio 6 of the indictment, I read and presented it to the witness. Understood by him, he said that: said affidavit is the same one that he gave on the referred-to occasion; in it is written all that he has testified; being necessary, he once again states and testifies anew; and he approves the repetition of its content. He confirms and upholds the matter, and he has nothing in it to remove, add, or amend. He responds.

3rd To the third question, the witness refers to what he already has stated. He responds.

4th To the fourth and final question, the witness said that all that he has said and testified is the truth, under burden of the oath that he has sworn, which he confirms and upholds. He did not sign because he does not know how. To all of which I, the judicial secretary, attest.

Before me,
27r *Antonio Pérez* |

Joan del Rodicio, teniente de promotor fiscal de esta ciudad, en la causa que por el Oficio de la Justicia sigo contra Josef Soller, mulato, sobre fingirse sacerdote y más que contienen los autos, que está recibido a prueba delante Vuestra Merced, con la jura debida, hago presentación de mi probanza y ratificación de testigos de la sumaria que está en poder del presente escribano. Suplico a Vuestra Merced se sirva haberla por presentada, mandando se junte a los autos y respecto está pasado el término de prueba hacer publicación de probanzas, y que se me dé vista para alegar lo que convenga a la vindicta pública y Oficio de la Justicia que defiendo. Pídola con costas, y para ello, etcétera.

Joan del Rodicio | 27v

Júntese a los autos y *treslado* a la otra parte. Lo decretó el señor licenciado don Juan Antonio Covillas, corregidor de esta ciudad y su tierra por Su Majestad, en Orense a siete de agosto de mil y seiscientos y noventa y tres años.

licenciado Covillas

Ante mí,
Antonio Pérez

En la ciudad de Orense a diez días del mes de agosto de mil y seiscientos y noventa y tres años, yo, escribano, hice saber y notifiqué el *treslado* de arriba a Baltasar de Lisasueta, procurador en nombre de Josef Soller. Y por él entendido, dijo que su parte no ha hecho probanza alguna. Y así consiente se lleven los autos para el de publicación y que se concluya la causa a difinitiva para que el Señor Corregidor se sirva dar la sentencia. Y usando con su parte de benignidad, le mande soltar de la prisión en que está ha tanto tiempo, padeciendo mucha necesidad. Esto respondió, de que doy fe.

Ante mí,
Antonio Pérez | 28r

Juan de Rodicio, teniente promotor fiscal de esta ciudad, en la causa de oficio contra Josef Soller, mulato, digo que habiendo presentado mi probanza y pedido publicación para tomar vista, Vuestra Merced se sirvió dar *treslado* a la otra parte que se hizo saber a su procurador, el cual concluye

I, Joan del Rodicio, this city's Deputy Prosecutor, in the case that I pursue through the Justice Office against José Soller, mulatto, regarding impersonating a priest and more that the proceedings contain, which is admitted as evidence before Your Grace with the proper oath, display my evidence and confirmation of witnesses of the indictment that is in possession of the present judicial secretary. I beseech Your Grace to deem it just to set the matter on record, ordering that the proceedings be gathered there since the evidentiary period to announce proof has passed, and that I be given approval to allege what may befit the public vengeance and the Justice Office, which I defend. I ask for it with costs and for that purpose, et cetera.

27v *Joan del Rodicio* |

Gather together for the other party the proceedings and notification. The Lord Don Juan Antonio Covillas, Esquire, Chief Magistrate of this city and its territory for His Majesty so ruled, in Ourense on the 7th of August of the year 1693.

Covillas, Esquire

Before me,
Antonio Pérez

In the city of Ourense on the tenth day of the month of August of the year 1693, I, the judicial secretary, informed and gave notice of the above communication to Baltasar de Lisasueta, the attorney representing José Soller. Understood by him, he said that his party has not produced any evidence, and so he consents that the proceedings be brought to the announcement stage and that the case be definitively concluded so that the Lord Chief Magistrate deem just to issue the sentence and, treating his party with kindness, to order him released from the jail in which he has been for so long, enduring great hardship. This he responded, to which I attest.

Before me,
28r *Antonio Pérez* |

I, Joan de Rodicio, this city's Deputy Prosecutor, in the legal case against José Soller, mulatto, say that having produced my evidence and having requested review for public announcement, Your Grace deemed just to notify the other party, who informed his attorney, who concludes the

a lo mismo. Porque suplico a Vuestra Merced se sirva mandar llevar los autos y en su vista dar auto de publicación de probanzas, y que se me dé vista de todos los autos para decir y alegar lo que me convenga por ser así de justicia, que pido con costas, y para ello, etcétera.

Joan del Rodicio | 28v

26 hojas Autos. Lo decretó el señor licenciado don Alonso Guerrero, canónigo, digo don Juan Antonio Covillas, corregidor de esta ciudad y su tierra por Su Majestad, en Orense a doce días del mes de agosto de mil y seiscientos y noventa y tres años.

Ante mí,
Antonio Pérez

Auto

En la ciudad de Orense a doce días del mes de agosto de mil y seiscientos y noventa y tres años, el señor licenciado don Juan Antonio Covillas, corregidor de esta ciudad y su tierra por Su Majestad, habiendo visto estos autos, dijo que hacía e hizo publicación de probanzas en esta causa con el término ordinario de la ley. Y mandó se junten a los autos y se dé vista y *treslado* a las partes para que digan y aleguen lo que les convenga. Y lo firmó.

licenciado Covillas

Ante mí,
Antonio Pérez

Notificación

En Orense dicho día, yo, notario-escribano de número, hice saber y notifiqué el auto de arriba al teniente promotor fiscal, y pidió vista. De ello doy fe.

Ante mí,
Antonio Pérez | 29r

same. For this reason I beseech Your Grace deem just to order the proceedings brought and to consider presenting an order publicly announcing the evidence. Please regard it as suitable for me to say and allege what may behoove me regarding all the proceedings, which I request with costs and for that purpose, et cetera.

28v *Joan del Rodicio* |

Proceedings. Lord Don Alonso Guerrero, Esquire, Canon, I mean Don Juan Antonio Covillas, Chief Magistrate of this city and its territory for His Majesty, in Ourense on the twelfth day of the month of August of the year 1693. 26 folios

Before me,
Antonio Pérez

Ruling

In the city of Ourense on the twelfth day of the month of August of 1693, Lord Don Juan Antonio Covillas, Esquire, Chief Magistrate of this city and its territory for His Majesty, having heard these proceedings, said that he would and did publicly announce the evidence in this case within the regular legal period. He ordered the proceedings be gathered together, and that notice and review be given to the parties so that they may state and allege what may behoove them. He so signed.

Covillas, Esquire

Before me,
Antonio Pérez

Notice

In Ourense on said day, I, a full notary, informed and notified the Deputy Prosecutor of the above ruling, and he asked for consideration. To that I attest.

Before me,
29r *Antonio Pérez* |

Joan del Rodicio, teniente de promotor fiscal de esta ciudad, en la causa criminal con Josef Soller, peregrino y mulato, por fingirse clérigo y otras cosas que los autos contienen, que con probanza en ellos dada, se ha de servir Vuestra Merced hacer y declarar como tengo pedido en mi acusación para que merezca el castigo que corresponde a semejante atrevimiento, procede y ha lugar por lo favorable. Y siguiente, y porque contra el sobredicho se justifica ser andante vagamundo de reino a reino, sin oficio ni ejercicio en que ejercite, su ociosidad, y siendo principio a la ruina de los hombres: aconseja la ley real lo que deben tolerar para que le sirva de castigo y ejemplo. Y asegurado este principio, se conoce e infiere su vida y costumbres cual será, y porque la malévola inclinación para el engaño le precisa dejándose llevar de ella y fingiéndose de sacerdote para por este camino incubrir sus maldades, haciendo abrirse corona y previniendo lo más que conduce al hábito de un eclesiástico, sin saber leer ni escribir, en lo cual debe de ser castigado aún más rigurosamente de la pena que corresponde al falsario que se muda el nombre o pervierte el estado para causar engaño. Y siendo tan desigual la diferencia, debe ser | castigado 29v
con más rigor, ejecutando en él el condigno. Así lo pido y concluyo con los autos a difinitiva. Justicia y costas, etcétera.

Joan del Rodicio *Joan Suares de Pardiñas*

Por concluso por esta parte y *treslado* a la otra. Lo decretó el señor licenciado don Juan Antonio Covillas, corregidor de esta ciudad y su tierra por Su Majestad, en Orense a diez y siete de agosto de mil y seiscientos y noventa y tres años.

licenciado Covillas

Ante mí,
Antonio Pérez

Notificación

En la ciudad de Orense y dentro de la cárcel real de ella, a diez y ocho días del mes de agosto de mil y seiscientos y noventa y tres años, yo, escribano, hice saber y notifiqué el auto de arriba a Josef Soller, mulato, preso en dicha cárcel. Y por él entendido, dijo | que afirmándose en lo que tiene 30r
dicho en sus declaraciones y respuestas, no tiene otra cosa que decir ni alegar. Sí, sólo suplica al Señor Corregidor que atendiendo a su sencillez

Joan del Rodicio, this city's Deputy Prosecutor, in the criminal case with José Soller, pilgrim and mulatto, for impersonating a priest and other matters that the proceedings contain, with the evidence given in them, proceeds and finds favorable that Your Grace must grant to do and testify as I have requested in my charge, that Soller might deserve the punishment that befits such impudence. Next against the abovementioned, because he justifies himself being a vagabond wandering from kingdom to kingdom without a trade or practice to exercise, his idleness, being the beginning of the ruin of men: royal law advises what they should tolerate so that it serves man as a warning and example. This principle guaranteed, who he will be is known and inferred from his life and habits because his malevolent tendency toward deceit requires him to be won over by it, impersonating a priest in order by this path to cloak his evil deeds, having a tonsure shaved and acquiring the rest of the items to prepare the habit of a priest, without knowing how to read or write, for which he should be punished even more harshly than the penalty that is suitable for the imposter who changes his name or misrepresents his status to engen-
29v der deception. The difference being so extreme, he should be | punished with greater severity, requiring of him that which is due. In this fashion, I request it and definitively conclude with the proceedings. Justice and costs, et cetera.

Joan del Rodicio *Joan Suares de Pardiñas*

Case concluded to the point of sentencing by this party and formally communicated to the other one. Lord Don Juan Antonio Covillas, Esquire, Chief Magistrate of this city and its territory for His Majesty, so ruled, in Ourense on 17th of August of the year 1693.

Covillas, Esquire

Before me,
Antonio Pérez

Notice

In the city of Ourense and within its royal jail, on the 18th day of the month of August of the year 1693, I, the judicial secretary, informed and notified José Soller, mulatto, imprisoned in said jail, of the above ruling.
30r Understood by him, he said | that confirming what he has said in his affidavits and responses, he has nothing else to say or allege. Yes, he only

y que su ánimo no ha sido en ninguna manera profanar ni ofender el estado sacerdotal sino por redimir la vejación de que no le prendiesen por esclavo en las partes por donde pasase, haciendo su peregrinación según lo tiene declarado, se sirva tener con él beninidad, mandándole soltar de la prisión donde se halla ha mucho tiempo desnudo, padeciendo mucha necesidad. Esto respondió, de que doy fe.

Ante mí,
Antonio Pérez

Otra a su procurador

En Orense dicho día, yo, escribano, hice saber el auto antecedente y respuesta de arriba a Baltasar de Lisasueta, procurador de Josef Soller, y por él entendido, dijo que repitiendo lo mismo que su parte dice en la respuesta | de atrás. Y afirmándose en ello, se aparta del *treslado* y pide se 30v
lleven los autos para su determinación, a que concluye. Esto respondió, de que doy fe.

Ante mí,
Antonio Pérez | | 31r–v 32r

Día 5 de septiembre [del año 1693]

En el pleito y causa criminal que [trata] de[l] Oficio de la Justicia y Juan de Rodicio, teniente de promotor fiscal en su nombre, de la una parte, y de la otra Josef Soller, mulato, reo acusado por usar de hábito sacerdotal sin serlo y otras cosas que refieren los autos, vistos, etcétera.

Fallo atento los autos y méritos del proceso, a que me remito, que por la culpa que de ellos resulta contra el dicho Josef Soller por vagamundo le debo de condenar y condeno a que sirva en las galeras de Su Majestad por dos años al remo y sin sueldo. Y habiendo empezado a cumplirlos, no los quebrante, pena de muerte de horca, y por esta mi sentencia difinitivamente juzgando, ansí lo pronuncio y mando.

licenciado don Juan Antonio Covillas Venero | 32v

beseeches the Lord Chief Magistrate, who, accepting his simplicity and that his intention has not been in any way to desecrate or offend the priestly caste but rather to put an end to harassment so that he should not be seized as a slave in whichever region he should travel, making his pilgrimage according to what he has testified, to deem just to treat him kindly, ordering him released from the jail where he has been naked for so long, enduring great hardship. This he responded, to which I attest.

Before me,
Antonio Pérez

The Other Party to His Attorney

In Ourense on said day, I, the judicial secretary, informed the previous ruling and above response to Baltasar de Lisasueta, attorney for José Soller, and understood by him, he reiterated the same thing that his party says
30v in his response | on back. Confirming it, he formally desists from the notification and asks that the proceedings be brought to their resolution, at which point he concludes. This he responded, to which I attest.

Before me,
31r–v 32r *Antonio Pérez* ||

The 5th Day of September of the year 1693

In the lawsuit and criminal case concerning the Justice Office and Juan de Rodicio, Deputy Prosecutor in its name, on one side, and on the other, José Soller, mulatto, a prisoner accused of using the habit of a priest without being one, and other matters to which the proceedings, hearings, et cetera, refer.

In consideration of the proceedings and merits of the trial, by which I stand, which on account of the guilt that results from them, I rule against said José Soller for being a vagabond. I should sentence and do sentence him to serve in His Majesty's galley ships for two years, rowing without pay. Having begun to fulfill them, he may not violate them, on penalty of death by hanging. Ruling definitively by this my sentence, in this fashion I pronounce and order it.

32v *Don Juan Antonio Covillas Venero, Esquire* |

Dada y pronunciada fue la sentencia de atrás por el señor licenciado don Juan Antonio Covillas, corregidor de esta ciudad y su tierra por Su Majestad. Según en ella firmó su nombre y dijo así la pronunciaba en Orense a cinco días del mes de setiembre de mil y seiscientos y noventa y tres años, estando presentes por testigos Juan de Fiuza, escribano de número de esta ciudad, Andrés Pérez, alcaide de la cárcel de esta ciudad, vecinos de ella, e yo, escribano, que de todo ello doy fe.

Ante mí,
Blas Antonio Cid

En la ciudad de Orense y dentro de la cárcel real de ella a cinco días del mes de septiembre de mil y seiscientos y noventa y tres años, yo, escribano, hice saber y notifiqué la sentencia antecedente a Josef Soller Chivo en su persona, que dijo escribiría al Señor Almirante de Castilla. Esto respondió, de que doy fe.

Ante mí,
Blas Antonio Cid

Son 29 hojas.

No hay tasa de costas por no haber de qué cobrarlas. | 33r

El fiscal de Su Majestad en este reino, en el pleito con Josef Soller en rebeldía, presenta petición y autos.

Apela. El fiscal de Su Majestad en este reino en vista de los autos hechos por el corregidor de Orense contra Josef Soller, mulato, que vienen por apelación, dice que de ellos consta ser el sobredicho vagamundo y esclavo fugetivo, y para ejecutar la fuga se fingió ser sacerdote valiéndose de otros tales para acreditarlo, con que alcanzó la cédula que se halla en los autos en la ciudad de Santiago, en la cual se le trata de sacerdote. Y habiéndose huido de dicha ciudad y entrádose en la de Orense se vistió de tal, profanando el estado eclesiástico, abriéndose corona. Y habiendo tenido sospecha dicho corregidor de si era el sobredicho tal sacerdote, le prendió, y

The previous sentence was given and pronounced by the Lord Don Juan Antonio Covillas, Esquire, Chief Magistrate of this city and its territory for His Majesty. He accordingly signed his name to it and said that he so pronounced it in Ourense on the 5th day of the month of September of the year 1693, being present as witnesses Juan de Fiuza, a full notary of this city, Andrés Pérez, warden of the jail of this city, residents both of it, and I, the judicial secretary, to all of which I attest.

Before me,
Blas Antonio Cid

In the city of Ourense and within its royal jail, on the 5th day of the month of September of the year 1693, I, the judicial secretary, informed and notified the previous sentence to José Soller Chivo in person, who he said he would write to the Lord Admiral of Castilla. This he responded, to which I attest.

Before me,
Blas Antonio Cid

There are 29 folios.

There is no amount of court costs on account of him not having anything
33r from which to collect them. |

His Majesty's Representative in This Kingdom, in the Trial with José Soller in Absentia, Presents a Petition and Proceedings.

His Majesty's Representative in this kingdom, in consideration of the proceedings made by the Chief Magistrate of Ourense against José Soller, mulatto, which come on appeal, says that from them, the abovementioned is documented as being a vagabond and fugitive slave. To carry out his escape, he pretended to be a priest, taking advantage of other such priests to authenticate it, by which means he obtained the document found in the proceedings from the city of Santiago, in which he is addressed as a priest. Having fled from said city and entered into that of Ourense, he dressed as such a personage, desecrating the priestly caste, shaving himself a tonsure. Said Chief Magistrate, having had the suspicion as to whether the abovementioned was in fact such a priest, seized

He appeals.

habiéndole tomado su declaración, dijo no ser tal sacerdote ni aún saber leer, variando en ella, deciendo ser natural de Italia y después confesar serlo de la isla de Santo Domingo, reino del Pirú, de que se conoce evidentemente el sobredicho vagamundo. Y aún del libro de cuenta que se le halló entre sus alhajas se presume ser ladrón. Y por ser los delitos tan graves y la sentencia dada por dicho corregidor contra el sobredicho muy begnina, apela de ella. Pide se supla a la que en derecho más lugar haya, que así conviene a la buena administración de justicia. Y concluye a definitiva. | 33v

Treslado

En la ciudad de la Coruña a trece días del mes de otubre de mil y seiscientos y noventa y tres años, estando en audencia pública los Señores Gobernador y Oidores de la Real Audencia de este reino, la presentó el fiscal de Su Majestad en este reino. Y dichos señores mandaron dar *treslado* a la contraria.

Seijas

Criminal *Figueroa*

Encomiéndase este pleito al licenciado don Juan de Montes, relator de esta Real Audiencia. Coruña y otubre, 13 de 1693. | 34r

El fiscal de Su Majestad en este reino, en el pleito con Josef Soller en rebeldía, de que es relator el licenciado don Juan de Montes, que se halla ausente, pide se pase al compañero, que así conviene.

Pásese. En audiencia pública. Coruña y otubre, 10 y seis de mil y seiscientos y noventa y tres *anos*.

Seijas | 34v

him. Having taken his affidavit, Soller said he was not such a priest, nor did he know how to read, wavering in his testimony, claiming to be a native of Italy and afterwards admitting to be one from the island of Santo Domingo, kingdom of Perú. From this, the abovementioned is clearly recognizable as a vagabond. He even is presumed to be a thief from the accounting book that was found among his valuables. Because these crimes are so serious and the sentence issued by said Chief Magistrate against the abovementioned so lenient, His Majesty's Representative appeals against it. He requests that the sentence be replaced by one that is more legally admissible, which in this way is in the interest of the good
33v administration of justice. He definitively concludes. |

Notice

In the city of A Coruña on the 13th day of the month of October of the year 1693, the Lords Governor and Judges of the Royal Appellate Court of this kingdom being at a public hearing, His Majesty's Representative in this kingdom introduced the appeal. Said lords ordered to notify the opposing party.

Seijas

Criminal *Figueroa*

May this lawsuit be entrusted to Don Juan de Montes, Esquire, Court Clerk
34r of this Royal Appellate Court. A Coruña, October 13 of 1693. |

His Majesty's Representative in this kingdom, in the lawsuit with José Soller in absentia, for which Don Juan de Montes, Esquire, who is absent, is the court clerk, requests that it be handed over to his colleague, which in this way is appropriate.

May it be handed over. At a public hearing. A Coruña, October 16 of the year 1693.

34v *Seijas* |

Ausente Montes

Por ausencia del licenciado don Juan de Montes se encomienda este pleito al licenciado Balboa, relator de esta Real Audiencia. Coruña y otubre 17 de 1693. | 35r

El fiscal de Su Majestad en este reino en el pleito con Josef Soller en rebeldía concluye a defenetiva y lleva término, etcétera.

En la ciudad de la Coruña a diez y seis días del mes de otubre de mil y seiscientos y noventa y tres *anos*, estando en audiencia pública los Señores Gobernador y Alcaldes Mayores de la Real Audiencia de este reino de Galicia, la presentó el fiscal de Su Majestad en este reino. Y dichos señores hubieron este negocio y causa por concluso en forma. Y en rebeldía se notificó en los estrados.

Seijas | 35v

Va del oficio para confirmar o revocar la sentencia de la justicia ordinaria. Coruña y otubre, 22 del 1693.

Domingo Pérez | 36r

Para despachos de oficio, dos maravedíes

SELLO CUARTO. AÑO DE MIL Y SEISCIENTOS Y NOVENTA Y CUATRO

Montes

En el pleito del Oficio de la Justicia y el fiscal de Su Majestad en este reino con Josef Soller Chivo, peregrino mulato, le remitieron en discordia los señores don Manoel Rodrigues de León, don Juan de Riaño y don Josef de Alvarado. Coruña y enero, diez y ocho de mil seiscientos y noventa y cuatro años.

Manoel Rodrigues de León *don Juan de Riaño* *don Josef de Alvarado*

Criminal *Figueroa*

Montes Absent

On account of the absence of Don Juan de Montes, Esquire, this lawsuit is entrusted to Balboa, Esquire, Court Clerk of this Royal Appellate Court.
35r A Coruña, October 17 of 1693. |

His Majesty's Representative in this kingdom, in the lawsuit with José Soller in absentia, definitively finishes and brings it to conclusion, et cetera.

In the city of A Coruña and the 16th day of the month of October of the year 1693, the Lords Governor and Senior Magistrates of the Royal Appellate Court of this kingdom of Galicia being at a public hearing, His Majesty's Representative in this kingdom introduced it, and said lords considered this matter and case to be concluded. It was formally communicated in the law courts that Soller was in absentia.

35v *Seijas* |

The appeal officially advances for the sentence of ordinary justice to be upheld or revoked. A Coruña, October 22 of 1693.

36r *Domingo Pérez* |

For legal offices, two maravedis

FOURTH SEAL. THE YEAR ONE THOUSAND SIX-HUNDRED NINETY-FOUR

Montes

In the lawsuit of the Justice Office and His Majesty's Representative in this kingdom with José Soller Chivo, mulatto pilgrim, Lords Don Manoel Rodrigues de León, Don Juan de Riaño, and Don José de Alvarado remitted it in disagreement. A Coruña, January 18 of the year 1694.

Manoel Rodrigues de León *Don Juan de Riaño* *Don José de Alvarado*

Criminal *Figueroa*

En discordia de los señores de arriba, se remite este pleito a los seño-
res don Bartolomé Escudero y don Juan Cachupín. Coruña y enero, 19 de 36v
1694. | | 37r

El fiscal de Su Majestad en este reino en el pleito con Josef Soller dice que habiéndose visto, se determinó en discordia. Y habiéndose nombrado señores jueces, el licenciado don Juan de Montes, relator, de él se fue a un negocio, por cuya causa no se puede ver con la aceleridad que conviene. Pide se mande llevar a otro relator, el cual le lleve mañana a la sala y que el escudero y relator de la semanaria le vayan a sacar del estudio de dicho don Juan, que así conviene, etcétera.

Pásese este pleito al licenciado don Gil de Balboa, el cual lo lleve mañana a la sala, y el relator y escudero de la semanaria lo saquen del estudio del licenciado Montes y lo entreguen al licenciado Balboa. En semanaria lo mandó el señor don Pedro Cachupín. Coruña y enero, veinte y seis de seiscientos y noventa y cuatro años.

Ante mí,
Varela

En la ciudad de la Coruña a veinte y seis días del mes de enero de mil seis-
cientos y noventa y cuatro años, yo, escribano relator, con asistencia de Gil
de Navaza, escudero de esta Real Audiencia, que asiste al Señor Semanero,
para efecto de dar cumplimiento al auto de arriba, fui con | su asisten- 37v
cia a casa del licenciado don Juan de Montes, relator de ella, para de su
estudio sacar el pleito que se intitula por *El fiscal de Su Majestad con Josef*
Soller. Y habiendo hecho pregunta por Juan de Lodeiro, su criado, para
que le manifestase, y hecho diligencias en su busca ansí por esta dicha
ciudad como por la Pescadería de ella algunas veces, no se le pudo dar
alcance. Y después, se abrió dicho estudio con la llave de él, que entregó
doña Catalina del Yago Montoto, mujer de dicho don Juan de Montes, y en
él se registraron todos cuantos pleitos había. Y no se pudo hallar al refe-
rido intitulado por *El fiscal de Su Majestad con dicho Josef Soller*. Y para que
conste y de que en orden a su busca, se hicieron vivas diligencias. Para la

The above lords being in disagreement, this lawsuit is remitted to Lords
Don Bartolomé Escudero and Don Juan Cachupín. A Coruña, January 19
36v 37r of 1694. | |

His Majesty's Representative in this kingdom in the lawsuit with José Soller says that having been heard, the case was decided in disagreement. Lord Magistrates having been named, Don Juan de Montes, Esquire, Court Clerk, left from the lawsuit on a business matter, for which reason he cannot be seen with the suitable rapidity. He asks that the case be ordered taken to another court clerk, who tomorrow should bring it to the courtroom, and that the squire and court clerk of the seminary should go remove it from the study of said Don Juan, which is advisable in this way, et cetera.

May this lawsuit be handed over to Don Gil de Balboa, Esquire, who tomorrow should carry it to the courtroom. The court clerk and squire of the seminary should remove it from the study of Montes, Esquire, and should deliver it to Balboa, Esquire. In the seminary, Lord Don Pedro Cachupín so ordered. A Coruña, January 26 of the year 1694.

Before me,
Varela

In the city of A Coruña on the 26th day of the month of January of the year 1694, I, the head court clerk, with the aid of Gil de Navaza, squire of this Royal Appellate Court, who helps the Lord Weekly Justice, with the inten-
37v tion of fulfilling the above order, went with | his help to the house of Don
Juan de Montes, Esquire, the case's court clerk, to remove from his study the lawsuit entitled *His Majesty's Representative with José Soller*. Having asked for Juan de Lodeiro, his servant, to show it to the squire and having taken steps to search for it in this fashion all over this said city as throughout its Fish Market neighborhood a few times, it could not be recovered. Afterwards, said study was opened with his key, which was delivered by Doña Catalina del Yago Montoto, wife of said Don Juan de Montes, and in it every case that was there was searched. The referred-to one, entitled *His Majesty's Representative with Said José Soller*, could not be found. May it be documented that energetic steps were taken having to do with its search. I

ejecución de lo que se ordena en dicho auto, lo pongo por diligencia. Y firmó dicho escudero con mí, escribano recetor, y de ello doy fe.

Gil de Navaza

Ante mí,
Antonio Fernández de Sobredo

make a written record for the carrying out of that which is ordered in said ruling. Said squire signed with me, the head court clerk. To that I attest.

Gil de Navaza

Before me,
Antonio Fernández de Sobredo

PART 3

Scholarly Supplement

Proper Names in the Dossier

Names appear in modernized form.

Aira, puerta de
Alayos, conde de
Algarborium
†...† Almeida Leiva
Alonso Guerrero
Andre da Costa do †...†
Andrés Pérez
Antonio Brabo da Silva
Antonio Correa da †...†on
Antonio de Castro
Antonio dos Santos
Antonio Fernández de Sobredo
Antonio Forneiro
Antonio González, Antonio González Siabal, Antonio Siabal, Antonio de Siabal
Antonio Pérez
Antonio †...† Velho
Aveiro
Baltasar de Lisasueta
Bartolomé Escudero
Berjano, viña de
Bernardo de Pando
Bernardo P†...†
Blas Antonio Cid
Caminha
Capellae Christianissimi Francorum Regis
Casas Consistoriales
Castilla, Almirante de
Catalina del Yago Montoto
Coimbra
Compostela, Jacobum in Compostella, Santiago
Convento de Tomar
Coruña, la
Cristo, Christo
Domingo Pérez
Domingos Sánchez
Fernan de Soiza Castelbranco Coitinho e Menezes
Figueroa
Fontaíña
Francia, Reino de
Francisco Pérez
Galicia, reino de
Gil de Balboa
Georgius Cornelius, Giorgio Cornaro
Gil de Navaza
Golegã
†...† Gonçalo
Gonçalo Teisera Coelho
Gregorio de Castro
Hispaniarum
Indias
Italia
Jacinto Suárez, Hiacinthus Suárez, Doctor
Jesús, Yesús
Joan de Rodicio, Joan del Rodicio
Joannes Andreas Rinaldarum
Jo†...† da Silveira
Joan Suares de Pardiñas
João Sánchez, Juan Sánchez
Josef
Josef de Alvarado
José Soller Chivo, Josef Soller Chivo, Josephum Soler, Joseph Soller
Juan Antonio Covillas Venero
Juan Cachupín

 | DOI:10.1163/9789004422704_012

Juan de Lodeiro
Juan de Montes
Juan de Riaño
Lisboa, Ullisipone
Luis de Mello
Madrid
Manoel Nunes
Manoel Rodrigues de León
María
Mariñamansa
Matías Sueyro
Menezes
Miguel de Albor
Miguel Manesca
Misericórdia, Misericórdias
Moreira
Nápoles
Nuno da Silva Seller
Orense
Palencia
Pedro Castro, Pedro de Castro
Pedro Debén
Perú, Pirú
Pescadería; Pescadería, Plazuela de
Portugal, reino de; Portogal, reino de; Portugallia
Real Audiencia, Real Audencia
Romam
Santarém
Santiago, apostol; Jacobi, Sancti
Santiago, Santa Iglesia de
Santa T†...††...†
Santo Domingo, la isla de; Santo Domingo en el Perú de Indias, la isla de; Santo Domingo en el Perú, la isla de; Santo Domingo, Reino del Pirú, la isla de
Seijas
Sexalbo
Soutullo
Tomar
Valença [do Minho]
Varela
Vasco Anfeiar de Menezes
Viana [do Castelo]
Zafra, Villa de

Aira, Puerta de. Appears as "Ayra" in the manuscript.

Alayos. Appears as "Alaios" in the manuscript. A region of the western Sierra Nevada range south of Granada, Spain.

Algarborium. The Algarves, the southernmost region in Portugal.

Alonso Guerrero. Church canon in Ourense.

Andre da Costa do †...†. Director of the Misericórdia of Viana do Castelo.

Andrés Pérez. Blacksmith.

Antonio Forneiro. Master barber.

Antonio González, Antonio González Siabal. The first surname appears as "Gonçalez" and "Gonzales" in manuscript. I choose the Spanish variant because González Siabal is not Portuguese. This is the barber who gives Soller a tonsure.

Antonio dos Santos. Warden.

Antonio Pérez. Main judicial secretary of that part of the case in Ourense.

Baltasar de Lisasueta. Appears as "Balthasar" in the manuscript. He is Soller's appointed public defender (*Procurador de Pobres*).

Bartolomé Escudero. One of the two additional justices named after the disagreement among the initial three appellate justices.

Berjano, viña de. Appears as "Berxano" in the manuscript.

Bernardo de Pando. The bailiff.

Blas Antonio Cid. Judicial secretary.

Capellae Christianissimi Francorum Regis. Translated as the "Chapel of his most Christian Majesty of France," this is a reference to the Chapel of the King of France (Capilla del Rey de Francia), also known as the Chapel of the Savior (Capilla del Salvador).[1] This chapel dates to the initial construction of the Romanesque Cathedral of Santiago de Compostela in 1075 and is located in the easternmost portion of the ambulatory.[2] The King of France for whom the chapel is named is Louis XI, who in 1447, as presumed heir to the French throne, provided enough income to supply the chapel with three chaplains to offer daily mass.[3] To this day, French pilgrims arriving to Santiago attend one of these daily masses given in French in this chapel.

Casas Consistoriales. The Town Hall of Ourense, to the patio of which the tailor is ordered to appear (figure 44).

Castilla, Almirante de. Juan Tomás Enríquez de Cabrera y Álvarez de Toledo, the last Admiral of Castile.

Catalina del Yago Montoto. In manuscript, her first surname appears as "Iago."

Cristo. Appears as "Christo" in the manuscript and is left as such in the Latin travel documents: "Christo," "Christi," and "Christianissimi." A reference to the Santo Cristo sculpture in the Ourense Cathedral (part 1, chapter 5).

Coimbra. Appears as "Coynbra" and "Coinbra" in the manuscript. City in Portugal.

Compostela, Jacobum in Compostella, Santiago. Appears as "Conpostela" in the manuscript.

Convento de Tomar. Appears as "Convento de Thomar" in the manuscript. This reference probably is to the Convento de Cristo in Tomar, a very important and vast monastic complex atop the highest point in town. Since the twelfth century, the complex served as the command post of the Knights Templar before they were forced to disband, and the Order of Christ assumed control and made it their headquarters in the fourteenth century. Kings Manuel and João III expanded the Convent of Christ in the sixteenth century. The Convento de Cristo was intimately linked to the Misericórdia of

1 López Ferreiro, *Iglesia de Santiago*, 4:138n1.
2 *Catedral de Santiago*.
3 Fernández Sánchez y Freire Barreiro, *Guía de Santiago*, 149.

Tomar in a common effort to provide hospitality and assistance to the poor, the sick, and travelers (part 1, chapter 5).

DOMINGOS SÁNCHEZ. Resident of Ourense.

FONTAÍÑA. The form "la fuente Eyña" appears in the manuscript as the name of a street that today is called Rúa Cervantes[4] (the southern stretch) and Rúa Barreira (the northern segment).

FRANCISCO PÉREZ. Witness.

GEORGIUS CORNELIUS, GIORGIO CORNARO. Appears as "Georgivs" in the manuscript. Consecrated Archbishop of Rhodes in 1692. Later, he became the first papal legate to Portugal to be elevated to Cardinal in 1697.[5]

GIL DE BALBOA. Court Reporter.

GIL DE NAVAZA. Squire of the Royal Appellate Court.

GOLEGÃ. Appears as "Gollegam" in the manuscript. Nearly 17 miles (27 km) from Santarém in the Extremadura Province of the District of Santarém, Patriarchate of Lisbon. It is in the watershed of the Tagus River.

GREGORIO DE CASTRO. Blacksmith.

HISPANIARUM. Spain.

ITALIA. The form appears as "Ytalia" in the manuscript.

JACINTO SUÁREZ, DOMINUS HIACINTHUS SUÁREZ, DOCTOR. Appears as "Hyacinthvs Svarez" in Soller's diploma. The Senior Cardinal in Santiago de Compostela who signs Soller's diploma.

JESÚS, YESÚS. The latter appears as "Iesus" in the manuscript. A reference in oaths to his attribute as a member of the Holy Family, that is, as the Biblical son of Mary and Joseph.

JOAN DE RODICIO, JUAN DEL RODICIO. Appears as "Rodiçio" in the manuscript. Deputy Prosecutor of Ourense.

JOANNES ANDREAS RINALDARUM. João André Rinaldo, secretary.

JOÃO SÁNCHEZ, JUAN SÁNCHEZ. Merchant who owns the book of accounts in Soller's possession.

JOSÉ SOLLER CHIVO, JOSEF SOLLER CHIVO, JOSEPHUM SOLER, JOSEPH SOLLER. Appears as "Josseph SSoller Chibo" in the manuscript. The Latin variants in the travel documents and that quoted in the Castilian are left in my edition as "Josephum" and "Joseph."

JOSEF. Biblical father of Jesus, husband of Mary, invoked in oaths.

JOSEF DE ALVARADO. One of the three appellate justices who disagree on the Soller case.

4 Álvarez González and López González, "Restos romanos."

5 Miranda, *Cardinals*.

JUAN ANTONIO COVILLAS VENERO. Lord Chief Magistrate of Ourense.

JUAN CACHUPÍN. One of the two additional justices named after the disagreement among the initial three appellate justices.

JUAN DE LODEIRO. Servant of Don Juan de Montes.

JUAN DE MONTES. Court reporter.

JUAN DE RIAÑO. One of the three appellate justices who disagree on the Soller case.

LISBOA, ULLISIPONE. The latter appears as "Ullysipone" in the manuscript. These names refer to Lisbon.

MANOEL RODRIGUES DE LEÓN. One of the three appellate justices who disagree on the Soller case.

MARÍA. Biblical mother of Jesus, wife of Joseph, invoked in oaths.

MARIÑAMANSA. Appears as "Mariña Mansa" in the manuscript. An intersection and neighborhood in Ourense.

MATÍAS SUEYRO. Appears as "Mathias Sueiro" in manuscript. Blacksmith.

MENEZES. Appears as both "Meneçes" and "Meneses" in the manuscript. I opt for the Portuguese variant, Menezes, since the name identifies individuals from Portugal.

MIGUEL DE ALBOR. Barber.

MISERICÓRDIA, MISERICÓRDIAS. Appears as both "Misericordia" and "Mizericordia" in the manuscript. A Portuguese religious assembly whose mission includes providing hospitality to pilgrims and feeding the poor.

ORENSE. The seat of the eponymous diocese in Galicia, this city was known as Auria, and from this name the related Auriense evolved to the Spanish Orense[6] and its Galician name, Ourense.

PEDRO CASTRO, PEDRO DE CASTRO. Tailor.

PERÚ, REINO DEL, CIVIDADE DE. Appears as "Ciuidade" in the safe-conduct. Translated as "kingdom of Perú," this named region does not refer to the Spanish viceroyalty of Perú but rather serves as a stand-in for all of Hispano-America. Soller's claimed birthplace of the island of Santo Domingo falls within the viceroyalty of New Spain (Nueva España), and so Perú must be interpreted more broadly.

PESCADERÍA; PESCADERÍA, PLAZUELA DE. Fish Market Plaza, the part of Ourense where the barbers have their shops (figure 44); a neighborhood of A Coruña lying outside city walls.

ROMAM. Rome, where Soller's travel documents indicate he was headed after Compostela.

6 Covarrubias, *Tesoro*, 1326.

SANTIAGO, APOSTOL; JACOBI, SANCTI. The latter appears as "Iacobi" in the manuscript.

SANTO DOMINGO, LA ISLA DE; SANTO DOMINGO EN EL PERÚ DE INDIAS, LA ISLA DE; SANTO DOMINGO EN EL PERÚ, LA ISLA DE; SANTO DOMINGO, REINO DEL PIRÚ, LA ISLA DE. This is the Caribbean island of Hispaniola (Española), today comprised of the Dominican Republic and Haiti. The geographic term "Perú" is a reference to the entire New World, as noted.

SEXALBO. Castilian Spanish variant for the Galician town known today as Seixalbo. Small town on outskirts of Ourense where Soller was apprehended.

TOMAR. Appears as "Thomar" in the manuscript. A monastery and city in Portugal.

ZAFRA. Appears as "Çafra" in the manuscript. This locale had various names given by the Celts (Segada) and Romans (Restituta Julia) before the Muslims gave it the name Zafar, which as a result of metathesis became the modern Zafra, although others say the name derives from that of either a Roman or Visigothic Captain. Fernando III reclaimed Zafra for the Christians in 1240. The city became so wealthy it came to be known as "little Seville." This wealth lead to the Portuguese sacking of the city in 1711,[7] less than two decades after Soller claims in 1693 to have visited here briefly before starting his pilgrimage to Santiago de Compostela in Lisbon. Based on my experience traveling here, a good amount of the historical center of this city predating the eighteenth-century attack survived the plunder.

7 Estrada, *Población general de España*, 328.

Linguistic Variants

Vocalic Alternation

aprendido : aprehendido
audiencia : audencia
confesión : confisión
definitiva : defenetiva : difinitiva : difinitivamente
delito : dilito
diciendo : deciendo
diligencia, diligencias : deligencia, deligencias
foliatura : foleatura
fugitivo : fugetivo
mismo : mesmo
pedido : pidido
peregrinación : perigrinación : peregrino
Perú : Pirú
Portugal : Portogal
portugués : portogués
proveer : prover
Real Audiencia : Real Audencia

Consonantal Oscillation

gn / n

benignidad : beninidad : begnina
ignorancia : inorancia : inora
insignia : insinia

ñ / nn / n

año, años : anno : anos
daños : danos

nm / mm / m

enmendar : emendar
inmediatamente : immediatamente : inmediatas

 | DOI:10.1163/9789004422704_013

ll / l

cabello : cabelo

s / ns

así : ansí

Alternation of Castilian Lexemes with Galician Words in the Castilian Text

año, años : anno : anos
bayeta : baeta
daños : danos
sastre : xastre

Galician and Portuguese Variants of Castilian Vocabulary within the Castilian Text

cabello : cabelo
caja : caixa

Oscillation of a Castilian Lexeme with Portuguese in Castilian Text

traslado : treslado

Morphosyntactic Alternation within Portuguese Travel Documents

da cidade : del cividade

Vocalic Oscillation in Portuguese Travel Documents

neste : niste

Scribal Errors

1r	sitio : sito
1v	con : co
1v	señal : senal
1v	cree : cre
2r	calzones : calcones
2r	cuyas : cuia
2v	alhajas : alaxa
2v	deligencia : deleixencia
2v	exceto[1] : exseto
3r	calzones : calcones
3v	Ø : alca[2]
3v	señal : senal
3v[3]	alzacuello : alcacuello
3v[4]	hízose : hicose
3v	rizo : riso
3v	hizo : hico
3v	alzacuello : alcacuello
4r	portogués : portogés
4v	declare : de clare
5r[5]	señal : senal
5r	declaración : decalarazion[6]
5v	mestizo : mestiso
5v[7]	señal : senal
6r	hizo : hico
8r	provido : provid[8]
8v	março[9] : marco
11v	hizo : hico
12v	vine : biene
12v[10]	señal : senal
14v	compañero : conpanero
15r	fianza : fianca
17r	suyo : su
18r	fiscal : fizcal
18v	hizo : hico
18v	alzacuello : alcacuello
21v	por : para
24v	Josef : Josephe
25r	afirma : afima
25r	inorancia : ynoraçia
25v	fiscal : fizcal
25v	examinado : exsaminado
25v	añadir : anadir
26r	fiscal : fizcal
26r	examinado : exsaminado
26r	fiscal : fizcal
26v	añadir : anadir
26v	4a : 3a[11]
29v	Ø : y seiscientos[12]

1 For the modern *excepto*.
2 The scribe appears to have begun and not finished writing a word.
3 Left margin.
4 Left margin.
5 Left margin.
6 Read under ultraviolet light.
7 Left margin.
8 There is a blank space following *provid* for the gendered form of the Portuguese participle to be added. It never was in this case.
9 Portuguese, in the *carta de guia*.
10 Bottom left margin.
11 It is the second consecutive instance of *3a* that I correct.
12 It is the redundant instance of this phrase I have deleted.

 | DOI:10.1163/9789004422704_014

29^{v}	necesidad : neçeçidad	34^{r}	compañero : conpanero
32^{r}	empezado : empesado	37^{r}	mañana : manana[14]
32^{v}	Ø : y Andrés Pérez[13]	37^{v}	Ø : con[15]

---

13 It is the redundant instance of this phrase I have deleted.

14 It is the second instance that I have corrected here.

15 It is the first word of this folio side, a redundant instance of *con* from the previous folio, that I have deleted here.

Case Notes

cov.

1 *Señores León, Riaño, y Alvarado*: the names of the three magistrates who initially rule on the appeal of Soller's case in the Royal Appellate Court of Galicia, or Real Audiencia.

1 *Visto en la discordia*: as the translation expounds, the appeal is "Adjourned in disagreement," meaning that the three magistrates above cannot agree unanimously. Absent unanimity, the Royal Appellate Court requires that the case be remitted to two additional magistrates, Don Bartolomé Escudero and Don Juan Cachupín, mentioned on folio 36^{r}.

1 *Josef Soller Chivo*: "Chivo" is a scribal insertion.

1 *Figueroa*: There are four clerk office centers (*escribanías de asiento*) named for the notaries who led them: Fariña, Figueroa, Gómez, and Pillado. López Gómez, *Real Audiencia*, 1:162.

1 *Relator Balboa*: after this text, "y ~~por su ausencia~~" is deleted.

1 *don Josephum Soler sacerdotem indianum*: this is as his name appears on his pilgrim's diploma from Compostela.

2 *Señor Corregidor*: a reference to the Chief Magistrate of Ourense.

fol.

1^{r} *Para despachos de oficio, dos maravedíes*: the amount of two maravedis represents the cost of the paper for official documents to scribes, notaries, and so on, who were obligated to use this specific kind of paper for which payment is a type of tax.

1^{r} *SELLO CUARTO. AÑO DE MILY SEISCIENTOS Y NOVENTA Y TRES*: this text appears to the right of the ten-maravedi Seal of the Kingdom of Galicia, within which appear a "10" on the left-hand side and "MS," the abbreviation for *maravedíes*, on the right. When these are official communiqués, charging two additional maravedis is a requirement. This seal is used with *papel del Sello cuarto*, meaning "fourth seal." Other denominations include *Sello primero*, *Sello segundo*, and *Sello tercero*, among others, and the ordinal number is determined by a variety of factors including subject matter, cost, weight, the geographical extent of the document's dissemination. *Sello cuarto* paper was used for documents dealing with items of lesser importance and more limited scope than royal decrees, international passports, and the like. See Felipe IV, "Título XXIV."

1r *Sexalbo*: a suburb of Ourense. This variant is Castilian Spanish for the Galician town that today is called Seixalbo, from "Seixos Albos," meaning "White Rocks" in Galician. The road to Seixalbo from Ourense was very challenging to walk or ride on during Soller's time (part 1, chapter 6).

1v *para saber si el susodicho es sacerdote o no y resolver la parte donde se ha de poner preso*: priests did not mix with the rest of the population, that is, they had their own law code, the rules of justice to which they were submitted, or jurisdiction. They were judged according to canon law, which was a branch of the European Common Law tradition known as *ius commune*.

2r *Alhajas que hayó en las alforjas*: written in a later hand. As with many of the annotations, it was added in A Coruña. These later annotations tend to be those of the Court Clerk, in this case Don Juan de Montes, and due to his absence, Don Gil de Balboa.

2r *Libro de Caja*: original lettering.

2r *En 25 de marzo de 93*: written in a later hand, possibly that of the Court Clerk.

3v *Declaración del reo*: written in a later hand, which typically would be that of the Court Clerk.

3v *Que hay 16 … tierra*: I deleted "Alca [*sic*]" immediately prior to bit of marginalia. The Court Clerk seems to have begun to write a word or phrase that he did not finish.

3v *dijo … la isla de Santo Domingo en el Perú de Indias*: a reference to Hispaniola, or the Caribbean island of Española, which presently consists of the Dominican Republic and Haiti. The term "Perú" is a geographic marker intended to represent the entirety of Hispano-America.

3v *barbero y arbolario*: used as a substantive here, the term *arbolario* was used in this period as both an adjective and a substantive. It alternated with *herbolario*, which is still in use as a sustantive.

5r *la calle de la Fontaíña*: this street in Ourense is known today as the Rúa Cervantes. An archeological excavation has uncovered the remains of the original fountain, "la Fuente Eyña" of the manuscript, that existed here. See Álvarez González and López González, "Restos romanos." The fountains and thermal baths found throughout Ourense have persisted since ancient times and are a chief reason for the city's initial Roman colonization.

5r *de la declaración*: found in the last line of the folio. I read this text under ultraviolet light.

7r *Gratis ubique*: this, the second line from the bottom, is printed and in ital-

ics. Meanwhile, in the rest of this safe-conduct (*salvi conductus*) italicized text represents handwritten text inserted into the printed document.

7r *Georgius Cornelius*: he had been elected and then consecrated as Archbishop of Rhodes in 1692, the year prior to this document's creation and of Soller's journey. See Miranda, *Cardinals*. See also the Proper Names appendix (part 3).

7r *domesticus*: a technical point, that the designation as Archbishop of Rhodes is a merely titular honor; that diocese was lost long ago to the Muslims, but someone gets to bear the title of prelate of that see in abeyance. The term *domesticus* means that this archbishop is counted a part of the papal household although resident elsewhere, in this case in Lisbon.

7r *NUNTIUS*: we use Nuncio in English for a papal ambassador or legate (there is one in Washington, DC); the term really means "spokesperson." The signatory to this document was resident in Lisbon.

7r *del cividade de Perú*: *cividade* is an Old Portuguese form deriving from the Latin *civitas*, (specifically its ablative singular declension, *civitate*), meaning *cidade* (in this case meaning "kingdom"), while Perú represents all of Hispano-America. See also the Proper Names appendix (part 3), the Note on the Translation (part 2), and In Search of Soller (part 1).

8r *com cavalgadura*: that Soller traveled on horseback would explain how he covered the roughly 80 kilometers over mountainous terrain between Coimbra and Tomar in a single day (from February 22 to February 23, 1693), but it does not explain why Soller suddenly reversed directions, switching from northward to southward. This credential (*carta de guia*) is dated Feb. 11, 1693, when Soller could have left from Lisbon. Starting here the pages are not numbered. Once again, the document contains printed text with handwritten text inserted. The first side of the document bears signatures, while the other side includes the dates and locations of his documented itinerary in Portugal during 1693. This sheet, effectively his pilgrim's credential, was folded in four parts at some point, probably when Soller had possession of it, in order to gather signatures from each locale he visted. See the chronology for dates and locations.

8r *Convento de Tomar*: top-right corner of the pilgrim's credential. A *convento* can house monks as well as nuns. The Convento de Cristo in Tomar lies to the northeast of Soller's starting point in Lisbon (figure 1) and roughly a mile up the hill from the Church and Hospital of the Misericórdia in Tomar. From the twelfth century, the complex served as the command post of the Knights Templar before they were forced to disband in the fourteenth century, and the Order of Christ assumed control

and made it their headquarters. Kings Manuel and João III expanded the Convent of Christ in the sixteenth century (part 1, chapter 5).

8^{r} *Joseph Soller para Valença*: there is a scribal strikethrough, "~~O Porto~~," in between the words "Soller" and "para" here.

8^{r} *provido*: there is a blank space following "provid" for the gendered form of the participle to be added. It never was in this case.

10^{r} *Cardinalis Mayor*: one of this historic privileges of the Cathedral of Santiago is that its canons are granted the title of Cardinal without being electors of the Pope.

10^{r} *Administrator Capellae Christianissimi Francorum Regis*: this Chapel of the King of France, located in the easternmost end of the ambulatory of the Cathedral of Santiago de Compostela, also known as the Capilla del Salvador. Pilgrims in Soller's day could confess in a variety of languages and obtain their diplomas here, and Soller's diploma indicates that he did just that. Jacinto Suárez's title as "Administrator" of this chapel means that he presided over the confessions that took place there, including Soller's. See the Proper Names index (part 3) for more details.

11^{r} *Soutoullo*: the individual whose signature appears must have been a lawyer who presents and gathers court documents.

11^{v} *don Juan Antonio Covillas*: scribal strikethrough, "~~Alonso Gue~~," between "don" and "Juan."

11^{v} *don Juan … noventa y tres años*: the text "No balga testado Alonso Gue" is deleted from the end of this, the first paragraph of the folio.

11^{v} *Antonio Pérez*: an unsigned and unidentified Spanish rubric appears beneath the final paragraph and before the signature of Antonio Pérez at the bottom of this folio.

14^{v} *Antonio Pérez*: the rubric of Juan Antonio Covillas appears without his signature immediately after end of the same paragraph and before signature of Antonio Pérez.

16^{v} *Antonio Pérez*: the rubric of Juan Antonio Covillas once again appears without his signature just after the close of the paragraph and before the signature of Antonio Pérez.

17^{v} *Auto*: just before this subheading at the bottom of the folio, an unsigned and unidentified flourish appears.

18^{r} *barbero arbolario*: used here as an adjective, the term *arbolario* could be used as either an adjective or a substantive during this period. It alternated with *herbolario*, which has fallen into disuse as an adjective when applied to herbal healing practices.

19^{v} *Antonio Pérez*: an unsigned rubric appears at the bottom of the folio just before this signature.

21^{r} *sencillez*: the middle syllable is a scribal insertion.

22^{v} *procurador de Josef Soller*: scribal strikethrough, "~~de ello~~," between "procurador" and "de Joseph Soller."

22^{v} *Esto respondió ... doy fé*: deleted "No bala testado de ello" after this text at the end of the second paragraph on this folio.

22^{v} *En la ciudad ... mes de junio*: in this text beneath the "*Otra* [*notificación*] *a Josef Soller*" subheading, the scribe corrects "junio" over "mayo."

24^{r} *se infiere ser ... contrario con papeles*: documents such as free papers (*una carta de libertad*), for example, or a dimissory letter attesting to his ordainment as a priest at home and to his right to give mass abroad. Soller is presumed to be a slave absent his possession of any such documentation.

25^{r} *necesidad*: the *s* is corrected over a *z*.

25^{r} *Siabal, barbero*: scribal strikethrough, "~~y~~," between "Siabal" and "barbero."

25^{v} *Antonio Pérez*: the rubric of Juan Antonio Covillas appears immediately prior to this signature at the conclusion of this paragraph at the top of the folio.

27^{v} *concluya*: the scribe corrects the *y* over an *i*.

28^{r} *etcétera*: this last word of the paragraph is a stand in for "I swear that which is necessary" (*juro lo necesario*).

29^{v} *y seiscientos*: I deleted a redundant instance of "y seiscientos" in the second full paragraph of this folio.

30^{r} *estado sacerdotal*: a reference to the three estates of the Old Regime—the Church, or those who pray (*oratore*); the nobility, or those who fight (*bellatore*); and the common folk, or those who toil (*laboratore*). Soller violated this hierarchy by impersonating a member of a higher estate. The reaction is so strong because the authorities sought to maintain the then-prevailing power structure, and also because of his mulattoness, which violates the force of the blood purity (*limpieza de sangre*) statutes.

32^{r} *Día 5 de septiembre* [*del año 1693*]: this text appears above the seal. The text contained in brackets is illegible, even when read under ultraviolet light. The most logical text, the year, has been inserted.

32^{r} *Rodicio*: corrected over illegible text.

32^{v} *y Andrés Pérez*: deleted as redundant after the initial appearance of this same name.

32^{v} *Señor Almirante de Castilla*: Juan Tomás Enríquez de Cabrera y Álvarez de Toledo, the last Admiral of Castile (part 1, chapter 7).

32^{v} *No hay tasa ... de qué cobrarlas*: a rubric appears after this text at the end of the folio.

33^{r} *en rebeldía*: in absentia. Soller is not present for this part of the trial, meaning that he does not appear in court for the appeal of his case despite the formal call for him to do so. In all probability, Soller escaped from his jail cell in Ourense. The implications of Soller's absence from trial are discussed in detail in part 1, chapter 6. Beginning with this folio, all the documentation of the case is generated in the Royal Appellate Court in A Coruña, while all the previous documentation is produced in Ourense.

33^{r} *esclavo*: the letter *b* of the unedited text's "esclabo" is corrected over an illegible character.

33^{r} *Y concluye a definitiva*: the rubric of the Prosecutor appears at the bottom of the folio after this text.

33^{v} *Treslado*: there are no records of having notified the accused party. That is, Soller never answers the charges against him as he always had done up to this point. The use of the term *en rebeldía* is evidence of his absence from trial. As noted previously (part 1, chapter 6), one might therefore infer that Soller managed to escape from jail as did so many others at this time.

33^{v} *la presentó el fiscal*: the scribe corrects the definite article *la* over the adverb *ya*.

33^{v} *Coruña y otubre, 13 de 1693*: a rubric appears at the bottom of folio after this text.

34^{r} *El fiscal de … que así conviene*: the rubric of the Prosecutor appears after this first sentence of the folio.

34^{v} *al licenciado Balboa, relator*: the name Balboa is written in another hand.

34^{v} *Seijas*: there is a rubric at the end of the folio after this name.

35^{r} *El fiscal de … lleva término, etcétera*: a rubric appears at the end of this, the first sentence of the folio.

35^{r} *concluye*: there is a scribal strikethrough of a redundant instance of the same word here.

35^{r} *Y en rebeldía se notificó en los estrados*: that is to say, Soller never arrived to the Court of Justice, one supposes, because he had escaped.

35^{r} *los Señores Gobernador y Alcaldes Mayores*: according to the *Ordenanzas de la Real Audiencia del Reino de Galicia* the Lord Governor does not have a vote on cases unless these are remitted to him in disagreement among all the Senior Magistrates.

36^{r} *Sello cuarto. Año de mil y seiscientos y noventa y cuatro*: beginning at this folio, the fourth seal stamp has been updated to match the new year, 1694.

36^{r} *Montes*: this text appears to the left of the stamp in the upper left-hand corner of this folio.

36r *Coruña y enero*: scribal strikethrough, "~~Relaciones los señores don~~," immediately preceding this text.

36r *Coruña y enero … noventa y cuatro años*: "No vala lo testado Relaciones los señores don" immediately following the end of this, the first paragraph, has been deleted. This is a reference to the suppressed scribal strikethrough from the preceding note.

36r *Coruña y enero … noventa y cuatro años*: the names of the three judges, Manoel Rodrigues de León, don Juan de Riaño, and don Joseph de Alvarado are indicated by their rubrics after first paragraph here.

36r *Criminal … enero, 19 de 1694*: a redundant instance of prior text, but with the correct date. Deleted before it after the first complete paragraph on this folio including scribal strikethroughs:

Criminal *Figueroa*

En discordia de los señores de arriva se remite este pleito
a los señores don ~~Bartolomé~~ Escudero … Coruña y enero
[~~rubric~~] 18 del 1692

The text "don ~~Bartolomé~~ Escudero" of this deleted material is written in a different hand.

36r *Criminal … enero, 19 de 1694*: a rubric appears at the end of this folio.

37r *mañana a la sala*: the text "a la sala" is a scribal insertion.

37r *Pide se mande llevar … que así conviene, etcétera*: the Prosecutor's rubric appears after this, the first full paragraph.

37v *su asistencia a casa*: a redundant instance of *con*, the first word of this folio, immediately prior to this text, has been deleted.

37v *la Pescadería*: the Fish Market neighborhood, which lies outside the walls of A Coruña.

37v *no se le pudo dar*: the passive marker *se* is a scribal insertion additionally elaborated as such in the deleted instructions at the end of the manuscript.

37v *todos cuantos pleitos había*: scribal strikethrough, "~~en el~~," in between *pleitos* and *había*.

37v *de ello doy fé*: The last two sentences after this one at the conclusion of the final paragraph of the manuscript have been deleted per the scribal instructions for which corrected text should be read and which text is not valid. Here are the deleted instructions: "Entre renglones se, vala. Y no vala lo testado fui, en el."

Bibliography

Manuscripts and Incunabula

O compromisso da Confraria da Misericórdia de Lisboa (*Agreement of the Brotherhood of the Misericórdia of Lisbon*). Lisbon: Assembly of the Misericórdia, 1520. Library of the Misericórdia of Lisbon, reference code PTSCMLSB/SCML/CR/07/02.

El fiscal de Su Majestad contra José Soller, peregrino mulato, por fingirse sacerdote y otros delitos (*His Majesty's Representative versus José Soller, Mulatto Pilgrim, for Impersonating a Priest and Other Crimes*). Royal Appellate Court of Galicia (Real Audiencia de Galicia), 1693–1694. Archive of the Kingdom of Galicia (Arquivo do Reino de Galicia), file bundle 26.339/13.

Libro de Acuerdos de la muy noble y leal Ciudad de Orense, Cabeça de Provincia, voto en Cortes, para el año de 1694, escrivanos Blas Antonio Cías y Juan de la Cruz, 1694. Archive of Ourense, call number 48.

Libro de Acuerdos de la muy noble y leal Ciudad de Orense para el año de 1693, siendo escribanos de Ayuntamiento Blas Antonio Cid y Juan de la Cruz, 1693. Archive of Ourense, call number 47.

Libros de Enfermos. Hospital Real Enfermos. Vol. 19. Arquivo Histórico da Universidade de Santiago de Compostela, January 1, 1693–August 2, 1693. http://arquivo.usc.es/ahus2/showInformacionNodo/1799543

Misericórdia de Tomar. *Lista dos passageiros e despesa com os mesmos*. 1808–1817. Archive of the Santa Casa de Misericórdia of Tomar, book 58.

Misericórdia de Tomar. *Procissão dos Santos Passos*. 1696–1697. Archive of the Santa Casa de Misericórdia of Tomar, book 20.

Misericórdia de Viana. *Libro de receita e despesa*, 1693. District Archive of Viana (Arquivo Distrital de Viana), call number 3.23.1.3.

Pedimentos. Royal Appellate Court of Galicia, seventeenth century. Archive of the Kingdom of Galicia, file bundle 421.

Registros de ida a Nueva España. Seville, Spain. 1727–1742. Archivo General de Indias, reference code: ES.41091.AGI/10.13.8.427//CONTRATACION,1481.

Sentencias. Royal Appellate Court of Galicia, 1614–1774. 1694. Archive of the Kingdom of Galicia, file bundle 32.

Primary Sources

Albani, Nicola. *Viaje de Nápoles a Santiago de Galicia: Manuscrito italiano de mediados del siglo XVIII depositado en el archivo del Centro Italiano di Studi Compostellani de*

Perugia (*Fondo Caucci ms. 1S*) Edited and translated by Isabel González. Madrid: Edilán, 1993.

Beleña, Eusebio Bentura. *Recopilación sumaria de todos los Autos Acordados de la Real Audiencia y Sala del Crimen de esta Nueva España, y providencias de su superior gobierno*. Vol. 1. México: Felipe de Zúñiga y Ontiveros, 1787.

Benedict, *The Rule of St. Benedict: The Abingdon Copy*. Edited by John Chamberlin. Toronto: Pontifical Institute of Mediaeval Studies, 1982.

Benedict, *The Rule of St. Benedict in English*. Edited by Timothy Fry. New York: Vintage Books, 1998.

Black Bride of Christ: Chicaba, An African Nun in Eighteenth-Century Spain. Edited, translated, and with an introduction by Sue E. Houchins and Baltasar Fra Molinero. Nashville, Tennessee: Vanderbilt University Press, 2018.

Cervantes Saavedra, Miguel de. *Don Quijote de la Mancha.*, Edited by John Jay Allen. 2 vols. Madrid: Cátedra, 2000.

Cervantes Saavedra, Miguel de. *Don Quixote: Fourth Centenary Translation*. Translated by Tom Lathrop. Newark, Delaware: Cervantes & Co., 2005.

Cervantes Saavedra, Miguel de. *Los trabajos de Persiles y Segismunda*. Edited by Stephen Hessel. Newark, Delaware: Cervantes & Co. 2011.

Cervantes Saavedra, Miguel de. *Trials of Persiles and Sigismunda, a Northern Story*. Translated by Celia Richmond Weller and Clark A. Collahan. Indianapolis, Indiana and Cambridge, Massachusetts: Hackett, 2009.

Claramonte y Corroy, Andrés de. *El valiente negro en Flandes*. Edited by Nelson López. Kassel, Germany: Edition Reichenberger, 2007.

Covarrubias Horozco, Sebastián de. *Tesoro de la lengua castellana o española*. Edited by Ignacio Arellano and Rafael Zafra. Madrid: Iberoamericana Vervuert, 2006.

Du Bois, W.E. Burghardt. *The Souls of Black Folk: Essays and Sketches*. Chicago, A.C. McClurg, 1909. https://books.google.com/books?id=lTXYAAAAMAAJ

Erauso, Catalina de. *Historia de la Monja Alférez, Catalina de Erauso, escrita por ella misma*. Edited by Ángel Esteban. Madrid: Cátedra, 2002.

Erauso, Catalina de. *Lieutenant Nun: Memoir of a Basque Transvestite in the New World*. Translated by Michele Stepto and Gabriel Stepto, foreword by Marjorie Garber. Boston: Beacon, 1996.

Felipe II. Pragmática de El Escorial de 13 de Junio de 1590. "Título XXX. De los Romeros y Peregrinos," 197–200. Vol. 1 of *Novísima recopilación de las leyes de España*. 6 vols. Madrid: Carlos IV, King of Spain, 1805.

Felipe IV. Cédula de 15 de Diciembre de 1636. "Título XXIV. Del uso del papel sellado en las escrituras, autos é instrumentos públicos," 149–168. Vol. 5 of *Novísima recopilación de las leyes de España*. 6 vols. Madrid: Carlos IV, King of Spain, 1805.

Fernández Catón, José María. *El Archivo del Hospital de los Reyes Católicos de Santiago de Compostela. Inventario de Fondos*. Santiago de Compostela: Secretariado de Publicaciones de la Universidad de Santiago, 1972.

Hospitales de San Roque y San Miguel. Catálogos e índices. Santiago de Compostela: CSIC Instituto de Estudios Gallegos "Padre Sarmiento," 1645–1720.

Um Instrumento Português de Solidariedade Social no Século XVI: O Compromisso da Misericórdia de Lisboa. Edited by Joaquim Veríssimo Serrão. Lisbon: Chaves Ferreira, 1992.

Künig von Vach, Hermann. *The Pilgrimage and the Path to Saint James*. Translated by John Durant. London: The Confraternity of Saint James, 1993.

Künig von Vach, Hermann. *Die Straß zu Sankt Jakob: der älteste deutsche Pilgerführer nach Compostela*. Edited by Klaus Herbers and Robert Plötz. Ostfildern: Thorbecke, 2004.

Laffi, Domenico. *Viaggio in Ponente a san Giacomo di Galitia e Finisterrae*. Edited by Anna Sulai Capponi. Naples, Italy: Edizioni Scientifiche Italiane, 1989.

Laffi, Domenico. *A Journey to the West: The Diary of a Seventeenth-century Pilgrim from Bologna to Santiago de Compostela*. Edited and translated by James Hall. Leiden, the Netherlands: Primavera, 1997.

Latino, Juan. *Carmen Austria*. In *The Battle of Lepanto*, edited and translated by Elizabeth R. Wright, Sarah Spence, and Andrew Lemons, 288–405. Cambridge, Massachusetts and London, England: Harvard University, 2014.

Lazarillo de Tormes. Edited by Francisco Rico. Madrid: Cátedra, 1998.

Liber Sancti Jacobi: Codex Calixtinus. Edited by Klaus Herbers and Manuel Santos Noia. Santiago de Compostela: Xunta de Galicia, 1998.

López de Úbeda, Francisco. *Libro de entretenimiento de la pícara Justina*. Edited by Enrique Suárez Figaredo. Barcelona, 2005. https://studylib.es/doc/6221586/la-p%C3%ADcara-justina

Magalotti, Lorenzo. *Viaje de Cosme de Médicis por España y Portugal (1668–1669)*. Edited by Ángel Sánchez Rivero and Ángela Mariutti de Sánchez Rivero, and illustrated by Pier Maria Baldi. 2 vols. Madrid: Sucesores de Rivadeneyra, 1933.

Manzano, Juan Francisco. *The Autobiography of a Slave. Autobiografía de un esclavo*: A Bilingual Edition. Edited by Ivan A. Shulman. Translated by Evelyn Picon Garfield. Detroit: Wayne State University, 1996.

Marvell, Andrew. "The Mower against Gardens." In *The Book of Restoration Verse*, edited by William Stanley Braithwaite. New York: Brentano's, 1910. http://www.bartleby.com/332/10.html

McQueen, Steve, dir. *Twelve Years a Slave*. Los Angeles, California: Regency Enterprises, 2013.

Misericórdia of Coimbra. *Compromisso da Santa Misericórdia da cidade de Coimbra e sua Instituição*. Coimbra, Portugal: University of Coimbra, 1830.

Morales, Ambrosio de. *Viage a los reynos de León y Galicia y Principado de Asturias*. Madrid: Antonio Marín, 1765. http://hdl.handle.net/10347/8267.

Naia, Giacomo Antonio. Viaje a Santiago de Compostela *de Giacomo Antonio Naia (1717–*

1719). *Texto integral en español.* Translated, edited, and with an introduction by Carmen Pugliese. Perugia and Pomigliano d'Arco, Italy: Edizioni Compostellane, 2012.
Northup, Solomon. *Twelve Years a Slave. Narrative of Solomon Northup, a Citizen of New-York, Kidnapped in Washington City in 1841, and Rescued in 1853, from a Cotton Plantation Near the Red River, in Louisiana.* Auburn, NY: Derby and Miller, 1853.
Peyron, Juan Francisco. *Ensayos sobre España.* In *Viajes de extranjeros por España y Portugal: desde los tiempos más remotos hasta comienzos del siglo XX*, 5:240–442. 6 vols. Valladolid, Spain: Junta de Castilla y León, Consejería de Educación y Cultura, 1999.
Quevedo, Francisco de. Lazarillo De Tormes *and* The Grifter (El buscón)*: Two Novels of the Low Life in Golden Age Spain.* Edited and translated by David Frye. Indianapolis, Indiana, and Cambridge, Massachusetts: Hackett, 2015.
Riva Palacio, Vicente. *Martín Garatuza.* Edited by Antonio Castro Leal. 2nd ed. Vol. 1. Mexico City: Porrúa, 1965.
The Souls of Purgatory: The Spiritual Diary of a Seventeenth-Century Afro-Peruvian Mystic, Úrsula de Jesús. Translated, edited, and with an introduction by Nancy E. van Deusen. Albuquerque: University of New Mexico Press, 2004.
Torres Villaroel, Diego de. *Vida, ascendencia, nacimiento, crianza y aventuras.* Edited by Guy Mercadier. Madrid: Castalia, 1972.
La vida y los hechos de Estebanillo González, hombre de buen humor. Edited by Antonio Carreira and Juan Antonio Cid. 2 vols. Madrid: Cátedra, 1990.

Secondary Sources

Abrahams, Roger D. *The Man-of-Words in the West Indies: Performance and the Emergence of Creole Culture.* Baltimore and London: The Johns Hopkins University Press, 1983.
Abreu, Alberto A. *Para a história de Viana do Castelo: Ensaios.* Vol. 3 of 3 vols. Viana do Castelo: Câmara Muncipal, 2007.
Alpuim, Maria Augusta d' and Maria Emilia de Vasconcelos. *Casas de Viana Antiga.* Viana do Castelo, Portugal: Centro de Estudos Regionais, 1983.
Álvarez González, Yolanda and Luís Francisco López González. "Restos romanos na rúa Cervantes no 11, na cidade de Ourense." In *Ourense. A Cidade, da Orixe ao Século XVI*, 84–92. Santiago de Compostela: Xunta de Galicia, Museo Arqueolóxico Provincial de Ourense, 2009.
Arellano, Ignacio. *Editar a Calderón.* Madrid: Iberoamericana, 2007.
Ares Queija, Berta. "Mestizos, mulatos y zambaigos (Virreinato del Perú, siglo XVI)." In *Negros, mulatos, zambaigos: Derroteros africanos en los mundos ibéricos*, coordinated by Berta Ares Queija and Alessandro Stella, 75–88. Sevilla, Spain: Escuela de Estudios Hispano-Americanos, Consejo Superior de Investigaciones Científicas, 2000.

Arribas Briones, Pablo. *Pícaros y picaresca en el Camino de Santiago*. 2nd ed. Burgos, Spain: Librería Berceo, 1993.

Asenjo González, María. "El Corregidor en la ciudad. La gestión de su oficio y la construcción del *habitus*, a fines del siglo XV y principios del XVI." *Studia Histórica. Historia Moderna* 39, no. 1 (2017): 89–124.

Badenas Zamora, Antonio. "Consideraciones acerca de la supresión de los casos de Corte." *AHDE* 82 (2012): 521–560.

Barriocanal López, Yolanda. *O camiño real de Castela a Santiago por Ourense, base do camiño de peregrinacion. Via da Prata*. Ourense, Spain: Museo Arqueolóxico Provincial de Ourense and Grupo Marcelo Macías, 2011.

Barros, Carlos. "La frontera medieval entre Galicia y Portugal." *Medievalismo* 4 (1994): 27–39.

BBC Mundo. "El video que reavivó el debate sobre el racismo en Colombia." *BBC Mundo*, September 16, 2015. http://www.bbc.com/mundo/noticias/2015/09/150916_colombia_video_racismo_ilm

Bento, Maria José Travassos de Almeida de Jesus. "Convento de Cristo—1420/1521—Mais do que um século." PhD diss., University of Coimbra, Coimbra, Portugal, 2014.

Berlin, Ira. "From Creole to African: Atlantic Creoles and the Origins of African-American Society in Mainland North America." *The William and Mary Quarterly* 53, no. 2 (April 1996): 251–288.

Berlin, Ira. *Many Thousands Gone: The First Two Centuries of Slavery in North America*. Cambridge, Massachusetts and London, England: The Belknap Press of Harvard University, 1998.

Bermejo Cabrero, José Luis. *Poder político y administración de justicia en la España de los Austrias*. Madrid: Ministerio de Justicia, Secretaría General Técnica, 2005.

Blackmore, Josiah. *Moorings: Portuguese Expansion and the Writing of Africa*. Minneapolis and London: University of Minnesota, 2009.

Blake, Robert J. "Sound Change and Linguistic Residue: The Case of [f-] > [h-] > [Ø]." In *Synchronic and Diachronic Approaches to Linguistic Variation and Change*, edited by Thomas J. Walsh, 53–62. Washington, DC: Georgetown University, 1989. https://repository.library.georgetown.edu/bitstream/handle/10822/555481/GURT_1988.pdf?sequence=1#page=65

Blázquez Miguel, Juan. *Yecla en el siglo XVII*. Yecla, Spain: Ayuntamiento de Yecla, Concejalía de Cultura, Caja de Ahorros de Murcia, Obra Cultural, 1988.

Blue, William R. "Carnival and Lenten Alternations." In *The Prince in the Tower: Perceptions of* La vida es sueño, edited by Frederick de Armas, 88–96. Lewisburg, Pennsylvania: Bucknell University, 1993.

Bravo Rodríguez, María José. "Matrimonio y vida sexual de las personas esclavizadas en la Granada del siglo XVII." In *Esclavitudes hispánicas (siglos XV al XXI): Horizontes socioculturales*, edited by Aurelia Martín Casares, 157–173. Granada: University of Granada, 2014.

Bristol, Joan Cameron. *Christians, Blasphemers, and Witches: Afro-Mexican Ritual Practice in the Seventeenth Century*. Albuquerque: University of New Mexico Press, 2007.

Burke, Peter. *Popular Culture in Early Modern Europe*. Aldershot, England: Ashgate, 1994.

Burshatin, Israel. "Written on the Body: Slave or Hermaphrodite in Sixteenth-Century Spain." In *Queer Iberia: Sexualities, Cultures, and Crossings from the Middle Ages to the Renaissance*, edited by Josiah Blackmore and Gregory S. Hutcheson, 420–456. Durham, North Carolina and London: Duke University, 1999.

Busto Duthurburu, José Antonio del. "Los escribanos en la conquista del Perú." *Notarius* 2 (1991): 161–163.

Bynum, Caroline Walker. *Christian Materiality: An Essay on Religion in Late Medieval Europe*. New York: Zone Books, 2011.

Cañizares-Esguerra, Jorge, Matt D. Childs, and James Sidbury, eds. *The Black Urban Atlantic in the Age of the Slave Trade*. Philadelphia: University of Pennsylvania, 2013.

Campos y Fernández de Sevilla, F. Javier. *"Las Relaciones Topográficas de Felipe II*: Índices, fuentes y bibliografía." *Anuario Jurídico y Económico Escurialense* 36 (2003): 441–574.

Cañizares-Esguerra, Jorge. "Demons, Stars, and the Imagination: The Early Modern Body in the Tropics." In *Racism in Western Civilisation Before 1700*, edited by Ben Issac, Miriam Eliav-Feldon, and Yossi Ziegler, 313–325. Cambridge, England: Cambridge University, 2009.

Carrasco Manchado, Ana Isabel. "'Simular' y 'disimular,' percepción de un concepto moderno en la Edad Media hispana." *Res publica* 18 (2007): 335–352.

Carretta, Vincent. *Equiano the African: Biography of a Self-Made Man*. New York: Penguin, 2005.

Carvalho, José Vieira de. *O Mosteiro de S. Salvador de Moreira (séculos XI a XIV). Subsidios para a sua historia*. Maia, Portugal: Instituição Valorizadora da Terra da Maia, 1969.

Catedral de Santiago de Compostela. Brochure. Santiago de Compostela Turismo. http://www.santiagoturismo.com/publicacions/folleto-catedral-de-santiago-de-compostela

Chamoiseau, Patrick. *Au temps de l'antan. Contes du pays Martinique*. Paris: Hatier, 1988.

Chamoiseau, Patrick. *Creole Folktales*. Translated by Linda Coverdale. New York: The New Press, 1994.

Chew, Samuel. *The Pilgrimage of Life*. Port Washington, New York: Kennikat, 1973.

Conde Guerri, Elena. "La tonsura como objeto de reglamentación canónica en las diócesis de occidente." In *Cristianismo y aculturación en tiempos del Imperio Romano*, edited by Antonio González Blanco and José María Blázquez, 291–299. Murcia, Spain: University of Murcia, 1990.

Copete, Marie-Lucie. “L’assistance aux prisonniers pauvres en Espagne (XVIe–XVIIe siècles): Entre mission et expérimentation.” *Archives de Sciences Sociales des Religions* 153 (2011): 23–42.

Cordero y Torres, Enrique. “Martín Garatuza.” In *Diccionario Biográfico de Puebla*, 271. Puebla, México: Centro de Estudios Históricos de Puebla, 1972.

Costa Buján, Pablo. “Evolución urbana y cambios morfológicos, Santiago de Compostela, 1778–1950.” PhD diss., University of A Coruña, 2013.

Cotta, Sergio. *Itinerarios humanos del derecho*. Edited and translated by Jesús Ballesteros. 2nd ed. Pamplona: Universidad de Navarra, 1978.

Cruz, Anne J. *Discourses of Poverty: Social Reform and the Picaresque Novel in Early Modern Spain*. Toronto, Buffalo, and London: University of Toronto Press, 1999.

Cuello Calón, Eugenio. “Contribución al estudio de la historia de la pena de muerte en España.” *Anuario de derecho penal y ciencias penales* 10 (1957): 9–40.

Cunha, Arlindo de Magalhães Ribeiro da. “A devoçaõ e a peregrinação jacobeias em Portugal.” *Ad Limina* 2, no. 2 (2011): 85–114.

Darnton, Robert. *The Great Cat Massacre and Other Episodes in French Cultural History*. New York: Basic Books, 1984.

Davis, Natalie Zemon. *The Return of Martin Guerre*. Cambridge, Massachusetts and London, England: Harvard University Press, 1983.

Dawson, Kevin. “The Cultural Geography of Enslaved Ship Pilots.” In *The Black Urban Atlantic in the Age of the Slave Trade*, edited by Jorge Cañizares-Esguerra, Matt D. Childs, and James Sidbury, 163–184. Philadelphia: University of Pennsylvania, 2013.

DeCosta-Willis, Miriam. “Self and Society in the Afro-Cuban Slave Narrative.” *Latin American Literary Review* 16, no. 32 (1988): 6–15.

Domingues, “Códices medievais de *ius commune* em Portugal: *Status Quaestionis*.” *Anuario de Estudios Medievales* 46, no. 2 (2016): 725–750.

Doña Teresa de Aguilera y Roche ante la Inquisición (1664). Edited by Magdalena Coll, Heather Bamford, Heather McMichael, and John H.R. Polt; translated by John H.R. Polt. Part 3. Berkeley, California: Research Center for Romance Studies, University of California–Berkeley, 2010. http://escholarship.org/uc/item/04c560kt

Earle, T.F. and K.J.P. Lowe, eds. *Black Africans in Renaissance Europe*. Cambridge, England, and New York: Cambridge University, 2005.

Estrada, Juan Antonio de. *Población general de España, sus reynos y sus provincias, ciudades, villas y pueblos, islas adjacentes, y presidios de África*. Vol. 1. Madrid: Andrés Ramírez, 1768.

Fernández Duro, Cesáreo. *El último almirante de Castilla Don Juan Tomás Enríquez de Cabrera: Duque de Medina de Rioseco, Conde de Módica, Osona, Cabrera y Melgar, Señor de las villas de Castroverde, Aguilar, Rueda y Mansilla, etc.* Madrid: widow and children of M. Tello, 1902.

Fernández Sánchez, José, y Francisco Freire Barreiro. *Guía de Santiago y sus alrededores*. Santiago: Seminario Conciliar, 1885.

Fogelman, Patricia and Marta Goldberg. "'El rey de los *congos*': The Clandestine Coronation of Pedro Duarte in Buenos Aires, 1787," document translation by Joseph P. Sánchez, Angélica Sánchez-Clark, and Larry D. Miller. In *Afro-Latino Voices: Narratives from the Early Modern Ibero-Atlantic World, 1550–1812*, edited by Kathryn Joy McKnight and Leo J. Garofalo, 155–173. Indianapolis, Indiana and Cambridge, Massachusetts: Hackett, 2009.

Fonseca, Jorge. "Black Africans in Portugal during Cleynaerts's Visit (1533–1538)." In *Black Africans in Renaissance Europe*, edited by T.F. Earle and Kate J.P. Lowe, 113–121. Cambridge, England, and New York: Cambridge University, 2005.

Foucault, Michel. *Discipline and Punish: The Birth of the Prison*. Translated by Alan Sheridan. New York: Vintage Books, 1979.

Foucault, Michel. *Surveiller et punir: Naissance de la prison*. Paris: Éditions Gallimard, 1975.

Fra Molinero, Baltasar. *La imagen de los negros en el teatro del Siglo de Oro*. Madrid: Siglo XXI Editores, 1995.

Fra Molinero, Baltasar. "Juan Latino and His Racial Difference." In *Black Africans in Renaissance Europe*, edited by T.F. Earle and Kate J.P. Lowe, 326–344. Cambridge, England, and New York: Cambridge University, 2005.

Fra Molinero, Baltasar. "Ser mulato en España y América: discursos legales y otros discursos literarios," In *Negros, mulatos, zambaigos: Derroteros africanos en los mundos ibéricos*, coordinated by Berta Ares Queija and Alessandro Stella, 123–147. Sevilla, Spain: Escuela de Estudios Hispano-Americanos, Consejo Superior de Investigaciones Científicas, 2000.

Franco Silva, Alfonso. "La mujer esclava en la sociedad andaluza de fines del Medioevo." In *El trabajo de las mujeres en la edad media hispana*, edited by Ángela Muñoz Fernández and Cristina Segura Graiño, 287–301. Madrid: Marcial Pons, 1988.

Fuchs, Barbara. *Passing for Spain: Cervantes and the Fictions of Identity*. Urbana and Chicago: University of Illinois, 2003.

Gallego Domínguez, Olga. *A cidade de Ourense. Unha visión a través dos séculos*. Boletín Avriense, Anexo 27. Ourense, Spain: Museo Arqueológico Provincial, 2001.

Gallego Domínguez, Olga. "Torres, puertas y cerca de la ciudad de Orense." *Boletín Avriense* 2 (1972): 241–278.

Gallego Domínguez, Olga and Francisco Fariña Busto. "As Casas Reales de Cimadevilla ou do Correxidor." *Boletín Avriense* 18–19 (1988–1989): 199–210.

Garber, Cecily. "Africans in Renaissance Europe." *The Ultimate History Project*, 2013. http://ultimatehistoryproject.com/africans-in-the-renaissance.html

García, Sebastián. *Guadalupe de Extremadura en América*. Guadalupe, Spain: Comunidad Franciscana de Guadalupe, 1990.

García Álvarez, Jacobo, and Paloma Puente Lozano. "Las Comisiones Mixtas de Límites y las representaciones geográficas de la frontera hispano-portuguesa (1855–1906)." *Revista de Historiografía* 23 (2015): 67–100.

García Álvarez, Jacobo. "La frontera hispano-portuguesa en el río Miño en el tratado de límites de 1864." In *Paisaje, cultura territorial y vivencia de la geografía. Libro homenaje al profesor Alfredo Morales Gil*, coordinated by José Fernando Vera Rebollo, Jorge Olcina Cantos, and María Hernández Hernández, 761–787. San Vicente del Raspeig, Spain: Universidad de Alicante, 2016.

García Iglesias, José Manuel. "La visita de Cosme III de Médicis a la catedral de Santiago." In *El viaje a Compostela de Cosme III de Médicis*, directed by Xosé A. Neira Cruz, 583–602. Santiago de Compostela: Museo Diocesano, 2004.

García Valdeiras, Manuel. "Intervencións arqueolóxicas na cidade de Ourense (1997–2007)." In *Estudos. Ourense: A cidade, da orixe ao século XVI*, coordinated by the Provincial Arqueological Museum of Ourense (Museo Arqueolóxico Provincial de Ourense), 133–183. Ourense, Spain: Xunta de Galicia, 2009.

Garrone, José Alberto, *Diccionario Jurídico*. 4 vols. Buenos Aires: LexisNexis Argentina, 2005.

Gates, Jr., Henry Louis. *The Signifying Monkey: A Theory of Afro-American Literary Criticism*. New York: Oxford University, 1988.

González Fernández, Isabel. "Compostela en las crónicas del segundo viaje por Europa de Cosme III de Médicis." In *El viaje a Compostela de Cosme III de Médicis*, directed by Xosé A. Neira Cruz, 231–249. Santiago de Compostela: Museo Diocesano, 2004.

González-Varas Ibáñez, Alejandro. "El *ius commune* y la convocatoria de concilios y cortes de León y Castilla en la edad media." In *El* ius commune *y la formación de las instituciones de Derecho público*, edited by Alejandro González-Varas Ibáñez, 109–164. Valencia: Tirant lo Blanch, 2012.

Greenia, George. "The Bartered Body: Medieval Pilgrims and Spiritual Transaction." *International Journal of Religious Tourism and Pilgrimage* 7, no. 1 (2019): 38–51.

Guillamón Álvarez, F. Javier and Jesús Pérez Hervás. "Los Forzados De Galeras En Cartagena Durante El Primer Tercio Del Siglo XVIII." *Revista De Historia Naval* 5, no. 19 (1987): 63–75.

Gutiérrez Estévez, Manuel. "Una visión antropológica del Carnaval." In *Formas carnavalescas en el arte y la literatura*, edited by Javier Huerta Calvo, 33–59. Barcelona: Ediciones Serbal, 1989.

Harney, Michael. *Race, Caste, and Indigeneity in Medieval Spanish Travel Literature*. New York: Palgrave Macmillan, 2015.

Heras Santos, José Luis de las. "Ejemplaridad, paternalismo y utilitarismo en la justicia de la España de los Habsburgo." *Estudios Humanísticos. Historia* 12 (2013): 185–213.

Heras Santos, José Luis de las. "Los galeotes de la monarquía hispánica durante el Antiguo Régimen." *Studia Histórica: Historia Moderna* 22 (2000): 283–300.

Heras Santos, José Luis de las. *La justicia penal de los Austrias en la corona de Castilla*. Salamanca: Ediciones Universidad de Salamanca, 1991.

Hernández Delgado, Alexander and Ignacio Ruiz Rodríguez. *Elena o Eleno de Céspedes: un hombre atrapado en el cuerpo de una mujer, en la España de Felipe II*. Madrid: Dykinson, 2017.

Hernández Figueiredo, José Ramón. "Apuntes sobre la geografía eclesiástica de Ourense: Tourém, Lama de Arcos, 'Couto Mixto' y 'pueblos promiscuos.'" *Cuadernos de Estudios Gallegos* 61, no. 127 (2014): 219–250.

Herwaarden, Jan van. *Between Saint James and Erasmus: Studies in Late-Medieval Religious Life: Devotion and Pilgrimage in the Netherlands*. Translated by Wendie Shaffer and Donald Gardner. Leiden and Boston: Brill, 2003.

Herzog, Tamar. *Frontiers of Possession: Spain and Portugal in Europe and the Americas*. Cambridge, Massachusetts and London, England: Harvard University Press, 2015.

Herzog, Tamar. "The 'Recopilación de Indias' and Its Discourse: The Spanish Monarchy, the Indies and the Seventeenth Century." In *Ius Commune*, edited by Dieter Simon and Michael Stolleis, 143–163. Frankfurt am Main, Germany: Vittorio Klostermann, 1993.

Hidalgo, Margarita. "El español de América en los archivos de la Inquisición: Nueva España 1527–1635." *Anuario de Lingüística Hispánica* XXVII (2011): 71–93.

Hotchkiss, Valerie R. *Clothes Make the Man: Female Cross Dressing in Medieval Europe*. New York and London: Garland Publishing, 1996.

Hurston, Zora Neale. *Mules and Men*. Edited by Henry Louis Gates, Jr. New York: Harper Perennial, 1990.

Irigoyen-García, Javier. *The Spanish Arcadia: Sheep Herding, Pastoral Discourse, and Ethnicity in Early Modern Spain*. Toronto, Buffalo, London: University of Toronto, 2014.

Jones, Nicholas R. *Staging* Habla de Negros*: Radical Performances of the African Diaspora in Early Modern Spain*. University Park, Pennsylvania: The Pennsylvania State University Press, 2019.

Jordan, Annemarie. "Images of Empire: Slaves in the Lisbon Household and Court of Catherine of Austria." In *Black Africans in Renaissance Europe*, edited by T.F. Earle and Kate J.P. Lowe, 155–180. Cambridge, England, and New York: Cambridge University, 2005.

Jordan, Winthrop. *White over Black: American Attitudes toward the Negro, 1550–1812*. Chapel Hill, North Carolina: The Omohundro Institute of Early American History and Culture at Williamsburg, Virginia, by the University of North Carolina, 1968.

Jusdado Ruiz-Capillas, Miguel Ángel. "Ius Commune y Common Law." *Cuadernos de Historia de Derecho* 15 (2008): 327–344.

Justo Martín, María Xosé. "A cárcere de Ourense no século XIX. Notas históricas." *Boletín Avriense* XI (1981): 195–226.

Kagan, Richard L. *Lawsuits and Litigants in Castile, 1500–1700*. Chapel Hill: University of North Carolina Press, 1981.

Kamen, Henry. "El rey hechizado que no lo fue." In *El rey loco y otros misterios de la España imperial*, written by Henry Kamen and translated by José C. Vales, 231–250. Madrid: La Esfera de los Libros, 2012.

Kamen, Henry. *Spain in the Later Seventeenth Century, 1665–1700*. London and New York: Longman, 1980.

Kendi, Ibram X. *Stamped from the Beginning: The Definitive History of Racist Ideas in America*. New York: Nation Books, 2017.

Konetzke, Richard. "La legislación española y el mestizaje en América." In *El mestizaje en la historia de Ibero-América*, edited by Magnus Mörner, 59–64. Mexico City: Editorial Cultura, 1961.

Lahon, Didier. "Black African Slaves and Freedmen in Portugal during the Renaissance: Creating a New Pattern of Reality." In *Black Africans in Renaissance Europe*, edited by T.F. Earle and Kate J.P. Lowe, 261–279. Cambridge, England, and New York: Cambridge University, 2005.

Lalami, Laila. *The Moor's Account*. New York: Pantheon Books, 2014.

Landers, Jane. *Black Society in Spanish Florida*. Urbana: University of Illinois, 1999.

Landers, Jane. "The African Landscape of Seventeenth-Century Cartagena and Its Hinterlands." In *The Black Urban Atlantic in the Age of the Slave Trade*, edited by Jorge Cañizares-Esguerra, Matt D. Childs, and James Sidbury, 147–162. Philadelphia: University of Pennsylvania, 2013.

Lawrance, Jeremy. "Black Africans in Renaissance Spanish Literature." In *Black Africans in Renaissance Europe*, edited by T.F. Earle and Kate J.P. Lowe, 70–93. Cambridge, England, and New York: Cambridge University, 2005.

Lobo de Araújo, María Marta and Alexandra Patrícia Lopes Esteves. "Pasaportes de caridad: las 'cartas de guía' de las Misericordias portuguesas (siglos xvii–xix)." *Estudios humanísticos. Historia* 6 (2007): 207–225.

López Díaz, María. "La Administración de la justicia señorial en el antiguo régimen." *Anuario de historia del derecho español* LXXVI (2006): 557–588.

López Ferreiro, Antonio. *Historia de la Santa A.M. Iglesia de Santiago*. 11 vols. Santiago de Compostela: Seminario Conciliar Central, 1907.

López Gómez, Pedro. *La Real Audiencia de Galicia y el Archivo del Reino*. 2 vols. Santiago de Compostela: Xunta de Galicia, 1996.

López Santaolalla, Miguel Ángel. "Picaresca y peregrinaje." Speech given in Villadiego, Spain, August 11, 2008. Asociación cultural las calzas de Villadiego, November 28, 2012. https://lascalzas.wordpress.com/2012/11/28/picaresca-y-peregrinaje-conferencia-calza-2008/

Loureiro, José Pinto. *Toponímia de Coimbra*. 2 vols. Coimbra: Câmara Municipal, 1960.

Lowe, Kate J.P. "Introduction: Black Africans in Renaissance Europe." In *Black Africans*

in Renaissance Europe, edited by T.F. Earle and Kate J.P. Lowe, 1–14. Cambridge, England, and New York: Cambridge University, 2005.

Lowe, Kate J.P. "The Stereotyping of Black Africans in Renaissance Europe." In *Black Africans in Renaissance Europe*, edited by T.F. Earle and Kate J.P. Lowe, 17–47. Cambridge, England, and New York: Cambridge University, 2005.

Ludmer, Josefina. "Las tretas del débil." In *La sartén por el mango. Encuentro de escritoras latinoamericanas*, edited by by Patricia Elena González and Eliana Ortega, 47–54. Río Piedras, Puerto Rico: Ediciones Huracán, 1985.

Maciel, Ana Ester Freitas. "A Misericórdia de Viana do Castelo: O braço do povo." PhD diss., Catholic University of Portugal, Braga, 2007.

Marchante-Aragón, Lucas A. "The King, the Nation, and the Moor: Imperial Spectacle and the Rejection of Hybridity in *The Masque of the Expulsion of the Moriscos*." *The Journal for Early Modern Cultural Studies* 8, no. 1 (Spring/Summer 2008): 98–133.

Martín Casares, Aurelia. "Repensar la esclavitud en el mundo hispano: reflexiones y propuestas metodológicas desde la Antropología histórica." In *Esclavitudes hispánicas (siglos XV al XXI): Horizontes socioculturales*, edited by Aurelia Martín Casares, 11–38. Granada, Spain: University of Granada, 2014.

Martínez Martínez, Faustino. "Ius commune, Utrumque ius: Tiempos de Derecho único, tiempos de juristas." GLOSSAE. *European Journal of Legal History* 13 (2016): 371–423.

Martínez Martínez, María José. "El Santo Cristo de Burgos y los Cristos dolorosos articulados." *Boletín del Seminario de Estudios de Arte y Arqueología* 69–70 (2003–2004): 232–233.

Massing, Jean Michel. *The Image of the Black in Western Art. From the "Age of Discovery" to the Age of Abolition. Europe and the World Beyond.* Edited by David Bindman and Henry Louis Gates, Jr. Vol. III, part 2. Cambridge, Massachusetts and London, England: The Belknap Press of Harvard University, 2011.

Mazzotti, José Antonio. "El Dorado, Paradise, and Supreme Sanctity in Seventeenth-Century Peru: A Creole Agenda." In *Creole Subjects in the Colonial Americas: Empires, Texts, Identities*, edited by Ralph Bauer and José Antonio Mazzotti, 375–411. Chapel Hill, North Carolina: The Omohundro Institute of Early American History and Culture at Williamsburg, Virginia, by the University of North Carolina, 2009.

Ménard, Caroline. "'Un esclavo que se llama Antonio': venta de dos esclavos asiáticos en Galicia a inicios del siglo XVII." *Cuadernos de Estudios Gallegos* 59, no. 125 (2012): 233–244.

Miranda, Salvador. "Giorgio Cornaro." In *The Cardinals of the Holy Roman Church.* Miami, Florida: Florida International University, 1998–2018. http://webdept.fiu.edu/~mirandas/bios1697.htm#Cornaro

Molas Ribalta, Pere, et al. *La transición del siglo XVII al XVIII: entre la decadencia y*

la reconstrucción, coordinated by Pere Molas Ribalta. Vol. 28, *Historia de España*. Madrid: Espasa-Calpe, 1993.

Molesky, Mark. *"This Gulf of Fire": The Great Lisbon Earthquake and Its Aftermath*. New York: Alfred A. Knopf, 2015.

Monteiro, António. "Obras de Misericórdia. Dar pousada aos peregrinos e pobres." *Boletim Informativo Santa Casa da Misericórdia de Santarém* 56 (2011): 10–11.

Montoro Ballesteros, Alberto. *Conflicto social, Derecho y Proceso*. Murcia, Spain: Secretariado de Publicaciones, Universidad de Murcia, 1980.

Morelli, Federica. "Pueblos, alcaldes y municipios: la justicia local en el mundo hispánico entre Antiguo Régimen y Liberalismo." *Historia Crítica* 36 (July–December 2008): 36–57.

Moro, Raffaele. "Las transformaciones de la memoria de un 'embustero' (México, siglos XVII–XIX)." In *Opinión pública y espacio urbano en la edad moderna*, edited by Carmen Serrano Sánchez, 211–222. Gijón, Spain: Ediciones Trea, 2010.

Morón, Manuel. *Reflexiones sobre la justicia penal*. Granada, Spain: Escuela Social de Granada, 1966.

Navarro Loidi, Juan and Pilar Merino Saenz. "The Units of Length in the Spanish Treatises of Military Engineering." In *The Global and the Local: The History of Science and the Cultural Integration of Europe. Proceedings of the 2nd ICESHS (Cracow, Poland, September 6–9, 2006)*, edited by Michal Kokowski, 447–455. Cracow: The Press of the Polish Academy of Arts and Sciences, 2007. http://www.2iceshs.cyfronet.pl/proceedings.html

Ortego Gil, Pedro. "Apercibimientos penales en la práctica criminal de la Real Audiencia de Galicia (siglos XVII y XVIII)." *Cuadernos de Historia de Derecho* 3 (1996): 11–41.

Ortego Gil, Pedro. "La aplicación de la pena de muerte en el Reino de Galicia durante la Edad Moderna." *Obradoiro de Historia Moderna* 9 (2000): 143–170.

Ortego Gil, Pedro. "El arbitrio de los jueces inferiores: su alcance y limitaciones." In *El Arbitrio Judicial en el Antiguo Régimen (España e Indias, siglos XVI–XVIII)*, edited by José Sánchez-Arcilla Bernal, 133–219. Madrid: Editorial Dykinson, 2012.

Owens, J.B. *"By My Absolute Royal Authority": Justice and the Castilian Commonwealth at the Beginning of the First Global Age*. Rochester, NY: The University of Rochester Press, 2005.

P.F.G. y C. "España pintoresca: Orense. Artículo primero." *Semanario pintoresco español*, 2, no. 7 (February 14, 1847): 49–51.

P.F.G. y C. "España pintoresca: Orense. Artículo segundo." *Semanario pintoresco español*, 2, no. 8 (February 21, 1847): 57–59.

Paül, Valerià and Juan Manuel Trillo-Santamaría. "Discussing the Couto Mixto (Galicia, Spain): Transcending the Territorial Trap Through Borderscapes and Border Poetics Analyses." *Geopolitics* 20 (2015): 56–78.

Paül, Valerià. "La construcción literaria de los paisajes fronterizos. Una reflexión a

propósito del Couto Mixto (Galicia y Portugal)." *Documents d'Anàlisi Geogràfica* 60, no. 2 (2014): 289–314.

Pérez Martín, Antonio. *El derecho procesal del "Ius Commune" en España*. Murcia: Universidad de Murcia, 1999.

Phillips, Jr., William D. *Slavery in Medieval and Early Modern Iberia*. Philadelphia: University of Pennsylvania, 2013.

Pike, Ruth. *Penal Servitude in Early Modern Spain*. Madison, Wisconsin: University of Wisconsin, 1983. https://libro.uca.edu/pservitude/pservitude.htm

Pinho, Joana Maria Balsa Carvalho de. "As Casas da Misericórdia: confrarias da Misericórdia e a Arquitectura quinhentista portuguesa." 3 vols. PhD diss., University of Lisbon, 2012.

Planas Roselló, Antonio. "El proceso penal en rebeldía en el derecho histórico de Mallorca. La pragmática de los procesos de ausencia de 1625." *MRAMEGH* 25 (2015): 105–136.

Planas Roselló, Antonio. "La recepción del *ius commune* en el Reino de Mallorca." *GLOSSAE. European Journal of Legal History* 13 (2016): 561–589.

Prato-Perelli, Antoinette da. *Las encomiendas de Nueva Andalucía en el siglo XVII: visita hecha por don Fernando de la Riva Agüero, Oidor de la Audiencia de Santo Domingo, 1688*. 4 vols. Caracas: Fuentes para la Historia Colonial de Venezuela, 1990.

PROLOPE, Grupo de investigación. *La edición del teatro de Lope de Vega: Las "Partes" de comedias. Criterios de edición*. Barcelona: Universitat Autònoma de Barcelona and Bellaterra, 2008.

Quintino, Carlos. "João Afonso e a assistência hospitalar na Santarém Medieval." *No país das maravilhas*. February 8, 2011. http://santaremportugal.blogspot.pt/2011/02/joao-afonso-e-assistencia-hospitalar-na.html

Ramey, Lynn T. *Black Legacies: Race and the European Middle Ages*. Gainesville, Florida: University Press of Florida, 2014.

Real Academia Española. *Diccionario de Autoridades*. 3 vols. Madrid: Gredos, 1969.

Real Academia Española. *Ortografía de la lengua española*. Barcelona: Espasa Libros, 2010.

Ribeiro, Victor. *A Santa Casa da Misericórdia de Lisboa (subsidios para a sua história): 1498–1898*. Lisbon: Academia Real das Sciencias, 1902.

Ribot García, Luis Antonio. "La España de Carlos II." In *La transición del siglo XVII al XVIII: entre la decadencia y la reconstrucción*, coordinated by Pere Molas i Ribalta, 61–203. Madrid: Espasa-Calpe, 2000.

Rincón García, Wifredo. "La Plaza Mayor española. Espacio para la sociedad y el poder. El ejemplo de Madrid." In *Arte, poder y sociedad en la España de los siglos XV al XX*, coordinated by Miguel Cabañas Bravo, Amelia López-Yarto Elizalde, and Wilfredo Rincón García, 265–278. Madrid: Departamento de Historia del Arte, Instituto de Historia, Consejo Superior de Investigaciones Científicas, 2008.

Río Barredo, María José del. "Burlas y violencia en el Carnaval madrileño de los siglos XVII y XVIII." *Revista de Filología Románica* 19, extra no. 3 (2002): 111–129.

Rodríguez Cao, Celso. "Excavación arqueolóxica en área nos soares n.o 18–20 da rúa Colón e n.o 29 da rúa Cervantes da cidade de Ourense." In *Estudos. Ourense: A cidade, da orixe ao século XVI*, coordinated by the Provincial Arqueological Museum of Ourense (Museo Arqueolóxico Provincial de Ourense), 117–121. Ourense, Spain: Xunta de Galicia, 2009.

Rodríguez Flores, María Inmaculada. *El perdón real en Castilla (siglos XIII–XVIII)*. Salamanca, Spain: University of Salamanca, 1971.

Rodríguez González, Avelino. *A Casa do Concello de Ourense*. Boletín Avriense, Anexo 34. Ourense, Spain: Grupo Marcelo Macías and Museo Arqueolóxico Provincial, 2015.

Sánchez Gómez, Rosa Isabel. *Delincuencia y seguridad en el Madrid de Carlos II*. Madrid: Secretaría General Técnica, Ministro del Interior, 1994.

Santa Casa da Misericórdia de Aveiro. *A Arte na Misericórdia Inventariar e Divulgar. Roteiro*. Aveiro, Portugal: Santa Casa da Misericórdia de Aveiro, 2007.

Santaolalla López, Fernando. "El voto de calidad del presidente del tribunal constitucional." *Revista Española de Derecho Constitucional* 85 (2009): 201–211.

Santos Fernández, Carlos. "Tres peregrinos del siglo XVII condenados por hurtos en el Hospital Real de Santiago." *Compostela: Revista de la Archicofradía Universal del Apóstol Santiago* 60 (2018): 33–39.

Saunders, A.C. de C.M. *A Social History of Black Slaves and Freedmen in Portugal. 1441–1555*. Cambridge, England: Cambridge University, 1982.

Schwaller, Robert C. "The Importance of Mestizos and Mulatos as Bilingual Intermediaries in Sixteenth-century New Spain." *Ethnohistory* 59, no. 4 (2012): 713–738.

Schwartz, Stuart B. *All Can Be Saved: Religious Tolerance and Salvation in the Iberian Atlantic World*. New Haven: Yale University, 2008.

Serrão, Joaquim Veríssimo. *A Misericórdia de Lisboa: Quinhentos Anos de História*. Lisbon: Livros Horizonte and Misericórdia de Lisboa, 1998.

Serrão, Vitor. "Portugal y las artes de la guerra." In *El viaje a Compostela de Cosme III de Médicis*, directed by Xosé A. Neira Cruz, 539–551. Santiago de Compostela: Museo Diocesano, 2004.

Singul, Francisco. *Vino y cultura medieval: Galicia y los Caminos de Santiago*. Santiago de Compostela: Apecsa, 2010.

Siraisi, Nancy G. *Medieval and Early Renaissance Medicine: An Introduction to Knowledge and Practice*. Chicago and London: University of Chicago, 1990.

Smith, Chantell. "From Juan to Juan: The Triumph of Poet and Subject in Juan Latino's *Austrias Carmen*." In *Slavery, Migrations, and Transformations: Connecting Old and New Diasporas to the Homeland*, edited by Toyin Falola and Danielle Porter Sanchez, 231–249. Amherst, New York: Cambria, 2015.

Soares, Mariza de Carvalho. "African Barbeiros in Brazilian Slave Ports." In *The Black Urban Atlantic in the Age of the Slave Trade*, edited by Jorge Cañizares-Esguerra, Matt D. Childs, and James Sidbury, 207–230. Philadelphia: University of Pennsylvania, 2013.

Sommer, Doris. *Proceed with Caution, When Engaged by Minority Writing in the Americas*. Cambridge, Massachusetts: Harvard University, 1999.

Somoza Medina, José. *As Lagoas: Un estudio de xeografía urbana*. Santiago de Compostela: Consellería de Cultura da Xunta de Galicia, 1996.

Somoza Medina, José. *Historia de Ourense: A cidade das pontes e os camiños*. Ourense, Spain: Duen de Bux, 2010.

Somoza Medina, José. *Ourense: La ciudad en el tiempo y en el espacio*. León, Spain: University of León, Secretariado de Publicaciones y Medios Audiovisuales, 2002.

Sousa, Fernando de, Jorge Alves, Gaspar Martins Pereira, and Jorge Ribeiro. "O Arquivo da Santa Casa da Misericórdia de Aveiro." *Boletim Municipal de Aveiro* 6 (December 1985): 1–23.

Stephens, Thomas M. *Dictionary of Latin American Racial and Ethnic Terminology*. 2nd ed. Gainesville: University of Florida, 1999.

Sweet, James. *Domingos Álvares: African Healing, and the Intellectual History of the Atlantic World*. Chapel Hill: University of North Carolina, 2011.

Sweet, James. "The Hidden Histories of African Lisbon." In *The Black Urban Atlantic in the Age of the Slave Trade*, edited by Jorge Cañizares-Esguerra, Matt D. Childs, and James Sidbury, 233–247. Philadelphia: University of Pennsylvania, 2013.

Taín Guzmán, Miguel. *La ciudad de Santiago de Compostela en 1669. La "peregrinación" del Gran Príncipe de la Toscana Cosimo III de Medici*. Santiago de Compostela: Teófilo Edicións and Consorcio de Santiago, 2012.

Thompson, I.A.A. "A Map of Crime in Sixteenth-Century Spain." *The Economic History Review* 21, no. 2 (1968): 244–267.

Tomás y Valiente, Francisco, "El 'Ius Commune Europaeum' de ayer y hoy." GLOSSAE. *European Journal of Legal History* 5–6 (1993–1994): 9–16.

Torquemada, María Jesús. *La Inquisición y el Diablo: supersticiones en el siglo XVIII*. Seville, Spain: Universidad de Sevilla, 2000.

Turner, Victor. "Variations on a Theme of Liminality." In *Secular Ritual*, edited by Sally F. Moore and Barbara Myerhoff, 36–52. Amsterdam, The Netherlands: Van Gorcum, 1977.

Twinam, Ann. *Purchasing Whiteness: Pardos, Mulattos, and the Quest for Social Mobility in the Spanish Indies*. Stanford, California: Stanford University, 2015.

Velázquez de la Cadena, Mariano. *A New Pronouncing Dictionary of the Spanish and English Languages*. Revised and enlarged by Edward Gray and Juan L. Iribas. New York and London: D. Appleton, 1900.

Vélez-Sainz, Julio. "Alternancias de carnaval y cuaresma en el *Buscón* de Quevedo

(Bajtin como puente entre el hispanismo estadounidense y el español)." *La Perinola* 14 (2010): 33–53.

Villalba Pérez, Enrique. *La administración de justicia en Castilla y en la corte a comienzos del s. XVII*. Madrid: Actas, 1993.

Vincent, Bernard. "San Benito de Palermo en España." *Studia Historica: Historia Moderna* 38, no. 1 (2016): 23–38.

Wach, Adolf. *Conferencias sobre la ordenanza procesal civil alemana*. Translated by Ernesto Krotoschin. Buenos Aires: Ediciones Jurídicas Europa-América, 1958.

Wright, Elizabeth. *The Epic of Juan Latino: Dilemmas of Race and Religion in Renaissance Spain*. Toronto, Buffalo, London: University of Toronto, 2016.

Yzquierdo Perrín, Ramón, Miguel Ángel González García, and José Hervella Vázquez. *La Catedral de Ourense*. León, Spain: Edilesa, 1993.

Index

Entries are to English, and other languages are cross-referenced; scholars mentioned in the text are indexed, those in the footnotes are not; the edition and translation of Soller's legal process are indexed by page and by folio number of the documents. Proper names of two categories of persons are signaled in the index: names that appear in Soller's trial and pilgrim's documents, along with their offices, are in **bold**; names of persons of black-African descent other than Soller himself are set in SMALL CAPITALS. Titles of texts, ships, and works of art are set in italic, with parenthetical identification of non-texts; page numbers in italics are for figures.

Abrahams, Roger D. 38
Admirabilis planta. *See* Marvel of Peru
Admiral of Castile. *See* **Enríquez de Cabrera, Juan Tomás**
Adoration of the Magi (*Epiphany*) (painting) *62*
adversarial procedure 19, 193
Africans, black, arrival in Europe 42–43
Afro-descended people 10, 12, 13, 16, 17n16, 23, 24, 26–30, 31, 36, 38, 42, 43–44, 45–46, 47, 48, 49, 50, 51–55, 55–63, 78, 84, 92, 112, 113, 114–118, 178, 179, 207, 209
  and priesthood 26–30, 75–79
  distribution 60
  devotion to San Benito of Palermo 32
  first Western intellectual 45–46
  free 27, 53–55, 118
  in Aveiro 133
  in Lisbon 114–115
  in Portugal 54–55
  in Seville 114
  legal regulation 179
  maritime workers 114, 207–208
  narratives 16–17
  noblemen (in painting) 116
  religious assimilation 61–63
  sentenced to galleys 179
  segregation of, in Lisbon 115
  speech communities 38 (*see also* creoles, Atlantic)
  and vagabondage 176–181
  voices, notional 17–18
Aira Gate. *See* Ourense
Alayos, Count of 56, 61, 197, 208, 241 (3ᵛ)
Albani, Nicola 98–99
Albor, Miguel de 9, 233 (1ᵛ), 314, 317
ALBUQUERQUE, AFONSO DE. *See* Albuquerque, Brás de
ALBUQUERQUE, BRÁS DE 54–55, 113, 117
Alemán, Mateo 97. *See also Guzmán de Alfarache*
Alfama District (Lisbon) 55
Alfonso VII of León, The Emperor (El Imperador) 156
Alfonso X, The Wise (El Sabio) 173n41, 185, 196
Algarborium. *See* Algarves
Algarves 42, 83, 253 (7ʳ), 313, 314
alguacil de vagabundos. *See* vagabonds: constable of
All Saints Royal Hospital (Lisbon) 109, *110*
Almadén Mines (Spain) 181, 206n18
Almeida Leiva *72*, 255 (8ᵛ), 313
Almirante de Castilla. *See* **Enríquez de Cabrera, Juan Tomás**
Alvarado, José de (Apellate Judge) 231 (cov. 1), 305 (36ʳ), 313, 316
ÁLVARES, ALFONSO 47n67
Andrade, Domingo de 151–152, 158
Anfeiar de Menezes, Vasco *72*, 255 (8ʳ), 314
ANGULO, CARLOS 12n11
ANTÓNIO, MESTRE 47n67
Apellate Judges (A Coruña: **José de Alvarado, Juan de Riaño, Manoel Rodrigues de León**) 231 (cov. 1), 305 (36ʳ), 314, 317
Archbishop, of Rhodes (Cornaro, Giorgio) 8, *74*, 253 (7ʳ), 313, 316
Arragel Bible 44
Arribas Briones, Pablo 85, 96
Assembly of Misericórdia 8, 66–73, 82–83, 103–162
  and blacks and slaves 112–113
  archive 69 (Viana do Castelo), 104–105 (Tomar)
  Coimbra 123–126
  Lisbon 106–113

Santarém 118–120
Tomar 129–133
Virgin Mary as symbol of 111–112
assimilation, religious, of African-descended persons 61–63
Atlantic world 16–17, *34*, 38, 54, 55–63, 114–115, 207–208
as black and urban 55, 61
See also creoles, Atlantic
Auristela (fictional pilgrim) 87, 93
Austrias carmen 46
Aveiro (Portugal) xix, 104, 133, *134–135*
Azevedo Sousa Martins, Teresa Raquel 104

Bacalhoa Palace (Azeitão, Portugal) 54–55, 116–117
Badapur, Thomas Gregorio 105
Balboa, Gil de. *See* **Court Clerk/Reporter**
Baldi, Pier Maria *108*, 119, 125, *126*, 142, *143–144*, 145
Balthasar (Wise Man of the Epiphany) 61–*62*
Barbaña River (Ourense) 154
barber-herbalist 84, 206, 241 (3^{v}), 272 (18^{r})
barbero arbolario. *See* barber-herbalist
barbers, ship-board, African-descended 206–207
Baron, Pablo 86
Bautista, Juan 29, 261 (12^{v})
beggars, Lisbon confraternities 66
Benedictine Rule 8
Benito de Palermo, San 32, *33*
Berardo Collection 116–117
Berardo, José ("Joe") Manuel Rodrigues 117
Berardo, Renato 54–55, 117
Berjano family (vineyard) 3, 233 (1^{v}), 313, 315
Berlin, Ira 55, 60
Bernardes, Manuel 109
black-African ancestry. *See* Afro-descended people
black-African descent. *See* Afro-descended people
blackness, equated with slavery, inferiority, and sinfulness 28–29, 40–45, 45–46, 52–53
transvalued in Juan Latino's work 46
black people. *See* Afro-descended people
blood-purity statutes 52, 123, 327 at 30^{r}
Bogotá 12
Book of Good Love 80
Book of Saint James 85
brand marks, slaves' 31, 50, 90
Brer Rabbit 37
Brueghel, Pieter, the Elder *80*
Brueghel, Pieter, the Younger 66, *67*
Burgas, Las (Ourense) 154–156
Burgos (Spain) 94–96
Buscón, El (*The Grifter*) 80, 97
Bynum, Caroline Walker 151, 161–162

Cachupín, Juan 307 (36^{r}), 313, 317
Cachupín, Pedro 307 (37^{r})
cacographies 223, 225
Calderón de la Barca, Pedro 80
Caminha (Portugal) xix, 139–141
Camino de Santiago. *See* pilgrimage: routes; Portuguese Way; Silver Way; French Way
Camino Real. *See* Royal Road
Capellae Christianissimi Francorum Regis. *See* Chapel of the King of France
Cardinal of Pilgrim's Diplomas (Santiago de Compostela: Jacinto Suárez) 5, 35, 102, 231 (cov. 1), 237 (2^{r}), 251 (6^{v}), 257 (10^{r}), 273 (18^{v}), 275 (20^{r}), 313, 316
Carlos I, King of Spain (Carlos V of the Holy Roman Empire) 46, 185
Carlos II, King of Spain, "El Hechizado" 25–26, 147, 171–172, 189, 190, 194, 208
Carnality, Sir (Don Carnal) 80
Carnaval. *See* Carnival
Carnival 80–81
CARRASCO, JUAN 193–194
Carretta, Vincent 60
carta de alforria. *See* manumission documents
Carta de Guía. *See* Pilgrim's Credential
Carta de Misericórdia. *See* Pilgrim's Credential
Casa do Corregidor. *See* House of the Chief Magistrate
Casa dos Bicos (House of Spikes) 55
Casas, Bartolomé de las 43
Casas Consistoriales. *See* Ourense: Town Hall
Casas Reais de Cimadevila. *See* House of the Chief Magistrate
Casado González, Gregorio ix–x, xii

- Casanueba, Juan de 86
- Cascaes (Portugal) 69
- case file 211–309
  - condition 15
  - contents:
    - adjournment 231 (cov. 1)
    - affidavit, procedural 235–239 (1^{v}–3^{r})
    - affidavit, Antonio González Siabal 249 (5^{v}–6^{r})
    - affidavit, José Soller 241–245 (3^{v}–4^{v})
    - affidavit, Pedro de Castro 251 (6^{r}–6^{v})
    - appeal 301–309 (33^{r}–37^{r})
    - arrest 233–235 (1^{r}–1^{v})
    - confession, Antonio González Siabal 259–261 (12^{r}–13^{r})
    - confession, José Soller 273–275 (18^{r}–18^{v})
    - confession, Pedro de Castro 257–259 (11^{r}–11^{v})
    - court costs, Antonio González Siabal and Pedro de Castro 271 (17^{v})
    - court costs, José Soller 301 (32^{v})
    - criminal claim/indictment 275–277 (20^{r}–20^{v})
    - deposit of valuables 239–241 (3^{r})
    - identification of the shops 245–247 (4^{v}–5^{r})
    - judgment 231–233 (1^{r})
    - notice 279 (21^{r}–21^{v}), 281 (21^{v}), 283 (22^{v}–23^{r}), 295 (28^{v}), 297–299 (29^{v}–30^{r})
    - notice and bail bond 263–265 (14^{v}–15^{r}), 269–271 (16^{v}–17^{v})
    - order to produce evidence 279 (21^{v})
    - ruling 239 (2^{v}–3^{r}), 245 (4^{r}–4^{v}), 251–253 (6^{v}), 247–249 (5^{r}–5^{v}), 263–267 (14^{v}–16^{v}), 271–273 (17^{v}–18^{r}), 295–297 (28^{v}–30^{r}), 299 (30^{r}–32^{v})
    - sentence 299–301 (32^{r}–32^{v})
    - subpoenas 287 (24^{v}–25^{r})
    - witnesses 287–293 (25^{r}–27^{r})
- case files, historical, interpretation of 199–201
- **cashbook, of João Sánchez** 89, 127–129, 231 (cov. 1), 237 (2^{r}), 239 (2^{v}–3^{r}), 243 (4^{r}), 273–275 (18^{v}), 277 (20^{v})
- **Castro, Antonio de** 247 (5^{r}), 313
- **Castro, Gregorio de** 9, 233 (1^{v}), 239 (2^{v}), 313, 316
- **Castro, Pedro de** (tailor) 6, 23, 29, 85, 168, 245 (4^{r}), 247 (5^{r}–5^{v}), 251 (6^{r}), 257–259 (11^{r}), 263–271 (14^{v}–17^{v}), 287 (25^{r}), 291 (26^{r}), 314, 317
- Catalan priest-pilgrims 5, 35, 75, 81, 84, 151, 243 (3^{v}), 273 (18^{v})
- cathedrals. *See* Santiago de Compostela: cathedral; Ourense: cathedral
- Catherine of Lancaster, Queen of Castile 54
- Catholic Monarchs 147, 174, 183
- cavalgadura 65, 73, 127
- Cervantes Saavedra, Miguel de ix, 64, 87, 91
- Céspedes, Eleno/Elena de 89–90
- Chafariz d'el Rey 114–118
- *Chafariz d'el Rey* (painting) 115–117
- Chamoiseau, Patrick 38
- *Chanson de Roland* (*Song of Roland*), and blackness 44
- Chapel of the King of France (Santiago Cathedral) 4, 149–151, 257 (10^{r}), 313, 315
- charges, de parte versus de oficio 19. *See also* case file: arrest; case file: claim/indictment
- Charles I, King of Spain (Charles V of the Holy Roman Empire) 46, 185
- Charles II, King of Spain, "The Bewitched" 25–26, 147, 171–172, 189, 190, 194, 208
- Chaucer, Geoffrey 54
- CHICABA (SANTO DOMINGO, TERESA) 17n16
- **Chief Magistrate (Ourense: Juan Antonio Covillas Venero)** 10, 18, 19, 22, 26, 28, 30, 128, 168, 172–176, 190, 195–196, 201, 208, 231–301 (1^{r}–32^{v}), 317
- churches, Misericórdia (Lisbon) 6, 109–*111*
  - Our Lady of Conception (Lisbon: Nossa Senhora de Conceiçao Velha) 109–111
  - San Francisco (Santiago de Compostela) 32, *33*
- *Chronicle of the Discovery and Conquest of Guinea, The* 36n15, 43. *See also* Zurara, Gomes Eanes de
- **Cid, Blas Antonio.** *See* **Judicial Secretary**
- City Council (Ourense) 170, 173–174
- cimarrones 54
- City of God 7
- cividade 35n11, 214–215, 253 (7^{r}), 317
- Claramonte, Andrés de 45, 50

clemency 18–19, 183, 281 (21^{v})
clerical regalia 6, 9, 23, 29, 53, 88, 89, 101–102, 164, 231 (cov. 1), 237 (2^{v}), 241 (3^{r}), 243 (3^{v}), 247 (5^{r}), 249 (5^{v}), 251 (6^{r}), 259 (11^{v}), 261 (12^{v}–13^{r}), 273 (18^{v}), 275 (20^{r}), 299 (30^{r}), 301 (33^{r})
clothing, equated with civilization 42–43
  significance 10, 53, 88
  sumptuary laws and race 53
  see also clerical regalia; disguise
Cocardon, François 186–187
Coelho, Antonio 194
Coelho, Gonçalo Teisera *72*, 255 (8^{v}), 313
Coimbra (Portugal) xix, 31, 89, 103, 123–129, 133, 190, 203, 231 (cov. 1), 237 (2^{r}), 243 (4^{r}), 255 (8^{v}), 273 (18^{v}), 277 (20^{v}), 313, 315
  University of 123–124
Colón, Fernando 154
Communion. *See* Eucharist
complex regular proceeding 20
Compostela. *See* Pilgrim's Diploma
Compromisso da Confraria da Misericordia 67–69, *68*
Concepción, María de la 41–42
confessions, in trials 199–200
Consello. *See* City Council
Constitution of 1812 (Spain) 27
Contreiras, Miguel 111
Convent of Christ (Tomar) 131–133, *132*
Convento de Cristo (Tomar) 131–133, *132*
conversos. *See* New Christians
Cornaro, Giorgio. *See* **Archbishop of Rhodes**
Cornelius, Georgius (Giorgio Cornaro). *See* **Archbishop of Rhodes**
Correa da … on, Antonio *72*, 255 (8^{v}), 313
Corregidor. *See* **Chief Magistrate**
Cortes of Cádiz 27
Coruña, A 13, 147, 190, 191, 192, 196–197, 202, 303–309 (33^{v}–37^{r}), 313, 317
Costa do …, Andre da *72*, 255 (8^{v}), 313, 314
Court Clerk/Reporter (Relator), Juan de Montes 192, 202, 231 (cov. 1), 303 (33^{v}–34^{r}), 305 (34^{v}, 36^{r}), 307 (36^{v}–37^{r}), 314, 317
  Gil de Balboa 231 (cov. 1), 305 (35^{r}), 307 (37^{r}), 313, 316
court documents 13–15, *14*. *See also* case file
Couto Mixto 24–25, 203–205
Covarrubias, Sebastián de 36–37, 179–180, 191
Covillas Venero, Juan Antonio. *See* **Chief Magistrate**
crab dance (jaibería) 39
creoles, Atlantic 31n1, 55–63
  cosmopolitan 60–61
  man-of-words 37–40
  storytellers 24, 38
cristianos viejos. *See* Old Christians
criollos. *See* racialization, social hierarchy
Crisólogo, Pedro 77–78
cross-dressing 89–91
cruces desperationis 219
Cruz, Anne 85
Cruz, Juan de la 53
Cuaresma, Doña (Lady Lent) 80

Darnton, Robert 16
Davis, Natalie Zemon 16, 31–32
Debén, Pedro 3, 9, 233 (1^{v}), 314
deceit, law of 85, 96–97, 265 (15^{r}), 269 (17^{r})
Deputy Prosecutor (Teniente Promotor Fiscal: Juan del Rodicio) 19, 22, 48–51, 52, 96, 101–102, 128–129, 149, 179, 185, 199, 273–299 (18^{r}–32^{r}), 313, 316
devotional images 7, 158, 160, 162
Diccionario de autoridades 191
Diego el Mulato. *See* Martín, Diego
dimissory letter 87–88, 181
disguise 37, 51, 84–93. *See also* "passing"
dissimulate/simulate 198
Domingo de Arechaga, Agustín 206
Don Quijote ix, 64, 91, 185
Dorado, El (legend) 37
double-consciousness 39
Dubois, W.E.B. 39

Ecclesiastical Judge (Provisor) 279 (21^{v})
Enríquez de Cabrera, Juan Tomás 61, 208, 301 (32^{v}), 313, 315
Epiphany (*Adoration of the Magi*) (painting) *62*
Equiano, Olaudah 60
Erauso, Catalina de 89–90
escribano, translation 213–214
Escudero, Bartolomé 307 (36^{r})

Esculi, Pierre 86
Española. *See* Santo Domingo
estates model, medieval 51
Estebanillo 31, 201
Estabanillo González 96–97, 142–143n113, 155
Estrudo. *See* Carnival
ethnic cleansing 44
Eucharist 3, 6, 67, 75
in Santiago Cathedral 147–153
Extremadura (Spain) 57–59

Falco, Antonio 105
features, Africanized. *See* phenotype
features, facial. *See* phenotype
Felipe II, King of Spain (Filipe I, King of Portugal) 46, 69, 77n47, 86, 87, 90, 174, 180–181, 183–184
Felipe III, King of Spain (Filipe II, King of Portugal) ix, 69, 91, 184
Felipe IV, King of Spain 15n10, 174, 194
Felipe V, King of Spain 194
Female Rogue Justina, The (*La Pícara Justina*) 97–98
Fernández de Sobredo, Antonio. *See* **Judicial Secretary**
Fernando III, "The Saint", King of Castile 157, 318
Fernando V, King of Spain 147, 174
Ferreiro, Antonio López 105
Ferreiro, José 32, *33*
Ferrer, Benito 199
Figueroa 231 (cov. 1), 303 (33^v), 305 (36^r), 313
Fight Between Carnival and Lent (painting) *80*
Fiscal. *See* **King's Representative**
Fiuza, Juan de 301 (33^r)
Fontaíña, Calle de (Fontaíña Street). *See* Ourense: Fontaíña Street
Forneiro, Antonio 245 (4^v), 313, 314
forzados (galley slaves) 185, 186, 189
Foucault, Michel 19, 20, 66, 84, 89, 172
France 16, 32, 65, 99, 160, 180
José Soller 31, 41, 243 (3^v)
Franciscans 32
free papers 41–42, 45, 47–49. *See also* manumission documents
French Way 155, 160. *See also* pilgrimage: routes
Fuchs, Barbara 87, 92
Fuero real (*Royal Code*) 183
fugitive slaves. *See* slaves: runaway

Galician Massif 142
GALINDO, FRANCISCO 53
Gallant Negro of Flanders 45, 50
galley slavery 24, 26, 175, 181–190
demographics 179
See also forzados
Garatuza, Martín 99–101, 198
García, Francesc 194–195
GARRIDO, JUAN 53
Gates, Henry Louis, Jr. 37
GODINHO, SIMÔA 110–111
Golegã (Portugal) xix, 120–*122*
González, Antonio 247 (5^v)
GONZÁLEZ PONCE DE LEÓN, JUAN 53
González Siabal, Antonio (barber) 5, 23, 29, 85, 168, 245 (4^r), 247 (5^r), 249 (5^v–6^r), 259–269 (12^r–17^r), 287–289 (25^r–25^v), 313, 314
gracias al sacar 78. *See also* whiteness
Grifter, The (*El Buscón*) 80
GRISO (Grupo de Investigación Siglo de Oro) 216
Grupo de Investigación Siglo de Oro (GRISO) 216
Guadalupe (Spain) 57–59
Guadalupe, Virgin of 57–58, *59*
Guerre, Martin 16, 32
Guerrero, Alonso 281 (22^v), 295 (28^v)
Guevara, Antonio de 187
Guinea 36, 43
Guzmán de Alfarache 97

Hall, James 145
Ham, Curse of 43–44
Hautefort, Ch.V. de 83
Henrique, Prince of Portugal 130
Herwaarden, Jan Van 85
Hieronymite Monastery of Bethlehem (Lisbon) *62*, 108–109
Hieronymite Monastery of Santa María de Belém (Lisbon) 62, 108–109
Hispaniola. *See* Santo Domingo

Holy Christ (statue), of Burgos 158, 161
of Ourense 7, 151, 157–162, 243 (4^{r}), 273 (18^{r})
of Saint Claire (Palencia) 158, 161
Holy House of Mercy. *See* Assembly of Misericórdia
Holy Week 79. *See also* Lent
horseback 65, 73, 127
hospices. *See* hospitals
Hospital of San Lorenzo (Hospital de San Lorenzo) (Ourense) 168
Hospital of San Roque (Hospital de San Roque) (Santiago de Compostela) 106
Hospital of the Holy Savior (Hospital de São Salvador). *See* Old Hospital
Hospital Real de Todos os Santos. *See* All Saints Royal Hospital
Hospital Velho. *See* Old Hospital
hospitality 92, 93–98, 138–139
infrastructure 8, 69, 85, 93–98
hospitals 65, 94, 96
in Aveiro 133, *134*
in Burgos 94–96
in Caminha 139
in Lisbon 109
in Ourense 168
in Santarém 119
in Santiago de Compostela 105–106, 147
in Tomar 130–131
in Viana 136–*137*, *138*
of the Assembly of Misericórdia 66, 69, 73, 109, 112, 130, 133–*134*, 136
hostels. *See* hospitals
House of Spikes (Casa dos Bicos) 55
House of the Chief Magistrate (Ourense) 175, *176–177*
Hurston, Zora Neal 40

illegitimacy 52, 54, 78, 84–85
illiteracy 70, 77, 79, 199
Soller's illiteracy 17, 79, 102
illiterates, in the case file, **Pedro de Castro** 251 (6^{r}), 259 (11^{v}), 269 (17^{r}), 291 (26^{v})
Domingos Sánchez 241 (3^{r})
José Soller 235 (1^{v}), 243 (4^{r}), 275 (18^{v}), 287 (25^{r}), 303 (33^{r})
imitation of Christ (imitatio Christi) 7
indiano (Soller) 35, 56, 253 (6^{v})
indianos (Spanish subjects of the Indies) 56, 74, 165n10
indios. *See* racialization, social hierarchy
Inquisition 45, 90, 197–200
inquisitorial procedure 19, 20–21, 193
Irigoyen García, Javier 52
Isabel I, Queen of Spain 44–45, 147, 174
Italy 31, 32, 65, 73
as Soller's origin 55, 56, 235 (1^{v})
ius commune 21, 182–183

Jaén (Spain) 41
jaibería (crab-dance) 39
jails 24, 170
escape from 189–190
in Ourense 169–171
James the Greater, Saint ix, 4–5, 6, 7, 54, 56, 64–65, 86, 143, 149, 151–153, *152*, 156, 157n171, 158, 162, 180, 235 (1^{v}), 237 (2^{r}), 243 (3^{v}), 257 (10^{r}), 273 (18^{r})
as Matamoros, Mataindios, Matanegros 54
Book of Saint James 95
See also pilgrimage: routes, Portuguese Way, Silver Way, French Way
Jesús, Úrsula de 17n16
Jimeno, Francisco 194
João II, King of Portugal 73, 123
João III, King of Portugal 109, 131, 315
John of Gaunt, Duke of Lancaster 54
Johnson, Thomas L. xiv
Juan of Austria 46
Judicial Secretary (**Escribano**) 213–214, 219, 220
A Coruña:
Seijas 303 (34^{v}), 305 (35^{r}), 314
Antonio Fernández de Sobredo 309 (37^{r}), 313
Domingo Pérez 305 (35^{v}), 313
Varela 307 (36^{v}), 314
Ourense:
Antonio Pérez 23, 29, 30, 32n2, 231–299 (1^{r}–36^{v}), 313, 314
Blas Antonio Cid 301 (32^{v}), 313, 315
jurisdiction 198–199

Kendi, Ibram 43
King's Fountain (Lisbon) 114–118
King's Hospital (Burgos) 94–96

King's Representative (**Fiscal; His Majesty's Representative**) 13, 22, 170, 191, 195, 196, 197, 214, 231 (cov. 1), 300–309 (33r–37r)
Künig von Vack, Hermann 94–95

ladino. *See* creoles, Atlantic
Laffi, Domenico 94, 95–96, 99, 145–146, 147, 148, 149, 153, 160, 161
Lagos (Portugal) 42
Lalami, Laila 31, 201
land held in common x, 174
Landers, Jane 53–54
Lateran Council, Fourth 20
LATINO, JUAN 45–46
Lazarillo de Tormes 100–101
legal system 21–22, 172–173, 182, 190–195, 213–215
Lent 9, 79–84
  processions 82–83
Lent, Lady (Doña Cuaresma) 80
León, Manoel Rodrigues de (**Appellate Judge**) 231 (cov. 1), 305 (36r), 314, 317
Leonor, Queen of Portugal 66, 70, 123
Lepanto, Battle of 46
libertos. *See* slaves: freed
Lieutenant Nun. *See* Erauso, Catalina de
Life is a Dream 80
liminality 60, 84
Lisasueto, Baltasar de. *See* **Public Defender**
Lisbon (Portugal) xix, 4, 5, 8, 9, *11*, 30, 35, 55, 56, 60, 62, 65–66, 67–70, 74, 79, 82, 102, 103, 106–118, *110*, 129, 207, 249 (6r), 253 (7r), 261 (12v), 277 (20v), 314, 316, 317, 318
  earthquake (1755) 106–108
  Treaty of 147
Lodeiro, Juan de 307 (37r), 314, 317
López de Úbeda, Francisco 97–98
López Ferreiro, Antonio. *See* Ferreiro, Antonio López
López Gómez, Pedro 15
López Santaolalla, Miguel Ángle 87
Lorenzo, Bishop of Ourense 156
LORENZO, DIEGO 77
Louis XI, King of France 149–151
Lowe, Kate 17
Lugo, Council of 156
Madrid 56, 57, 96, 193, 199, 241 (3v)
Magalotti, Lorenzo 108, 112, 119, 120–121, 124, 143–144, 145
Maghreb 115
Manesca, Miguel *72*, 255 (8r)
Man of Sorrows 158
man-of-words, creole 37–40. *See also* creoles, Atlantic
Manuel I, King of Portugal 54, 67–78, 109, 111, 117, 123, 131, 136
manumission 49
  documents 49
MANZANO, JUAN FRANCISCO 17
marcas de fuego. *See* brand marks, slaves'
María of Aragón, Queen of Portugal 111
Mariñamansa 4, 233 (1r), 314, 317
maroons 54
Martín Casares, Aurelia 56
MARTÍN, DIEGO, CAPTAIN 53
Martínez de Araque, Antonio 168
Martín Garatuza 100–101
Martins, Teresa Raquel Azevedo Sousa 104
Marvel of Peru (*Mirabilia peruviana Admirabilis planta*) 36
Marvell, Andrew 36
Mataindios, Saint James 54
Matamoros, Saint James 54
Matanegros, Saint James 54
Mass. *See* Eucharist
Meaus (Spain) 204
Medici, Cosimo III de' 79n58, 82n65, 108–109, 121, 124, 127, 135n93, 139, 142, 143–144, 145, 149, 151
MEJÍAS, FRANCISCO 53
Meléndez, Juan 36
Mello, Luis de *72*, 255 (8r)
Méndez Silva, Rodrigo 168
Menezes, Fernan de Soiza Castelbranco Coitinho e *72*, 255 (8r)
Menezes, Vasco Anfeiar de *72*, 255 (8r), 314
mercury, mines (sentence) 181, 206–207, 208, 209
MÉRIDA, JUAN DE (fictional character) 45, 50
mestizos 58, 77n47, 92, 177–178
  José Soller as 48, 50, 235 (1v), 249 (5v), 251 (6r)
  See also racialization: social hierarchy
MEXÍAS BEJARANO, DIEGO 77

Miño River 8, 109, 139, 141, 142, 153
Mirabilia peruviana. *See* Marvel of Peru
miscegenation 52. *See also* illegitimacy
Misericórdia. *See* Assembly of Misericórdia
Monsuriu, Jerónima 42
Montalvo, Francisco de 36
Montero, Jerónimo de 194
Montes, Juan de. *See* **Court Clerk/Reporter**
Moor's Account, The 31
Morales, Ambrosio de 155
Moreira (Portugal) xix, 129, 133–135
moriscos ix, 52, 64n1
  expulsion ix, 91–92
Mozarabic Route 153
"Mower, The" 36
mudéjar architecture 56, *57*, 140, *142*
mulato, peregrino. *See* José Soller, peregrino mulato
mulattos. *See* Afro-descended people
Mules and Men 40
Müntz, Eugenio 83

Naples 32, 235 (1^{v})
Navaza, Gil de 307–309 (37^{r}–37^{v}), 313, 316
New and Very New Compilation 184–185
New Christians (conversos) 44–45
Noah 43
Northup, Solomon 47–48
Nossa Senhora de Conceiçao Velha (Lisbon: Our Lady of Conception Church) 109–110
Nueva y novísima recopilación 184–185
Nunes, Manoel *72*, 255 (8^{r})

Old Christians 45
Old Hospital (Viana do Castelo) 136–*137*, *138*
Ordás, Diego de 37
Original Poor Pilgrim's Hospital (Santarém) 119
Orinoco River 37, 193
Ourense xix, 3, 7, 8, 65, 103, 153–162, 163–202
  Aira Gate (Porta da Aira) 4, 60, 165–168, *167*, 233 (1^{r}), 313, 314
  cathedral 7, 156–157
  Fish Market Plaza (Plazuela de Pescadería) 164, 245 (4^{v}), 307 (37^{v}), 314, 317
  Fontaíña Street (Calle de Fontaíña) 164–165, 247 (5^{r}), 313, 316
  plan *166*
  Town Hall (Casas Consistoriales) 168–169
outsider 12n1, 13, 23, 48, 51, 84

Palácio da Bacalhôa. *See* Bacalhoa Palace
palenques. *See* maroons
Palermo (Italy) 32
Panama 77
Panasco, João de Sá 115–116
Pando, Bernardo de 9, 233–237 (1^{r}–2^{r}), 241 (3^{r}), 271 (17^{v}), 313, 315
Panza, Sancho (fictional character) ix, 64n1, 91, 189
parchment (skin), of devotional sculpture 160–161
Pardiñas, Joan Suares de 277 (20^{v}), 281 (22^{r}), 285 (24^{r}–24^{v}), 297 (29^{v}), 313
pardos 52–53, 61, 77–78. *See also* Afro-descended people
Pareja, Juan de 47
"passing" 89–90, 92
Passion of Christ 157–158
  Lenten reenactment 82–83
Paul, Saint 7
peninsulares. *See* racialization: social hierarchy
people of black-African descent. *See* Afro-descended people
people of color. *See* Afro-descended people
peregrino mulato. *See* José Soller: peregrino mulato
Pérez, Andrés 239 (2^{v}), 241 (3^{r}), 265 (15^{r}), 269–71 (17^{r}), 301 (32^{v}), 313, 314
Pérez, Antonio. *See* **Judicial Secretary**
Pérez (de) Mariño, Vasco 158
Pérez, Domingo. *See* **Judicial Secretary**
Pérez, Francisco 241 (3^{r}), 313, 316
Periandro (fictional pilgrim) 87, 93
Perú, Kingdom of 18, 35–37, 241 (3^{v}), 253 (7^{r}), 273 (18^{r}), 277 (21^{r}), 303 (33^{r}), 314, 317
perulero 36
Peter, Saint 7
P.F.G. y C. 157

phenotype 28–30, 31, 40–42, 44–46, 49, 50–52, 54, 58, *59*, 77, 92, 110–113
and slavery 44–46
in case file 235 (1^{v}), 243 (3^{v}), 247 (5^{r}), 249 (5^{v}), 251 (6^{r}), 261 (13^{r})
See also skin, dark
Phillips, William D. 17, 41–42
physiognomy. *See* phenotype
Pícara Justina, La (*The Female Rogue Justina*) 97–98
picaresque novels 80, 96–98, 124–125
pigmentation, skin. *See* skin, dark; phenotype
pilgrimage 6–9, 64–66, 81
as disguise 84–93
as penitential 81
legal regulation 87–88
routes, of Saint James (Camino de Santiago) *11*, 94, 97, 112, 139. (*See also* French Way; Mozarabic Route; Portuguese Way; Silver Way)
pilgrim documents 15, 17, 31, 48, 88, 96–97, 103–104
in case file 251 (6^{v}), 253–257 (7^{r}–10^{v})
See also Pilgrim's Credential, Pilgrim's Diploma, Pilgrim's Passport
pilgrims 13, *113*
Christ as pilgrim *138*
false 86–88, 93–98
fictional 87, 93–94, 106, 188
fictional, German (*Don Quixote*) 91–92
See also picaresque novels
Pilgrim's Credential (Carta de Guía, Carta de Misericórdia) xix, 4, 8, 15, 69–73, *71*, *72*, 88, 96, 225, 253–255 (8^{r}–8^{v}), 277 (20^{v}). *See also* pilgrim documents
Pilgrim's Diploma (Compostela) xix, 4–5, 15, 35, 75, *76*, 149, 223, 231 (cov. 1), 237 (2^{r}), 243 (3^{v}), 257 (10^{r}–10^{v}). *See also* pilgrim documents
Pilgrim's Passport (Salvi Conductus) xix, 4, 8, 15, 35, 73–75, *74*, 88, 223, 253 (7^{r}–7^{v}). *See also* pilgrim documents
Pisa (Italy) 83
Plazuela de Pescadería. *See* Ourense: Fish Market Plaza
pogroms against Jews 44
Poor Laws 26
Porta da Aira. *See* Ourense: Aira Gate
Portuguese War of Secession 147
Portuguese Way *11*, 102, 103, 127, 139. *See also* pilgrimage: routes
poverty, aid to poor 66
legitimate poor versus delinquents 23–25, 66, 85–91, 97, 183–184
See also vagabonds
priesthood 10, 27
and race 27–30, 75–79
priestly regalia. *See* clerical regalia
printing press and forgery 100–101
procedimiento ordinario complejo 20
Procurador de Pobres. *See* **Public Defender**
PROLOPE Research Group 216
Provisor. *See* **Ecclesiastical Judge**
Public Defender (**Procurador de Pobres: Baltasar de Lisasueta**) 18, 28, 191–192, 277 (20^{v}), 279 (21^{r}), 283 (22^{v}), 293 (27^{v}), 299 (30^{r}), 313, 314
public vengeance 19, 199, 215, 275 (20^{r}), 293 (27^{r})
Puerta de Aira. *See* Ourense: Aira Gate
purification 9, 10, 155–156
removing lice 10n38

Quevedo, Francisco de 80, 97. *See also* *Grifter, The*
quicksilver. *See* mercury

race, categories, constructed 45. *See also* phenotype; skin, dark; whiteness
racialization, of persons of black-African descent 44
of sentences 179
of slavery, inferiority, and sinfulness 28–29, 40–45, 45–46, 52–53
social hierarchy 50–51, 92–93, 207–208
racial profiling 13, 40
Raleigh, Sir Walter 103
Ramey, Lynne 43–44
Ravello, José Sebastião *72*, 255 (8^{v})
Real Audiencia del Reino de Galicia. *See* Royal Appellate Court of Galicia
Real Hospital de los Reyes Católicos (Santiago de Compostela) 86, 105–106, 147
Reformation 65
Rhodes, Archbishop of (**Giorgio Cornaro**). *See* **Archbishop of Rhodes**

Riaño, Juan de (**Appellate Judge**) 231 (cov. 1), 305 (36^{r}), 314, 317
Ricote (fictional character) ix, 64, 91–92
Ricote Valley (Murcia) ix
Rinaldo, João André (Joannes Andreas Rinaldarum) 253 (7^{r}), 313, 316
rituals of exclusion (rituels d' exclusion) 19, 112
Riva Palacio, Vicente 100–101
Road to Santiago. *See* pilgrimage: routes, Portuguese Way, Silver Way, French Way
Rodicio, Juan or Joan del. *See* **Deputy Prosecutor**
Rodrigues Berardo, José ("Joe") Manuel 117
Rodrigues de León, Manoel (**Apellate Judge**) 231 (cov. 1), 305 (36^{r}), 314, 317
Rome 64, 73
  José Soller 5, 7, 8, 25, 31, 75, 93, 203, 253 (7^{r}), 314, 317
  Trials of Persiles and Sigismunda 87, 93
Royal Apellate Court of Galicia (**Real Audiencia del Reino de Galicia**) 13, 15–16, 24, 30, 192, 195, 196–201, 229, 303–307 (33^{v}–37^{r})
Royal Code (*Fuero real*) 183
Royal Hospital of the Catholic Monarchs (Santiago de Compostela) 86, 105–106, 147
Royal Medical College 207
Royal Residences at the City Summit. *See* House of the Chief Magistrate
Royal Road (Ourense) 4n8, 165
Ruiz, Juan 80
Ruta Mozárabe 153. *See also* Silver Way

Saenz de Rojas, Diego Eugenio 193–194
Saint James, Book of 85
Salgueiro Doce, Lucía 105
Salinas, Buenaventura de 36
Salvi Conductus. *See* Pilgrim's Passport
Salzedo, Lourenço de 62
Sánchez, Domingos 241 (3^{r}), 313, 316
Sánchez, João. *See* **cashbook**
San Juan Bautista (packet boat) 206
Santarém (Portugal) xix, 118–120, *120*, *121*
Santa Semana. *See* Holy Week
Santiago (Apostol). *See* James the Greater, Saint: Matamoros; Mataindios; Matanegros
Santiago de Compostela (Spain) xix, 4, 5, 7, 8, *11*, 35, 56, 60, 64–66, 74, 79, 82, 96, 98, 102, 103, 105, 143–153, *144*
  cathedral 105, 147–153, *150*, 243 (4^{r}), 253 (7^{r}), 273–275 (18^{v}), 301 (33^{r}), 315
Santiago, Knight of 115, 117
Santiago, Military Order of 115
Santiago, Voto de 146–147
Santo Cristo (statue). *See Holy Christ*
Santo Domingo 18, 32–35, 56, 60–61, 75, 77, 165n10, 197, 208, 215, 235 (1^{v}), 241 (3^{v}), 273 (18^{r}), 277 (21^{r}), 303 (33^{r}), 314, 317, 318
SANTO DOMINGO, TERESA (CHICABA) 17n16
Santos, Antonio dos 239 (2^{v}), 265 (15^{r}), 271 (17^{r}), 313, 314
seals (documents) 4, 15, 74, 75, 149, 209n38
  in case file 230 (1^{r}), 304 (36^{r})
  stamped, how transcribed 219
Seguín, Pedro 157
Seijas. *See* **Judicial Secretary**
Seixalbo (Portugal) 4, 165, 168, 233 (1^{r}), 318
Seller, Nuno da Silva *72*, 255 (8^{r})
Semanero (**Weekly Justice**) 202, 307 (37^{r})
sentences, arbitrary punishments 183
  in absentia 190–195
  José Soller 181–190. (*See also* case file: sentence)
  utilitarian 183–184
Seven Acts of Mercy, The (painting) 66
Seven Divisions, The 183
sex/gender change 89–90
Siete Partidas, Las. See The Seven Divisions
Sil River 153
Silva, Antonio Brabo de *72*, 255 (8^{v}), 313
Silva Seller, Nuno da *72*, 255 (8^{r})
Silveira, Jo … da *72*, 255 (8^{r}), 313
Silver Way (Vía de la Plata) *11*, 56, 103, 153–154. *See also* pilgrimage: routes
simulate/dissimulate 198
skin (parchment), of devotional sculpture 160–161
skin, black. *See* skin, dark
skin, dark 3, 5, 28, 30, 40–43, 45, 46, 50, 52, 77, 78, 88, 90, 111, 113, 118
  equated with enslavement 28, 44–46
  geographic distribution 118
  sign of illegitimacy 84–85

See also phenotype; racialization: social hierarchy
skin tone. *See* skin, dark
slavery, and vagrancy 178
equated with blackness 28–29, 41–42, 48–49
index of debased status 53
ports 114
trade 38, 43, 114–115
slaves, distribution 117–118
ethnic diversity 41, 56
freed (libertos) 28, 49
imprisoned 112–113
in Madrid 60
in Zafra 60
narratives 17
permission to meet 118–119
runaway 23, 48–50
Smith, Chantell 46
social conditions, Hapsburg Spain 23–26, 146–147
social groups 21–23, 112–113
during Lent and Carnival 81
legal exemptions 181
fiscal exemptions 22–23, 44, 173, 205
social hierarchy. *See* racialization, social hierarchy
Soiza Castelbranco Coitinho e Menezes, Fernan de *72*, 255 (8^{v})
Soller, José, 18th-century ship captain 206–209
Soller Chivo, José, arrested as fugitive slave 49, 243 (3^{v})
charges 19, 275–277 (20^{r}–20^{v})
in Santiago de Compostela 105–106
itinerary xix, *11*, 50, 69, 103–162
itinerary anomaly 127–129
missing documents 88, 181
sentence 175, 181–185, 299–301 (32^{r}–32^{v})
peregrino mulato 231–233 (cov. 1–2, 1^{r}), 259–261 (11^{v}–12^{r}), 275 (20^{r}), 285 (24^{r}), 289 (25^{v}), 293 (27^{r}, 28^{r}), 297 (29^{r}–29^{v}), 299 (32^{r}), 301 (33^{r}), 305 (36^{r})
Sommer, Coris 40
Somoza, Juan Antonio 42
Song of Roland (*Chanson de Roland*), and blackness 44
Sousa Martins, Teresa Raquel Azevedo 104
Soutullo 257 (11^{r}), 259 (12^{r}), 263 (14^{r}), 266 (16^{r}), 314
Spanish subjects of the Indies (indianos) 56, 74, 165n10
Spikes, House of (Casa dos Bicos) 55
Suares de Pardiñas, Joan 277 (20^{v}), 281 (22^{r}), 285 (24^{r}–24^{v}), 297 (29^{v}), 313
Suárez, Jacinto *See* **Cardinal of Pilgrim's Diplomas, Santiago de Compostela**
Sueyro, Matías 233 (1^{v}), 239 (2^{v}), 314, 317
sumptuary laws. *See* clothing
Sweet, James 114, 179

taxes 22–23, 44, 173, 205
Teisera Coelho, Gonçalo *72*, 255 (8^{v})
Teresa, Countess of Portugal 156
Tesoro de la lengua española. *See* Covarrubias, Sebastián de
Treasury of the Spanish Language. *See* Covarrubias, Sebastián de
Thirty Years' War 65
thurible, Santiago de Compostela 148–149
Toledo, 1449 Rebellion 44–45
legislation against vagabonds 184
Tomar (Portugal) xix, 82, 103, 104, 127–133
tonsure, José Soller 5–6, 9, 10, 23, 29–30, 40–41, 55, 74, 81, 88, 89, 99, 101–102, 233–235 (1^{r}–1^{v}), 243 (3^{v}), 245 (4^{r}–4^{v}), 247–249 (5^{r}–6^{r}), 259 (11^{v}–12^{r}), 261 (12^{v}), 267 (16^{v}), 273 (18^{v}), 274 (20^{r}), 285 (24^{r}), 297 (29^{r})
Torres Villaroel, Diego de 86–87, 124n74, 139, 179, 180n62
torture 199–200
Trabajos de Persiles y Sigismunda, Los. *See* *Trials of Persiles and Sigismunda, The*
Trent, Council of 65
"tretas del débil." *See* "tricks of the weak."
trials 18–24
appeal 196–198
in absentia 190–199
Trials of Persiles and Sigismunda, The (*Los Trabajos de Persiles y Sigismunda*) 87, 93–94, 106, 188
"tricks of the weak" (tretas del débil) 13, 37
Tuy (Spain) 109, 129, 139, 142, *143*
Twelve Years a Slave 47–48
Twinam, Ann 26–27

University of Coimbra 123–124

vagabonds 12n1, 23, 97–98, 176–181
constable (alguacil) of 85
definition in Covarrubias 179–180
illustration as pilgrims 180
legal regulation 178
presumed of Afro-descended people 178
Valdés, José Manuel 78
Valença do Minho (Portugal) xix, 8, 70, 79, 96, 109, 139, *141*, 141–142, *143*, 255 (8r), 314
Varela. *See* **Judicial Secretary**
Vega, Pedro de la 154–155
Vega y Verdugo, José de 145–146, *146*
Velasco, Diego de 156
Velázquez, Diego de 47
Velho, Antonio ... *72*, 255 (8v)
Venido, Juan 174
Verástegui, Francisco 168
Vía de la Plata. *See* Silver Way
Viana do Castelo (Portugal) xix, 82, 104, 135–139, 255 (8v), 314
Vida es sueño, La 80
Vila Nova de Gibraltar (Lisbon) 109
Villalba Pérez, Enrique 20
Villavicencio y Salazar, Martín de. *See* Garatuza, Martín
vindicta pública. *See* public vengeance
Virgin Mary, as mediatrix 112
of Guadalupe 57–58, *59*
Our Lady of Grace (Tomar: Nossa Senhora da Graça) 129–130, *131*
symbol of Assembly of Misericórdia 111–112

Weekly Justice (Semanero) 202, 307 (37r)
West Indies 35, 37, 38
whiteness 12n1, 27–28, 44, 52
purchasing (gracias al sacar) 27
unmarked and superior 44
whitening 78, 117
wool 52
Wise Men (Christian Epiphany) 61–62, *62*
Witimer, first Bishop of Ourense 156
Works of Mercy 68
Corporal 66, 67, 82, 170

Yago Montoto, Catalina del 307 (37r), 313, 315
Yáñez de Noboa, Pedro 173

Zafra 56–58, *58*, 60, 93, 241 (3v), 314, 318
zambos. *See* racialization: social hierarchy
Zurara, Gomes Eanes de 36n15, 42–43

www.ingramcontent.com/pod-product-compliance
Ingram Content Group UK Ltd.
Pitfield, Milton Keynes, MK11 3LW, UK
UKHW022224051026
15624UKWH00002B/348

9 789004 417779